OHIO STATE ATHLETICS
1879–1959

OHIO STATE ATHLETICS

1879 - 1959

By
James E. Pollard

COPYRIGHT, 1959
BY THE ATHLETIC DEPARTMENT
OHIO STATE UNIVERSITY

ERRATA

9th page, picture section, upper right, wrong picture used for Bill Smith

p. 151, 3rd line from bottom, re Vanderbilt—first appearance *since 1909*

p. 161, line 11, re 1944 team—undefeated in *nine* games

Ibid., lines 12, 13, over-all record, *16* won, etc., for percentage of *.889*

p. 163, line 7, Illinois score, *16 to 7*

p. 164, line 20, Pittsburgh score, *41* to 0

p. 170, line 19, Washington State score, 35 to 7

p. 173, line 8, Washington, *not* Washington State

p. 175, line 15, *eleven* Conference championships

Ibid., line 16, ... In *382* games

Ibid., line 17, won *256*, lost *101*, and tied *25* for a percentage of *.713*

Ibid., line 18, lost *78* and tied *17*

Ibid., line 19, percentage of *.666*

Ibid., line 23 (Wilce), Conference games, won 37, lost *30*, tied 4

Ibid., line 26 (Brown), Conference games, won 9, lost 6, tied *1*

Ibid., line 27 (Widdoes), Conference games, won *16*, lost 2, tied *0*

Ibid., line 29 (Fesler), all games, won 21, lost 13, tied *3*

Ibid., line 30 (Hayes), all games, won *54*, lost *16*, tied 4

TABLE OF CONTENTS

Part I
Beginnings and Growing Pains, 1879–1911

Introduction	ix–x
I. The Seeds Are Sown	3– 10
II. Official Attitudes	11– 22
III. Competitive Beginnings	23– 35
IV. Early Football, 1889–1897	36– 53
V. The 1898 Crisis and Reorganization	54– 60
VI. General Development, 1898–1911	61– 73
VII. Football, 1898–1911	74– 93
VIII. Track, Basketball and Baseball, 1898–1912	94–102

Part II
Expansion and Competition, 1912–1959

IX. The 1912 Reorganization and the Big Ten	105–116
X. The Stadium and Its Aftermath	117–130
XI. Football, 1912–1958	131–176
1. The Wilce Era, 1913–1928	131–159
2. Willaman and Schmidt, 1929–1940	150–158
3. Brown Through Fesler, 1941–1950	158–169
4. The Hayes Phase, 1951–	169–176
XII. Other Sports	177–211
Baseball	177–181
Track and Cross Country	181–188
Basketball	188–194
Swimming	194–200
Golf	200–202
Other Sports	202–208
Intramural Athletics	208–211

Part III
Athletic Administration, 1912–1959

XIII. The Physical Plant	215–232
XIV. The Administrative Side	233–257
XV. Problems and Policies	258–288

TABLE OF CONTENTS (*Continued*)

ILLUSTRATIONS..*follow* 150
CALENDAR.. 289
INDEX... 301

INTRODUCTION

A history of athletics at the Ohio State University has been in the making for more than a decade. Originally it was a special project of the University Development Fund, sponsored by the Alumni Varsity "O" Association. It was undertaken by the late Athletic Director L. W. St. John upon his retirement in 1947. In this he had the devoted help of Miss Carrie Dudley, longtime secretary in the Athletic Department.

This dual choice was a happy one. Mr. St. John, a Varsity football player in 1900, returned to the campus in 1912 as business manager of athletics and in a multiple coaching capacity. Shortly he was made athletic director but retained his coaching chores. Miss Dudley came to the campus soon after. For the next thirty-five years they were intimately concerned with the University's athletic growth and knew personally the hundreds of men who passed across its athletic stage. Some time after Mr. St. John's death the work passed into the hands of the writer who, it happened, came to the campus the same year Mr. St. John returned to it and, as it turned out, had a longtime connection with the department in various ways.

Many persons have helped with the "digging" and in the completion of the work. Special mention should be made of Miss Dudley who, among other things, went laboriously through the dusty files of the *Lantern* and the *Makio* and who filled eleven notebooks with clues, data and pertinent references. Various "oldtimers" helped such as the late Carl E. Steeb, '99, longtime Board of Trustees secretary, active in the Stadium campaign and a member of the first basketball team, and Prof. Charles W. Foulk, '94, a player on the first football team. Thanks are due also to Athletic Director Richard C. Larkins for advice and assistance, to the Athletic Board for its patience, and to numerous members of the athletic staff for their help.

An exhaustive history of Ohio State athletics would require volumes. What is set down here is the running story with significant high spots or particular details. Because of the sweep of policy involved considerable attention has been given to the administration of athletic activities. Football has been emphasized to some extent also because it has drawn the greatest public interest and because it has provided most of the athletic bread and butter.

Unfortunately, Athletic Board minutes and other official records prior to 1912 appear to have been lost or, worse, destroyed. The sources of information relied upon for the early period were the files of Columbus newspapers from 1879 on, files of campus publications—the *Lantern*, *Wahoo* (an interim paper), the *Makio*, the *Alumni Monthly* (originally a quarterly), and official records such as University faculty minutes and those of the trustees, and the annual reports of the president.

Appreciation is due to the historical division of the campus photography department for most of the pictures used. Others came from the files of the *Alumni Monthly*.

As might be expected, some of the early accounts do not always agree as to the scores of games or vary in other respects. As far as available material permitted these have been checked, rechecked and cross-checked for accuracy.

The question of selection was sometimes difficult. Doubtless some things have been omitted that should have been recorded while others that were included might well have been left out. The primary purpose was to tell the story of the origin and growth of Ohio State athletics and to let the essential facts speak for themselves.

JAMES E. POLLARD

Columbus, Ohio
June 17, 1959

PART I

BEGINNINGS AND GROWING PAINS
1879–1911

I
THE SEEDS ARE SOWN

LIKE TOPSY, college athletics at most U. S. colleges and universities with men students "just growed." This was true at Ohio State in the late 1870s and early 1880s where a simple sports program of sorts emerged from the natural competitive urge of healthy young men who, then as now, needed a satisfying muscular outlet.

Against the later backdrop of the great horseshoe Stadium and the adjacent Field House, Arena, and Natatorium, it is hard to imagine the primitive beginnings. But they were to be found in the open field adjoining the old North Dorm, long since torn down, which stood west of Neil Ave. and a little north of Eleventh Ave. The campus of those early days was remote from the city which years later flowed northward and engulfed it. But the students of that day, mostly men, were dependent largely upon their own resources for entertainment and particularly for recreation.

Baseball was common but basketball was not to make its appearance on the campus until nearly twenty years later. Track and field competition in the form of annual Field Days and Class Days occurred fairly soon. Before 1890 some one turned up at the "dorm" with a strange object called a football and before long another major Varsity sport was born. In time, too, what began as impromptu "pickup" games evolved into competition with outside teams. Some of these were from nearby colleges such as Ohio Wesleyan, Otterbein, Denison and Kenyon, but also included were Y.M.C.A., "Deaf Mute" and even occasional high school teams. In football, as will be seen later, the Columbus Barracks (in modern times Ft. Hayes) team was a fairly regular opponent for some years.

As this was written there were men still living who remembered when Varsity sports began to emerge in the 1880s and when the athletic field ran down hill to the west of Neil Ave. north of Eleventh Ave. Still more could recall the move to Ohio Field at Seventeenth Ave. and High St. after the turn of the century. This followed the erection of the Armory and Gymnasium in 1898. It was on Ohio Field that Ohio State athletics began to attract national attention with the first championship football teams of 1916 and 1917. This led presently, after further successes following the end of World War I, to the Stadium era and to the expansion that followed.

Many names, many faces and many events make up the total Ohio State tapestry which depicts the evolution of the intercollegiate and intramural sports programs over a span of three-quarters of a century. The simple, spontaneous urge of the 1880s has become long since a complex of big business, with annual receipts of $1,500,000 a year and with an investment in plant and equipment, exclusive of the men's and women's gymnasiums, of nearly $8,000,000. It would cost considerably more than that to reproduce the physical facilities that make up the University's modern athletic plant.

No one planned it that way. Certainly neither students, faculty nor trustees of the early 1880s had the remotest idea of all that would grow out of the impromptu ball games on the dormitory field or the annual Class and Field Days on the grass and roadway in front of University Hall.

Competitive sports on the Ohio State campus may be said to have passed through four stages. The first, roughly from the late 'Seventies to the early 'Eighties, was spontaneous and unorganized. The second, during much of the 'Eighties, saw the beginning of contests with outside teams, some college and some not. The third, in the 'Nineties, was marked by three developments: the organized scheduling of games, the emergence of a group of Ohio colleges which were natural competitors in what after the turn of the century became the "Big Six," and the appearance of hired seasonal coaches, particularly for football. The last and most important phase, as far as Ohio State was concerned, began in 1912 with the University's formal admission to the Western Conference.

Although athletics on an organized intercollegiate basis were a decade away, sports were a campus activity at least as early as 1879, or six years after the University opened its doors. The *Lantern*, in its third issue, March, 1881, made a plea for spring sports, particularly baseball and track. "We want this year a nine that can play and win with any of the college or local clubs about here," it commented editorially. "That we can have such a nine, no one who saw the make-up of last, and year before last can doubt." But it argued for players who not only had ability but were "willing to make some sacrifice to the success of the club." It went on:

The Baseball Association have hitherto been willing to do all in their power to further the success of the nine, but the players have sadly disappointed their friends in not taking sufficient interest in their work.

But in addition to the base ball, we should enter into other athletic sports. An Athletic Association is what is needed, one that will institute a regular series of games, offer prizes, and get the members awake to the sport. Surely amongst two hundred and fifty men there ought to be some who can make good records in the various sports common to colleges. Now and then we hear of some one of the students making a good jump or a capital run, why not bring all under a system, that the best men may be pitted against each other, and the students at large get the enjoyment on some Saturday of a Field Day . . . .

Form an athletic association, select the men for the ball team, start some athletic sports, and do it too, before it be too late; the more that join in the movement the easier and pleasanter it will be. The benefit and pleasure and the pride that every student of O.S.U. will feel in a series of victories and good records will far outbalance some little sacrifices of time, comfort and *laziness*.

This plea evidently had some effect for the next issue reported the holding of a meeting "for the organization of an Athletic Association," which "though not enthusiastic was successful." A committee was appointed and there was talk of arranging "a Field-Day on the second Saturday of April." On this slim evidence the beginnings of organized athletics seem to have been made on the campus in the spring of 1881.

But unorganized sports had a place also. Under the heading of "Local," a brief note in the same issue reported: "Foot-ball is in the order of the day at the Dorm, and nearly every evening witnesses a jolly game. Any one is at liberty to join the sport, for in this game the saying 'The more the merrier,' holds true." The same issue reported that the committee "to secure members for the Athletic Association is meeting with encouraging results. Nearly the entire number of students have already signified their willingness to aid in the support of the association." If the movement succeeded, "some rare sport during next term" was predicted. It emphasized that the chief interest "will be centered in the base-ball nines."

There was a good deal of apathy and inertia to overcome. The May, 1881 issue of the *Lantern* reported that the "meeting of the Athletic Association for the purpose of adopting a constitution and by-laws and electing officers, was poorly attended. The officers elected are without doubt well chosen, but the same can not be said of all the committees. There was too much hurry about the whole matter." There was still talk of a field day "on the first Saturday in May" and to insure success the writer urged "each member" of the association to "enter for one or two of the games in which he has an interest" and argued that whether the student "can 'do anything' or not, is purely a secondary consideration."

Officers of the original association were: W. K. Cherryholmes, president; A. J. Heinlein, vice president; M. N. Mix, secretary; J. R. Lovejoy, treasurer. These committees were chosen: Base Ball—A. J. Heinlein, J. Wikoff, W. F. Rice. Foot Ball—E. S. Howells, C. R. Vanderberg, M. P. Dozer. General Athletics—H. B. Dahl, H. R. Pool, F. Shedd.

In the fall of 1881 the *Lantern* urged renewed activity on the part of the Athletic Association. "The grounds which were given it," the paper pointed out, "should be fitted up in the proper manner, so that the Association could claim them as a permanent possession. A little action now may secure a valuable acquisition, which carelessness may deprive it of, for a time at least, if not permanently."

Interest in athletics continued in the spring of 1882 but the emphasis as before was on baseball. It was suggested that teams from Capital University, the Deaf and Dumb Asylum, and the University "engage in a regular series of contests during the present term, instead of playing at odd times, as in the past." Commenting on an Athletic Association meeting, the *Lantern* expressed the hope that "some neat uniform will be adopted by the Association, as contestants in uniform always feel more comfortable, can do better work, are more sightly, and, in fact, are in better shape in every way than if not uniformed.

The second annual Field Day was set for May 20, 1882. There was progress in other directions also. To quote the *Lantern:*

> The plan, submitted to the Athletic Association by its committee, for the arrangement of its grounds was adopted and the grounds have been staked out. The catcher's fence of the baseball grounds will be situated in the vicinity of the small grove adjacent to the grounds, and the batting will be to the southeast. An elliptical race-track, an eighth of a mile in circumference, was staked out encompassing the base ball diamond. It was thought best to lay out a straight hundred yards course, and this was done, the track set apart for this being near to and parallel with the fence forming the north boundary of the grounds. It will take considerable work to have these grounds in readiness for Field Day, but they should be finished by that time by all means. Already several energetic members of the Association have, by taking hold with their own hands, put the ball diamond into excellent shape, for which they deserve considerable credit.

Field Day, 1882, was considered to be an improvement on the first one, held in 1881. The program ran more smoothly and there were fewer delays, but one criticism was that more contestants were needed. The campus was remote from downtown Columbus and one comment sounded strange in terms of the later Stadium era: "Some of the visitors at the O.S.U. from another college, during Field Day, were highly pleased with the exercises of the day, with their reception, and with the University. Their principal objection was that it was so far from town. Yes, it is far from town—half an hour's ride in the cars, and away from clouds of dust, heat and impure air. . . ."

The *Lantern* justified what to some of its readers might appear the "undue prominence" given in its columns to "athletic sports." "It should be remembered," it pointed out, "that a few weeks in the spring term is all the time that we, who have not the advantages of gymnasium, have for these exercises." It called such matters not merely "affairs of pleasure, they are urgent necessities." It argued that "As a general rule, the best athletes are the best students. . . ."

The November, 1882 *Lantern* bewailed the lack of interest in baseball. "It is strange that in so large a body of active students," it remarked, "it is almost impossible to find nine competent men who are willing to spend a little time in practicing base-ball. It was rather humiliating to our boys to be compelled to take two outsiders with them when they played the Delaware club on the 21st." Ohio State won, 15 to 7.

An account by one of the players, under the head of "Base Ball Notes," explained that "On account of the non-appearance of two players at the time of departure for Delaware, the boys were compelled to take along an out-sider. This should never occur again; and when players agree to do, they should fulfill their promise." The final game of the "season" was played November 11 at Westerville, Ohio State winning 9 to 7.

Football was still in the future although it was coming over the horizon. In the notes under "Local," the *Lantern* asked "Where is the foot-ball? What a grand game could be had on the campus. Why not give us a challenge game among the classes?"

There seems to have been a Base Ball Association separate and apart from the general Athletic Association. The May, 1882 *Lantern* noted that "Professor Lazenby followed the commendable example of Professors Mendenhall and Lord, and added another to the generous donations to the Base Ball Association. Let the good work continue." Elsewhere it was reported that Mendenhall and Lord gave $5 each. The same issue reported that "The regular College nine was again organized late in April, with A. J. Heinlein, Captain, and Al. A. Moore, Manager." In its first game the team defeated "the Deaf Mutes," 5 to 3. Next it defeated the city high school team, 23 to 17, but lost to Otterbein, 10 to 8.

Sports were not as seasonal in those early days as later. Several years later, for example, football was played in the spring until the weather got too warm. And baseball was played in the fall as well as in the spring.

The October, 1882 *Lantern* reported that "The College B.B.C. [Base Ball Club] held a meeting the 22nd of Sept. for the purpose of organizing, and to fill vacant places with players." A game was played the next day between two "picked nines," i.e., from the club membership. It was reported also that "The grounds will have to be moved farther towards High Street, as the new Chemical Laboratory interferes."

The second volume of the *Makio,* the campus yearbook, in 1882 devoted six pages to athletics. Under "Athletic Association of the O.S.U.," it listed the officers along with the names of eighty-two members. Several of them were nationally known in later years. Besides the Field Day, a Class Day was held. The events for the latter were much the same as for the former. But Class Day came during the commencement season. The accompanying 1881-82 "Calendar" listed "Athletic sports" or Field Day for May 20, while "Class Day and athletics" was June 20. Under "Base Ball," the "College Nine" and the four class teams were shown. There was also a "Cricket Club."

In the next decade athletics grew slowly. The Athletic Association was still in existence, but there was now also an "O.S.U. Athletic Stock Association," incorporated under the laws of the state, and of which Prof. Benj. F. Thomas was president. This association was incorporated for $2000 with shares at $1 each. Dr. C. B. Morrey, a member of the first football team, raised an echo of this past in January, 1950 when he asked the Athletic Board about the possibility of redeeming a $100 stock certificate for a fence built around the playing field adjoining the old North Dormitory "back sometime in the 1890s." In the fall of 1953 W. N. Zurfluh, '94, of Louisville, Ky., sent Director Richard C. Larkins one of his "stock certificates of the first and only Ohio State University Athletic Association Company that built the first grandstand in Dr. Detmer's cow pasture where we played our football games in the early Nineties."

By 1882 there was also an Ohio Intercollegiate Athletic Association, of which Robert J. Watson, of Kenyon, was president. By 1890 there was a "State Field Day" as well as the campus Field Day. The former was a forerunner of the later Ohio Conference or "Big Six" meet for the state track championship. There was by now, too, a state tennis tournament in which Ohio State was champion.

Under a basic Western Conference requirement to which the University subscribed years later, intercollegiate athletics must be under faculty control. But in the early years there was only the voluntary Athletic Association to which students belonged and to which some faculty members contributed small sums of money. From the scanty records it appears that the association suffered frequently from apathy or from a crippling lack of money. From time to time there were campus "benefits" of one kind or another designed to relieve the financial stringency, but the needs always outran the funds available.

As noted, an Athletic Association of sorts was in existence in the first decade of the life of the University although it lacked authority and was ineffective. On September 30, 1882 the Columbus *Dispatch* mentioned a meeting of the association the day previous. On June 20, 1881 in connection with the Class Day exercises it was reported that they would be followed by "the summer meeting of the Athletic Association" but no further details were given.

The association had a hard time getting the breath of life and went through several reorganizations. From time to time the *Lantern* used its editorial whip in trying to get some action from the association. Thus in October, 1884 it urged the association "to get to work" and repeated the plea in the next issue in which it asked "What has become of the Athletic Association?" But in June, 1885 the paper reported that interest in athletics was increasing.

Various members of the early faculty helped to keep the spark of athletic interest alive. Apparently the earliest of these was Prof. William Rane Lazenby, a Cornell alumnus, who held the chair of horticulture and botany. He was also the first secretary of the School of Agriculture. This was before the University had colleges or deans. Among his other duties Prof. Lazenby was responsible for the care of the campus grounds. The November, 1885 *Lantern* spoke of his efforts to raise the standard of athletics.

Another pioneer was Prof. Albert H. Tuttle who had joined the faculty during the University's second year of operation as professor of zoology and comparative anatomy. In the fall of 1885 he took charge of a class in gymnastics. By 1888, however, he resigned to go to the University of Virginia.

Various schemes and devices were tried in an effort to raise money for athletics. The June 6, 1888 *Lantern* reported the results of a "pronouncing bee" the proceeds of which were to go to athletics. Attendance at games was slim and money was hard to come by. The December 7, 1888 *Lantern*, speaking of alumni attendance, remarked that "Athletic sports have been unsatisfactory."

In the early 'Nineties the athletic stock company was formed for the support of University athletics with stock at $1 a share. This resulted in a measure of support but it proved inadequate and ineffective. The June 23, 1892 *Lantern* carried a financial statement of the stock company which showed a balance of $24.98.

Receipts for the year were as follows: from stockholders, $465; rent of grounds, $10; "two balls sold," $2; games, $460.20; lawn tennis, $3.50; and local field day, $31.25. Expenditures, similarly, were listed as: paid on fence and grand stand, $377.70; "stationary [*sic*], etc.," $30.30; baseball, $452.77; tennis, $36.90; local field days, $9.50; state field day, $35.50; and "Football (new)," $4.50.

"Subscriptions to the Stock Company," the account added, "are coming in slowly, but as may be seen by the above statement the Association is not yet out of debt. . . . If the O.S.U. Athletic Company had not been formed as it was, athletics in Columbus would have been a mere side show. . . ." An accompanying list showed that 106 "stockholders" had paid their subscriptions, amounting to $465, in full as follows: students, $255; faculty, $183; and others, $27. Eleven faculty members, including one "Incognitus," paid from $1 to $50. "Incognitus" gave $1 and Prof. Benj. F. Thomas $50.

Before the turn of the century—and later—interest was high in college literary societies. The debater or elocutionist was a big man on the campus and there was great interest in statewide contests. This kind of interest began to decline. But the *Lantern* of April 28, 1892 was of the opinion that this waning interest could hardly be explained by the growing interest in athletic sports. And under the heading of "Bless Them," the November 19, 1892 *Lantern* reported a contribution for football by the women's Browning Dramatic Society.

The Athletic Association continued to face recurring financial difficulties. After the 1896 Thanksgiving football game with Kenyon, the *Lantern* in its December 2 issue declared "Through gross mismanagement and reckless extravagance the association has fallen deeply into debt. The receipts from the game have been enough, fortunately, to fulfill the obligations incurred and leave the progress of athletics, if not encouraged, at least unhampered."

But in three months there was talk of a "benefit" for the association 'to put the baseball team on its feet." The '"benefit," in the form of a concert, was held March 19, 1897 in the chapel. The March 24 *Lantern* called it an "unqualified success" both musically and financially but it failed to say what the profits were.

II
OFFICIAL ATTITUDES

A DOZEN years passed after the University opened its doors in 1873 before any official mention was made of sports. This came about in 1885 and 1886 in reports by Prof. Lazenby who had charge of University grounds. He recommended specifically in 1885 that "all grounds needed for field sports be put in the best possible condition for the use of students just before the opening of each college year, and that the care of them thereafter be left to the various organizations that use them." The next year he recommended that the trustees provide $150 to "keep the ball ground, tennis courts and the track of the general athletic grounds in excellent order." Physical culture, he pointed out, was being "regarded more and more as a necessary requisite for the best intellectual development. . . . As long as the university has no gymnasium, a reasonable degree of encouragement should be given to field sports."

Apparently little or nothing was done about the matter for in 1888 Lazenby repeated his recommendation in slightly different form. This time it was for a request for funds "sufficiently large to keep the ball grounds, tennis courts and quarter-mile track in good order." He also urged the draining and grading of the athletic grounds east of the chemical laboratory so that they "could then be used by the athletic association and also by the battalion for drill and dress parade."

When the chemistry building was destroyed by fire in February, 1889 a new one was built where two tennis courts had been. These, Lazenby reported, had cost "the university tennis club" $50 and he urged that the University replace the courts. He added that another $50 "would keep the ball-grounds in fairly good order."

By 1890 athletics had gained enough prominence to warrant substantial mention in the president's annual report. There was "a new and unprecedented interest in athletics," President W. H. Scott reported, with teams for "base ball, foot ball and lawn tennis." The baseball team, moreover, had made "a tour" to play three games which caused "an absence of about two and a half days from college exercises," i.e., classes. There was also "one match game of foot ball with the team of another college" which was unidentified. As a result of this increased interest, a request was made to the trustees "to provide more extensive grounds and enclose them." A faculty committee drew up a plan to this end. President Scott had more to say on the tendencies, dangers and need for control. He went on:

> The advantages of cheerful and hearty physical exercise are so important as to be worthy of encouragement by the faculty and the board; and these advantages are no doubt secured to some extent by the present system of athletics. But a well regulated system would secure them in a far greater degree with far less risk. Most of the time there is but little practice; then comes a tremendous overstrain. Lawn tennis is not liable to this criticism, as the practice is more regular, and the match games are less violent. To foot ball, on the other hand, the criticism is especially applicable, and in this game accidents are frequent. Another evil that attends the present system of athletics is its interference with university work. This is particularly true of intercollegiate games. An effort is made to restrict them to Saturdays and other holidays, but it is apparently impossible to play them without more or less neglect of regular studies, not only at the time when they are played, but during the period of training for them.
>
> The faculty has adopted no plan for regulating these games so as to abate the evils that already exist or to prevent those that seem likely to arise. We have great confidence in the loyalty and earnestness of our students. Some of the most loyal and earnest are members of the various teams, and others are zealous friends and supporters of the association. Yet the history of athletics in the Eastern colleges, and the manifest tendency of those of Ohio, indicate that some limits should be prescribed.

The catalogue for 1890-91 also made some formal mention of athletics. "The campus affords an excellent opportunity for general athletics," it reported. "The students have an athletic association, under the auspices of which an annual 'Field Day' is held, members of the association competing for prizes in the various contests usual on such occasions. There are also clubs in archery, lawn-tennis, base ball, and foot-ball, who meet teams from other colleges at proper times. Much interest is taken in these sports by the students, and the Faculty."

At commencement time in 1890 the students petitioned the trustees for help in the following petition signed by 182 of them:

> Whereas, $48,947.53 was expended last year on the brain development of the Ohio State University students, while no gymnasium is provided for their physical development, we, the undersigned, respectfully request the Board of Trustees to enclose an athletic field, containing a quarter mile track, tennis courts, for match games, base ball and foot ball grounds, or, that the sum of $200 be set aside, annually, to be expended under the direction of the Athletic Association on base ball, foot ball, tennis and general athletics.

The petition was referred to the president and the executive committee. Five months later a faculty committee recommended that "As we have no gymnasium, special pains should be taken to furnish facilities for field sports." Specifically, it urged that "the present ball ground, situate between the large Dormitory and the new Veterinary building, be made an athletic field," with "a base ball diamond, foot ball grounds, and a quarter of a mile cinder track, the whole thing enclosed by a light board fence of suitable height."

It was pointed out that there was ample ground to do this "without interfering with class room work or detracting to any considerable extent from the orderly appearance of the campus." A grandstand seating 300 was recommended also, with "additional spectator seats on either side," and with "a special practice ground for foot ball" so that baseball and football could be played at the same time without interference. To this end, it was estimated that at least 5½ acres would be needed and that the expense would be $1950, of which $500 was for fencing, gates and ticket office, $450 for grading and leveling, $350 for the track and straight-away, and $650 for the grandstand and side seats. The committee consisted of Profs. Lazenby, C. N. Brown and B. F. Thomas. After hearing the report, the trustees voted $200 for the athletic association "to be expended under its direction for the furtherance of its objects."

A year later there were two further developments. One was a petition from the football team, referred by the secretary of the faculty, asking to be excused from military drill "in order that they might devote that hour to foot ball practice." This had the indorsement of the athletic association managers and of the commandant, with the suggestion that football practice, if the petition was granted, "be made subject to the same rules as govern military drill." On this condition the request was approved by a vote of 3 to 2, with the stipulation that the commandant and Prof. Lazenby see that the conditions were enforced. At the same meeting the athletic association managers petitioned the trustees to fence the athletic grounds and erect a grandstand at an estimated cost of $1150. This was refused "because of lack of funds."

In the spring of 1892 matters took a slightly different turn when the trustees granted the athletic association permission to erect a fence and grandstand "on the grounds south of the dormitories" at a place to be designated by the chairman of the executive committee and the secretary of the board. Plans for the grandstand were to be submitted also to the executive committee for approval. In line with the previous action in excusing the football squad from military drill, the trustees also granted a request "to have certain members of the base ball team" excused. Nine students were in this group.

Although the full effects were not evident at once, help in expanding the athletic program now came from an unexpected quarter. This was the passage by the General Assembly of an act requiring "provision to be made at all educational institutions supported in whole or in part by money received from the state for teaching physical culture and calisthenics." This was called to the attention of the board by Trustee John B. Schueller. The leverage thus supplied led in time to direct provision for the armory and gymnasium that had been needed so long. At the June 21, 1892 board meeting Dr. Schueller made a long report "on the subject of providing for teaching physical culture at the university, as required by an act of the legislature." For the time being the report was filed.

Despite the lack of what a later day would have regarded as even minimum athletic facilities, the University catalogue for some years in the early 'Nineties carried an optimistic statement as to the opportunities for physical training. It read:

For the physical development and training of students the practical instruction in military tactics is found to be a most valuable aid. In addition to this, the University grounds afford excellent opportunities for general athletics, and the students support well organized clubs in baseball, football and lawn-tennis. These general sports are participated in by large numbers, and friendly contests are occasionally held with other colleges. Besides the special clubs named above, the students have an athletic association which holds an annual "Field Day," in which prizes are given to the victors in the various contests usual on such occasions.

In June, 1894 the application of the athletic association "to let the base ball grounds to outside parties during the summer vacation" was refused by the trustees, who placed the grounds during vacations under the control of Prof. Thomas F. Hunt. The board ordered also that in the future the use of the grounds would "not be allowed for games in which the university clubs are not contestants." Later that same month the trustees deferred the proposed removal of the athletic grounds "until next year."

From time to time the general faculty concerned itself with athletic matters. In the winter of 1893 it took an action on athletic eligibility that resulted in student disapproval. The Alcyone Literary Society, one of the two major men's groups, had a debate on the question. And the February 21, 1893 *Lantern* reported a resolution of disapproval of the faculty action. Three days later the *Lantern* referred to student indignation over the matter. There was reference in the February 28 issue also to a student "mass" meeting on this.

The cause of the student discontent lay in an action taken February 18 by the faculty to the effect that "no student or preparatory pupil of the Ohio State University be allowed to take part in intercollegiate games unless his record in the past has been above average. The President of the University is to decide what constitutes such record." Apparently the students thought the rule too exacting for they petitioned the faculty to reconsider the matter. This was done at the March 8, 1893 faculty meeting.

The earlier rule was amended to read that "no student or preparatory pupil of the Ohio State University be allowed to take part in intercollegiate athletic games, who has, within the two preceding terms, incurred a failure in any subject or has incurred conditions in more than five hours' work. This regulation shall go into effect at the opening of the University year 1893-94." The amended rule was less stringent and was not to take effect until the start of the next school year.

While the trustees at least twice had given their consent that under close supervision certain athletes might be excused from military drill they did not regard this as a change in policy. In the fall of 1894, at any rate, they declared by resolution "That the former action of this board excusing students taking part in athletic contests from military drill was only intended to be temporary and not a general rule." On the same occasion, at the suggestion of President W. H. Scott, "the use of the athletic grounds was granted for a contest between two other college clubs," not otherwise identified.

To anticipate, the building of the new gymnasium and armory in 1897-98 marked a new day for the University in the realm of physical training, indoor athletics, and military training. This development was signalized by the appointment of Dr. Christopher P. Linhart as "director of the gymnasium and instructor in hygiene and physical training." Linhart was to remain until 1904.

The University under James Hulme Canfield, its fourth president, (1895-99) meanwhile took something of a lead in what a later day would have called a housecleaning for intercollegiate athletics. It was one of the first to indicate its willingness not only to follow but to implement the code drafted by Ohio college presidents at their meeting during the 1895 holidays. On February 27, 1897 the faculty went a step further by adopting a set of rules governing not only athletics but other student activities.

The regulations, the March 3, 1897 *Lantern* reported, were the "consummation" of faculty and student efforts "to place O.S.U. athletics on a basis of absolute purity." The rules follow:

1. No person shall represent the O.S.U. in any athletic games or other public events who is not a student doing full work in the regular course.
2. No student shall take part in any intercollegiate contest except he has been in regular work for at least six months of the academic year in which said contest takes place. Students who enter from other colleges and receive credit for at least one year in the law course or in any other four year course, are exempt from this during the first year of their residence.
3. Intercollegiate games shall be played against bona fide students only.
4. All schedules of intercollegiate games involving absence from this city must be submitted within a reasonable time to the Faculty for their approval.
5. Every student association which receives money from contributions, solicitation or sale of tickets from persons other than its members, shall keep exact account of the amounts received, with all necessary vouchers, and shall submit the same for auditing twice a year by a committee consisting of one member from one of the associations and one of the Faculty.
6. The report of the auditing committee shall be published, and a copy furnished the President of the Faculty and the secretary of the Faculty.
7. The rules shall be published for the information of the Faculty and the student body and shall take effect immediately.

This action was discussed in other Ohio college papers. It also drew favorable comment by recognized sports authorities in the East.

During the school year 1897-98 all student rules and regulations were reviewed and the resulting code appeared in printed form in the fall of 1898. Six applied directly to athletics as follows:

58. The Faculty members of the Athletic Board shall constitute a committee with power to approve all schedules of athletic games. . . .
61. Athletic games are forbidden during the hours in which regular University classes are held.
62. No person shall represent this University as a contestant in any intercollegiate game or other public event, who is not a *bona fide* student of the University, doing full work, and not delinquent in his studies.
63. Except by permission of the General Faculty, on recommendation of the Faculty members of the Athletic Board, no student of this University shall play in any intercollegiate contest unless he has been in regular attendance during six consecutive months of the academic year immediately preceding July 1st of the calendar year in which the contest occurs. Students who enter this University from other colleges and receive credit for at least one year in the law course or in any four-year course, are exempt from this rule during their first year of residence.

64. No student may engage in any intercollegiate athletic contest until he has passed a physical examination satisfactory to the Director of Gymnasium.

In March, 1898 the trustees referred to the farm committee the question of "the location of the athletic grounds and location of fences enclosing" with the provision that "the university be at no expense for fencing or otherwise improving or repairing said grounds." The farm committee in a report dated April 15, 1898 recommended that the athletic grounds be relocated near the northeast corner of the campus "at the south end of the long pasture which lies north of the president's house." This site required no general grading, would interfere little with farm operations, was near the new gymnasium and close to "the most effective street railway, which is a considerable advantage." The trustees adopted this program May 5, 1898.

CONFERENCE BEGINNINGS

The growth of early athletics on the Ohio State campus seemingly paralleled that on other Ohio college campuses. Natural rivalries began to spring up at least by 1884 when there was talk of forming a state intercollegiate athletic association. One of the early advocates of this was the editor of the Kenyon *Advance*. This idea was taken up by the *Lantern* and others. Presently the Ohio Conference was organized. Rules were adopted and intercollegiate schedules began to be drawn.

What was described as the first annual contest of "The Inter-Collegiate Athletic Association of Ohio" took place at 2 p.m. May 31, 1884 on the Ohio State grounds. The program was made up of eleven events with "an elegant goblet offered the individual winner." The meet was won by Wooster with 31 points, Kenyon 24, Ohio State 17, and Denison 8. The cup was won by L. M. Snyder, of Kenyon. The boxing matches were called off "because of the non-arrival of the gloves in time." The winning marks were well below those of a modern high school meet: 100-yd. dash, 11⅕ sec.; 220-yd. dash, 25¾ sec.; running broad jump, 17 ft., 9 in.; 440-yd. run, 60 sec.; high jump, 4 ft. 10 in.

The next spring a further effort was made to promote the intercollegiate idea. The Columbus *Dispatch* of April 14, 1885 reported that an Athletic Association committee had been appointed to correspond with the colleges of the state regarding an intercollegiate contest. On May 13 it noted that a local field day would be held May 23 and that "successful contestants at this contest will represent the State University at the Inter-Collegiate contest" at Wooster on the second Saturday in

June in which six colleges were expected to participate. But when May 23 came the field day had to be postponed because 9 inches of rain fell in 11 hours. The paper had no later report on any state meet.

But Wooster was the host on May 22, 1890 to the "Ohio State Inter-Collegiate Field Day." Ohio State entered a squad of nine men. Wooster, Denison, Buchtel (later Akron), and Kenyon were the other participants.

Despite this earlier intercollegiate competition, the *Dispatch* on May 24, 1890 reported the results of what was described as the "first meeting of the Ohio Inter-Collegiate Athletic Association." Wooster, Ohio State, Kenyon and Denison participated. One of the events was "kicking football." A Denison man won this event with a boot of 135 ft., 6 in. Ohio State entrants won the 100-yd. dash, the shot put, the pole vault, and the mile run.

The state "field meet" in 1896 was held June 6 at Westerville. Nine colleges were represented. Oberlin was first with 48 points and Ohio State second with $20\frac{1}{3}$. The 1897 meet was held at the Columbus Driving Park and again Oberlin was first and Ohio State second. The outcome was clouded a bit because of charges that the winner of the 880-yd. run, who placed second also in the hurdles, was a "professional," according to the May 31 *Dispatch*. Ohio State, the May 30, 1898 *Dispatch* reported, "easily won" the third annual state field day with 58 points.

During the 1895 holidays, meanwhile, the presidents of Ohio colleges, concerned as to irregularities in college athletics, met in Columbus and drew up a set of regulations to counteract professionalism and other unhealthy influences. The proposed set of rules was to become effective whenever any five Ohio colleges signified "their intention of abiding by the rules." As reported by the January 15, 1896 *Lantern* the eight proposed regulations were:

1. No student shall take part in intercollegiate athletics during the first year of his connection with the college unless he bring special commendations as to his high school scholastic attainments and especially as to his industry, faithfulness and general success in his student undertakings.

2. No student shall take part in intercollegiate athletics during the first year of his connection with the college, unless he is a candidate for a degree and a full and unconditioned member of the class with which he claims graduation or is a regular and unconditional member of some established course in the institution.

3. It shall be an absolute and essential condition precedent of every intercollegiate game that the managers of the contesting clubs shall interchange, not less than ten days prior to the game, full lists of

participants, which lists shall be certified by the presidents of the respective colleges as containing only the names of actual and bona fide students of the colleges in good and approved standing.
4. In any intercollegiate game no person shall be chosen as umpire or referee, or for any other similar position, who has any connection whatever with either of the colleges contending.
5. Any student properly charged and duly disqualified by the umpire or referee with slugging or any other form of foul play, shall be debarred from playing in any intercollegiate game in the remainder of the college year unless reinstated by the approval of the presidents of three non-participating colleges.
6. The use of profanity or any obscenity by any member of a team shall be strictly forbidden by the managers and captains of such teams.
7. When any member of a team fails or has charged against him any conditions in the work of the term preceding that in which any intercollegiate game is played, such student shall not be allowed to play in such intercollegiate game until his conditions have been made good.
8. No student shall be allowed to receive any form of compensation for engaging in athletics.

The account made no mention of whether President Canfield attended but it is likely that he did. By a coincidence there was evidence elsewhere that President William Oxley Thompson, of Miami University, who was to succeed Canfield at Ohio State, took part. "At the University here," the *Lantern* commented with reference to the code, "they will also be construed as to be binding in our relation with colleges outside the state and those within the state that have not come under the new regulations." But a month later it noted that only three colleges had approved the code.

College presidents were not the only ones interested in the matter of intercollegiate athletic rules. Student representatives from eight Ohio colleges attended a meeting February 8, 1896 and drew up an alternate set of regulations, modifying those drafted by the presidents. The institutions represented were Cincinnati, Otterbein, Wittenberg, Denison, Kenyon, Oberlin, Ohio Wesleyan and Ohio State. Ed H. French represented Ohio State.

"The belief seemed quite general," the February 12, 1896 *Lantern* explained, "that the desired results could be secured with less trouble and greater satisfaction than under the plan proposed by the College Presidents association." Two things were proposed: a permanent organization among the colleges of the state, and "to adopt a set of rules and regulations that would forever prevent the taint of professionalism from creeping into the college athletics."

A constitution was framed which was to be submitted to the colleges of the state. The organization was to be known as The Intercollegiate Athletic Association of Ohio. Its objects were "To establish a state authority in collegiate athletics and the advancement and improvement of amateur athletics among Ohio colleges." The first annual state field meet under auspices of the new association was set for May or June, 1896 in Columbus and an arbitration commission was provided to resolve disputes.

Students evidently took exception to the proposed rules as drawn up by the college presidents. The November 4, 1896 *Lantern* said that an alternate set of rules, slightly modifying those drafted by the presidents, had been drawn up and would "soon be considered." It observed that "In every rule pertaining to individual players the erroneous idea is at the bottom that to engage in athletics is a great privilege which is granted by the great generosity of the Faculty." It called this "hideous in the extreme."

Early in his regime on the campus, President Canfield expounded his ideas on athletics in a talk to the athletic association. "The way to put athletics on a proper footing," he said, "is to make the Association include and foster every kind of legitimate out-door sport. We need to have foot-ball and play it well, in a clean and gentlemanly way, whether we win or not, for that matter . . . ."

The fact was that toward the turn of the century intercollegiate athletics were in a state of ferment. Definite faculty and administrative control was supplanting the earlier laxity and irregularities. Groups of colleges and universities with common interests and problems were being organized with standards for eligibility and competition and with definite codes of rules and regulations.

President Canfield evidently attended such a meeting in January, 1897 at Madison, Wis. This was a meeting of university presidents at which a committee on athletic games was set up. Canfield transmitted this committee's report to the faculty in June, 1897. This was referred in turn to the faculty committee on student organizations of which Prof. Ernst Eggers was chairman. Eggers reported back at the October 13, 1897 faculty meeting but the minutes gave no details of the "progress" noted.

Just what meeting Canfield attended the previous winter is not clear. That it was not a meeting of what became the Land-Grant College Association seems borne out by the fact that the proceedings of that group make no reference to any such item or committee. It could have been a meeting of the National Association of State Universities, since Ohio

State belonged to both groups. The latter group took shape in 1896 but no proceedings were published prior to those for 1901. Despite the lack of a definite record, it seems clear that both inside and outside of Ohio college and university presidents as well as their faculties had a sense of growing concern and responsibility for college athletics.

Within Ohio this common interest, both educationally and athletically, centered largely in the Ohio Conference and especially in its most influential members known as the Big Six: Western Reserve, Case, Oberlin, Wooster, Ohio Wesleyan, and Ohio State. In the Midwest a similar grouping involved the Big Nine or the Western Intercollegiate Conference which Ohio State was to join in 1912.

The presidents of Ohio colleges met again during the 1896 holidays and continued their discussion of athletics. The January 13, 1897 *Lantern* spoke of the presidents and deans as having met in Columbus during the vacation period. The dates were not given but the account said in part:

> President Canfield opened the evening session with a talk on "Athletics," in which he gave voice to his own feelings and those of the student body in stating that the movement in our institution was towards cleaner athletics. President Meyers of Cincinnati College explained fully the condition of affairs there and pledged the support of his institution to pure athletics. President Thompson of Miami presented the following resolution which was at once adopted:
>
> "That it is the sense of this body that colleges in the association shall not make dates next year with colleges not certifying to the student list of players; and that we further recommend that 10 days' notice be interpreted to mean 'sufficient notice.'"

Thus slowly but steadily were the colleges of Ohio, and those elsewhere, moving in the direction of higher standards and joint control of athletics.

Intercollegiate athletics were also a topic of discussion at the 1897 and 1898 meetings of the Ohio College Association. At the 1897 meeting June 29-July 1 in Toledo, college athletics came under review as part of a conference on college problems. The topic was assigned to E. L. Hall, professor of Latin at Hiram College. Hall admitted that "a great deal can be said in favor of college athletics," but he dealt chiefly with their "most objectionable features."

In his opinion student athletic associations regarded their debts or other financial obligations lightly. On the playing fields, he added, "Profane language is not uncommon; the use of tobacco in its vilest and filthiest form is noticeable; betting is carried on by persons who have no means to squander in this way; players are hired who have no connection with the college or institution for which they play; . . . ." To him professionalism was one of the worst features. And when games were played in large cities with many students attending, he went on, "It is a common thing to see college decorations used in ornamenting saloons, and to see the college colors flaunted in places that are worse than saloons; . . ."

He took a dim view also of newspaper coverage of college sports. Such reports, he asserted, gave to the player "who is above average a prominence which leads him to over-estimate his own importance." Reports of college games were generally printed, moreover, on the sports pages "in connection with accounts of prize fights, horse races and contests between bull dogs and game cocks, or any other animals that may be induced to fight for the amusement of human brutes." He objected likewise to "the hooting and yelling" and hideous noises at college games and to the "desecration" of Thanksgiving by games played on that day.

At the next year's O.C.A. convention at Put-in-Bay, there was further discussion of "Inter-Collegiate Athletics." The participants were President J. W. Bashford, of Ohio Wesleyan, and Profs. A. C. Pierson, of Hiram, and G. H. Young, of Wittenberg. Bashford said he favored college athletics but declared that they were "subject to great abuses." He advocated the adoption in Ohio of the rules of "The American Athletic Association," which, in essence, forbade professionalism or pay for summer play, required high scholarship, and had a 4-year limit on participation by any individual athlete. In Pierson's view college athletics were "demoralizing," he objected to the interference with school work, and said there was "some drinking on the road after a successful game of ball."

Young declared himself heartily in favor of "local college athletics" or what a later day would have called interclass or intramural sports. At Wittenberg, he said, "our local athletic association was so involved financially that it could not run the risk of having a team in the field at large, so attention was turned to local athletics" in which there were five class teams.

III
COMPETITIVE BEGINNINGS

EARLY athletics on the campus were, as noted, a simple matter of doing what came naturally. Much of this, as indicated, centered at the North Dorm. Thus in the spring of 1882, for example, the *Lantern* reported that the Dormitory Athletic Association had purchased boxing gloves. The same issue noted also that football once more was engrossing the attention of men students. And the June, 1882 issue even had some comment on overemphasis on sports on the campus.

For the next fifteen years there was frequent mention of the lack of indoor facilities and of the need for a gymnasium. Until a separate building could be provided for this purpose application was made to the administration to set aside space in University Hall or some other building. These efforts came to nought although indoor drill was held for some years in a basement room in University Hall. In 1887 there was even talk of a stock company to underwrite a gymnasium.

In the early years two sites were used successively for athletic grounds. One was on the north side of the campus, extending northward from about where Derby and Hayes Halls were built later. But this location was too valuable for such a purpose and the May, 1883 *Lantern* reported some of the space taken from the athletic grounds for other purposes. The next site used regularly was the field west of Neil Ave., north of the North Dorm and about opposite where Oxley Hall was erected years later. This site ran downhill toward the Olentangy River, a fact which gave some advantage, for example, to the football team which had the higher ground. This location gave way around the turn of the century to what became known as Ohio Field, which ultimately occupied all of the area from 17th Ave. and High St. north to Woodruff Ave., and west to the "woods."

Four decades afterward, Prof. Joseph N. Bradford, '83, longtime University architect, recalled the early days of sports on the campus. As reported in the February, 1920 *Alumni Monthly,* he said that the earliest interest in what might be termed athletic contests was in the spring of 1877 or 1878 and consisted of foot races. The "track" was the gravel road from High St. to the main building. Professors served as officials and the "stadium" was the front steps of University Hall.

About 1886, he continued, the first effort was made to develop a real athletic field. This occupied the site of the later chemistry building near where Derby Hall now is, and extending to a point near the road in front of where Lord Hall was built later. Its main feature was a "well built" quarter-mile track. Spectators stood and the most exciting events were the bicycle races on the old "high wheelers."

Increasing interest in athletics, he went on, soon required a better place for practice and for the games. The next field was in the area west of the site of the later Oxley Hall "across the Neil Ave. driveway." This was partly fenced on the east and partly on the north and south sides. On the south side of the field was "a very primitive stadium," which actually was a rickety wooden stand seating about 200. Prof. Bradford said this field was the site of the first intercollegiate baseball game on the campus and of the first senior-faculty game.

Prof. James E. Boyd, '91, longtime head of the department of mechanics, also provided a brief description of the early days centering in the "Dorm" in the July, 1910 issue of the *Alumni Quarterly*. "The first training table at the University was furnished there and at the club's expense for one of the football teams," he said. "Before we had enclosed grounds for athletics the supplies which the teams received were bought by subscription. One fall a collection of about thirty dollars was raised at the Dormitory to supply the football teams with suits . . . ."

As noted, baseball seems to have been the original sport on the campus. Tennis, track (Field and Class Days), and football soon followed. But basketball did not begin to flourish until the gymnasium became available in 1898 and other sports such as swimming and golf came much later. Tennis was fairly popular. At one time there was a court where the Thompson Memorial Library now stands and there were others on the site of one of the early chemistry buildings and on the edge of a grove of trees west of Neil and Eleventh Aves. between the North Dorm and the "Little" Dorm.

Selection of University colors and the emergence of college cheers come in 1878 about the time of the advent of competitive sports on the campus. The colors chosen were scarlet and gray. From the limited evidence this was the work of a committee composed of two men and two women students. (See p. 25.) Cheerleaders also began to make their appearance although they were first known as "yell masters."

One of the first Ohio State yells was the "Wahoo." There were two explanations for the "Wahoo" yell. One what that it was derived from the "wahoo bush" (*Euonymus*) whose berry was bright scarlet with gray hulls. But Charles Fox, Ag. '90, in a letter in the May, 1923 *Alumni*

Monthly, scoffed at this. According to his recollection the "Wahoo" yell became prominent about 1889 and was a product of the North Dorm. There were two versions of it, he said, "one for girls, Y.M.C.A. work and refined meetings—the other for practical field work."

"Wahoo!" he added, was a favorite expression of a man named Clark. "Wahoo Tonic," then a popular "medicine," was sold in the vicinity of Broad and High Sts. by "an old medicine fakir" who extolled its supposed virtues. Many years later "Wahoo" was changed in the yell to make it rhyme with Ohio but this was derided by oldtimers.

The old yell went like this:

> Wahoo, Wahoo!
> Rip, zip, bazoo!
> I yell, I yell,
> For O. S. U.,
> Wahoo, Wahoo!

The other version was:

> Wahoo, Wahoo!
> Rip, zip, bazoo!
> I yell, I yell,
> I yell like hell!
> For O. S. U.!

According to the Hooper volume of the University History series, the University colors were "adopted in the spring term of 1878 by a committee consisting of Alice Townshend Wing, '80, Curtis C. Howard, '78, Sioux Glover, '82, and Harold R. Pool, '81. The first colors selected were orange and black, but as these were found to be the colors of Princeton, they were changed to scarlet and gray. There was no significance in either selection, the only purpose of the committee being to have a pleasing combination. The original colors are preserved in the Library."

The early sports activities on the campus in baseball, tennis and the Field and Class Days are dealt with here. Because almost from the first it attracted considerable attention, football is described separately.

BASEBALL

At the outset baseball and the annual Field and Class Days were operated on a hand-to-mouth basis in that they had little or no coaching, little or nothing in the way of furnished equipment, and very skimpy financial support. As early as the spring of 1881 the *Lantern* reported a baseball game between the University and the Capital University "Mutuals." Ohio Wesleyan was another early opponent, sometimes referred to as "Delaware." In June, 1883 the *Lantern* asked "Is Wooster afraid to play OSU?" The same issue reported that the athletic association had decided not to pay the expenses of the "boys" to Wooster for a game, while in a game with Ohio Wesleyan a "Delaware" player suffered a broken leg. The July issue stated bluntly that Ohio State baseball playing was "a poor excuse."

Baseball was played on the campus at least as early as 1879. Under the heading of "Local Mention," the Columbus *Dispatch* of May 26 that year in giving the scores of games reported "Acme 22, State University 11." On June 4, 1880 it announced that "The State University and Anderson base ball clubs will play at the Barracks Saturday at 2:30 P.M. The elegant grounds and the auspices surrounding the respective clubs that have played there guarantees fine amusement under most favorable circumstances. Ladies have been present at games played heretofore." The outcome was not reported. On October 26, 1882 the *Dispatch* noted that "The defeat of the Ohio Wesleyan university base ball club by the Ohio State University club created little excitement owing to the clubs being out of practice."

Out-of-town games soon came into the picture. On May 3, 1883 the *Dispatch* reported that "The Athletic Association will go on an excursion to Delaware on Saturday, to witness a game of base ball between O.S.U. and Delaware." Progress was being made meanwhile at home. "The base ball grounds," the paper added under "State University Notes," "are being put in good condition, and the Athletic Association proposes fitting up their new grounds for permanent use, laying out a track for running and walking, erecting hurdles, bars, etc., with a grand stand for the accommodation of visitors sometime in the new [*sic*] future." Two weeks later the University team was to go to Wooster for a game.

But progress was slow and organization was lacking. "Owing to the kindness of Professor McFarland," the *Dispatch* told its readers April 2, 1885, "the base ball grounds at the dormitory are being placed in excellent condition." It added that there would be a game there on Saturday "between picked nines." On May 1 following it reported that "The base ball club met today and instructed a committee to procure uniforms," adding that the manager was trying to arrange for a game with "the Barracks" the next day.

Baseball in those days was a fall as well as a spring sport. The *Dispatch* of October 3, 1885 said that "The first ball game of the season was played on the dorm grounds yesterday afternoon between the college nine and a picked nine from town." The score was 24 to 6 "in favor of the college." The same issue reported a movement under way "to consolidate the Athletic Association, the Base Ball Association and the Tennis Club under one head, while each retains its individuality. The united organization would include almost every student and a vigorous effort would be made to secure better facilities for athletic training."

Interest in sports both on the campus and in the city was sporadic and apathetic. The campus was still far out in the country. This situation was reflected in an item in the *Dispatch* for November 12, 1887: "The athletic sports on the dormitory grounds this afternoon were poorly attended, only about a score of visitors being present. A game of tennis was played, and a game of base ball was to take place later." Baseball in the fall continued at least into the early 'Nineties. On October 30, 1891 the *Dispatch* reported that "The base-ball team of the University will cross bats to-morrow afternoon for the last time this season, with the Capital University team, on the grounds of the latter."

An Ohio college league of sorts was in existence at least as early as 1890. That spring a schedule was announced which included the teams of Denison, Kenyon, Buchtel, Wooster and Ohio State. Large scores were not uncommon. In the spring of 1893, for example, Ohio State won from Wittenberg 11 to 8 and from Kenyon 18 to 7 but lost to Adelbert (Western Reserve) 19 to 7, then "pulverized" Denison by the "hilarious" score of 17 to 3. The 1892 Ohio State team won seven straight games and the "championship." The Varsity nine was listed as "champions, 1892," playing five games in October, 1891 and fourteen in the spring of 1892. Of these it won fifteen, lost three and tied one.

In the spring of 1895 enough players were out to have two teams in uniform, one in "the regulation scarlet and gray, while the second team have secured the uniforms of the old Columbus professional team."* That season was marked by what apparently was the first game with Michigan, then as later described as "'champions of the West." The game had its climax in a 9th inning "rhubarb" when after continued wrangling over the officiating Michigan took its team off the field and the crowd erupted in disorder. Part of the *Dispatch* accounting for April 18, 1895 follows:

* "Effie" Norton, a former outfielder turned pitcher, was a star on this team. The next year he pitched for the Washington Senators.

STUDIENTS LOSE THEIR MINDS

DISGRACEFUL SCENES ON THE O.S.U. FIELD

The game of baseball between the teams of Ann Arbor and the Ohio State University terminated disgracefully yesterday. After over two hours of wrangling and with ball playing, the contest ended in what bordered on a small-sized riot. Rowdyism, mistaken for college enthusiasm, prevailed to such an extent that the policemen and a few sensible alumni of the university alone, prevented a conflict which would undoubtedly have resulted disastrously for both sides. . . .

The score was 4 to 4 in the 9th and Ohio State had a runner on second base. Michigan objected to the umpire. The home team was exonerated and the rooters were blamed for what followed. The Michigan team left the field.

In February, 1897 the *Lantern* was looking forward to a resumption of athletics "after a period of repose during the winter months." Among the sports anticipated in the spring were "baseball, Field Day events, Tennis, Bicycling and Golf." All of these were known on the campus except golf and it was expected that a golf club would be organized that spring.

The *Lantern* recalled that in the spring of 1896 the "innovation" of bringing in a coach was tried with good results. The coach, who evidently worked only during March, 1896 was "Kip" Selbach, of Columbus, a former student, who was an outfielder for Washington, then in the National League. As a result, the *Lantern* declared that the Varsity nine "outclassed" every team it played in '96 except possibly Michigan. But while the paper had announced that Selbach would again coach "during the month of March," it was now doubtful because of the perennial lack of funds. There was talk of another "benefit" to help the situation but the outlook was not favorable.

What seems to have been the first baseball victory over Michigan occurred in April, 1897 when the home team won 12 to 11 by scoring four runs in the 9th inning. Yet on a trip two weeks later Ohio State lost successively to DePauw 11 to 3, to Northwestern 15 to 6, and to Michigan 11 to 4. There was an echo from Cleveland that spring following a game with Western Reserve. Under a Cleveland dateline, May 14, the *Dispatch* reported: "There's a kick at Western Reserve over 'ringers' having played in the game against O.S.U. last week. President Thwing threatens to oust the team for the season."

Another development that would have been regarded as strange in later years involved a game scheduled with Ohio Wesleyan. It appeared in this *Dispatch* item for June 1, 1897: "Delaware, O., June 1. DePauw University filled the Ohio State's date yesterday with Ohio Wesleyan owing to the Ohio State's president refusing to allow the team to play on Memorial day." In the final game that spring Ohio State defeated Indiana 24 to 2. In the spring of 1899 in a game here with Washington & Jefferson the visiting pitcher struck out twenty of the home team. The visitors won 7 to 4.

TENNIS

Tennis was popular in the early 'Nineties. On October 21, 1892, for example, the *Wahoo,* which succeeded the *Lantern* for a time, reported a match won by the University doubles team of Farber and Jenkins from the Columbus Tennis Association pair. The scores were 6-4, 4-6, and 6-4. The paper said "the space west of the court was crowded with enthusiastic spectators." Match tennis was played in the fall in those days as well as in the spring.

Campus facilities for tennis were limited and somewhat primitive by later standards. On October 26, 1892 the *Dispatch* reported that "a return game of lawn tennis is to be played Saturday at the residence of Governor Foster." Yet in the spring of 1887 the *Dispatch* mentioned that the lawn tennis association had four playing courts. On October 26, 1886 the *Ohio State Journal* noted that "The cold wave has practically killed lawn tennis playing." In June, 1890 the *Dispatch* reported that Ohio State had won the intercollegiate tennis tournament, both singles and doubles.

FIELD AND CLASS DAYS

"Field Days" were one of the earliest manifestations of sports at the University. In the early years two of these were held each spring, one open to all students "regardless of race, color or previous condition," as a *Dispatch* account put it on April 29, 1881, and the other in connection with a Class Day program. Before many years a state "field day" was held and in time this grew into the Ohio Intercollegiate Conference championships, known as the "Big Six" meet.

At the outset the campus "field day" was held near the main building. The short races were run on the roadway and the longer ones went around the building. These meets, which included bicycle races at different distances, were held later on the first regular athletic field. Still later they were held at the State Fair Grounds or at the Driving Park in southeast Columbus.

On the 1881 occasion referred to above, the *Dispatch* said:

Saturday, May 7th, will be a field day at the State University. The students . . . will indulge in athletic sports. They desire the presence of all their sisters, cousins and aunts, and as many more as can spare the time. It is proposed to convert a portion of the grass covered campus into a temporary gymnasium. Jumping, running, boxing, pole leaping, hammer throwing, fencing, base ball, foot ball and other sports involving muscular exhibition by young men, will be the order of the day.

The races will be of at least one hundred yards in distance. High jumping will be preceded by running and by standing [*sic*]. The hop, step and jump will be one of the exercises.

The gentlemen are in the flower of youth and early manhood. It is believed their friends will be present to smile upon them one week from tomorrow, May 7th.

The program came off on schedule but some of the events listed originally, such as "foot ball," did not materialize. There was a boxing match, a tug-of-war with seven men to a side, a 1-mile heel-and-toe walk, a wheelbarrow race, and a sack race. The 100-yd. dash was run in 11 seconds and the 220-yd. dash in 27½ seconds. The pole "leap" was won at 6 ft., 6 in., or less than a later day high jumper could do. The "running long jump" reached 17 ft. and the baseball throw 212 ft.

The June, 1881 *Lantern* reported the results of the first Field Day as "gratifying" with nearly 1000 in attendance. The "exercises" were held on the campus. But the paper suggested the need for more entries and for better arrangement of the program. It complained also of the "crowd of small boys" and urged at the next Field Day "to have *no one* on the lawn except the contestants and the judges." It recommended also that the band be "draughted" for the occasion.

"A badge, made of heavy blue silk," the account added, "on which was printed the name of the Association, and the name of the event in which the contestant won, was presented to the winner in each event. The college colors were attached to the badge, adding considerably to its appearance."

The Class Day exercises occurred in connection with the commencement season. The events were much the same as for the Field Day, but a top award, known as the Franklin Prize, went to the individual scoring the most points. This was presented by Prof. Albert H. Tuttle, of the faculty. The 1881 Class Day meet was scheduled for June 21 but the *Dispatch* of the next day did not give the results.

Thirteen events were announced for the 1882 Field Day, including shooting, the ⅓-mile run, a 2-mile go-as-you-please, and a blind man's race. At that year's Class Day "athletic exercises," the *Dispatch* reported that the Franklin Medal was won by S. S. Devol, while Charles Easterly "by the aid of a pole, vaulted over a string eight feet eight inches high," or 6 inches higher than the previous record. Some of the weights used varied considerably from those of a later day. A 22-pound shot was thrown 21 ft., 9 in., and a 9-pound hammer 93 ft., 8 in.

Better marks were made in the 1882 Field Day events than a year earlier. Some of the events, by later standards, were oddities such as the triple standing jump and the ⅓-mile run. The attendance was estimated at 1200, including apparently a visiting contingent from Ohio Wesleyan who got mention for "the tall plug hats of the Delaware seniors."

Marks made on that occasion were: 100-yd. dash, 11½ sec.; 1-mile walk, 9 min. 30½ sec.; running broad jump, 17 ft. 8½ in.; standing high jump, 4 ft.; pole vault, 8 ft., 2 in.; hammer throw (9 lbs.), 76 ft., 9 in.; shot put (22 lbs.), 22 ft. 9 in.; running hop, step and jump, 39 ft., 5 in.; ⅓-mile run, 1 min., 32½ sec.; 3 standing jumps, 28 ft., 3½ in., and 2-mile go-as-you-please, 13 min., 55 sec.

Bad weather interfered with the 1883 program since the quarter-mile track, the hurdle track and the horizontal bar were not in readiness, the June 2, 1883 *Dispatch* noted. The sports, it said, "had to be conducted as usual in front of the College building this afternoon." In addition to the usual potato and sack races, there was a "knights tournament," with four contestants of whom two were mounted on the shoulders of two others. The object was to dismount the opponent.

The hammer broke after a number of throws and that contest had to be declared off and the mile run likewise because of some irregularity. There were other complications when the individual high point winner, with 18 points, was declared ineligible and the top prize went to D. F. Snyder who had 11 points.

For some reason a Field Day program was held in November, 1884. The *Dispatch* of November 4, 1884 noted that athletic contests for the Franklin and Lazarus prizes were "in progress this afternoon." The former was a gold medal, valued at $25, and the latter was a silver medal donated by the Lazarus brothers. The program consisted of fourteen events, including an obstacle race.

An idea of the paucity of physical facilities of the time may be had from a small item in the *Dispatch* of May 6, 1885. It reported that the board of trustees at a recent meeting had voted $50 "to equip a female gymnasium for the female students under the direction of Professor Tuttle."

After the regular Class Day exercises of June 23, 1885, "the audience adjourned to the east lawn to witness the athletic sports," according to the next day's *Dispatch*. For the high point man the prize was $10 worth of books. This time, among other things, there was a fat man's race. The broad jump was won by "Mr. McPherson." This was William McPherson, later a distinguished chemist and for more than twenty-five years dean of the Graduate School. He did 17 ft., 9 in. in the broad jump and also won the high jump, the running hop, step and jump and the standing broad jump and was second in the 2-mile go-as-you-please. He was high man with 31 points.

In 1886 the Field Day "exercises," already postponed a week, had to "be abandoned because of the lateness of the hour." Several weeks later the Class Day exercises were postponed similarly "on account of rain."

"Athletic exercises" or a Field Day were still scheduled late in the fall of 1886. They were to have been held November 6, but had to be postponed because of bad weather. On the program were two bicycle races, one for the slowest and one for the fastest rider. It was then announced that the events would be held the next Saturday but no mention was made of the results.

In addition to the Franklin Prize, merchandise prizes came into vogue for the winners of Field Day events. Apparently they were contributed by merchants. In 1890, for example, a silver cup was the prize in the 50-yd. dash, two pairs of slippers in the 100-yd. dash, a silk belt in the 220-yd. dash, a pair of tennis shoes in the 440-yd. dash, six linen handkerchiefs in the standing broad jump, a $2 hair brush for the standing broad jump (with weights), a book of Longfellow poems in the running hop, step and jump, a box of cigars in the running broad jump, a pearl handled knife in the standing high jump, a $3 hat in the pole vault, a dozen photographs in the hammer throw, a cash prize of $2 in the sack race, a razor in the quarter-mile walk, and a scarf pin in the slow bicycle race.

One of the great athletes of the mid-'Nineties was Ed H. French, brother of Prof. Thomas E. French, '95, the University's first—and long-time—Western Conference faculty representative. Ed French was a "one-man gang" both in football and in track. In the 1894 Field Day in a 16-event program French won seven firsts, a feat which, in its way, matched in part the marvelous doings of the fabulous Jesse Owens nearly forty years later. French won the 100-yd. dash, the shot put, the high kick, the standing hop, step and jump, the standing high jump, the running broad jump, and the 440-yd. dash. The winner of the 1-mile bicycle race in that meet with Perry Okey, later a well known Columbus figure.

Between 1890 and 1896 new campus marks were set for the various track and field events. There were still no indoor facilities. In 1896 W. F. Genheimer won the medal for the best all around athlete. As given by the 1897 *Makio*, the campus records were:

Event	Record	Athlete	Year
50-yd. dash	5⅖ sec.	Hobart Beatty	1892
100-yd. dash	10⅖ sec.	R. M. Burns	'96
220-yd. dash	24 sec.	C. W. Withoft	'92
440-yd. dash	55 sec.	S. H. McKee	'96
880-yd. run	2 min. 10⅘ sec.	Homer C. Howard	'96
Mile run	5 min. 4⅕ sec.	C. E. Lane	'95
120-yd. hurdle	19⅕ sec.	Hobart Beatty	'92
16-lb. shot put	34 ft. 11 in.	W. F. Lavery	'90
16-lb. hammer throw	79 ft. 3 in.	M. L. Blose	'96
High jump	5 ft. 3 in.	E. M. Bloom	'90
Broad jump	18 ft. 3 in.	Hobart Beatty	'91
Hop, step and jump	43 ft. 3 in.	Hobart Beatty	'92
Standing high jump	4 ft. 6 in.	W. S. Scott	'92
Standing broad jump	10 ft. 5 in.	W. S. Scott	'91
Standing hop, step, jump	30 ft. 4 in.	W. S. Scott	'91
High kick (hitch)	8 ft. 7 in.	Homer Howard	'96
Pole vault	9 ft. 1 in.	W. A. Landacre	'90
¼-mile bicycle race	34⅘ sec.	F. Mundhenk	'96
½-mile bicycle race	1 min. 15⅘ sec.	F. Mundhenk	'96
1-mile bicycle race	2 min. 25⅗ sec.	F. Mundhenk	'96
2-mile bicycle race	5 min. 20 sec.	A. DeLoffre	'95

Occasional dual meets were also held. Ohio State won a "field day" with Kenyon in May, 1895 at the State Fair Grounds. George W. Rightmire, a tall, gangling senior, who was to become the University's sixth president, won the standing broad jump and the hammer throw and was second in the hop, step and jump and in the shot put.

Until it had better facilities of its own the University had to resort to other places such as the State Fair Grounds and the Columbus Driving Park for outdoor sports. But there were complications at times. In 1896, for example, the state board of agriculture in the words of the May 27 *Dispatch* "refused to permit the university athletic association to use the state fair grounds for field day exercises. Heretofore the state fair grounds had been secured without any trouble and no one had any idea they would be refused this year. The only other place available in the city with a race track is the driving park and it is impossible to secure that.

However field day must be held and if nothing else can be done it is probable the bicycle races will be declared off and the other events held at the university ball park. The roads on the campus will have to be used for the running races. . . ."

The solution was to take the affair to "the driving park at Westerville" and this was done May 29, 1896 with a half holiday from classes. Again merchandise and other material prizes were given to the individual winners such as a $5 umbrella, a $5 cane, $2 in laundry trade, meal tickets worth $3.50 at the Coffee Kitchen, a $5 lamp, a pair of $2.50 bicycle pants, a set of boxing gloves, and a revolver, no less, along with a pair of $7 opera glasses, $5 on a suit, and a pair of $4 football shoes. Records were broken in the hammer throw, the 100-yd. dash, the hitch kick, the 440-, 880-, 1- and 2-mile runs, and in the bicycle races. In the last Fred Mundhenk was credited with a new world's collegiate record in the 2-mile bicycle handicap race. Mundhenk, starting from scratch, outraced other riders with handicaps, in 5 min., $29\frac{1}{5}$ sec. The old record was 5 min., 42 sec. Mundhenk won a gold medal for his effort. W. F. Genheimer topped the meet with 31 points.

When the new gymnasium was under construction in 1897 there was criticism because no provision was made for a running track. This was remedied in the early winter when it was announced that a "mezonene" story would be added to provide a canvas-covered track with seats at that level for 1000 spectators. This brought the total seating capacity for indoor events such as basketball to around 3000.

The *Lantern* had come out that year for an expanded sports program. In the January 13, 1897 issue it advocated editorially "Athletics that will bring out every student. Besides football and baseball there should be tennis, golf, hare and hounds [cross country], and even walking clubs" as well as "a boating course on the Olentangy" which would provide skating in the winter. It also urged class teams and "a permanent location of the athletic field." This last, to be described later, was to come the next year. That same year, however, the "all around athlete" was discouraged to the extent that participants in the annual Field Day were limited to two events each.

The spring of 1898 was notable for the fact that the new athletic field northwest of what later was 17th Ave. and High St. was used for the first time despite its unfinished state. At almost the last minute the Field Day exercises, which were to have been held at the Driving Park, were transferred to the new site on May 21. "To this end," the *Dispatch* reported May 13, "work on the new grounds is to be pushed with the greatest expedition." It was hoped to have the grounds ready but this proved in vain as the *Dispatch* told its readers on the day of the meet. The field, it said, "has only been fenced within the last week and consequently there has been no time to prepare a running track and the runners are somewhat handicapped in having to run on the sod." Even so the final of the 100-yd. dash was clocked in $10\tfrac{3}{5}$ seconds.

IV
EARLY FOOTBALL—1889–1897

WHILE the first varsity football was not played on the campus until the spring of 1890 the dormitory grounds west of Neil Ave. were the scene of impromptu football activity as early as 1881. There was mention, for example, of "foot-ball" in connection with the 1881 Field Day. Under the heading of University News, the October 8, 1887 *Dispatch* reported that "A new foot-ball was obtained to-day at the dormitory, and promises to furnish considerable amusement for the boys." On October 25, 1887 this item appeared: "A foot-ball team has been organized and will play a picked eleven on the dorm grounds late this afternoon." Two weeks later the paper reported further: "Two foot-ball teams have been selected by the Athletic Committee to take part in the contest on field day, next Saturday." There was no further mention that fall.

Competitive football made its unorganized appearance on the campus at least as early as 1886. The *Makio* of that year, speaking for one of the upper classes, reported that "The freshmen had the audacity to challenge us to a game of football." The 1888 *Makio* accounted not only for the baseball, tennis, bicycle and fencing clubs but for a "Foot Ball Team." There was no mention of any games but eleven players were named,— a center and six "rushers," i.e., linemen, three right and three left, as well as two halfbacks, a quarterback, and a "goal" or fullback. If there was any organized football during the school year 1888-89, the *Makio* was silent about it.

The first football on the campus, as indicated, centered around the North Dorm. But it was not long before talk began of meeting teams from other Ohio colleges. Thus the April 21, 1887 *Lantern* reported that Marietta College students had sent word that they were "willing to play us a game of football." Footballs themselves were so rare they belonged to individual students. The May 26, 1887 *Lantern* spoke of one belonging to Erwin Schueller. And the October 6, 1887 issue reported that there would be a game of football but it did not say with whom. A little later the paper mentioned a game between the Columbus Buggy team and the college team.

In 1893 the *Dispatch* recalled the beginnings of college football in Ohio, although the details were a bit at variance with the apparent facts.

In its November 27, 1893 issue it said: ". . . figuratively speaking the students of the colleges of Ohio had never seen a foot ball until the fall of 1890, when several of them organized an Intercollegiate Association and Columbus was represented by the O.S.U. eleven. The game did not receive a very enthusiastic reception, as it was, locally, a new one, and consequently a very small number . . . were acquainted with it." But interest in it, the account added, increased rapidly.

George N. Cole, '91, was credited with being one of those influential in introducing football to the campus. In the spring of 1889 some of the North Dorm students had been practicing with a football, perhaps home-made, but certainly not "store-bought." Cole told fifty years later how he took up a collection for a "real" football. Cole had gone to school in Columbus with Al S. Lilley who then attended Lawrenceville preparatory school and Princeton. Lilley and K. L. "Snake" Ames, an early Princeton All-American, were in Columbus later.

Cole helped to get Ohio State football going in two ways: he wrote to Spaulding's, one of the first athletic supply houses, for a football rules book and he asked Lilley whether he would coach the team. The rule book, in Cole's words, was "all Greek to the boys." Lilley agreed to do the coaching—there was no salary—and, according to Cole's account, Lilley, who lived on Main St., would ride an Indian pony to the practice grounds. Ames spent an afternoon teaching the squad to kick.

"Anything went but brass knuckles," Cole said in an interview in 1938, "and there was none of this fancy forward passing or razzle-dazzle. It was all power stuff and wedge work—the flying wedge, a sheer power play, was then in vogue. It was all right to step on a man's face, but you had to be careful how you did it."

Some years earlier, when the Stadium campaign was beginning to shape up in 1919, Athletic Director L. W. St. John and Prof. Thomas E. French addressed the New York alumni on the Stadium project. Afterward Cole, who was present, gave other details of the beginnings of football on the campus. He was quoted in the February, 1920 *Alumni Monthly* about the receipt of the football from his father, and what followed:

> In a few days a beauty of a pigskin contraption came, but he had made a mistake, so we thought, and we would have to return it, and it was accordingly repacked. But that afternoon someone broke into my room . . . and took out the alleged football, and a gang of the boys used it, playing a sort of mongrel soccer, mostly perspiration and wind—for we didn't know how real football was played.

So we had to keep it, much to our disgust, for that ball was eliptical [*sic*] and no one had heard of such a thing before. But we looked up the matter, sent for a book of rules and got a team together of which old Caesar Morrey was the mainstay.

They all had suits of heavy muslin. My place on the second team did not assure me with a suit so I got a suit of painter's white overalls and jumper, and after proper cutting-down, puckering strings, and an old blanket cut up for padding, it was quite a comfortable outfit to be thrown across the lot in. But I would note right here that the suit was always engaged weeks ahead by someone on the first team . . .

One afternoon late in the season I managed to get Snake Ames, who was captain of the Princeton football team about 1890 and who had been a classmate in Columbus schools to come out and show us a bit of class. I can still hear the crack of his kick!

M. C. Lilley, Jr., and A. S. Lilley who had also gone east to the old East Main Street School before playing on Yale and Princeton teams were also obtained as early coaches and before long things were just humming.

No admission was charged in those days of real sport—teams just came down and we put them up at the North Dorm. I had the big room over the "office" and as a rule they undressed in there to play in the big field west of Neil Avenue opposite what is now Oxley Hall . . . .

The *Lantern,* nearly a decade afterward, gave this account of the beginnings of football on the campus in its issue of December 7, 1898:

The game of foot ball took root at the Ohio State University in the fall of 1889, when a few students used to "gather on the green" of the old athletic field and kick a foot ball around the place a few hours in perhaps a few afternoons each week. But there was nothing like an organized foot ball team. That came in the spring of 1890, when a rudimentary team was formed with the remote idea of perhaps playing a game some day. That day came on April 1, 1890,* when the team went to Delaware for a game with the Ohio Wesleyan University. Neither team knew much about the game . . . .

Eleven years later in another story on the beginnings of football on the campus, the *Lantern* gave further details. In its December 1, 1909 issue it said that a score of years earlier "Wooster was the only school in Ohio with a regularly organized University team."

In the spring of 1890, the game finally reached the stage of Varsity competition with another college team, that of Ohio Wesleyan. This was twenty-one years after the first intercollegiate game in the United States between Rutgers and Princeton. The Ohio State-Ohio Wesleyan game was played May 3, 1890 at Delaware and the former won, 20 to 14. Neither the *Dispatch,* the *Ohio State Journal* nor the Delaware *Demo-*

* Actual date May 3, 1890.

cratic Press, a weekly, made any direct mention of the game at the time. Earlier the April 4 *Ohio State Journal* said "The football team has ordered suits and will go to Delaware next Saturday in style."

The April 25, 1890 *Lantern* meanwhile renewed the plea for support of the athletic association, noting that "The tennis teams, foot-ball team, and, particularly, the baseball team, are working hard." The same issue gave the lineup of the football team which, it added, "is ardently at work under Captain Jones" who played "center rusher." "Tomorrow the team goes to Delaware," the paper added, "to down the O.W.U.'s. The fellows are in fine shape, and clad in their new uniforms present a fine appearance."

For some reason the game was delayed a week. In the meantime there were injuries. "Along with the athletic boom," the next issue of the *Lantern* reported, "E. D. Martin, the efficient half-back of the foot ball team, broke his collar-bone in practice. Rane '91 and Laughlin '90, both met with injuries which necessitated their withdrawal from the foot ball team and Field Day. The injury to Mr. Rane is especially deplored, since he is one of the best of both the foot ball and base ball clubs . . ."

This same May 9, 1890 *Lantern* carried this account of the football game with Ohio Wesleyan, the first intercollegiate game for Ohio State. The account began:

FOOT BALL

O.S.U. vs. O.W.U.

Last Saturday, May 3rd, the O.S.U. foot ball team went to Delaware to play the first game since the organization of our team.

Neither team had practiced much, but our boys knew a little more about the game than the Delaware team. This fact gave us quite an advantage, and to it can be attributed the victory.

The team left for Delaware at 6 a.m. and the game was called for 9:30. Ohio State kicked off. Presently Large, the Ohio State quarterback, "got hold of the ball and made a fine run" and a touchdown. The goal was kicked and Ohio State made two more touchdowns in the first half to one for Ohio Wesleyan. Score at the half: Ohio State 14, Ohio Wesleyan 6.

With 10 minutes to play in the second half, Ohio Wesleyan tied the score. The *Lantern* account went on:

At this time, Morrey got the ball, and by a fine run, really made a touch down. The umpire, however, ruled that the runner had crossed the line. This put the ball "in play" within four feet of O.W.U.'s goal line.

To attempt running here would have been useless. The order was given to form the wedge three times in succession. On the first wedge the ball was advanced about three feet, and on the second it crossed the line by about a foot.

To kick a goal, from the position to which the ball was carried out, was indeed difficult, as it was far to the left of the goal. Large was equal to the occasion, however, and sent the ball spinning directly between the posts. After this there was but four minutes' time left. A great deal of work was done in this time but nothing was accomplished.

O.W.U.	Position	O.S.U.
Clark	Center Rusher	Jones
Ganer	First Right	Lincoln
Hyer	Second Right	Miller
Liehly	Right Tackle	Johnston
Tracey	First Left	Folk*
Clark, Chas.	Second Left	Richardson
Albright	Left Tackle	Huggins
Saylor	Quarterback	Large
Jones and Roll	Half Backs	Morrey and Kennedy
Robinson	Full Back	Hegler

*C. W. Foulk

Ohio State touchdowns were made by Large, Morrey, Foulk and Kennedy, and for Ohio Wesleyan by Saylor, Ganer and Shaw. Large kicked two goals after touchdown and Saylor one. About 700 persons were reported present. For Ohio State, Jesse Jones was captain and E. T. Ellis, manager. Several of these players were well known in later years—Paul Lincoln as a wealthy industrialist, Foulk as a longtime professor of chemistry in the University, and Morrey for many years head of the bacteriology department there.

The accounts in the *Ohio Wesleyan Transcript* and the Delaware *Gazette* were similar. In its April 17 issue the Ohio Wesleyan paper spoke of "the coming game" and said the team had "been in training in the gym nearly all winter and out of doors since the weather will permit." It, too, spoke of the game as to be played "next Saturday afternoon," adding that "This will be the first game of foot ball, that has been played according to Rugby rules in the O.S.U. for many years. Give the boys a good crowd."

The *Gazette* of May 3, 1890 had this account:

The first game of Rugby foot ball that has been played in this city for many years was played this morning on the athletic grounds, between the O.W.U. and O.S.U. teams. The game was a spirited one, and, from the interest aroused, it is safe to say that foot ball has taken a firm hold upon both students and citizens.

At the end of the 1st half the score stood at 14 to 6 in favor of O.S.U. Columbus making her points from 3 touch downs and one kick over goal. O.W.U. from one kick over goal from a touch down. In the 2nd half O.S.U. made 6 points on a kick over goal from a touch down. O.W.U. made 8 points on two touch downs.

Foulk, r.e.g.; Large, q.b.; Morrey, h.b., of the O.S.U. team made several very brilliant plays, while Jones, h.b.; Saylor, q.b.; Tracy, r.g., did excellent work for the O.S.U. team.

Had our boys worked a little harder and displayed a little more head work in the first half of the game, there is reason to believe that the result would have been different.

On May 6, 1890 the *Dispatch* said that the second football game of the championship series would be played against Denison the following Saturday in connection with the annual Field Day. When the day came the Field Day had to be postponed until the next Saturday because of bad weather, but again there was no report of such a game having been played at the later date. On May 9 the *Dispatch* reported that "A challenge has been received by the O.S.U. foot ball team from the Ohio Wesleyan college team, which will undoubtedly be accepted." This was not described, however, as a return game.

The *Lantern* (May 3) that reported the Ohio Wesleyan game was annoyed editorially over "The action of Denison in claiming a game from the O.S.U. which was never played and which was not to be played on the day when Denison proposed." The *Lantern* contended that the game was contingent upon faculty action for "O.S.U. to leave." Evidently this was not granted and the *Lantern* thought it "peculiar" that "Denison would have us forfeit the game." If Denison, it went on, "is not afraid of the O.S.U., pray meet us once more. We want fair play and plenty of it."

The May 15 *Ohio Wesleyan Transcript* reported that "The Foot Ball Eleven expect to petition the Faculty today for permission to play the Ohio State boys next Saturday or some other convenient day." Evidently nothing came of this.

The sport was resumed that fall on the Ohio State campus. On October 20, 1890 the *Dispatch* carried the information that "Saturday afternoon the Ohio State University foot ball team will meet the team of Wooster University at Recreation Park for the opening game of the inter-collegiate series. Our boys will use every endeavor to win, and a splendid contest may be expected." Five days later, despite the optimism, it reported that the home team was shut out 64 to 0. Among other things it noted that "A number of ladies were present and attempted to cheer the O.S.U. boys to victory, but to no avail, as there was not the remotest possibility of their winning."

The 1891 football season was another formative year. "Capt. Lincoln enrolled the past week twenty-five men from which to select his foot ball material," the October 7 *Lantern* told its readers. "This is business, and if energetic work can be done now, we have great prospects. 'Wind' is what our team lacked last year, and without which we shall have the same reverses this year."

On the campus and in Ohio intercollegiate circles the sport began to be better organized that fall. In its October 22 issue the *Lantern* carried a discussion of football signed "C.W.F." This was Charles W. Foulk, manager, who had played on the '90 team. "At O.S.U.," he wrote in part, "our prospects for having a good team are much brighter than last fall. Most of the old men are back and three or four players have been found among the new men." He went on:

> We are placed at a disadvantage with other colleges in the fact that we have only one hour a day for practice, while some places have three or four hours. We do not ask for more than that every man in the team should be on hand promptly for that one hour.
>
> Foot ball is yet a comparatively new game at O.S.U. We lack experienced men as coaches. But interest is now aroused. The generous way in which faculty and students have responded to our call for money to purchase suits, shows this, and if we don't win at least a *few* games this fall it will be for some cause not apparent now.

The team began its season the previous Saturday by playing Otterbein at Westerville. Only thirty students accompanied the squad. Otterbein won, 42 to 6. Under "Notes," the *Lantern* reported: "Game Saturday afternoon, probably with Wittenberg or Kenyon. Let the college 'en masse' attend."

The *Lantern* had this to say about the Otterbein defeat: "Can not our institution of 600 students furnish as good men as smaller colleges of from 200 to 500. The fault lies not so much with the team as with the college . . . . If we can orate, if we can play lawn tennis, if we can play base ball, we can play foot ball. If we can find material for the former, we can for the other. . . ."

At a meeting October 24 at Kenyon with "delegates" from five colleges participating, an intercollegiate schedule was drawn up with rules governing the "agreement." (By faculty action Wooster students lately had been forbidden to take part in intercollegiate sports.) The participating colleges were: Buchtel (Akron), Adelbert (Western Reserve), Denison, Kenyon, and Ohio State. The rules were as follows:

> All ties to be played off.
> Each college plays four games; two at home, two away.
> Each team pays its own expenses.
> Visiting team shall have referee first half of the game and umpire second half.
> Managers shall not act as umpires or referees.
> In case of ties involving Adelbert, Denison or Ohio State they were to be played off, respectively, at Cleveland, Newark or Columbus, the profits and expenses to be divided.

This agreement was drawn up apparently by student "delegates" and managers. The Ohio State representative was C. B. "Caesar" Morrey and the manager was C. W. Foulk. This meeting had in it the germ of what became the Ohio Conference. As a result of it, Ohio State had a 4-game schedule: at home against Adelbert on November 11, at Kenyon on November 14, at home against Denison on November 26, and against Buchtel at Akron on December 5.

In a game at Recreation Park, at what later was Whittier and High Sts., Adelbert won with ease, 50 to 6. "The result of Wednesday's football game," the November 19 *Lantern* commented, "has sadly confirmed the the fact that there must be an awakening in our interest in athletics if we wish to be recognized with any degree of respect among the colleges of Ohio. The faculty has already met us half way and granted excuse from drill to the first and second elevens. It now rests with the students to do the rest." The *Dispatch* called the game "a match of boys on one side against men on the other."

In the second game Kenyon won, 26 to 0. The *Lantern* contended, however, that the game "wasn't so unequal as the score would indicate." It called the Kenyon grounds "very poor" and charged the umpire, furnished by Kenyon, with being "clearly and stubbornly unfair and prejudiced."

In the third game, played Thanksgiving morning, however, Ohio State won from Denison, 8 to 4. In preparation the squad had worked out in "the drill house" and this, the *Lantern* said, "won the game." For the final game, against Buchtel, the team left Columbus at 6 a.m., arriving in Akron at 11:30. Ohio State won, 4 to 0, and the December 10 *Lantern* remarked that "Both teams played like high school boys."

For years, with occasional interruptions, a Thanksgiving game with Kenyon was a highlight of the sports year in Columbus. Although it was much the smaller school Kenyon had the upper hand for some years. The first game in this series, which always had overtones of a society affair, was played November 27, 1890. Kenyon won 18 to 10.*

These early football seasons were full of ups and downs—often, it seemed, with more downs than ups. Football as an intercollegiate sport was growing in popular appeal but most of the attention was centered on the Eastern teams. On the Ohio scene an intercollegiate group or conference emerged, as noted, and the non-conference games were regarded, and were sometimes referred to, as "practice" games. For a while there was even a kind of "tournament" in connection with the State Fair. This was a pre-season affair.

College football in the 'Nineties was marked also by charges of "brutality" (some of this at least growing out of the use of "wedge" or mass play), of the use of alleged "ringers" or non-students, and the playing of coaches on their own teams. There was talk in college facilities of abolishing football, but somehow it survived even though college teams on occasion played games in mid-week or scheduled as many as three or four games in one week although this was rare.

The campus was still somewhat remote and distant from the city but the downtown papers began to give more space and attention to Ohio State football. By the same token the public began to show more interest and enthusiasm. The first long account, with a top-of-the-page headline, in the *Dispatch* appeared in connection with the 1892 Thanksgiving Day game with Kenyon. The game was scheduled for 9 a.m. on the dormitory field but through some misadventure it was not played until afternoon. "For the first time," the November 23 *Dispatch* emphasized, Ohio State "has a foot ball eleven that can bid defiance to any other team in Ohio." It had praise for the "coacher" Fred B. "Jack" Ryder of Columbus, (Williams, '92) whom the paper described as "a mighty man and a mighty player." (Ryder in after years was a well known Cincinnati sports writer.)

The *Dispatch,* same issue, gave this description of football training:

Every fellow arises at 7 o'clock and breakfasts at training table at the "dorm" on rare beefsteak, poached eggs, fried potatoes and dry bread. The forenoon hours are devoted to study and recitation and at noon an hour is spent at rehearsing signals and individual practice, after which comes dinner on rare

---

* Homer Howard, quarterback in those days, told the writer Kenyon once had the choice of a cash guarantee of $85 or 60 per cent of the gate. It took the cash. The receipts were $1134.

roast beef and other substantials. At 4 o'clock the men practice team work with the second University eleven until dark, when they take a run of several miles and then rub down, eat supper and go to bed . . . .

Ohio State won the game with Kenyon, 26 to 10. The game was marked by the use of a new formation described as "the Ryder wedge." The referee was S. P. Bush, master mechanic of the Panhandle [Pennsylvania R.R.] shops, later a well known Columbus industrialist.

A gloomy financial picture for the 1892 football team was painted by the *Wahoo* of September 27 that year. It gave figures showing the "estimated cost" of the football season was $550 against "probable receipts" of $250. The cost included these items: coaching, $110; "unsettled obligations," $130; training table, $40; uniforms, $50; footballs, $20; advertising, $30; trips to Denison and Adelbert, $175. The anticipated income included "probable receipts," $150; subscriptions unpaid, $55; "on hand," $45.

The 1893 season was a somewhat different story. Ohio State played Kenyon twice, losing both—the first 42 to 6 and the second on Thanksgiving Day 10 to 8. After winning from Wittenberg the Varsity lost to Oberlin 38 to 10. The latter game was marked by the appearance of "the newly organized O.S.U. band" which was to "parade the city" the morning of the game and "give a concert before the game." On the personal side the October 31 *Dispatch* reported that "Clarence Withoft, the full back of the O.S.U. foot-ball team is able to be around again. His last injury was the breaking of three ribs. He always plays in hard luck."

Kenyon won on Thanksgiving Day by the narrow score of 10 to 8. The *Dispatch* account of November 30, the day of the game, broke off early in the second half with the score tied 4 to 4. It reported 4000 "people witness the exciting struggle," and that "hilarious students" were "wild as the game progresses." The score was 4 to 0 in Ohio State's favor as the first half ended, but Kenyon scored in the "first 4½ seconds of the second half." The crowd poured onto the field and tore down a portion of the fence. "The game had to be stopped," the *Dispatch* said, "until the police cleared the grounds." Meantime "The University band played and the crowd became so enthusiastic as to break down the fence north of the field." A 70-yard run by Nagel, an Ohio State back, was called the most "brilliant play of the whole game."

There was talk that fall, however, of legislative action to curb the "brutal" game as it was then played. The December 1 *Dispatch* carried this item:

Cincinnati, O., Dec. 1. There is trouble ahead for football players and enthusiasts in Ohio. Already two members of the next Legislature have announced their intention of presenting bills looking to radical regulation, if not suppression, of the game in this State. The almost daily report of broken limbs and not infrequently fatal casualties has had its effect. There will doubtless be lively opposition, however, to the measure.

A possible antidote was reported the following spring in the "invention" of a new game called "roller-ball." This, the April 19, 1894 *Dispatch* told its readers, "is intended to supersede foot-ball and its brutality." The new game called for the use of a ball 3 feet in diameter. There is no record that the "invention" caught on.

Football meanwhile was taking stock of itself and efforts were made to meet some of the criticism by rule changes which minimized the dangers from "the flying wedge," a mass momentum play, as it had been used. But as always were found to circumvent the rule at least partially. The October 3, 1894 *Dispatch* noted:

> Foot ball players have discovered that the wording of the new rule which prohibits the forming of a wedge more than five yards back of the line will permit of a play that was evidently overlooked by the rule makers. A wedge can be formed five yards back of the line, but at the same time ten or fifteen yards to the right or left of the center rush. In this way the men can get started well and then by a sudden turn can push through the line with great momentum. This play is being practiced on the quiet by several of the big elevens.

M. C. Lilley, of Columbus, a Yale alumnus, began as coach of the team in 1894. But the early results were disappointing and there were rumors of dissension on the team. The November 21 *Lantern* reported that "A change in the coach was also deemed necessary and was accordingly made, Mr. Fred Ryder, the coach of '92 and '93, taking the place made vacant by the resignation of Mr. Lilley." Ryder did better.

The first game of the regular 1894 season was October 6 against Antioch. The *Dispatch* that day remarked that "The games during the State Fair cannot be counted in the season's list of games because the season had not opened." A week later it noted that "The Ohio State University foot ball team was defeated by Wittenberg in the State Fair tournament. This game was protested before the State Board of Agriculture, but was disallowed." (Members of the winning team received uniforms as prizes, as Homer C. Howard told the author in 1959. Ohio State played Buchtel also during the fair.)

A new kick-off rule was in effect that fall to lessen injuries from the old close wedge or compact flying wedge play. The October 23 *Dispatch* pointed out the rule that "only three men can start before the ball is in hand is aimed at the momentum play so prevalent in the big games last year." The new rule, as quoted, read: "No momentum mass plays shall be allowed .... Nor shall more than three men group for that purpose more than five yards back of the point where the ball is put in play."

The 1894 Thanksgiving game with Kenyon was another gala affair although the November 28 *Dispatch* said it was "for blood." The paper gave these team statistics: Ohio State line, average weight, 178, Kenyon, 172; Ohio State backs, 158, Kenyon, 162; Ohio State team, 171; Kenyon, 168. On the day of the game the *Dispatch* reported: "Early in the afternoon the cars were crowded going to the grounds, while elegant traps and tally hos sped gaily northward amid the salutes of the friends of the contesting teams." Ohio State won, 20 to 4.

The November 30 *Dispatch* said "O.S.U. put up one of the finest games she has ever played, and it was vim, vigor and victory from beginning to end. One of the pleasant features of the contest was that it was free from slugging or other dirty work, and none of the players were injured." Men from the 17th Regiment, stationed at Columbus Barracks, were present to keep "the field clear and maintain order on the outside."

In 1895 the team lost to Otterbein at Westerville, 14 to 6, and there were charges that the referee, "an old Otterbein student," gave the losers "the worst of it in the first half." A month later there was satisfaction, however, when Cincinnati was beaten on its own field. One account read: "Roling [*sic*] in mud and water, on a foreign field, with no home crowd to cheer them on, with two good men out of four, the State university football team won a gratifying though not totally unexpected victory against the University of Cincinnati." The score, 4 to 0, was "indicative of what a hard and bitterly contested game it was."

That season Ohio State had four games scheduled in eight days although only three were played. One with Starling Medical, of Columbus, came to nought when Starling "failed to fulfill its engagement" on Wednesday. Ohio State next defeated Kentucky 8 to 6 at Lexington and the next day, Saturday, played Centre College at Danville. In the Kentucky game after Ohio State scored twice, the November 16 *Dispatch* reported, "Kentucky put their coach, Mason, in the game, who played half-back at Cornell last year." Centre won the game there, 10 to 0.

A squad of sixteen men made the trip to Kentucky for the two games. After its return the November 20 *Lantern* said that the team "was in very poor shape after Friday's game . . . and felt like anything but playing football Saturday." The paper had its version of alleged rowdyism at the first game. "Some rowdies in the crowd," it said, "presumed to take exception to the decisions of Referee Wasson and Umpire Waite, but the Kentucky team and college men were careful that the officials were protected." It added: "Both Kentucky teams played clean ball and were well satisfied with the decisions of Referee Wasson. The Lexington so-called 'riot' was greatly exaggerated. The 'small boy' was the principle [*sic*] factor as usual . . . ." (A stronger version of the rowdyism was recounted in the December, 1923 *Alumni Monthly* by Quarterback Homer Howard.)

Ohio State again won the Thanksgiving game with Kenyon by the narrow score of 12 to 0. Under the heading of "VIVE LA O.S.U.," the November 29 *Dispatch* said "The game was a hotly contested one and was won in an exciting finish. After the play the crowd went crazy and carried the winners off the field." Two days earlier the paper remarked that "Mr. Ryder, O.S.U.'s coach, has filled his place with ability and judgment." The game ended the season and whatever the result, the paper added, "the players will then seek the barber shops to be shorn of their lengthy locks." This was a reference to the long hair worn by players of that day.

Early in the 1896 season Ohio State lost to Cincinnati, 8 to 6. There must have been criticism for the October 12 *Dispatch* quoted the coach as commenting, "I'm satisfied—why not the public?" That was the year of the McKinley "front porch" campaign. A feature of the football season was that the Ohio State-Otterbein game was played October 17 in Canton, McKinley's home. There is no evidence that he attended, but Ohio State won, 12 to 0. The day before the game the *Dispatch* told its readers "It is known that representatives from over 25 colleges will be on hand and the day will be given over to Mr. McKinley and football." The game evidently was started so late that "by mutual agreement" it was called on account of darkness.

A sidelight on playing conditions in those days had to do with an Otterbein player. On the Monday after the game the *Dispatch* noted that Dempsey, the Otterbein left end, played "under very adverse circumstances. He entered the game in a dazed condition—the result of the long ride on the train in the morning—and in tackling Crecelius [the Ohio State left guard] on the 6th play of the game he received a broken nose. In spite of this he remained in the game."

The *Lantern* account of the Otterbein game at Canton paralleled that in the downtown papers. The team went to Canton on Friday afternoon but the start of the game was delayed the next afternoon until 3:45 because of the "late arrival of the O.S.U. delegation in Canton."

The score at the half was 0 to 0 but in the second half Ohio State made two touchdowns to none for Otterbein. Six minutes remained to play after the final touchdown but, the *Lantern* said, "Otterbein had enough and the game was called on account of darkness." Then the Ohio State rooters gave Canton something to talk about. "Those Canton people have become accustomed to parades and cheering," the *Lantern* reported, "but they had not heard a crowd of 200 rooters from the O.S.U." In their enthusiasm the visitors hired a tallyho to take the victorious team to the railroad station.

At the start of the 1896 season a regular coach had not been hired. As an interim coach, Sid Farrar, a former Princeton player, who was a Starling Medical student, was engaged. The September 23 *Lantern* said he would "undoubtedly make an excellent coach." Farrar saw the team through its first few games when he was replaced by Charles A. Hickey, who had captained the 1895 Williams College eleven.

Following the Cincinnati game, the October 14 *Lantern* remarked that Hickey's "new system of which so much had been expected, did not succeed because the men need a great deal more coaching before they can play Mr. Hickey's system successfully." The same issue voiced relief that rumors to the effect that the Athletic Association intended to let Farrar play fullback had proved groundless.

It said also that while Farrar's work as coach had been satisfactory, "because Mr. Hickey is just out of school his coaching will probably be a little more up to date. The opinion prevailed that Mr. Farrar had been permanently engaged as coach, but this was a mistaken idea." Hickey was hired when it developed that Sweetland, of Union College, was not available.

To round out an apparently unhappy season, Ohio State lost the traditional Thanksgiving game to Kenyon, 34 to 18. The crowd, estimated at 8000, the November 27 *Dispatch* reported, "filled the stands and lined the field. . . . They stood upon the fences, on top of the carriages, the tally-hos and drags." Again darkness fell and the game was called before time was up.

The rooters had plenty of pre-game enthusiasm. Some, equipped with brooms, chanted:

        O.O.O.S.U.!
        We won't do a thing to you

Another Ohio State yell was:

> Well, well, well;
> Well, well, well.
> Won't we give those fellows—
> Olligazinsta—Bing bazan.

"A new feature of the O.S.U. games," the November 27 *Dispatch* remarked, was the sale of candy, pop-corn and peanuts by vendors in the grand stand and on the grounds. Huge chrysanthemums were also offered for sale." Homer Howard, quarterback, finished the season with a record of nineteen consecutive goals after touchdown.

Besides playing the Otterbein game at Canton and the switch in coaches, there were other developments during the 1896 season. There were charges of using "ringers" as an aftermath of the game with Wittenberg, the Varsity captain was dropped in midseason by faculty action, and in one two-week period the team played four games. The *Lantern* reported early in the fall that the Athletic Association directors had "decided to fit the team out in new uniforms, consisting of scarlet sweaters and gray moleskin pants with scarlet and gray striped jerseys and stockinettes. This will make by far the best uniform which the team has ever had."

The team won its first game under Farrar but ran into trouble under Hickey. The first team lost to Cincinnati, 8 to 6, on the latter's field chiefly because of fumbles. On the same Saturday the "second" team defeated "Chillicothe," 10 to 8. Just before the Oberlin game, played there, Captain Ed French was barred from further play because of low scholastic standing. He accompanied the squad to Oberlin but Ohio State lost, 16 to 0. In the October 28 issue the *Lantern* demanded, "Who defeated the O.S.U. team? The Oberlin team or the O.S.U. faculty?"

In the meantime, the *Lantern* added, a petition signed by 600 students asked President Canfield and the faculty to reinstate French on the ground that he was not given sufficient notice. The faculty heard the matter at a special meeting and drafted a lengthy reply to the student petition denying the request. It pointed out that the player "had been industriously working up the foot-ball team and as industriously cutting classes. . . . Ten days ago he was notified that he was practically out of college, and was advised to withdraw, which was done." It called the student request "unwise and even impossible."

A game with Washington & Jefferson had been scheduled for later in the season but this was canceled and "two games at home were arranged on very short notice." On Thursday (November 5) Ohio Wesleyan defeated Ohio State, 10 to 4, and on Saturday Ohio State won from the Barracks, 10 to 2. The latter game ended in a dispute. On Wednesday of the next week Ohio State and the Ohio Medics played a scoreless tie, but on the Saturday following Wittenberg trounced the home team, 24 to 6.

Charges that Wittenberg used "ringers" followed the defeat. Specifically, the November 18 *Lantern* quoted the Notre Dame *Scholastic* as saying that Nicholas Dinkle, Notre Dame '95, "is spending his spare moments playing right tackle on the football team at his home in Springfield, O." The lineup showed that Dinkle played quarterback. The Wittenberg left end, the *Lantern* added, "is known to have graduated from Wittenberg in '95," while its left guard was described as a "student" at a Springfield business college.

"We do not mean to criticize Wittenberg," the *Lantern* continued, "for if they choose to play this kind of a team it is their privilege. The criticism is due to the O.S.U. in playing a team of this kind." In further explanation of the loss, the paper added, "in the first half, having the wind and also the slope of the field in their favor, they had no trouble in making the necessary 5 yards." An Ohio State end suffered a broken nose in the game.

On the basis of their respective records, the November 25 *Lantern* predicted just before the Thanksgiving game with Kenyon, "Judging from form this year everything points to a victory for O.S.U." But Kenyon won, 34 to 18. As the December 2 *Lantern* headline put it: "O.S.U. FALLS A VICTOR TO THE SUPERIOR MANAGEMENT AND COACHING OF THE KENYON TEAM." A Kenyon man had scouted the Ohio State-Wittenberg game, noted the lightness of the former's backfield, and in two weeks converted a 190-pound guard into a halfback. The ex-guard scored two of Kenyon's five touchdowns. The question was asked why Kenyon with only seventy-five students was able to master Ohio State. It was estimated 4000 saw the game.

In 1897 the team won only one game, lost seven and tied one. It lost to Case, 14 to 0, and to the Barracks, 6 to 0, somewhat unexpectedly tied Otterbein, 12 to 12, lost to Oberlin, 44 to 0, to Cincinnati (there), 24 to 0, and to West Virginia (there), 28 to 0. Ohio Wesleyan instead of Kenyon was the Thanksgiving opponent "upon the Western league Columbus baseball grounds," and won, 6 to 0.

The high point of the season, however, was the first Ohio State football game with Michigan. This was played October 16, 1897 at Ann Arbor. Michigan won, 34 to 0, all of the scoring being done in the first half. Just previously Michigan had played Ohio Wesleyan and the Michigan faculty board of control objected to the fact that Fielding H. Yost, later for many years the famous "Hurry Up" who coached championship Michigan teams, had played on the Ohio Wesleyan team he coached, despite promises to the contrary. As the October 18 *Dispatch* told it, the Michigan authorities adopted resolutions objecting to the fact that

the Ohio Wesleyan university played Mr. Yost, their coach, after having promised not to do so, and after having introduced another man as Mr. Yost, promising that the man should not play, and that not being Mr. Yost at all. Resolved, That the managers of all athletic teams of the University of Michigan are hereby directed to make no engagements with any team representing Ohio Wesleyan University.

A month later, according to the November 23 *Dispatch,* the Michigan authorities replied to recent Oberlin charges of "brutality, ungentlemanliness, dishonesty" and more following a recent Michigan-Oberlin game.

The Ohio State season had begun with a new coach and the usual high hopes but by the end there were few bright spots to look back upon. The new coach was David F. Edwards who, according to the September 15, 1897 *Lantern,* was "graduated from Princeton last year and was secured by the board of directors after a careful search in all quarters. Edwards was the staunch half back of his alma mater's eleven."

Early in the season the annual game with the Ohio Medics ended in a row with the Medic team leaving the field and Ohio State claiming a victory by forfeit. The Medics were ahead by one touchdown when the squabble occurred. Hawkins, the Ohio State captain, scored from about a yard out. The Medics at once protested, arguing that Hawkins had been "pushed" over the line by Coach Edwards, but the referee refused to allow the claim. "One O.M.U. man, green with rage," according to the *Lantern,* "sprang on Capt. Hawkins while he was down and attempted to catch him by the throat with his teeth." It was at this point that Edwards "jumped in and pulled the man off," the account continued. The game was recorded as a forfeit.

The next week the team lost to Case, 14 to 10, and then followed the game with Michigan. Next came Otterbein and then Oberlin, the latter winning, 44 to 0. The crowd numbered only 600 and "the dust hung like a canopy over the University field." Ohio Wesleyan, the

Thanksgiving opponent, won 6 to 0, before a throng of about 1000. The *Lantern* took some satisfaction in the fact that, "Delaware, with all their trick plays taught them by their crafty coach, Yost, could only score one lone touchdown."

But in its December 8 review of the season, the campus paper demanded some changes before another season and advocated alumni coaching. "The experience the Ohio State University has had during the past two years with high salaried eastern coaches who were supposed to know the game, but who didn't, has taught a lesson not to be forgotten soon. If the Ohio State University could secure the services of several of its alumni to coach the team next year as is done in the University of Michigan and the Eastern schools, it would undoubtedly put a winning team on the gridiron and would meet with the hearty approval of the alumni, faculty and student body."

Fred E. Butcher, '01, active in athletics at the time, told years later how in February, 1897 a stranger applied for the football coaching job. This was Fielding H. Yost, then coach—and player—at West Virginia University. Yost gave such a vigorous demonstration of his physical prowess, first on a student and then on a faculty member, that the latter phoned Butcher to get rid "of that wild man." Yost went to Ohio Wesleyan and later to Michigan and for years was a thorn in Ohio State's football side.

V
THE 1898 CRISIS AND REORGANIZATION

THE school year 1897-98 was highly important in the emerging history of Ohio State athletics and physical education. Between September, 1897 and June, 1898 these events occurred: the first director of physical training, Dr. C. P. Linhart, was employed; the new gymnasium was dedicated and put into immediate use, giving the University indoor sports and physical education facilities for the first time; the Varsity basketball squad played its first intercollegiate schedule; because of the athletic debt amounting to $1400, the faculty in February, 1898 refused to approve future Varsity schedules until the students took some definite action to pay off the debt; this resulted in a concerted plan to liquidate the debt; and this led to the organization of a new athletic organization with a board of control.

The faculty that year overhauled University rules and regulations, including those governing athletics. The trustees also assigned a site to the north of the new gymnasium for a new athletic field. This became known as Ohio Field.

President James H. Canfield at the June 2, 1897 faculty meeting transmitted to the faculty a report of the Committee on Athletic Games which, he said, was appointed at the January, 1897 meeting of university presidents held at Madison, Wis., previously noted. This report, mentioned earlier, was referred to the faculty committee on student organizations of which Prof. Ernst A. Eggers was chairman. At the October 13, 1897 meeting Eggers "reported progress" in the matter, but the minutes gave no details. Prof. Nathaniel W. Lord gave notice of his intention to propose a standing committee on athletics.

This he did at the December 8, 1897 faculty meeting with a 4-point plan for a 3-member standing "committee of the faculty on athletics" with power "to associate itself with one representative of the Alumni and one representative of the Athletic Association and shall constitute a Board of Control with power to decide all questions not specifically covered by Faculty rules." This was, in effect, to bring athletics under organized faculty control.

At the January 19, 1898 faculty meeting a committee consisting of Profs. Lord, Eggers and J. V. Denney offered a 7-point plan for an Athletic Board of Control. The faculty adopted this plan. The board was to be composed of the director of physical training *ex officio* and four other faculty members elected by the faculty, a resident alumnus and a representative of the "Student Athletic Association." The board was to choose its own officers but the treasurer was to be a faculty member or the alumni member. The board was to make "all necessary rules and regulations" and was to have disciplinary powers.

This proposal went before the board of trustees at its March 4, 1898 meeting where it was referred to Dr. Canfield and Trustee Paul Jones to confer with the faculty and take such action as in their opinion "will best subserve the interests of the University." Meanwhile the faculty at its February 9 meeting had voted to go ahead with the new athletic board of control but any "discipline to be subject to review by the president until the trustees conferred full disciplinary powers." But when Trustee Jones, an alumnus, appeared by invitation at the March 9 faculty meeting he said that the faculty plan was doubtful because in the trustees' opinion "it would be illegal to confer the power of expelling and suspending students from the University, upon a Board of Control composed in part of students and alumni." In other words, such power resided only in the faculty and trustees.

The urgency of the over-all situation was reflected in the fact that the faculty met seven times between January 19 and March 30, 1898 compared with the usual frequency of once a month. Some phase of athletics was a major item of discussion each time. In view of the trustees' opinion, the faculty at another meeting March 11 rescinded its earlier action setting up the 7-man board and all rules and regulations regarding athletics in force on January 19 were "hereby revived and declared to be in power."

At the February 9 faculty meeting Prof. Eggers had reported that the Student Athletic Association had a balance on hand of 2c and debts of $1419.74. It was hardly surprising that this situation came to a head at a faculty meeting February 18 when the faculty declined to approve a proposed schedule of baseball games for the 1898 season. Instead, the faculty voted that it be returned to the signer, Rufus H. Patchin, the student manager, "with the statement that having investigated the condition of college athletics and having found that the good name of the University has been used by those representing college athletics to incur a large indebtedness involving the credit of the University, the University Faculty, therefore, decline to receive and consider any petitions concerning athletics until the majority of students of this University, in proper form and by a responsible organization, present evidence that they are willing and able not only to provide for the present indebtedness but to submit plans by which the future expenses of athletics will be paid." The motion was adopted 17 to 2 and President Canfield ruled also that under the motion a schedule of proposed basketball games "could not be received or considered." The February 23 *Dispatch* in reporting the action said in sum it meant "No pay, no play."

This action was a blow to student plans for spring sports but it was also a blessing in disguise since it resulted 1) in immediate action to liquidate the debt, and 2) in a plan for a new athletic association which would exercise joint faculty-alumni-student control over athletics. But the March 2 *Lantern* complained that "If there were to be no games this spring, the fact should have been announced sooner. For that matter, prompt action should have been taken two years ago. . . . We cannot afford to be without a base ball team, nor can we let it be said that the Athletic association succumbed to financial disasters. . . . Give money, give benefits, and most of all, give wise suggestions."

At a student "mass" meeting held March 8 it was reported not only that the athletic association was heavily in debt but that its constitution could not be found. Prof. Thomas presided and Dr. Canfield was among those who spoke. The latter suggested that a constitution be adopted for a new association and steps were taken to solicit all campus societies and organizations as well as individual students for voluntary contributions toward lifting the debt. There were proposals also for "benefits" to raise money to this end. One was for a dance to be held in the new gymnasium but the faculty turned this down in view of the standing rule against dances on the campus. But a concert in April by campus musical organizations netted $50 toward the athletic debt and the proceeds from the first indoor track meet in the new gymnasium were also earmarked for this purpose. One of the soloists at the benefit concert was Oley Speaks who was famous as the composer of such well known songs as "The Road to Mandalay," "Sylvia," "Morning," and others.

The primary purpose of the athletic organization, to quote the *Makio*, "was to create an association under such a constitution as would insure its financial stability." The account went on: "Partly through mismanagement, but chiefly through lack of interest and patronage on the part of the students, the old association had become hopeless in debt. It was desired to form an organization that would insure the hearty co-operation of all the students."

The new officers were F. E. Butcher, president, and B. W. Hough, secretary. Hough some twenty years later stood high in the Ohio National Guard and later was a Federal judge. Team managers were W. T. Leonard, track; R. H. Patchin, baseball; and J. O. Leslie, football.

The bulk of the money raised came from subscriptions. The April 20 *Lantern* reported that about $400 had been subscribed by the faculty, provided the remainder was raised by students and others by May 1. The signs were hopeful since all but about $100 of this had been paid or pledged. But hard cash was difficult to come by and a week later the *Lantern* said that unpaid subscriptions amounted to $191.25. In view of the improved financial outlook, meanwhile, the faculty relented in its stand against intercollegiate games for the baseball team which finally opened its season April 30, defeating Otterbein, 15 to 6.

The April 27 *Lantern* also carried a detailed statement and plea from Prof. Thomas on the athletic debt fund. This showed student subscriptions of $397.75, and from societies and fraternities of $153.50, a total of $551.25. The students had paid $303.25 but organizations only $24.50. "The Athletic Board of Managers," Thomas remarked, "can do nothing further until this amount is paid. . . . If this is not done, the attempt to pay the debt must be abandoned and all athletics suspended indefinitely." But it did not come to this.

In the meantime, as noted, the new athletic association had been organized. This was brought to the attention of the faculty at its March 30 meeting, called "to consider certain communications from the newly formed Athletic Association." One was a letter from Hough as secretary of the association requesting the faculty to elect three members to "the Board of Directors of said association." Next was a report showing the means taken to lift the debt of the old association. Although the minutes gave no details they were presumably those described above. The third item was the constitution of the new association.

It was to be known as the Athletic Association of the Ohio State University. All students, alumni and those "officially connected" with the University were eligible to membership by signing the constitution. Regular meetings were to be held in October, January and May.

It provided also for an Athletic Board consisting of three faculty, three resident alumni (not faculty members), and four students. The last were to include managers of the football, baseball and track teams and a fourth who was to be secretary. Faculty and alumni members were to be chosen by those bodies. It was provided further that "The

Board shall have absolute control over all matters pertaining to athletics in the University provided that their action shall not conflict with the rules established by the University faculty."

This meant a new day for organized athletics on the campus. It meant joint faculty-alumni-student control instead of the apathetic, uncertain conditions of the earlier associations. It meant financial responsibility. The faculty gave its approval at once to the new plan and elected Profs. Linhart, William McPherson and F. C. Caldwell. Linhart's appointment had been authorized in August, 1897 at a salary of not to exceed $180 a month. His appointment was effective January 1, 1898, with Miss Stella Elliott as gymnasium assistant at $60 a month to handle the limited women's program.

That the financial outlook had improved was shown by a May 11 faculty minute to the effect that the Athletic Board treasurer had $601.01 cash on hand and that "The Board promises to pay the remaining debt." At this meeting the faculty also adopted a resolution "That the report of the Faculty members of the Board of Control in regard to the payment of the debts of the old Athletic Association shows that the conditions under which consideration of athletics by this Faculty will be resumed have been fulfilled; and that the resolution stopping such consideration be hereby repealed."

In the spring of 1898 the trustees, as noted, provided for a new athletic field close to the new gymnasium. This was done on recommendation of the farm committee so as to bring all athletic activities, indoor and outdoor, in close proximity. The location was "the field just north of the President's residence." But there were certain stipulations as follows:

1. The debts of the Athletic Association shall first be fully paid and sufficient funds be raised by subscription or otherwise among the students, faculty, alumni and friends to fit up the new grounds in appropriate and creditable manner, with the aid herein afterward promised.
2. On these conditions the farm workmen and teams shall take down and remove to the new grounds all available material in the old fences and grand-stand, and we recommend that the Board appropriate not to exceeed $500, furnish needed new material and erect the necessary fence and an open grand-stand around and on the new grounds and aid in other needed improvements on said grounds.
3. Suitable fences shall be built to throw the old athletic grounds into economical farm use, . . .
4. All work in fitting up the new grounds shall be promptly done, in time for this year's athletics, as a final condition to aid offered above.

Immediate action was taken toward these ends for the May 18 *Lantern* reported that "All last Saturday student volunteers were working on the fence, and by evening the north and west sides were completed and the south side partly done." In view of the financial situation it was arranged also to have the annual Field Day on May 21 on the new field, as noted, rather than to rent an outside field even though much remained to be done on the new site.

At the trustees' meeting of May 5, 1898 Profs. McPherson and Linhart informed them that "the debt of the athletic association was practically provided for." Upon learning this, the trustees ordered the athletic board to "proceed at once in fitting up the athletic grounds" in accordance with the plan described. In June, 1898 upon request of the athletic board the trustees repealed their earlier rule against permitting games on the University grounds "unless the university teams shall take part." Instead the athletic board was given discretion to charge a "reasonable" rental for the use of the grounds by others where an admission fee was charged.

A long felt need was realized when the gymnasium was completed. It had facilities for both men and women and a main floor with a canvas-covered running track above. The women were housed in the east end and the men's lockers and swimming pool were on the west side. An innovation was the requirement of "physical training" for all students, although some of the faculty looked askance at this. This was not wholly surprising, Dr. Canfield remarked in his annual report for 1898. But the year, he insisted, "completely demonstrated the wisdom of the undertaking, and of the methods employed." Another new requirement was that "all who are to take part in any athletic event must first submit to a rigid physical examination."

The means to finance a grandstand for the new field were finally found in what now seems a curious way. In June, 1900, President W. O. Thompson presented to the board a form of contract for the erection of the structure whereby it was stipulated that Dean George B. Kauffman, of the College of Pharmacy, who was also president of the Kauffman-Lattimer Co., wholesale druggists, was personally to lend the money. As a consideration, a committee from "the university faculty and executive corps" was to be "given control thereof, collect the receipts for admission thereto, and pay therefrom the principal and interest of the sum so advanced." The contract was approved.

Despite the move to and improvement of the new site there was still some uncertainty in the early 1900s as to the ultimate location of the athletic field, or University Field as it was first known. There was still occasional talk of another site. In time, however, after several starts and stops, the trustees decided to adhere to the High-Woodruff location, except that the area was expanded so as to make 17th Ave. the southern boundary and with some expansion westward to what was known as the University grove.

Yet there was talk of a move to another site in the spring of 1903 and this kept up with variations for several years before a final decision was reached as to Ohio Field as it came to be known ultimately. Meanwhile the Athletic Board was given permission to extend the field to Woodruff Ave.

Profs. B. F. Thomas and George W. Rightmire appeared before the April, 1903 trustees' meeting to ask for "the use of a tract of ground west of the university woods extending along Woodruff avenue 800 feet and southward along the edge of the woods 500 feet as a new site for the athletic field." They submitted also a plan of the proposed improvement with a cost estimate. The trustees approved the change of site. But they changed their minds somewhat when it developed that the proposed change would "interfere with the proposed site for new buildings." Action on the matter was then deferred.

The Athletic Board faced what for the time was heavy expense in developing Ohio Field. This involved the erection of a grandstand and bleachers, "skinning" the baseball diamond, and laying out a quarter-mile running track. That funds were still scarce was borne out by the fact that any surplus from a sophomore dance at Buckeye Lake in the spring of 1903 was to be turned over to the Athletic Board. Another straw in the wind was the report that since there were no funds for a training camp like that provided by some colleges, the pre-season training for the 1903 football squad would have to be held in the gymnasium. One addition that fall, however, was to employ an assistant football coach instead of depending upon volunteer help from former players and others.

VI
GENERAL DEVELOPMENT, 1898-1911

OPENING of the new gymnasium in the winter of 1898 was a turning point on the campus for both athletics and physical education. Its completion, signalized by "a delightful entertainment" in February, 1898, made possible year-round training quarters, facilities for indoor activities, and the adoption of a broad physical education program for both men and women students that was soon made compulsory for all. The year before the gymnasium came into use, however, the faculty surprisingly took two steps which would have been regarded later as lowering the standards for athletics. One was to permit men with one "condition," or a subject in which a student had not passed his work, to participate in sports. Generally he could remove this "condition" by earning a passing mark in a second examination. The other step was to permit freshmen to play on Varsity teams.

In a little more than a year after the athletic reorganization described in the preceding chapter the University had a new president in Dr. William Oxley Thompson, formerly of Miami University, who was to serve in that capacity for the next twenty-six years. During that long period he showed more of an active interest in physical education and athletics than any of his predecessors. The November 8, 1899 *Lantern* reported the new "prexy" as having been at the previous Saturday's football game carrying a scarlet and gray banner.

Athletics were still in a "growing pains" stage on the campus. The May 24, 1899 *Lantern* spoke of athletics as "daily assuming a more and more important position" in University life. The new athletic field was still incomplete and there was need, the paper pointed out, of a suitable place "for the training and practicing of running, jumping, etc." It urged that the track men be taken to the Driving Park or some similar place for practice.

Occasionally there was renewal of the talk that the athletic field would yet be moved to a new site. In December, 1904 the *Lantern* told of a new survey to be made of the field north of the campus power plant to "ascertain the possibility of moving the athletic field." There was some criticism also that the gymnasium running track was not sufficiently available for the use of the track squad. This problem was resolved by giving the squad "entrance" to the gymnasium floor at 4 o'clock on class days.

Some uncertainty continued over the athletic field. In June, 1905 an Athletic Board committee asked the trustees to allocate a portion of the field west of the woods on the north side of the campus and north of the power plant "to the Athletic Association for the purpose of an athletic field." The trustees complied and set apart the site requested "permanently for athletic purposes" under Athletic Board control. But the board rescinded this action later.

In the end it was decided to retain and expand the existing field. The November 15, 1905 *Lantern* reported that a new field would be "established" on the site of the old one and that elaborate plans had been worked out to this end. But some opposition developed from North Side merchants since a petition was circulated opposing the new field on the N. High St. site.

A major change in athletic administration was the appointment of Dr. H. Shindle Wingert in the dual capacity of director of physical education and athletics. Dr. Wingert succeeded Dr. Linhart, who resigned. Until Dr. Wingert's arrival, Dr. W. C. Mills, who had been Athletic Board president, was in charge. This superseded a graduate manager policy that had been in operation.

The position Dr. Wingert assumed was a new one. As the October 10, 1905 *Lantern* described it, he was to have general charge of the gymnasium, physical education classes and athletics. In addition, he was to be the University's representative in "all affairs connected with the management of athletics." Dr. Wingert came from Lehigh University where he had held a similar post and was to serve in his multiple capacity until 1912 when the University was admitted to the Western Conference. Not long after his arrival the *Lantern* reported that "the tennis association has been made part and parcel of the athletic association." The policy under the new administration was to consolidate athletic activities and to centralize authority for them. A year after Wingert's arrival the University was invited to join the American Intercollegiate Association.

President Thompson meanwhile had his first lengthy official say about college athletics. In his annual report for 1905 he saw athletics as a general as well as a local problem and as an inescapable part of the college scene. But he was of the opinion that college faculties must "recognize not only their *right* but their *duty* to lead in all forms of college athletics." Some faculty effort had been made in this direction but he was not sure that it had "done all that could be done" or that the results were "entirely satisfactory." He continued:

An absorbing interest of the public, of alumni, and of students has created an atmosphere not always the purest. For ten years or more, commendable efforts have been made to regulate the excesses, irregularities, and professionalism of athletics. There has been evident improvement in the rules; what is most needed at present is to improve in the ethical standards of all persons interested in athletics. Conformity to athletic rules is too much of a technicality and not enough of a principle . . . . The suspicion that seems to be in the minds of people interested in athletics, is itself a greater evil than some of the abuses complained of. Athletics like every other form of amusement or business must eventually rest on sound ethics; . . . It is unfortunate in the extreme that the public mind is so eager for amusement that it becomes indifferent to the ethical conditions surrounding the game . . . . It is a manifest waste of energy . . . to spend time in denouncing athletics; what is needed is efficient leadership by men to whom principle is dearer than anything else. If university faculties are set for the education of youth, it is little more than a corollary to add that they can not ignore the ethical conditions existing in college sports . . . . It would be gratifying to some if there were no athletic problems; but so long as there are institutions there will be students and so long as there are games there will be problems. We shall never reform athletics simply by rules; we shall reform it only when we have inspired young men to cling to high ideals and to be governed by sound ethics . . . .

In June, 1906 the trustees authorized another long step forward when they approved a faculty plan for the "readjustment" of physical education for men and athletics. This called for the employment of an official in the dual capacity of head of the combined department of physical education (men and women) and director of the gymnasium. He was to be responsible for the gymnasium and for physical education for men along with general supervision of athletics.

This last included the making of team schedules with responsibility for all coaching, training, and athletic contests. The appointee was also to have charge of all athletic equipment, make all purchases and approve all bills in connection with such activities and appoint assistant coaches and trainers subject only to Athletic Board approval. To this post, as noted, Dr. Wingert was appointed.

Further refinements in athletic rules were adopted in the early part of 1906 by both the Ohio Conference, of which Ohio State was a member, and by the Western Conference which it was to join six years later. The new "Big Six" (Ohio) rules centered in three things: only undergraduates enrolled in regular or special courses could participate, they must have been enrolled previously for at least a full college year, and participation was limited to three years. Pre-season training and the training table were abolished but the members were unable to agree on proposals to do away with professional coaching, to shorten the football season to eight games, and to abolish Thanksgiving Day games, according to the March 14 *Lantern*. Twelve Ohio colleges and universities were represented.

About the same time the Big Nine had similar changes under consideration. A week later the *Lantern* reported that "Football reform has at last crystallized in the Big Nine by the adoption of a series of drastic rules very much the same as those agreed upon in Ohio. The rules include prohibition of freshmen upon athletic teams, enforce one year's residence, and the three-year rule is embodied, and also the requirement which bars all graduates."

Campus athletic conditions remained somewhat unsettled during the winter of 1906. One result, the *Lantern* said, was to "upset everything regarding the new field." Another factor was an athletic deficit as shown by an Athletic Board financial statement early in the new year. That winter, growing out of a "mass" meeting January 25 in the chapel, an athletic carnival took shape. This was called a "carnival of Sports" and was to be "under auspices of each and every organization and each and every man, woman, and child at Ohio State.

The chapel meeting, the January 31 *Lantern* said, was given over to "a discussion of the present serious condition of athletics." Prof. Rightmire, who had been graduate manager of athletics, described how operating costs had gone up. In 1898, he said, the season gate receipts amounted to $1575 and the costs included $300 for the football coach and $83 for the training table. Currently, he added, the expense of salaries alone had risen to $3300 a year. The carnival for the benefit of athletics was finally held April 21. The proceeds amounted to about $750 which, the April 25 *Lantern* said, "would place the association upon a firm financial footing."

The three or four years prior to 1912 marked a period of growth and physical improvement in Ohio State athletics and vague stirrings toward better things. Among the latter was a growing feeling that the University ought to broaden its field of competition, particularly with other state universities in the Western Conference. But there were serious and practical obstacles to the accomplishment of this end as will be seen.

There was also a shift in the football coaching policy and by the end of this brief period a start had been made toward the hiring of full-time, year-round coaches and trainers instead of merely seasonal ones. There was a brief experiment with the Yale system of football coaching and there was serious discussion of trying to set up a system of alumni coaching like that in effect on some campuses.

During 1908-09 substantial improvements were made to "U" Field.

These cost $30,000, a considerable sum for those days, and were met partly from athletic receipts and partly from borrowing. The "unsightly" old board fence at the south end of the field was replaced by "an iron railing which allowed an unobstructed view of the field and the campus beyond." New bleachers had been erected on the east side of the field, fronting on High St. The trustees gave permission to add 10 feet to the south end, making the total area approximately 800 by 500 feet.

The new fence was regarded as something special. It ran for 172 feet along High St. from the south end of the east bleachers to the southeast corner of the field, then 400 feet across the south side, and up to the grandstand on the west side. It was 8 feet high, with eight covered gates on the south side, with "registering" turnstiles flanked on each side by ticket offices. According to a description in the first issue of the *Alumni Quarterly*, it had "heavy brackets and a frieze of rough-cast, with ornaments and the name OHIO FIELD done in Hartford faience" to give "individuality." There were also flagpoles "on which the colors of visiting teams are displayed along with the University pennants. This little courtesy has occasioned favorable comment."

There were also two 16-foot exit gates near the southeast and southwest corners of the field, and along the south curve of the quarter-mile running track surrounding the football field was a 4½-foot railing. During football games a "brown canvas wall" was stretched along the railing to cut off the view from the outside. One effect of the improvements was "to quiet all remarks from the property owners in regard to the location of the field."

To the foregoing, Prof. French, who wrote the description, added a prophetic note: "It is hoped that this is only the beginning of the final Ohio Field. The fence will be continued around the entire enclosure, with perhaps behind the bleachers a concrete wall paneled for bronze tablets to be left by future classes; and with the continued splendid financial management and the support of the alumni the dream of a magnificent concrete stadium in horse-shoe shape may be realized sooner than anyone would expect." Another thirteen years were to pass before the dream of such a stadium came into being and then it was on the banks of the Olentangy and not on the site of Ohio Field.

The 1909 *Makio* was enthusiastic over the improvement of Ohio State's athletic fortunes during that school year. "The completion of 'Ohio Field' at the beginning of the present school year," it observed, "marked a new epoch in Varsity athletics. State students and all other followers of University teams have at last come into their own. . . .

With an equipment second to none and with an abundance of material to represent it in every branch of sport, Ohio State has now taken a position in athletics among the leading universities of the land. The decisive defeat of Vanderbilt in football last November, the near-victory over Michigan, the remarkable performances of the basketball team against Wabash, Michigan, and Rochester, and the showing made by the Varsity relay teams at Philadelphia have all served to spread the name and fame of Ohio State over the length and breadth of the land."

These accomplishments, it went on, were largely the result of "the improved College Spirit which can be found in these days on and about the campus." In proof it cited "the ever memorable snake dance which escorted the football team to the station on its way to Vanderbilt, and which, more than any other one thing, was responsible for the return of the team to a point where it could display championship form after sustaining three crushing defeats." It was estimated that nearly 1000 students took part in the snake dance.

Also in the first issue of the *Quarterly* referred to was a report by Prof. William Lloyd Evans, '92, on behalf of the alumni members of the Athletic Board. He described the general condition of athletics as "excellent" and noted that the spirit of the student body toward visiting teams was "one of friendship and good sportsmanship, the consequence of which has been the establishment of intercollegiate relations of which the Alumni may feel justly proud." For the improvements to Ohio Field a field committee had been appointed to correct the inadequacies and provide for future needs. In the enlargement of the field, Prof. Evans emphasized, "the University grove to the west has in no way been encroached upon." The three principal improvements, besides those noted, were a new gridiron, a new baseball diamond, and a standard quarter-mile track, with the new bleachers along the east side of the football field.

The playing field improvements were completed by October 1, 1908. These gave an additional seating capacity of 4200, or a total of 6100. These immediate improvements cost $19,000. The new field was dedicated November 21, 1908 at ceremonies preceding the Oberlin-Ohio State game. Mrs. W. O. Thompson "christened" the new athletic grounds "Ohio Field" with water from the campus spring. In contemplation was a new grandstand having a capacity of 5000 or 6000. In a year or two a new student bleachers was built north of the old grandstand along the west side of the field. The old grandstand, festooned for some years with tinkling glass "bells," stood until Ohio Field was abandoned after the Stadium was built in 1921-22. With temporary bleachers at the north and south ends of the football field, Ohio Field had an ultimate capacity of about 14,000.

"In arranging the plans for this year," Prof. Evans' report in the *Quarterly* went on, "the question as to the advisability of changing from the present system of coaching to the graduate system was taken up by the Athletic Board. At present the system consists in the employment of the services of a professional coach and the captain of the preceding year's team. After a full and thorough discussion of the problem, it was decided to retain the present system for another year, modifying it by the addition of one more graduate coach. Although the present plan is not intended as a solution of the problem, we believe that it is a move in the right direction." Credit was given to half a dozen former Varsity players for "assistance and advice."

Baseball had been suspended as a Varsity sport in 1907-08 because of the improvements under way on Ohio Field. A student petition with 600 names asked the board to provide a temporary diamond but "expenditure of funds in this direction was deemed inadvisable." Baseball was also something of a problem in that interest was greater in informal baseball for which there were twenty teams representing colleges and other campus interests. It was pointed out that only 165 season tickets were sold for baseball at $1 each, of which forty were bought near the end of the season to qualify their purchasers to vote in the annual election of student managers of Varsity teams. The two outdoor track meets with Michigan and Oberlin were also "poorly attended," yet the board closed the year was a balance of about $500.

It was recommended: "1) That if intercollegiate baseball is to be continued as a sport, a varsity game be scheduled on Alumni Day in commencement week; 2) That the Alumni should cooperate in every way possible to make the proposed inter-scholastic meet of next spring one that will make the University better known among the high schools of the State, and to keep this permanently annual; 3) That, when possible all Alumni who were members of athletic teams lend their assistance in the matter of coaching teams or advice in the directing of athletic affairs in the University."

Prof. Evans also reviewed the 1909 football season. A crowd of 7000 saw the game with Case, the greatest attendance "ever known at any Ohio State athletic event." But the three games lost—to Michigan, Case and Oberlin—were the three Ohio State wanted most to win, and Case won permanent possession of "the silver loving cup" emblematic of the state championship for the last nine years. For the Michigan game the regimental band and a thousand Ohio State students went to Ann Arbor.

Total athletic receipts were $17,292.81 and expenditures $16,777.24, including $5944.34 for improvements and repairs to Ohio Field, and $3000 for coaching and assistance. This left a balance of $515.57 and uncollected accounts of $370. At that, receipts apparently were about $2000 less than for the previous year.

Despite the employment of Howard Jones, of Yale, as football coach for 1910 there was renewed discussion of graduate coaching. To get the ideas of former Varsity athletes, Prof. Joseph Russell Taylor, '87, editor of the *Quarterly,* sent out a circular asking for their opinions on the subject as well as for general suggestions for the improvement of athletics. He received replies from men as far back as '91 and as recently as '09.

"Not one man expressed favor for the graduate system at the present time," Prof. G. W. Rightmire wrote in the *Quarterly*. There was "general agreement that we are not now prepared to take up graduate coaching; the solution of our coaching problems proposed is rather to continue to employ a professional coach, the best we can obtain, and to arrange a system of graduate assistance." This latter was to be accomplished by having the football manager correspond with "football graduates to find whether they can return for the football season" and whether they could stay "two or three days a week or more" and on this basis "formulate a schedule for the season," i.e., of voluntary, unpaid graduate assistance to the head coach. It was suggested that two or three men could be "put up" at the new Union and that the Athletic Board could probably pay their travel expenses.

Rightmire summed it up thus: "The suggestion is that these men report to the head coach, and take their orders from him; under his direction devoting their attention to individual players in the positions which they themselves filled in their college days." This plea was made: "All who see this number of the Quarterly will kindly map their time as far ahead as possible, and then write to the football manager; stating when during the next football season it will be convenient to come back; stating how long a stay can be made, and if it is possible to come several times or at stated intervals; and mentioning the dates specifically. . ." This would make it possible to set up a schedule of such help. Another academic change in prospect was the switch from the term to the semester system.

Apparently there was some criticism of "the large number of small colleges appearing on the athletic schedules" and a feeling that "several state universities should be played annually besides Michigan," although it was realized that it would be hard to break into longstanding relationships. Rightmire listed three "distinguishing features" Ohio State athletic policy should have in the next few years: systematic alumni help in football coaching, the establishment of athletic relationships with several more state universities, and the holding of the annual interscholastic track meet for Ohio high schools. "If these features are added to the splendid facilities and the clean sportsmanship that have come during the last few years," he concluded, "our athletics will have been placed on a large and permanent basis."

One other development occurred in the early summer of 1910. This was the announcement of the intention to proceed with the building of new and permanent bleachers on the west side of Ohio Field comparable in size to the new east side bleachers.

There was renewed reference to the dissatisfaction with the athletic schedules, especially football. The Vanderbilt game, for example, was dropped after two years because Vanderbilt was "located badly, geographically speaking." Rightmire spoke again of the desirability of athletic relations with Indiana, Illinois and possibly Chicago and other members of the Western Conference. Formerly members of that conference played only five games each fall but were now permitted seven. But as Rightmire noted, "the Conference has recently decided that each college shall play games only with other Conference teams, consequently Ohio State cannot expect games with Western Conference teams unless it becomes a member of the Conference."

"Whether it should become a member is a matter of policy," he went on, "and when it is remembered that the Conference prohibits its members from playing with the University of Michigan so long as Michigan remains out of the Conference, the question resolves itself into one of determining whether Ohio State should go into the Conference if possible and forego the Michigan game, or continue the Michigan game and make no effort to get into the Conference. The effect of endeavoring to get into the Conference is problematical and it is not seen that Ohio State has any stronger claim to present than other western universities that have been excluded. It certainly would be inadvisable to sever relations with the University of Michigan. This university has done more for Ohio State athletics than almost all other forces combined. . . . If Michigan should go back into the Conference, then

Ohio State should make an effort to enter the Conference, for wider and more valuable relations can be built up with the Western Conference universities than can be built up outside of that Conference."

He described an ideal schedule as calling for annual games with Michigan, Illinois and possibly Indiana and the stronger Ohio teams. This account is repeated at some length because, despite his doubts of the moment, it was to be Rightmire who successfully pleaded Ohio State's case so well that, without Michigan, it was admitted to the Conference in 1912.

Another idea taken for granted in future years was also ventilated. This was Homecoming although the name was not yet used. Toward the end of his account Rightmire referred to the practice of some universities of using a big football game as "the occasion of a general return of the graduates who visit the University and get into touch with the old institution again." He suggested that such a gathering might feature the Syracuse game in '11 and the Michigan game in '12. "We might inaugurate what might be called Ohio night," he suggested, "and on the evening preceding the game have a spread and some toasts and renew acquaintances, and live again some of the experiences of our own scholastic youth."

On the fiscal side he paid tribute to W. C. Mills who had been a member of the board and had served as graduate manager and treasurer. "In a number of instances," Rightmire reported, Mills had "borrowed money on his own responsibility to take care of current expenses." From receipts of the past four years, Rightmire noted further, the improvements to Ohio Field had been entirely paid for. The greatest need that remained, he added, was for training quarters which might cost from $10 to $20,000 and where "the men of the various teams might live under proper sanitary and dietary conditions" and where "the men at their own expense could live well." He suggested that some "well-disposed alumnus has here an opportunity to immortalize his name" by providing such a building. But if opportunity knocked no alumnus heard.

Under Ohio Conference rules as amended to September, 1910, meanwhile, intercollegiate athletics were under faculty control in the member institutions and the rules were designed to keep participation on an amateur basis and to permit only eligible students to take part. Participants must be bona fide students and the one-year rule was in force. No one was to participate "for more than three years in the aggregate," although playing in the first contest only after the opening of a given season was not to count if the athlete did not play thereafter in that season. No student was to play under an assumed name, and any person who played on a college team when not a student was barred thereafter from intercollegiate athletics in the Conference.

No one was to compete who "receives any gift, remuneration or pay for his services on the college team," and anyone was barred from competition "who has ever used, or is using, his knowledge of athletics, or his athletic skill for gain." Playing on professional or semi-professional teams was barred. All intercollegiate games must be played on grounds owned by or under the control of one or both of the participating colleges. Each candidate for a varsity team must sign a statement as to his eligibility "under the letter and spirit of the rules adopted."

College football teams could play "only with teams representing educational institutions" and teams other than varsity teams "only with teams of their own institutions." Pre-season training, e.g., football during the summer vacation, and the maintenance of a training table were forbidden. No student could participate "who is found by the faculty to be delinquent in his studies," and a player who failed to complete the work of that term or semester "shall not be permitted to compete in the same sport in his next year of residence."

The year 1911-12 was one of decision with large consequences for Ohio State athletics. The October, 1911 *Quarterly* carried a statement on "Athletic Policies" by Prof. Rightmire. This was a condensation of a fuller statement published in the first issue of the *Lantern* that fall.

"We are in more or less of a transition period in our intercollegiate relations, not only in football but in all other athletic games," Rightmire wrote. "The stronger Ohio colleges will always find a place on our schedules, but we are now definitely trying to enlarge the scope of these schedules. It is not, of course, that we have beaten the state, and are looking for larger game; . . . the other colleges themselves, our equal rivals on the field, look to us to represent the state in interstate athletics. It is not presumptuous for us to think that we could hold our own in greater contests; outside the few great teams, football in Ohio is as good as it is anywhere; . . . It does not seem advisable to open such relations east; the distances are too great, and return games in many cases impossible. Our natural field is the west."

He pointed out again, however, that Western Conference policy was "that its members shall play among themselves." In football, moreover, each Conference school had to schedule at least four games with other members, leaving only three other games. It was still Conference policy, moreover, to permit no games between Conference members and Michigan. Rightmire repeated his earlier observation that if Ohio State was admitted to the Conference it would be at the expense of its relations with Michigan. "It seems clear from every standpoint," he commented, "it is unadvisable for Ohio State to do anything which would sever football relations with the University of Michigan."

But there was always the possibility that the attitude of Michigan toward the Conference, or vice versa, might change in the next few years and time proved this to be correct. "If that comes to pass," the future president went on, "our case is clear; we should immediately apply, and keep on applying, for admission into the Western Conference." In the meantime the best hope was to open baseball and track relations with Illinois and possibly Indiana and Purdue. Rightmire reported that efforts to this end were being made.

He had a prophetic word about athletic income and the cost of maintaining sports like baseball and track which produced little revenue. Any deficits on this account had to be met from football. "It will probably always be the case," he observed, "that football must earn the money to float all the other games; and a conservative policy in reference to sending teams on long trips outside the state, or in bringing teams here from any distance outside, must necessarily be pursued." He spoke of it as "folly to undertake games that create a deficit," but he was insistent that the University "should by all means continue games wtih Michigan." Time proved him right on most of these points.

He touched on two other matters: eligibility requirements and athletic facilities. "It is a well-known fact," he remarked, "that eligibility requirements at Ohio State are higher than in most of the western universities." On this point he did not specify, but when Ohio State was admitted to the Western Conference a year later it had to revise its eligibility requirements sharply upward. And as time proved, joining the Western Conference had the effect of raising general University standards in certain respects.

In the matter of facilities, Rightmire said the University now had "a fair diamond, the best football field in the state, and as good a track as there is in the whole country." He called the seating capacity of Ohio Field "ample for the present." He could not know but in six years the place would be bursting at the seams for football games, due partly to the increased enrollment but in particular to the first spectacular success in football that was soon to come. But for the time being further improvements were postponed. During the past year the new west bleachers had been built and the east bleachers painted at a total cost of $7000. Coaches and trainers, he added, cost $5000 and there was a $4000 deficit for the year, mostly from baseball and track.

During these emergent years there were other developments, for example, with regard to other sports such as gymnastics, tennis and fencing. There was some controversy also over the Varsity "O" toward which cadet officers and even Varsity debaters had aspirations. To go back a bit, requirements for the "O" were modified in the spring of 1905. The June 2 *Lantern* reported that under the new rules a football letter could be awarded to any player who had played "in five full games or an equivalent in halves of the last eight games scheduled" or by playing in the Michigan game and the final game of the same season. In basketball the requirement was to play in six full games or equivalent halves. In track it was to score a first or two seconds in a meet and to compete in an event in the Big Six meet.

Fencing bobbed up in the sports picture in the winter of 1909 with the announcement that a tryout would be held for places on the Varsity team. The first intercollegiate fencing meet in which Ohio State took part was in April, 1909 and the team lost to the University of Cincinnati, 5 to 4. That spring also there was a revival of interest in tennis. And with the coming of a new track coach (Riley) early in 1909 Ohio State announced plans for a relay carnival to be held that spring on Ohio Field. Western Conference teams and others from schools and colleges in nearby states were to be invited.

In the spring of 1911 a long smoldering controversy over the Varsity "O" broke into the open. The Varsity "O" Association formally protested the wearing of "O's" by members of the Military "O" Association. The latter came into being in the spring of 1906 and its members, mostly cadet officers, were granted an "O" in recognition of military service on the campus.

The Military "O" Association appealed to President Thompson "to vindicate the legitimacy of its letter" and demanded an apology from the Varsity "O" Association. It expressed a willingness, whenever the apology was received, to discuss the matter. The demand was ignored. In the meantime, Dr. Thompson, in a letter, recalled having given his approval for a military "O" but on the "distinct understanding that it should not be a duplicate or infringement upon the Athletic 'O' . . ." To one unfamiliar with them the two "O's" were confusing, but the military "O" continued to be awarded for some years.

VII
FOOTBALL 1898-1911

Ohio State football fortunes were a bit sad again in 1898 but brightened considerably in 1899 when J. B. C. Eckstorm was hired to coach. For three seasons—1899, 1900 and 1901—Eckstorm, a recent Dartmouth captain and star, achieved a fine showing and widened Ohio State's football horizons. Those three teams won twenty-two games, lost only four and tied three. The 1899 team was undefeated but had one tie. This was the best showing over such a period until the first Western Conference championship teams of two decades later under J. W. Wilce.

But coaching was still on a seasonal basis and the situation left much to be desired. From 1898 to 1911, inclusive, there were seven football coaches. Only two of these stayed longer than two seasons—Eckstorm from 1899 to 1901 and Al Herrnstein from 1906 through 1909. None had faculty status and only one of the seven was employed on an all-year basis. This was E. R. Sweetland, who served in 1904 and 1905, coached track as well as football and served as Varsity trainer.

The year 1898 was marked by the brief Spanish-American War which had minor overtones on the campus, and by the use of the new athletic field. As it turned out, this was to serve for twenty-four years until the Ohio Stadium era. At the start of the '98 season there was complaint, as voiced in the October 1 *Dispatch,* that "the grass is so long that it interferes with the running of the men" and that some students "persist in their determination to follow the players all over the field and hear everything the coach has to say .... Strangers have mixed in with the spectators during practice and secured the team's signals during the practice hour."

In '98 Coach F. B. "Jack" Ryder was in charge with some help from two former Varsity players. Once more the team had indifferent success. It began by defeating Heidelberg, 17 to 0, lost to the Ohio Medics, 10 to 0, beat Denison, 34 to 0, and then lost in succession to Marietta, 10 to 0, to Western Reserve, 49 to 0, to Case, 23 to 5, and to Kenyon, 29 to 0.

There was an echo of the Spanish War in the second game with the Ohio Medics played November 19. Mayor Samuel L. Black, of Columbus, suggested that a percentage of the receipts be donated toward a monument of the 4th Ohio Volunteer Infantry, a local unit that had served in the war. The Athletic Board agreed to make the game "a benefit for the monument fund in honor of the fallen heroes of the Fourth Ohio." The Medics won again. The *Lantern* said later that "a neat little sum" would be turned over, but there was no mention of the amount realized from the "benefit."

There was clamor that fall for a renewal of the Thanksgiving rivalry with Kenyon instead of Ohio Wesleyan. But the latter was scheduled although until a few days before the game there was doubt whether it would be played because of a dispute over the choice of officials. Ohio Wesleyan was chosen because it was willing to take a smaller percentage of the gate receipts than Kenyon had been getting. The game was finally played, Ohio State winning, 24 to 0.

The outlook was better for 1899. As early as April the *Lantern*, in commenting on prospects, predicted "in 1899 O.S.U. will, in all reasonable probability have the best foot ball team she has had in years." One reason was the selection of Eckstorm as coach. He had played four years for Dartmouth which was champion of its league in his senior year. He had coached the '98 Kenyon eleven.

As the May 27, 1899 *Dispatch* put it: "Coach John B. C. Eckstorm, who will have charge of the State university on the gridiron next fall, dropped into the city yesterday and met about 40 candidates who expect to fight for a position on the 'varsity next season . . . . Coach Eckstorm met the candidates again today and gave them some instructions in punting and starting and other preliminary work, which he wants them to practice on during the summer months so that they will be better able to get right down to work next fall." This was spring training of sorts.

The new regime got immediate results. In the first game Ohio State defeated Otterbein, 30 to 0, and Wittenberg was the next victim, 29 to 0. The October 4 *Dispatch* reported also that "a training table has been started on Eleventh Avenue" but only eight men were sent there.

A member of the squad was E. G. "Rastus" Lloyd, years later a state senator, who had played for Otterbein. That fall, in fact, he had played for Otterbein against Washington & Jefferson. Evidently a question was raised as to whether Lloyd could then play for Ohio State. But as the October 12 *Dispatch* told its readers, "under the circumstances the athletic committee of the Ohio State university is unable to see any reason why Lloyd should not play on the O.S.U. team so long as he meets all the requirement of the literary standard of the university."

A training table of sorts was established about that time. Coach Eckstorm noticed some of "the bigger and better material sitting in the stands watching practice." When he asked them why, they told him some of them lived outside the city on farms and had to leave the campus early to do farm chores in the evenings. Asked for suggestions, one of the men said that if a training table could be set up and jobs found that would not interfere with practice and so the "farm boys" could stay overnight in town, they would consider coming out for football. A common table was arranged in a private home but no jobs were provided, Dr. Eckstorm told the writer in June, 1959.

A high point of the season was the important game with Oberlin at Oberlin. Eckstorm and eighteen players left the day before for Wellington. Five more players were to come the next morning on the special student train for which more than 300 rooters were "assured." Ohio State defeated Oberlin in football for the first time, by a score of 6 to 0, when Capt. Del Sayers, left tackle, recovered an Oberlin fumble and ran 25 yards for the game's only touchdown. Part of the somewhat ecstatic *Dispatch* account of October 30 read:

> Oberlin, O., Oct. 30.—Smiling with perfect indifference in the face of rheumatism, pneumonia and grip, the Ohio State university football team met the Oberlin aggregation in a quagmire Saturday afternoon, wallowed with this for 50 minutes in mud and rain, buried them under a decisive and crushing defeat, and waded proudly and victoriously from the field amid the deafening yells of 350 enthusiastic O.S.U. students, who had cheered the 'varsity boys on to victory.

The mud was described as "six inches deep." There was special satisfaction in the fact that Oberlin had been state champion. Ohio State next defeated Western Reserve, 6 to 0, Marietta, 17 to 0, and the Ohio Medics, 12 to 0.

"Secret practice" was ordered for the game with the Medics in which there was great local interest. There was some doubt whether Lloyd would play as he had not played in several games. But he notified the manager that if provided with a suit he would be out. As indicated, Ohio State won, 12 to 0, what the November 20 *Dispatch* called "the most exciting football game ever seen in this city." That evening the "entire student body" with the band at its head had a "shirt tail parade" down High St. as far as Rich St., crying "Wahoo, wahoo, Rip, zip, bazoo, I yell, I yell for O.S.U., Wahoo, wahoo," and chanting the score, "One, two, three, four" to twelve.

For the first time there was published mention of betting on the outcome. "The betting on next Saturday's game," the November 15 *Dispatch* remarked, "is still at even money and promises to remain that way till the game starts. . . . One bet of $700 even was made yesterday with a member of the Ohio State eleven taking the O.S.U. side of it. It is understood that his father furnished the 'mazuma.' The O.S.U. money which was left at the Dispatch office has not yet been covered."

A week after the Medic game Muskingum was obtained at the last minute to fill an open date and lost, 34 to 0. Then came the annual Thanksgiving game with Kenyon. The home team won, thanks to a goal from placement by Sayers. In the first half Ohio State was three times inside the Kenyon 20-yard line. The crowd was estimated at 6000. On the outcome Ohio State for the first time claimed the state championship with nine wins, no defeats and one tie, and with 185 points to 5 for its opponents. The December 2 *Dispatch* contended: "Ohio State University finds nothing in the field to dispute her right to the state championship."

The Eckstorm period marked a new era in Ohio State football. The team got sound coaching, it won the state title, downtown Columbus began to prick up its ears at the success, the local newspapers devoted more space to football and, perhaps most important, football began to make money. There were other signs of the times: the band began to figure seriously in the football scheme and automobiles began to be seen at games. But there was still no grandstand on the athletic field and spectators followed the opposing teams on the field.

After the successful 1899 season the Athletic Board promptly rehired Coach Eckstorm for the next two seasons. Carried away by the 1899 success the board early in the new year began to discuss the idea of playing teams outside of Ohio in 1900. Steps were taken also a little later looking to plans for a grandstand and a running track on the new athletic field.

The 1900 season was also highly successful. It was highlighted by a win over West Virginia and, in particular, by a 0 to 0 game with Michigan at Ann Arbor which was regarded as a "moral victory" for the invaders. By September 21 a score of men were out for "light work." "The regulars are a little slow in getting to work," the *Dispatch* reported that day, "but they will all be on the field by next Monday afternoon when Coach Eckstorm will put in his appearance and proceed to shape up an eleven for the game on the following Saturday with Otterbein." Five days later the paper noted that "The uncertainty which has surrounded the football prospects of the State university came to a sudden close yesterday afternoon by the long delayed appearance of Coach Eckstorm" who had been expected for a week. The first game was only four days away.

Otterbein fell, 20 to 0. The game the next week with Miami was canceled because of "an epidemic of fever" on the Miami campus. Ohio University was obtained instead and also lost, 20 to 0. The next week Cincinnati was beaten, 29 to 0, on its own field and again there was a "night shirt parade" that evening to downtown Columbus. High St. businessmen burned red fire and the team was met at the station with a tally-ho drawn by four horses. A member of the squad was L. W. St. John, a promising freshman, who a dozen years later was to return to the campus as a coach in three sports and presently athletic director.

But all was not sweetness and light for in mid-October the *Dispatch* reported "the worse [*sic*] practise of the year" and said the work of the squad was "handicapped by the absence of proper clothing for the players." Evidently there had been a delay in placing the order.

As the game with the Ohio Medics approached there were charges of professionalism against the latter and the game was in doubt. The Athletic Board went so far as to take formal action against permitting the Varsity to play the Medics but the issue was settled when one Medic player was dropped. In the meantime Ohio State defeated Oberlin, 17 to 0, West Virginia, 27 to 0, and Case, 24 to 0. Then the Medics trounced the University team, 11 to 6. Perhaps this bore out a *Dispatch* headline of some days earlier:

O.S.U. ELEVEN
NEED TO GUARD AGAINST
SWELLING HEADS

Unusual interest was shown in football on the campus that fall. Before the Oberlin game fifty-two players were out for the team. Prior to the Michigan game hundreds of students showed up at the Varsity practices—300 one day and 500 the next, plus the band, according to the *Dispatch*. Five hundred turned out for a rally at the gymnasium the day the squad left for Ann Arbor. Renick H. Dunlap, captain of the '95 team, helped with the coaching to give the staff a partial alumni flavor. He handled the second team.

Any regrets over the outcome of the Medic game were forgotten in the joy over holding Michigan 0 to 0 on its own field. It was estimated that 900 rooters followed the team to Ann Arbor. There was a prophetic note in the jubilant *Dispatch* story on the game under the headline: "OHIO STATE PROVED HER RIGHT TO RECOGNITION IN WESTERN FOOTBALL." The story began:

Ann Arbor, Mich., Nov. 24. Another star has risen on the western football horizon. No longer can the "Big Nine" be referred to in western football discussion to the exclusion of the great Buckeye state. Hereafter it will be the "Big Ten" for it will be impossible to ignore the Ohio State university, whose football team scored a triumph on Regents field this afternoon by playing the great Michigan eleven to a standstill and successfully defended their goal against the attack of the heavy Michigan backs through two bitterly contested twenty-five minute halves.

The paper reported that the Ohio State line was outweighed from 20 to 55 pounds per man and asserted that Ohio State clearly outplayed Michigan. Actually the game was played in very bad weather, sleet beginning to fall just before the game began. At that Ohio State carried the ball from its own 15-yard line to Michigan's 19 where it lost the ball on a holding penalty.

Five days later to climax a second successive championship season, Ohio State defeated Kenyon, 23 to 5, in the Thanksgiving Day game. For this occasion the Athletic Board expanded the seating facilities of the new field by renting Sells Bros. circus seats. With only 700 grandstand seats this increased the capacity to about 2000 besides standing room. Ohio State was one of five Ohio college teams that fall to lose only one game to an Ohio opponent, but its over-all record, with 213 points to 26 for its opponents, gave it unquestionably the top ranking. So the campus and the town faced the new century with football fever at a higher pitch than they had ever known.

An innovation that fall was the erection of a score board on the field. Near the close of the season it was reported that the gross receipts would approximate $6000. Total attendance for the season was given as 13,000. Another report was that Michigan was eying Coach Eckstorm. Perhaps as a sign of Ohio State's rise in athletics Michigan agreed to play their 1901 game in Columbus instead of Ann Arbor. Another byproduct of this new success was the erection of bleachers at an estimated cost of $1000.

This 1900 football team was one of the two or three best of the early Ohio State elevens from 1890 to 1912. It won eight games, lost only one and tied Michigan. Only three opponents were able to score upon it.

There were other marks of progress that season. The new grandstand was in use. The Athletic Association began the season in good financial condition for a change. There was wider community interest in football and as a spur to this the Athletic Board put season tickets on sale.

But the 1901 season was somewhat less successful than the two preceding ones. The team won five, lost three and tied one game while another was canceled. It was the only season in the entire history of Ohio State football in which a player was killed. The victim was John L. Sigrist, center. He suffered a fatal injury early in the second half of the game with Western Reserve on October 26 and died on the following Monday afternoon. He was hurt in a pile-up.

The incident caused a stir on the campus. Some advocated the abolition of football or at least the cancellation of the remainder of the schedule. In the end only the game with Ohio Wesleyan, scheduled for the next Saturday, was abandoned.

The school year had opened with unusual activity in athletics, especially football. The trustees had appropriated $1000 for the erection of bleachers and the Athletic Board had borrowed money on personal notes to provide a tier of boxes for the grandstand.

The Western Reserve game was hotly contested but Ohio State won, 6 to 5. Sigrist was hurt in a hard scrimmage and was carried off the field. At Grant Hospital it was found that his neck was dislocated and he was partially paralyzed. He said he had tried to buck the line with his head. There was talk of an operation to relieve him and for a time there was hope of his recovery, but he died at 1:30 p.m. Monday. His death shocked and saddened the campus.

Prof. J. A. Bownocker and another member of the Athletic Board conferred with President Thompson and it was decided to call off the game with Ohio Wesleyan. In the evening the president met with the Athletic Board and arrangements were made for the funeral. Next morning the body was escorted to the University chapel by a detail of cadets. After short and impressive services the body of the dead athlete was accompanied to the Union Station by the student body from where it was taken to his home at Congress, Ohio, for burial.

On the evening of November 1 memorial services for Sigrist were held in the chapel. Some of the speakers attacked football and denounced the sport as inhuman and brutal. One, however, defended the game and was authorized to say for Sigrist's brother Charles, a fellow student, that it was his wish that the game go on. The attitude of Charles Sigrist had much to do with the decision of the Athletic Board to complete the schedule. Two of Sigrist's brothers were members of the football squad later.

Some favored abandoning the remainder of the schedule while others were for prohibiting the game altogether. The Athletic Board was in a trying position. It had gone to considerable expense in preparing for and advertising the remaining games yet it did not wish to offend those who were so shocked by Sigrist's death. It was decided to submit the matter to a vote of members of the Athletic Association and to the football players. At a meeting in the gymnasium the football men and Athletic Association members voted to go on with the schedule.

But some faculty members were strongly against this. At a faculty meeting November 4, Prof. N. W. Lord offered a resolution canceling the schedule. This was warmly discussed, but was finally defeated by a vote of 18 to 8. When the schedule was resumed the team lost to Michigan, 21 to 0.

In January, 1902 Perry Hale, a onetime Yale star, was engaged as the new coach. Eckstorm, after three years with the Varsity, was to tutor the Ohio Medics. In the spring a play by Strollers, campus dramatic society, was announced for the benefit "of the athletic fund."

There was spring training again in 1902. The *Lantern* called a trainer "the most crying need in our system of athletics." Another sign of bad times was the announcement that spring that the track team had disbanded and "much to our regrets we have no meets this year." That year also there had been no Varsity basketball for lack of funds.

Under Coach Hale there were a number of innovations in the fall of 1902. In an early issue the *Lantern* commented on the absence "of head harness and nose guards" in the first game. The next week the paper reported that Hale had had "hand holds" fastened to the backs of the belts of all the halfbacks. This was still the day of the flying wedge and of mass formations. Hale himself was the victim of a thief who took his uniform so that for part of a week he had to appear on the field in civilian clothing.

There was as yet no organized cheering at football games although it had been pointed out that other schools had "yellmasters." That fall the *Lantern* urged students to "yell a little in your room." Another item in the same column suggested that "It might be well to practice yelling a little when you wake up."

Despite high hopes the 1902 season saw the worst drubbing a

Michigan team ever administered to Ohio State. The final score: 86 to 0. It became legendary, however, that even at the half, when the score was already 45 to 0, Ohio State cheerleaders kept calling for the yell

> We can, we can
> We know we can,
> We know we can
> Beat Mich-i-gan!

The game was so one-sided the *Lantern* reported it as the opinion of many Michigan people that Ohio State would not be given a place on Michigan's schedule the next season. But it was.

There were compensations, however, that fall. Kenyon was beaten "by the largest score ever," and Illinois, in the first meeting between the two teams, was held to a scoreless tie. And after Ohio Wesleyan was defeated by the margin of a field goal, Indiana not only got off with a tie but, according to the *Lantern,* was "lucky to escape defeat." One outcome of the season was that Hale was re-engaged as coach for the next year. It was also reported that he would enroll as a student.

As a means of helping to meet the costs of improving the athletic field, students were urged to subscribe 50c each. In an interim report Prof. Rightmire, treasurer, said he was "much pleased" with the progress of the "Athletic Fund." The Athletic Board also made an appeal to alumni to support the fund.

In 1903 Ohio State invaded Michigan again but lost, 36 to 0. The season was only fairly successful with eight victories and three defeats. Early in December the *Lantern* reported doubt that Hale would be back for the 1904 season and a month later the issue was still undecided. Presently, however, E. R. Sweetland was hired as coach and took over the track coaching also. There was no spring football practice.

On the administrative side Carl E. Steeb, University bursar, was elected treasurer of the board in place of Prof. Rightmire, who resigned. Another change of importance was the resignation of Dr. C. P. Linhart as director. He was followed January 1, 1907 by Dr. H. S. Wingert.

Sweetland, who was to remain two years, was the University's first all-year coach. The 1904 squad was small in numbers and early that fall the coach and Capt. "Texas" Thrower made a plea for more men to come out for the team. Among other things that season was marked by the erection of new bleachers on the east side of "U" Field as it was still known. The Athletic Board voted that fall not to sell season tickets but announced individual game prices. This aroused no objection but there was criticism when all the seats in the grandstand and nearly all of the desirable bleacher seats were reserved.

Football fortunes were better in 1904. On the administrative side, Vernon H. Davis, '00, a former Varsity player, was hired as graduate manager of athletics. He succeeded Prof. Rightmire, of the law school, who had given part time to the duties. A football training table was in operation. The scale of football ticket prices was almost unbelievable by Stadium era standards. For the Otterbein, Miami, Muskingum and Denison games admission was 25c. For the Case, Illinois and Kenyon contests it was 50c and for the de luxe games with Michigan and the Carlisle Indians it was $1.

Advertising in Columbus and nearby cities was used to swell the attendance. "The big games will be advertised in all cities and towns within easy reach of Columbus," the September 28 *Lantern* reported. "Seats to accommodate 1,500 people will be placed along the east bleachers before the big games open up. The team will soon appear in brand new suits. Eighteen or twenty will probably be purchased."

One of the season's high spots was the Michigan game, played on "U" Field. This was one of Yost's famous teams with the great Willie Heston as captain. Michigan won, 34 to 6, before a record crowd of 5402 of whom 550 were from Michigan, but not until after a scare. Michigan scored in the first half but a touchdown by Marquardt, of Ohio State, matched this and early in the second half Ohio State was ahead, 6 to 5. Then the roof fell in and Heston alone scored three touchdowns.

The *Lantern* went into ecstacies. Its October 19 headline cried: "Wolverines Return Home Humbled by Score—Practical Victory for 'Varsity." The account of the game boasted that "for the first time in years Michigan faced a score against her . . . and for six and a half minutes they were a defeated team." Yost was quoted earlier as saying "O.S.U. has a stronger team than any other western college except Michigan, Chicago, Wisconsin and Minnesota." One player was ejected from the game for slugging.

Earlier in the season the Varsity had defeated Otterbein, 34 to 0, and swamped Miami, 80 to 0. A week after the Michigan game Case was beaten, 16 to 6. Next the team lost to Indiana, 8 to 0, and then to Oberlin, 4 to 2, but won from Kenyon, 11 to 5. The Thanksgiving game was with the Carlisle Indians who won, 23 to 0. There was a rumor that the

Indians did not use their first team. But the November 30 *Lantern* spiked this by pointing out that eight of their men had also played for the famed Indians against Harvard and the Haskell Indians.

Both Ohio State and Case claimed the 1904 state championship. This was submitted to "Prof. St. John, of Oberlin" [Wooster?] to arbitrate. The decision was that there was no Ohio championship that year as far as possession of the emblematic trophy was concerned and that it should be so engraved. A financial report after the close of the season showed total receipts of $15,845.45 and expenditures of $13,696.21. Expense items included $1300 for salaries, $1123.60 for a training table and $25 for "mending."

Sweetland was rehired for the season of 1905 in the dual capacity of trainer and coach and was to be consulted in schedule making. The Athletic Board ended the year in good financial condition. A sensation of the time was the exposure of Cassie Chadwick, of Cleveland, who looted certain northern Ohio banks of hundreds of thousand of dollars. One of these was an Oberlin bank. Ohio State was reported to be the loser of about $150 as a result of the Oberlin bank "trouble." In March, 1905 Sweetland issued a call for spring practice.

Football hopes were high in the fall of 1905 but the realization was somewhat less than the anticipation. Season athletic books were again put on sale at $2 and the Varsity had a new assistant coach in L. J. Bingham, who had a Colgate background. Members of the football squad were put on notice that football "material," i.e., equipment, was merely loaned to them and must be returned at the close of the season. The *Lantern* commented that other Ohio colleges had developed a process of "loading" for games with Ohio State. To sharpen the Varsity, Sweetland planned a game between it and a team made up of alumni and former stars. He tried also to arrange for a number of midweek games to test the Varsity. An innovation that season was the organization of a rooters' club.

With perhaps two exceptions the 1905 team lost the "big" ones and the schedule was marred by a dispute with Denison which resulted in the latter's forfeiture of the game and a rupture in athletic relations between the two schools. The incident grew out of a charge that Denison was playing three men who were ineligible under Ohio Conference rules.

The opening game with Otterbein resulted in a 6-to-6 tie. But as the *Lantern* explained, the squad had "gathered together just two or three days" before the game, had had no scrimmage and nothing more than signal practice. On the next two Saturdays, Heidelberg and Wittenberg were taken care of, 28 to 0, and 17 to 0, respectively. Then came the Denison game.

Ohio State had protested earlier the use of the allegedly ineligible men on the grounds of professionalism and other irregularities. In an effort to save the game this dispute was dropped at game time, but another developed over the length of the halves to be played. Ohio State held out for the regulation 35-minute halves but Denison insisted upon "short" ones—time not given. When the team captains could not agree the referee ruled in favor of Ohio State which won the toss and lined up to play when the whistle blew. But Denison did not and after waiting two minutes the game was declared forfeited.

There were two other results of this action. One was a financial loss since Ohio State had to refund the money for the tickets sold. A report after the close of the season showed that 2187 tickets had been sold on which the refund amounted to $1078. For some reason total refunds came to $1206 for a net loss of $128. As a final result the Athletic Board closed the year with what at the time was a heavy deficit. Happily the rupture, like others, did not last long and athletic relations were resumed when Ohio State played Denison in basketball at Granville and received courteous treatment.

A week after the Denison affair Ohio State defeated DePauw, 32 to 0. Next came a 0-to-0 tie with Case described as "the fiercest seen in Ohio for years." In the following weeks Ohio State defeated Kenyon, 23 to 0, lost to Michigan, 40 to 0, defeated Oberlin, 36 to 0, and Wooster, 15 to 0, but lost to Indiana, 11 to 0, on Thanksgiving. This was the only season Ohio State ever had twelve football games although only eleven were played. And whatever the cause, Coach Sweetland entered Protestant Hospital for the treatment of what the *Lantern* called "nerve ailments." There was some talk of a new coach for 1906 but Sweetland was re-engaged although, as it turned out, he did not serve.

It was during the 1905 season that "Carmen Ohio," the University alma mater song, was born. "Carmen Ohio" is in reality a hymn. It was written by Fred A. Cornell, w'06, on the way home from Ann Arbor following the defeat by Michigan. Cornell wrote the words and borrowed the music of an old Spanish hymn. Although the music is hardly suited to such occasions, especially when it is dragged, "Carmen Ohio" has been sung faithfully for many years, first on Ohio Field, and since 1922 in the Stadium and on many foreign fields.

To anticipate, a demand developed years later for a new Varsity song that was appropriate for football. At its March 9, 1928 meeting the Athletic Board authorized a prize of $500 "for a new football song with original words and music, . . ." Earlier "Across the Field," one of the most stirring college football songs in America, was born. Words and music were written in 1915 by William A. Dougherty, '17, '20, manager of the 1916 Western Conference championship team. The third Varsity football song, "The Buckeye Battle Cry," was the work—words and music—of Frank Crumit, musical comedy star and brother-in-law of George M. Trautman, in 1919.

Shortly after the close of the 1905 season, Graduate Manager Davis reported that receipts were only a little more than half of the total for the previous season. The January 17, 1906 *Lantern* said that at least $1000 had to be raised at once to save the situation. "If order is not brought out of the present chaos of dissention and knockerism," it declared, "the faculty is likely to settle down upon the situation and forever bar athletics from the institution." A financial report showed receipts of $11,108.55 as against disbursements of $9611.03. But there were "fixed liabilities" of $2995, including $2860 still due on salaries. The "net deficit" that had to be provided for was given as $2022.50.

The 1906 season got off to a start that spring. As a first item Coach Sweetland was publicly exonerated of using "improper influence" in recruiting athletic prospects. Second, because of substantial changes adopted by the rules committee, it was planned to have spring practice. Next was the withdrawal of Captain-elect R. C. Reemsnyder from school, leading to the election of James F. Lincoln to replace him. But the plans for spring practice ran into a road block in the campus military department and had to be abandoned.

There was a faculty investigation of a campus carnival for the benefit of athletics but it was held and was described as "eclipsing" all former events in terms of success. The net profit, reported later, was $980.46. This was turned over to the Athletic Board. By that fall the cup of optimism was running over again and plans were reported to make "U" Field "one of the finest in the country." Ralph W. Hoyer, captain of the '05 team, was named assistant coach and L. J. Bingham, Colgate, '02, also helped.

The '06 season brought another state championship and the team lost only to Michigan. The team, under Coach Al Herrnstein, of Chillicothe, a former Michigan player, won its first three games—Otterbein,

41 to 6, Muskingum, 17 to 0, and Wittenberg, 52 to 0. Michigan, which Herrnstein had scouted personally in its game with Case, defeated Ohio State, 6 to 0, thanks to a place kick and a safety.

Oberlin and Kenyon were beaten next by identical scores, 6 to 0, as was Case, 9 to 0, at Cleveland. But Wooster held the Varsity to a 12 to 10 score and in the Thanksgiving game with the Ohio Medics victory was by the narrow margin of 11 to 8. The Medic scores were on two drop kicks by Jack Means, one of them for 52 yards. This kick was claimed as setting a record but for some reason was never accepted in the record books. Means was later for many years a member of the University's medical faculty and a well known football official.

The season had its other moments. At the Oberlin game (there), the townsmen and students got somewhat out of hand in what the *Lantern* called "rowdyism and ruffianism." What triggered the outburst was not only that Ohio State had scored a touchdown but that a long run for a seeming touchdown by an Oberlin player was disallowed on the ground that he had stepped out of bounds on the Ohio State 37-yard line. Mud, stones and even a can of paint were thrown and a home team player was struck by a stone supposedly intended for an official.

Despite the impressive showing the season ticket sale to students was disappointing. There was even talk early in the season of calling off the sale because of what the *Lantern* called "Inexcusably Miserable Student Support of the Liberal Offer of the Board." In two weeks the sale was less than enough to meet the expenses of the first two games.

In all, the team won eight games and lost one, scoring 154 points to 6 for its opponents. It was the first Ohio State team whose goal line was uncrossed and was understandably called "the best team that has ever represented O.S.U." Perhaps the climax of the season was the return of the state championship trophy at a University convocation. The trophy, a huge cup, was given originally by Ohio State students in 1900 as emblematic of the state title. The successful season was reflected also in fatter gate receipts. A financial report, noted in the February 20, 1907 *Lantern,* showed receipts of $18,650.60 as against expenditures of $11,259.19, leaving a balance of $7391.41. Receipts from games away from home yielded only $1871.38.

By ordinary standards the '07 team had a successful season but the Varsity lost the state championship. The team won seven and lost two games, and tied one. The losses were to Michigan, 22 to 0, and to Case, 11 to 9. The title hinged on the latter game. The tie was with Wooster, 6 to 6. Wooster was coached by L. W. St. John. Several months after the close of the season Dr. Wingert reviewed it in his first annual report. This was the first year of the operation of the 1-year residence rule which, to quote the *Lantern*, "made great inroads upon the otherwise available material."

Another development of the '07 season was a resumption of relations with Ohio Wesleyan and with Denison. To offset this, however, relations were broken with Kenyon during the season because of what the *Lantern* called "unsportsmanlike actions." This step followed a rough game between the two teams in mud and water.

Early in the new year ex-Captain H. J. Schory was named assistant coach for the '08 season. For reasons not given there was no spring practice. Coach Herrnstein was back that fall, there was hope of selling 2000 season tickets, and there was a new score board "to enable rooters . . . to follow the plays and keep track of the downs."

New regulations concerning the forward pass were in force and the *Lantern* for the first time mentioned "Signor Angelo" who over the next forty years was to become a legendary campus figure as Tony Aquila, groundskeeper extraordinary. In Ohio State's first game that fall the forward pass was used successfully once. The new east bleachers were also in use for the first time that season. An early season setback was at the hands of Wooster.

The season had its ups and downs. Michigan was held to a 10 to 6 score and Ohio State adherents got a tremendous bang out of this and out of the fact that Halfback Millard Gibson ran 70 yards for a touchdown. In the next game Ohio State defeated Ohio Wesleyan, 20 to 9, coached by Branch Rickey who years later was best known as a baseball genius. But a little later the Scarlet and Gray was beaten by Case, 18 to 7. Vanderbilt was defeated, 17 to 6, at Nashville and the season closed with victories over Oberlin and Kenyon.

Seventeen Varsity "O's" were awarded for the season, including one for the head cheerleader. The season was a success financially so that with $700 pledged the continuation of baseball was assured for the spring of 1909. Coach Al Herrnstein was re-engaged for 1909 with Walter D. "Rink" Barrington, former quarterback and captain, as assistant. The cheerleader "O" went to Harry E. "Mother" Ewing, who subsequently declined the honor in the belief that such letters should go only to active players.

In a signed article in the '09 *Makio*, Herrnstein reviewed the '08 season and "its greater significance" to the University. He cited the unexpected results of the games—losing to teams where victories had been counted upon and making the best showing against Michigan and Vanderbilt. Gibson's touchdown run through the entire Michigan team was only the second time Ohio State had ever scored on Michigan. Gibson's season performance, to quote the *Makio,* won for him "mention by Walter Camp as an All-American possibility,—the first time that this honor has been accorded to a State player. . . ."

A call for spring practice preliminary to the '09 season was issued in February with the actual call in mid-March. Again in '09 the team had a good season on the whole, winning seven and losing three games. But the three games lost were the "big" ones—to Michigan, 33 to 6, to Case, 11 to 3, and to Oberlin, 26 to 6. Otterbein, Wittenberg, Wooster, Denison, Vanderbilt and Kenyon were shut out and Ohio Wesleyan was beaten, 21 to 6. Vanderbilt was called the "champions of the South." Its coach, Dan McGugin, a brother-in-law of Coach Yost, of Michigan, scouted the Ohio State-Michigan game. Herrnstein was coach for the fourth straight year which was also his last.

The Michigan score was somewhat one-sided but the October 20 *Lantern* called Michigan lucky. It pointed out that "State outrushes Wolverines, but succeeeds in scoring only one touchdown." Ohio State made nine first downs in the first half but no score, while Michigan with only five first downs scored 21 points that period. Fifteen hundred Ohio State rooters followed the team to Ann Arbor. The round trip was $2 and admission to the game 50c.

The Rev. George B. Cutten, pastor of First Baptist Church, Columbus, was a volunteer assistant Varsity coach during the '08 and '09 seasons. In the words of the *Lantern* his "services . . . have contributed materially to the success of two Varsity football seasons." Years later Cutten was president of Colgate University.

Despite the relative success of the team football receipts in 1909 fell nearly $3000 below those for 1908. In December, 1909 it was reported that the Athletic Board had about $7500 left of which $3000 was earmarked for coaches' salaries and it would have to get along on the remainder until proceeds from the 1910 season became available.

Dr. J. B. C. Eckstorm, the former coach, was team physician in the fall of 1909. An innovation that season was the arrangement for a committee representing the Student Council to welcome visiting teams on their arrival. An unfortunate development in mid-season was the "retirement" of a Varsity end from the team because of what the *Lantern* called an "unfortunate refusal to obey orders."

A major addition to the staff resulted from the employment of

Stephen J. Farrell as Varsity trainer and track coach as of January 1, 1910. Farrell was to remain through the seasons of 1910-1912 and later went to Michigan in a similar capacity. In his younger days Farrell was a champion sprinter and formerly coached track at the University of Maine and at Yale.

Still another major change was the hiring of Howard Jones, former coach at Yale and All-American end there, as head football coach for 1910. He won distinction later as coach at Iowa and at Southern California. As time proved he was the last but one of the seasonal or transient football coaches for Ohio State. He set April 25 for the opening of spring practice. An early plea was that "more men are needed" for the squad.

Football on the campus began to take on a new look early in 1910 with the hiring of the new coach and the new year-round trainer, followed by spring practice. Jones was the older brother of the equally famous "Tad" Jones. Howard Jones had coached at Yale the previous season and would bring with him, the January 12, 1910 *Lantern* said, "the eastern style of play which will be a bit new." He was to be assisted by Sumner "Doc" Welch, former Ohio Wesleyan player. Primarily Welch would have charge of the freshmen.

Jones made his appearance on the campus late in April. As the April 27 *Lantern* put it, he "started practice Monday and Tuesday afternoons and has now run back to his business in Excello, Ohio." The business was a paper mill. But a week later the paper said only eighteen men were out for practice where there should be forty. "Coach Howard Jones will be with the men off and on," it added, "and wants all the available material to be on hand."

That spring also the Athletic Board considered a plan to sell all-year season student books at a blanket price of $5 instead of the practice of separate season books. The season football ticket sold for $2.50, for basketball $1.75, track, baseball and tennis $1 each or a total of $7.25. The all-year plan was subsequently adopted.

The board took steps also to expand the seating capacity of Ohio Field by authorizing the construction of new bleachers on the west side. These were to extend, the June 8, 1910 *Lantern* reported "from the north end of the gridiron to the north end of the old covered stand, which will see service for at least one more season." The new stand was to follow the general line of the east bleachers. But the old grandstand was to continue to serve for another dozen years until Ohio Field yielded to the Ohio Stadium.

The 1910 season saw a number of major changes. The coaching staff was described as the best Ohio State had had "in years." There were major changes in the football rules: there were now four "periods" to the game instead of two halves, limitations were put on the forward pass, and the flying tackle was banned. There was some feeling that the new rules were a handicap.

Purchase of year-round tickets was required for membership in the Athletic Association. But the sale lagged and as classes began the *Lantern* reported that it was necessary to sell 1000 but so far students had bought only 153. By the time the season opened the sale reached 500. A minor development was the refusal of the Athletic Board executive committee to grant anyone the "peanut and popcorn privilege," i.e., concession, for the 1910 season.

The high spot of the season was the 3-to-3 tie with Michigan before a crowd of 6500 on Ohio Field. Neither team was able to cross the other's goal line but Michigan managed a field goal from the 22-yard line and Captain "Prep" Wells offset this with one from 35 yards out. But this unaccustomed success against Michigan was marred afterward by what the *Lantern* called "celebrating the event in dissipation," i.e., too much conviviality.

In its next game, moreover, the Varsity showed a letdown and was tied by Denison, 5 to 5. The team lost the championship in large part because of a defeat by its old rival, Case, by a score of 14 to 0 at Cleveland.

Two things marked the close of the season. One was the resignation of Jones who was succeeded by Harry Vaughn. The latter, also from Yale, was recommended by Jones and by Walter Camp. The other development was Athletic Board action in restricting the number of football "O's" granted. Jones recommended fourteen players but in its initial action the board approved only nine. The December 14 *Lantern* ran a picture of the squad two-thirds of the way across page one with the caption, "Out of this big squad only nine men are granted 'O's' by the Athletic Board." A few days later at the time of the football banquet the board granted three more, along with three "R's"—Reserve.

Prof. Rightmire reviewed the season in the January, 1911 *Quarterly*. The Case game was played under protest because "the Case management seemed unreasonable in the matter of selecting officials." For several years it had become increasingly difficult to agree upon officials for this game, whether in Columbus or Cleveland, and efforts failed to have them chosen by A. A. Stagg or others.

Under the revised rules, Rightmire continued, "the game was full of surprises." And cheering, he added, had "become the striking feature of a football game at Ohio State." Speaking of the coach, Rightmire wrote that "Howard Jones with the Yale system was an unqualified success." Jones operated on the theory that "the defensive team should be as nearly perfected as possible before the fancy offensive game was undertaken." In this fashion the team defeated Western Reserve and Cincinnati and, for the second time, tied Michigan. It started its offensive game against Case but lost. Still, as Rightmire pointed out, "No clean touchdown, by straight football, was made against the team."

While the account gave no explanation, Jones left after the one season. Coaching assistance was given by Thomas H. "Tommy" Jones, '09, Millard Gibson (punter), Ralph W. Hoyer (center), Sansenbacher, Bryce and Barrington—all former Varsity players. This was the apparent result of the partial "graduate" system for which a plea had been made earlier.

There were other innovations. One was separate coaching for the freshmen under "Doc" Welch. "He has successfully inaugurated," Rightmire explained, "the new policy of the athletic board in giving attention to the first year men ... with the idea of both finding out what material there may be in the freshman class and developing it as much as possible." It all seemed very primitive by contrast with the extensive recruiting and screening that came about in later years. Some 740 of the new all-year athletic tickets were sold for $5 each or to about one-fourth of the student body.

There was prophetic note after the close of the 1910 season by Prof. William Lloyd Evans, of the Athletic Board, that football schedule difficulties could be solved if Ohio State joined the Western Conference. There was talk that Wisconsin might be on the 1911 schedules and that the Michigan Aggies were desirous of a place on the schedule.

Football began on a hopeful note in the fall of 1911. The schedule had Syracuse as an added attraction. The Athletic Association treasurer reported that the finances were in good shape although there were unpaid notes at the bank. Year-round athletic books were again put on sale at $5. Fifty men reported for practice under Coach Vaughn, with "Prep" Wells, former Varsity captain, as assistant.

Under the prevailing system cheerleaders were chosen at a student election. H. S. Atkinson, a basketball star at the time and later a longtime trustee of the University, was the head cheerleader. It was announced also that any Varsity "O" man, graduate or undergraduate, could get a ticket to any athletic contest by calling at Dr. Wingert's office.

Close games marked the early part of the season. Otterbein was defeated, 6 to 0, and Miami, 3 to 0. There were newspaper reports of a Varsity training table but the *Lantern* emphasized that the players ate at the Ohio Union at their own expense. Two special trains took Ohio State rooters to the Michigan game but Ohio State lost, 19 to 0. Coeds sold tags to help send the band to Michigan where it made a late appearance.

The team lost later to Case, 9 to 0, and tied Oberlin, 0 to 0. This led Cleveland and other newspapers to ask "What's the trouble at Ohio State?" The Athletic Board sent a squad of twenty-five to Oberlin, plus the cheerleader. This was the first time the board had paid the cheerleader's expenses to a game away from home.

Near the end of the season the *Lantern* gave its own answer as to what was "wrong." It blamed the showing on insufficient equipment, the "evil" effects of military drill, a lack of student spirit, and ineffective work by the Varsity "O" Association. It also cited "frugality" on out-of-town trips. Coach Vaughn declared that a big change in spirit on the campus was needed. The athletic management gave its side of the "frugality" on the Oberlin trip.

Coming events, meanwhile, were casting their shadows. A *Lantern* story reported President Thompson as favoring relieving Dr. Wingert from team management. Another story told of an impending revision of the Athletic Association constitution. And Vaughn was given a rousing sendoff when he left to return to Yale to resume his law studies.

The '11 season under Vaughn had been what a later generation would have called "so-so." Still, as the *Quarterly* reported candidly in its January, 1912 issue, "Much praise is due Coach Harry Vaughn for the things that he accomplished. It must be remembered he was very much handicapped by the fact that but three men who could really be called regulars remained as a nucleus of the team which he was to construct. As he was unfamiliar with Ohio State football and had no coaching experience, it was doubtful whether he could make good." Yet it was pointed out that only two touchdowns were scored all season against Ohio State by "straight" football.

There was a bright side to the picture, too. For the first time since the extensive improvements to Ohio Field were begun the Athletic Association was out of debt, having paid off $3500 in notes. The only remaining improvement contemplated was to extend the west bleachers southward and move the old grandstand to the baseball diamond. This was never done.

VIII

TRACK, BASKETBALL AND BASEBALL, 1898-1912

ALTHOUGH the new University Field came into use in the spring of 1898 it had no running track for some time. As late as the spring of 1900 track and field meets were still being held at the Columbus Driving Park. Cross country running made its appearance at least as early as the fall of 1898. That season the Athletic Board authorized a cross country run on Thanksgiving Day. The November 16 *Dispatch* reported that the three best runners were to be rewarded with "ribbon badges."

It was not surprising that the competitive urge to run and jump, reflected first in the early Field and Class Days, continued after the turn of the century. But the physical resources were still meager and support in the way of coaching or finances was very limited. Until Sweetland's time, 1904-06, there was a succession of seasonal coaches. And it was not until the arrival of Steve Farrell in 1910 that track began to reach maturity on the campus.

For more than a decade the Big Six track meet, emblematic of the Ohio intercollegiate track championship, was the high spot of the outdoor track season in the state. This meet was inaugurated in 1903. It was run by the Intercollegiate Athletic Association, made up of Oberlin, Case, Western Reserve, Wooster, Ohio Wesleyan, Kenyon, Miami, Cincinnati and Ohio State. In the ten meets held through 1912 Ohio State won seven and Oberlin three.

Oberlin invariably had one or more outstanding stars. In the 1911 meet the feature race was between Baker, of Oberlin, and Wikoff, of Ohio State, at two miles. Wikoff won in the then record time of 9 min., 45 sec. In the 1912 meet he again won and lowered his mark by one second. Ohio State again won the team championship.

To go back, track facilities were improved somewhat in the spring of 1905 when the trustees authorized the building of a track in "the south field," i.e., near Eleventh Ave. But as the April 19 *Lantern* explained, "The location was not such that a full quarter mile track could be installed, but the present one is not far short." A month later, however, the paper complained that "The pasturing of University cows in the fields along Eleventh avenue has aided utterly in ruining the new track." Despite these handicaps the Varsity closed the season by winning the Big Six meet with 61 points to 45 for Oberlin which was second.

There was an element of hoodlumism present at home contests that spring, especially baseball. This led to a long letter in the May 10 *Lantern* from Prof. Rightmire, former graduate manager, pleading for an attitude of fair play toward visiting teams.

The 1906 season was another good one in track. In dual meets the team defeated Indiana, 63 to 32, and Purdue, 60½ to 51½. It also won the fourth annual Big Six meet, scoring nine firsts.

In those years, as noted, there was a succession of track coaches. The February 13, 1907 *Lantern* referred to Arthur Pearse "who practically coached the track team of 1906." Pearse was completing his medical work at O.M.U. In the spring of 1907 George D. Corneal was named coach. For two years Corneal had been assistant to the famous Mike Murphy, of the University of Pennsylvania.

Under Corneal the squad had a good season. It won the annual Big Six meet with 59 points. It narrowly lost to Purdue at Lafayette, 61 to 56, with the results of two events disputed. And a quartet of Buckeye runners took second in the special 1-mile college relay at the Pennsylvania Relays. Money was a problem, as always, and to send the runners to Penn $160 was raised, besides what the athletic treasury could spare. The girls' glee club contributed $25.

Early in 1908 W. J. McCarty, of Cornell, was named track coach. As an undergraduate he had starred at Boston College in the dashes and broad jump. At Cornell he was assistant to the famous Jack Moakley, longtime coach there. Under McCarty the Varsity again won the Big Six meet and a relay team placed third in a 1-mile event at the Penn Relays. McCarty was enrolled in the Veterinary College while coaching. Cross country was still struggling for recognition but without much encouragement or support. In the fall of 1908 students were asked for donations to help the cross country team.

Evidently McCarty coached only one year for one Riley is in the records as having coached in 1909. In March he announced a "novice" track meet to be held in the gymnasium. The hat was passed that spring to send 4-mile and 1-mile relay teams to the Penn Relays where the latter placed fourth. An effort was made next to employ E. T. Cook, of Chillicothe, as coach. Cook was a star at Cornell and had won the pole vault at the London Olympics in 1908. But Cook declined because to accept would have cost him an impending trip abroad.

The head track coaching duties fell instead into the capable hands of Steve Farrell in January, 1910. As noted elsewhere, Farrell was to serve as head trainer for all Varsity teams as well as track coach. He coached for three seasons. In his prime, in the '80s and '90s, Farrell was regarded, to quote the May 11, 1910 *Lantern,* as "the greatest sprinter in the world, running all distances from one hundred yards to the half mile with almost unvarying success." He came to the campus from the University of Maine.

What became the annual state high school track championships were begun meanwhile under University auspices. These were begun in the spring of 1908. There was some talk of abandoning the meet in 1908. What was described as the third annual meet was held on Ohio Field in June, 1910.

Prof. William Lloyd Evans, in the *Alumni Quarterly,* spoke of Farrell's first season as track coach. The account pointed out that "In less than five months, in the face of every sort of discouragement and hard luck, Farrell has succeeded in developing a very mediocre array of hopefuls into a team of world beaters." Oberlin was defeated in the annual meet, 60½-56½, yet Ohio State finished second to Oberlin in the Big Six meet, 44⅗ to 40⅕. In this meet seven new records were set and Metcalf, of Oberlin, scored 26 points.

Through a combination of circumstances track began to come into its own during those years. One was the hiring of Farrell. Another was the appearance and development of several individual stars, notably Garnett Wikoff, middle distance runner, Clement C. Cooke, sprinter, and H. M. Crellin and Robert B. Criswell, also distance runners. Under Farrell's tutelage the team not only achieved success in dual meets but individual athletes and relay teams were successful in outside meets such as the Penn Relays and special meets in Chicago and elsewhere.

Finances were still a problem, however, and in March, 1911, for example, the Student Council was raising money to send Farrell and Wikoff to a meet in Chicago. Both Cooke and Wikoff were Columbus products. They were to have the distinction of being members of the U.S. Olympic team at Stockholm in 1912. Wikoff went to the Chicago meet referred to and won his event. In an outdoor meet with Ohio Wesleyan, Cooke won four firsts. He not only ran the 100- and 220-yd. dashes but competed in the broad jump and shot put.

When the question of sending Cooke and Wikoff to the U.S. Olympic tryouts at Chicago arose in the spring of 1912, the Athletic Board was hard put for money. At a May 17 board meeting it was moved that "on account of the stringent financial condition of the Board, these men not be sent to Chicago at the expense of the Board." The motion was reconsidered and lost, but another motion to appropriate $50 to send the two men to Chicago carried. Student contributions apparently made up the difference. Both men qualified.

In those days competition in the annual Big Nine track championships was open to other schools. Because of the success of the Ohio State squad that spring the Athletic Board at its May 27 meeting approved the sending of Farrell and five athletes to the Conference meet at Purdue at board expense. The men were Wikoff, mile and 2-mile; Lee, half mile; Rogers, quarter mile; Copeland, sprinter; and Kesler, pole vault.

It developed that the Big Nine regarded Wikoff as ineligible for the meet.* At a special board meeting, the board withdrew its approval to send the men to Purdue "on account of Capt. Wikoff being barred from the meet." At the same time the board approved the payment of "all of Wikoff's expenses to Chicago to the Olympic tryouts," but not to exceed $50. At still another meeting May 28, the telegram stating that Wikoff was not eligible to compete in the Big Nine meet was "read and discussed" but no further action was taken.

In 1912 in Farrell's last season as Varsity coach, the team again won the Big Six. The two outstanding men, as noted, were Wikoff and Cooke. Outdoors Wikoff defeated Metcalf, the Oberlin star, in 9 min., 40⅖ sec. This was faster than the Big Nine record but was 15⅕ seconds off the U.S. intercollegiate mark. In June both men went to the Olympic tryouts and won their events. Cooke tied the world's record for the 200 meters in 21⅗ seconds and placed third in the broad jump. Wikoff was first in the 5000 meters in 15 min., 37⅕ sec. Both men then went on to New York to compete in the finals against the Eastern winners, won places on the U.S. team and left for Stockholm.

At Stockholm, unfortunately, neither man was in the money. Cooke was bothered by a football knee although he lasted until the semi-finals. There were workouts aboard ship en route and Wikoff's left leg began to bother him. Despite the handicap he entered the race but was unable to finish his heat. He was taken back to the ship where he was confined for a week.

BASKETBALL

With the completion of the new gymnasium in the winter of 1898 basketball took a regular place as a Varsity sport. At a meeting in mid-January, the *Lantern* said, between thirty and forty men turned out

* Because he and Cooke had represented the Cleveland Athletic Club.

"to consider the organization of a basket ball team to represent the Ohio State University." In its February 16 issue the paper added that the team had "played its first game" with North High School as the opponent. The collegians won, 13 to 3, but the account gave no lineup. "With a little practice," the paper said, "the team met the Columbus North High school team in a game on the floor of the new gymnasium last Tuesday evening."

The gymnasium, as noted, was formally opened with a reception. "Monday evening the new gymnasium," the February 23, 1898 *Lantern* reported, "was the scene of a most delightful entertainment." The reception was "tendered to the students, alumni, ex-students, trustees and faculty by the O.S.U. Alumnae Club, the Faculty Women's Club and the Scarlet and Gray." There was nothing athletic, however.

The March 1 *Dispatch* noted that the Varsity basketball team had played the Barracks on the new floor but it neglected to mention the score. On March 9 it told of the Varsity meeting the Y.M.C.A. "at the auditorium." The collegians won by the strange score of 12 to 0. Yet there seems to have been some basketball activity as early as 1897 since the February 11, 1900 *Lantern* reported that a claim of Coach Edwards for services in 1897 was settled. George M. Karshner, '00, in a letter in April, 1955, said that in the fall of 1897 he asked President Canfield for permission to "start the game at State" and Canfield approved. Karshner added: "We played our first game at the old Goodale St. armory" against the local Y.M.C.A., "defeating it."

The 1899 team did well. The May 24 *Lantern* said it had won the "championship of the state in per centage of points won, but tied with Urbana in number of games won." In those days college teams played against local or town teams as well as against other college teams.

The 1899 team provided one of the few bright spots in Ohio State athletics that year. It won twelve out of fifteen games and closed the regular college season by defeating Kenyon, 14 to 11. The *Lantern* described it as "the only winning team in any line of athletics that O.S.U. has had for three years." Besides college opponents, it played Y.M.C.A. and other "town" teams. Kenton, for example, was played three times. The Varsity played Urbana twice, losing there but winning at home. The *Lantern* regretted that "such a team receives so little support from the university body, and so small an amount of encouragement from the Athletic association."

Play was sometimes rough. In a game at Kenton in February, two Ohio State players—Karshner, right forward, and Reed, right guard—

appeared on the floor with football headgear and nose guards. According to the February 15 *Lantern* account, "The umpire and referee insisted that Karshner and Reed should doff their foot ball gear, but they wore them throughout the game."

Poor attendance at one of the early games in 1900 was laid to the fact that it was scheduled the same night the debate team performed. On this the *Lantern* said the Athletic Board "cuts their own throats" in so doing. There were rumors also in the downtown papers that the basketball team was at swords' points with the board over lack of basketball representation on the board. There was even criticism of basketball games being scheduled in the evening.

A fine record was made by the '05 basketball team. It won eleven and lost only two games and claimed the state championship. It scored 501 points to 253 for its opponents. Among its victims were three future Western Conference opponents. It defeated Wisconsin, 25 to 22, Purdue, 26 to 23, and Indiana, 66 to 12. But it lost to Minnesota, 27 to 25. The other defeat was by Oberlin (there) while the team defeated Oberlin in Columbus. Hegelheimer was captain.

Another state championship was won in 1906 when the team lost only one game—again to Oberlin. The 1907 team was only moderately successful, winning seven and losing five games. A feature of the season was a resumption of athletic relations with Denison which were broken after the 1905 football dispute. The 1907 game, played at Granville, was won by Denison, 23 to 11. "The reception accorded the State team by Denison officials and students," the February 13 *Lantern* said, "were of the most cordial kind and relations were reopened with the Baptists college in the most auspicious way."

But a breach with Ohio Wesleyan, for reasons not clear, remained unhealed. The above issue of the *Lantern* remarked, "No great advances have been made in the matter of resuming athletic relations with Ohio Wesleyan." An innovation of the 1908 season was the appearance of a gymnastic team before the game and between halves of the January 11 game with Wittenberg.

Next to football, basketball became the most popular Varsity sport in the pre-Western Conference years. The gymnasium had a maximum seating capacity of some 2000. To do this chairs and low, temporary bleachers were placed in every available spot. Under these conditions the playing floor was very close to the "ringside" seats and in vigorous play every now and then a player would find himself catapulted into the nearby seats.

The basketball squads were small both in numbers and in the size of the players by contrast with modern day groups. In the 1908-09 season, for example, only five "O's" were awarded owing to the "strict enforcement" of Varsity rules. Yet this team won all but one of its twelve games. The Varsity won the state title again in 1910 under Coach Tom Kibler by defeating Oberlin (there), 22 to 17. Kibler served also as baseball coach.

A curious but not uncommon situation in those years arose during the 1910-11 season as the result of temptation to play on outside teams under assumed names while playing Varsity basketball. This had several results: four of the six regular players were suspended, only one "O" was awarded at the close of the season, and where the team showed a tendency to "run away" from its opponents during the first half of Varsity games, it let down perceptibly during the second half.

For college players to play on outside "semi-pro" teams, generally under aliases, was fairly common in the first decade of the 1900s. Such teams were sponsored by merchants and others from whom the players received money and/or merchandise. The issue came to a head on the campus at the close of the 1911 season when it began to be noised about that players on the squad might not be granted their Varsity letters. This was confirmed presently when, after hearing the evidence and considering the circumstances, the Athletic Board voted the letter to only one player. Before reaching its decision the board referred the professionalism charges to a Varsity "O" Association committee.

This situation was discussed at some length in the April, 1911 *Alumni Quarterly* by its editor, Prof. Joseph Russell Taylor, under the heading "Lessons from the Basketball Season." Toward the end of the season, he commented, "the papers began to publish the reason for this: between the Varsity games, and mostly under assumed names, the men on the team were playing on outside teams," as, for example, the night before the last game with Oberlin, the most important on the schedule.

The Varsity "O" Association made an investigation and suspended from the association the captain and three other regular players, but exonerated two others. The Athletic Board disqualified the first four but, as Taylor pointed out, "by the rules of the Ohio Athletic Conference they disqualified themselves by the use of assumed names." One of the two exonerated by the Varsity "O" Association was also disqualified "by his own admission that he played under an assumed name in one game before the Varsity season opened." But because of his "faithful training and excellent service," the board recommended his reinstatement.

Much the same problem existed with respect to playing summer baseball under assumed names contrary to college athletic regulations. This and playing on outside basketball teams during the regular season developed gradually and were fairly common occurrences. Prof. Taylor quoted the cage captain (Spangler) as saying, "We have learned our lesson; all we can hope for is an honorable reinstatement before we leave college."

The basketball coaching chores for the 1911-12 season, the last one before permanent, full-time coaches were provided, fell to Stockton A. "Sox" Raymond, '05, a former Varsity player. Raymond had the assistance of H. J. Hegelheimer, '07, another former Varsity player. At the close of the 1911 season Coach Kibler had resigned to become manager of the Chillicothe team in the Ohio State League.

BASEBALL

As described earlier, difficulties beset the 1898 baseball team, especially because of the strong faculty stand against approving any schedule until something was done to meet the athletic debt. This action jolted the campus because there was no warning of it.

When a way out of the dilemma was found, as noted, a schedule of seven games was finally announced. "The unsettled state of affairs in the way of athletics at the University this year" was given as the explanation for so few games. Home games were played on the new athletic field, but a year earlier the team practiced "on the open lot at the corner of Neil and Eleventh avenues."

During this period, however, baseball remained one of the major sports, with success in some years and not in others. Coaching was still at a minimum and at best was on a part-time basis.

One of the stalwarts on the 1902-03-04 baseball and basketball teams was George "Ho" Bellows, of Columbus, the tallest man on either squad. Bellows who later became one of the most distinguished American painters of his generation played shortstop on the baseball team and right forward on the basketball squad. The 1903 records gave his fielding average of .928 but a batting mark of only .160.

Disputes over the eligibility of baseball players occurred from time to time. One of these developed near the end of the 1907 season when Kenyon challenged two Ohio State players. The men had played regularly in earlier games, including one with Michigan, and there had been no challenge. Ohio State insisted upon playing the pair, Davis, the captain and centerfielder, and Barrington, shortstop. But the game was canceled when the opposing team refused to play on these terms.

Early in 1908 there was again question of the baseball outlook for financial reasons. But the picture brightened when the *Lantern* reported that 400 students had pledged themselves to buy season books at $1 each. Dr. H. S. Wingert, the new athletic and physical education director, in his first annual report dealt among other things with baseball. He spoke of "an effort to suspend 'Varsity baseball for one year in order to give it a trial on a recreative basis," i.e., what later would have been called intramural. As reasons for this he cited the lack of support, the small number of students directly interested, and the great demand for the use of the one playing field by class, college and fraternity teams.

On the eve of the 1910 season the fate of Varsity baseball was again in doubt. At the end of January the Athletic Board adopted a resolution that it was "the sense of the Board that the University should support a baseball team." But efforts to revive it failed and three weeks later the Varsity team was dropped for the time being because of a lack of interest and insufficient subscriptions. "Recreative" baseball was substituted.

There was also gloom over the baseball prospects in the spring of 1911 because eighteen members of the squad were reported as down in their school work and therefore ineligible. There were several applicants to succeed Coach Kibler, resigned, and the board belatedly named J. R. Willoughby, a Starling-Ohio medical student, as coach early in April. In 1912, the last season before the advent of full-time coaching, the interim coach was Dow A. "Red" Baird, a former Varsity pitcher. At the time he was a student in the law college.

PART II

EXPANSION AND COMPETITION
1912-1959

IX
THE 1912 REORGANIZATION AND THE BIG TEN

THE year 1912 was perhaps the most important single year in all Ohio State athletic history. It was not only a year of decision but one of transition. It was marked, in particular, by five major developments: the organization of the Athletic Board under faculty control, the separation of athletics and physical education, the hiring of year-round coaches with faculty status, the admission of the University to the Western Conference, and the scheduling of the first Conference football games for the 1913 season. There were other items of lesser significance.

Three men were to stand out in the epochal transition of the University from a leading member of the Ohio Conference to the "baby" member of the Western Conference. First was Thomas Ewing French, '95, second chairman of the reorganized Athletic Board and who was to be the University's faculty representative in the Western Conference from 1912 until his death in 1944. He had been active and influential in athletic affairs prior to the reorganization. He was credited later with being the "daddy" of the Stadium idea and the record shows that he began to dream of a concrete horseshoe-shaped structure at least as early as 1908.

The second was George W. Rightmire, also '95, who as an undergraduate had been active and prominent as a participant in the annual Field Days. A member of the law faculty, he served for a time as graduate manager of athletics. But in particular it was Rightmire, later president of the University during the troubled years from 1926 to 1938, who successfully presented the University's "case" for admission to the Western Conference.

The third man, who returned to the campus with the reorganization that was effective in the fall of 1912, was Lynn W. St. John, w'04, who became a nationally known figure in intercollegiate athletics. In the fall of 1900 he was a freshman halfback on the football squad of that year but had to drop out of school shortly because of his father's death. In time he coached at Fostoria High School, then at the College of Wooster (football, basketball and baseball—and numbered the famous Compton brothers among his players), and then at Ohio Wesleyan where he was director and coach. While there he commuted for two years to Starling-Ohio Medical College, in Columbus, where he studied medicine in the mornings and returned to Delaware on the noon interurban to his athletic duties.

"Saint," as he was known best to his players and to the public, returned to the Ohio State campus in the fall of 1912 in a multiple capacity: as football line coach, as head basketball and baseball coach, and as athletic business manager. With the departure of Athletic Director John R. Richards early in the winter of 1913, St. John suddenly found himself athletic director. The evidence is that the Athletic Board did not even consult him on the move but simply promoted him and then notified him. This had two results: it ended whatever hopes he entertained of a medical career and it put him on the long road to eminence in the Western Conference and in the intercollegiate athletic world, particularly in the National Collegiate Athletic Association.

The athletic reorganization on the campus was overdue. For nearly six years the management had been in the hands of Dr. Wingert who was also director of physical education. Stated simply, Dr. Wingert had too much to do, especially in the face of the mounting importance of athletics and the rapid growth of the University. But under the prevailing system he had the "power to formulate all playing schedules, which made him the sole intercollegiate representative of the University; he had authority to purchase all supplies and equipment for athletes, and the power to determine the quantity and quality of such equipment; he had charge of Ohio Field, and of the arrangement for games, and, finally, he supervised all coaches and trainers, and nominated them to the Athletic Board for election."

Under this setup the Athletic Board was little more than a rubber stamp agency. It had few real powers and these were largely advisory and by way of ratifying actions already taken. But it had control of the purse strings as far as athletic funds were concerned and all contracts involving athletic matters were valid only upon board approval. "This system seemed to work satisfactorily for a time," Rightmire wrote in the *Quarterly* in the spring of 1912, "but it became apparent that, under the limited manning of the Department of Physical Education, the Director was overloaded with duties."

Besides the growing desire to be admitted to the Western Conference, there had been growing dissatisfaction with athletic conditions on the campus. The old Athletic Board was unwieldy, consisting of thirteen members: three faculty, the physical education director, three resident alumni, the Board of Trustees secretary, and five students, including the four team managers and the secretary of the Athletic Association.

The faculty, the students and the alumni all took a hand in the situation. Students brought to the faculty in December, 1911 a proposal to give undergraduates control of athletics by reconstituting the board with five student members, two faculty and two alumni. On the ground that it would develop their responsibility, President Thompson seems to have favored the proposal. But the faculty at a special meeting December 18 refused to ratify it. In January, 1912 a two-way faculty inquiry was begun, one as to the situation on the campus and the other as to how athletics were administered elsewhere.

The Athletic Board at a meeting January 22, to quote the January 24 *Lantern*, "unanimously agreed to petition the Conference for admission" even though this meant the severance of athletic relations with Michigan. The latter was out of the Conference on the issue of the training table. A committee of three, Profs. Rightmire and Alonzo H. Tuttle, both of the law school, and Carl E. Steeb, '99, secretary of the trustees, presented the University's case January 26, 1912 before the Conference. The actual presentation was made by Rightmire. This followed a visit to the campus in mid-January by Prof. H. W. Johnstone, of Indiana University, president of the Conference. Johnstone talked favorably of the chances of the University's admission which was granted finally in June.

In the meantime a Franklin County (Columbus) alumni committee consisting of Clarence D. Laylin, '04, J. Howard Galbraith, '83, and Homer C. Howard, w'97, was inquiring into the "causes of dissatisfaction with the present system," according to the February 14 *Lantern*. Another faculty committee consisting of Profs. Tuttle, French and J. A. Leighton was also at work. Tuttle and Leighton visited the Chicago, Northwestern and Illinois campuses to see at first hand how they ran their athletics and French did likewise at Michigan. In Ohio, Western Reserve, Case and Oberlin were visited similarly.

The two main conditions of membership in the Conference were adherence to rules based upon amateur standing and scholastic eligibility and faculty control of intercollegiate athletics. This was accomplished at Ohio State by the report of the committee on athletics which was effected March 5. The report, adopted February 14 by the faculty, was ratified February 21 by the trustees.

"The control of intercollegiate athletics," the faculty report began, "shall be vested in an Athletic Board of Control." The board had nine members, five from the faculty, and two each representing the alumni and students. The faculty members, to be appointed annually by the president, were to constitute the faculty committee on athletics and eligibility. The alumni members were to be chosen annually by the

Alumni Association and the two student members were to be "elected annually by the members of the Athletic Association." (The holder of an annual student athletic book was automatically an association member.)

The board was given power to "appoint the Athletic Director, engage all coaches and trainers, approve all schedules and expenditures, and appoint all student managers and other assistants." The "immediate direction" of intercollegiate and intramural athletics was to be in the hands of the athletic director who was "responsible to the board of control." His functions were to "arrange the schedules of all intercollegiate and intramural contests," subject to the board's approval; to "supervise all trips and all arrangements for the carrying on of intercollegiate and intramural contests"; to "look after the interests of the intercollegiate teams"; and to "endeavor to promote a general participation in outdoor athletics among the students of the University." He was also to report to the board "on all matters relating to his department."

Another major change was the hiring of full-time coaches for the major teams with faculty rank and tenure. On this point the report "recommended that as soon as practicable and as far as possible all coaches of teams shall be employed for the regular academic year and when satisfactory, continued in their office from year to year. In the view of the Committee it is highly desirable that all coaches should be permanently identified with the life of the University." For all practical purposes this policy was put into effect with the school year 1912-13 and has continued ever since.

The original members of the Athletic Board as reorganized were as follows: faculty—Profs. A. H. Tuttle, George W. Rightmire, Thomas E. French, C. A. Dye, and J. A. Leighton; alumni—J. H. Galbraith, '83, and C. D. Laylin, '04; students—I. N. Jenkins, '12, and W. Henry Grant, '12. Some of the faculty members had been active in the earlier days and Ohio State athletics owed much to them for their zeal and devotion in the formative years. Galbraith was on the Columbus *Dispatch* staff, and Laylin, an attorney, was later for many years on the law faculty. Jenkins, one of the most active students, in after years was elected to Congress from a Chicago district.

The March 5 reorganization meeting was called to order by Rightmire who moved that Tuttle serve as temporary chairman. Officers elected were Rightmire, president; Tuttle, vice president; and Grant, secretary. A committee consisting of Leighton, Tuttle and Jenkins was appointed to revise the bylaws. R. M. Royer, longtime University purchasing agent, was treasurer. Rightmire was authorized to "O.K. all bills now owed by the board." During the remainder of that school year the athletic administration was carried on by committees.

An accompanying financial report, of the same date, showed receipts of $19,926.21, expenditures of $16,594.99, a cash balance of $2971.22, and $2198.00 in outstanding bills—all for salaries, leaving a net balance of $773.22. The breakdown showed that Harry Vaughn, football coach the previous fall, was paid $2000, and "Prep" Wells, his assistant, $250. Steve Farrell, track coach and head trainer, was on for $1800 and Stockton Raymond, basketball coach, was down for $150 salary. Also at the March 5 meeting a committee of three was named—French, Tuttle and Laylin—"to entertain applications for the position of Athletic Director," and to submit the names to the board.

One byproduct of all this was a delay in the election of the 1912 football captain. Don Barricklow, tackle, was finally chosen March 4. Another effect was to abandon the method of choosing Varsity team managers at campus-wide elections. From now on they were to be chosen by the board.

In the meantime the Western Conference itself was in some difficulty. There was dissatisfaction with the way it was run. Much of this, according to the March 27, 1912 *Lantern*, centered at the University of Illinois where students had petitioned the faculty to withdraw from the Conference. This, to quote the *Lantern* further, was on the grounds that the "method of regulation of athletic affairs is cumbersome; that permanent policy agreeable to all is impossible; that the summer baseball compromise is far from a solution of the problem; competition with Michigan is desirable and should not be denied, and that the implied slap at Director George Huff [of Illinois] is unjust."

The presidents of eight of the Conference universities met in Chicago in March because of "growing dissatisfaction with the existing conditions of government of the Western Intercollegiate Conference." They set at rest, however, the rumor that the Conference would be dissolved.

In a report on the campus athletic reorganization in the *Quarterly*, Prof. Rightmire wrote: "This Board must now fit itself into the athletic situation, bring the student body more intelligently into co-operation with it, and arouse a keener interest and more intelligent interest among the Alumni and ex-students; . . . The Board must also bring the University more strikingly to the attention of the High Schools of the State, and help create a deeper feeling that Ohio State is coming closer to the front each year in all lines of amateur athletics, . . . The largest question now is who will make the best Director obtainable and a committee is already at work trying to frame the answer. . . .

"It is hoped that our athletic horizon can be widened by admission to the so-called 'Western Conference,' which includes the State Universities of Indiana, Illinois, Iowa, Minnesota, and Wisconsin, and Chicago, Northwestern and Purdue Universities. Our application is under consideration, and will probably be acted upon during this month; the prospects are very favorable. In that conference, athletic competition will, generally, be on a higher plane than Ohio State has hitherto been able to reach, and the effect upon us should be a stimulating one, and no enduring reason appears why we should not at a very early day be the athletic peer of any of these universities . . . ." These last were strong words but George Rightmire was a better prophet than even he knew for in four years Ohio State was to win its first Western Conference football championship.

At an Athletic Board meeting March 11 two actions of some importance were taken. One was the adoption of new bylaws. The other was a request to the University trustees that one of the few remaining faculty houses on the campus, known as the Thomas house, fronting High St. at 16th Ave. and convenient to Ohio Field, "be converted into a headquarters for the Athletic Department, and be equipped by the University for that purpose." Approval was given shortly, the conversion was made, and the structure served as the Athletic House until the new men's physical education building was completed in 1931.

A small addition to the west end of the first floor housed the shower room, lockers for various athletic squads were installed in rear rooms downstairs and upstairs, with a training (rubbing) room at the head of the rear stairway upstairs. What had been a parlor was used as a squad meeting room, and athletic department offices were quartered in a large room upstairs facing High St. There was always the possibility that one of the women secretaries, on her way to or from the bathroom at the rear of the second floor hall, might encounter a nearly nude athlete en route to or from the locker rooms and the training room where "King" Brady and later "Doc" Gurney functioned.

The bylaws cited above contained the usual routine provisions for organization, operation and the duties of officers and of members of the coaching staff. While the athletic director was given a good deal of responsibility, the board reserved the "appointment and dismissal of coaches and trainers" to itself. And in case "of any disagreement or conflict between the Director of Athletics and the coaches or trainers, the matter in dispute shall be referred to the Athletic Board for final adjudication."

Various items show on what a modest scale Varsity athletics were conducted in those days. A request to send a cheerleader with the basketball squad to a game with Oberlin was denied. A question arose as to who should pay for the repair of "lockers on the Gymnasium floor, broken by track athletes." It developed that the earlier board had paid for such repairs the cost of which in this case was reported later as $2.35. At the close of the 1912 basketball season authority was given "to purchase seven (7) sweaters at $4.75, and to arrange for a light banquet at Ohio Union for the basketball men." The "banquet" cost 50c a plate and board members paid for their own.

Two months elapsed before an athletic director was named. In the meantime the impending changeover was made at the cost of dispensing with the services of Steve Farrell who had served well as Varsity trainer and track coach. Farrell was well regarded, especially by the track men. In a formal resolution May 13, 1912 the board explained that "on account of the reorganization" it found it impossible "on account of financial conditions to employ more than two high class men for the entire management and coaching of all athletic teams, thereby rendering it necessary for each man to coach two athletic teams in addition to performing numerous other duties."

The board regretted "that it must part with the services of Mr. Farrell, and takes this occasion to express its appreciation of his earnestness and ability as a coach and trainer and his great success not only in accomplishing results, but in winning the confidence and loyalty of the athletes." It promised also to do all in its power "to assist Mr. Farrell in becoming located at some other institution, and stand ready to give the strongest recommendation of Mr. Farrell's ability and success whenever it may be desired." It also voted him a bonus of $200 "in appreciation of his excellent services." The students gave him a silver cup and a purse collected at the Big Six netted him $129 more. Farrell promptly caught on at the University of Michigan where he made an outstanding record also as trainer and coach.

At a number of meetings between March and May the special committee on hiring an athletic director reported no progress. But at the May 9 meeting it made two momentous recommendations. The first was that John R. Richards be engaged as athletic director and head coach of football and track at $3500 a year. The other was that L. W. St. John be employed as "Manager of Athletics, head coach of Baseball and Basketball, and assistant coach of Football at a salary of $2000.00 per year." After a nearly 3-hour discussion the recommendations carried unanimously.

Richards was brought from the University of Wisconsin. He had coached also at Colorado College and at Shurtleff College. He was a vigorous man in the prime of life, direct and sometimes brusque. It fell to him to coach the last Varsity football team before the University entered active Western Conference competition. But his first season was also his last since he resigned voluntarily but rather suddenly not long after the close of the season to accept other employment. In the meantime he had begun work with the indoor track squad.

For St. John, who was to emerge as the most important individual in the University's athletic and physical education picture for the next three decades, his employment, as noted, was in the nature of a homecoming. He was a man of great energy and talent, and an outstanding organizer and administrator. He had had strong teams at both Wooster and Ohio Wesleyan in three sports—football, basketball and baseball. As indicated, he was to have primary responsibility for basketball and baseball under the new Ohio State setup and was to assist with football. In addition, he was, in effect, athletic business manager. In the spring of 1912, meanwhile, Farrell again coached track, Dow A. "Red" Baird had charge of baseball, and R. F. Foster, Central Ohio tennis champion, was named tennis coach.

During the early months of 1912 the University's request for admission to the Big Nine awaited final action. At the March 25 board meeting, for example, the minute stated: "Mr. Rightmire reports that no definite action has yet been taken by the Western Conference as to the admission of Ohio State." As a matter of fact the board minutes are silent as to when the Conference acted favorably. But the Conference records show that it was April 6, 1912. By that fall Ohio State had taken its place as the "baby" member of the Conference in which it was to play an increasingly strong role in the years ahead.

While the University continued athletic relations with Ohio colleges and remained a member of the "Big Six," it was now headed for "big time" competition, especially with other leading state universities in the Midwest, plus Northwestern and Chicago. In view of its rapid growth after 1912, events proved that membership in the Conference was thoroughly justified. Time was to prove also that quite apart from intercollegiate athletics this relationship was to be highly fruitful to the University in other directions.

The so-called Western Conference was organized in 1895 with seven members. Its purpose was to encourage intercollegiate competition among a select group of like-minded universities in the Midwest. While the presidents of the member schools were directly responsible for its original formation, their authority in this field was delegated to faculty representatives, one from each member school. For this reason the proper name of the group was the Intercollegiate Conference of Faculty Representatives. It was known popularly, however, as the Western Conference or Big Nine.

In January, 1908 Michigan had withdrawn from the Conference in protest against "retroactive provisions" of certain Conference enactments. Actually this resulted from a dispute over the training table issue. Michigan held out for an authorized training table and gave up its membership when the Conference would not yield. With the admission of Ohio State and the loss of Michigan the number of members remained at nine. In view of the longtime athletic relations between the two schools, Ohio State officially expressed its hope that Michigan would return to the fold. This it did in November, 1917.

At the Sept. 21, 1912 board meeting, meanwhile, Prof. French was elected its president, a position he was to hold for a good many years. He served also as the University's faculty representative in the Conference. In recognition of the long and valuable services of Prof. Rightmire, who resigned as president, the board voted him "complimentary tickets for the foot ball season." (Complimentary tickets were much harder to come by in those early days than they were later.) Dr. O. V. Brumley, of Veterinary Medicine, filled the vacancy on the board.

In those early days the Big Nine was still in a primitive stage. It had as yet no commissioner. It was, in fact, a two-headed sort of affair with the faculty representatives in one group and a corresponding group of alumni on the other. Where French represented the University in the faculty group, Vernon C. Ward, '03, of Chicago, was the alumni representative. The Western Inter-Collegiate Athletic Association was a corporation, with one share of stock for each member institution. At the November 27, 1912 board meeting French was authorized to take over Ohio State's share of stock.

Various problems had to be overcome in the transition from Ohio and Big Six circles to the Big Nine. One of these concerned the matter of letter awards and another major problem was athletic eligibility under the higher standards of the Big Nine. At the November 13, 1912 meeting the board voted that the Varsity "O" be granted "only for merit in intercollegiate competition and the board approve the form of Varsity letter submitted upon the condition that it be awarded in such competition only." Much later, at a meeting March 28, 1916, the board voted to ask President Thompson to give it "the sole right of awarding the 'O'."

New enthusiasm was in the air that fall (1912) for the reorganized and revitalized athletic program. Prior to the opening game with Otterbein there was a rally with a "giant" bonfire. This was the autumn of the Wilson-Roosevelt-Taft presidential campaign and Wilson was to speak in Columbus that night. But "Prexy" Thompson, a friend of Wilson, stayed away from the political meeting to attend the football rally.

There were other signs of Ohio State's new athletic status. The Western Conference, however, did not accept the University's invitation to stage the annual Conference cross country run over the Varsity course. The Athletic Board took notice of the increased interest in football by expanding the seating capacity of Ohio Field to 6000. Even before the season was over rumors began to be heard that Director Richards might leave his new job to become recreation director for the city of Chicago. For a time it was hoped that he could be persuaded to stay, but before Christmas the board accepted his resignation, effective January 1.

No mention is made in the board minutes of Richards' resignation. But those for the December 18, 1912 meeting read: "Prof. Tuttle moves that Mr. St. John be made Director Athletics, Seconded—Carried." His salary was increased to $2500, effective January 1. He used to say later that the board acted without consulting him and its action came as a complete surprise to him. His salary was further increased at the December 7, 1914 board meeting to $2750 and was set at $3000 for 1915-16.

Also at the December 18, 1912 meeting the board authorized the employment of Carl Rothgeb, coach at Colorado College, as football and track coach at $2500 a year "to take such position as soon as possible." The board also recorded "its deep appreciation of the services which Mr. Richards has rendered to the Ohio State Athletics both in the way of management and more efficient Athletic System and of bringing a broader vision of the place of athletics in University education."

Rothgeb declined presently and the upshot of this unexpected development was the hiring of John W. Wilce, a University of Wisconsin alumnus, as football coach. Wilce, who was outstanding as a Badger football and basketball player and on the crew, had coached freshman football at Wisconsin. He was to make an enviable record for the next sixteen years as director of football and of intramural athletics. Thus began a University connection that was to last until his retirement in 1958.

One result of this over-all situation was to expand the coaching staff to three full-time men. Where Richards was athletic director and head football and track coach, and Rothgeb, an Illinois alumnus, was to have been head football and track coach, Wilce was hired as football coach. Wilce had been teaching and coaching at LaCrosse, Wis., high school.

The new man for track was Frank R. "Riley" Castleman, a 4-sport man at Colgate, who was brought from the University of Colorado as track coach and to assist with football. Wilce had the general football responsibility, St. John coached the line, and Castleman assisted with the backs for several years. All three were to remain permanently at the University and contributed greatly to its rise in intercollegiate athletics.

In the meantime Indiana, Wisconsin and Northwestern were scheduled as the initial Conference football opponents for the 1913 season. As part of the revised and expanded sports program Varsity wrestling was provided for and twenty men responded to the call for wrestlers. Another change in the changeful year of 1912-13 was the addition of soccer as a recognized sport. The board added this to the growing list of activities in April, 1913 and arranged to provide for two playing fields. One unexpected development that spring was the aftermath of the tremendous March flood which took a heavy toll of life in Columbus and elsewhere in the state. Along with all other students on the campus Varsity athletes returning to school were required to be vaccinated against smallpox.

Soon after his arrival April 11, Coach Wilce began spring football practice. Fifty men turned out for the squad and much time was spent on fundamentals. George Little, former Ohio Wesleyan star, helped with the coaching. Coach Castleman called a meeting of cross country candidates. Only six letters were awarded in basketball and the Oratory Council petitioned for the admission of Varsity debaters to the Varsity "O" Association.

Purdue was the opponent in the first Western Conference baseball for Ohio State and Wisconsin similarly provided the first Conference competition in outdoor track. In the Penn Relays that spring the Ohio

State 4-mile team took third place and the squad finished ninth in the Conference meet. A committee was set up to "look into the matter of Military and gymnasium 'O's."

Edith D. Cockins, for many years University registrar, was authority for the statement that on the basis of Western Conference standards only a handful of men from the 1911 squad would have been eligible to play in 1912. The transition, however difficult, was beneficial. This was illustrated by the case of a well-known player on whom the eligibility committee reported after the close of the 1912 season. The minutes show that the ruling accepted was that "with the information at hand we are unable to say that R—— will be eligible to play next year." As time proved he was not.

X

THE STADIUM AND ITS AFTERMATH

WITH the sudden growing pains following admission to the Big Nine it was only a question of time until Ohio Field would be outgrown. The space there was limited and the High St. frontage was too valuable for permanent athletic use. The Athletic Board began to take notice of this situation. At its May 28, 1913 meeting it authorized the appointment of a committee "to confer with President Thompson for discussion of the plan of moving the athletic field to a new place." At this meeting, the minutes show, the committee on improvement of the present seating capacity reported that "it does not favor any extensive improvement upon the present equipment" although it was for keeping "the present equipment in repair." Nearly a decade was to elapse before the Stadium was to become a reality.

Because of his long, intimate and influential connection with the project as it developed, Prof. French was generally credited with being the father of the stadium idea. But there is evidence that Prof. F. W. Ives, a Wisconsin alumnus, was the first to give tangible support to it. Ives, a member of the engineering drawing department of which French was chairman, offered $100 toward the building of a stadium.

A preliminary discussion of the idea was under way soon after the close of the 1916 championship season. At a February 3, 1917 board meeting the sole topic of discussion was "the plans for the new stadium." The minutes gave no details.

In the summer of 1918 the idea of a new athletic plant and stadium was still germinating. At an August 13, 1918 board meeting, Prof. French reported on "the new plans of Architect Smith for the new Athletic Field and Stadium." Again no details were given but it was Architect Howard Dwight Smith, '07, who finally drew the plans for the horseshoe-shaped, double deck stadium finally built in 1921-22 and completed in time for the 1922 football season.

There was further discussion of the idea of a new athletic plant and stadium in the early months of 1919. At the March 21 board meeting, for example, "General discussion of plans for a new field constituted the business for the evening."

Money was the great problem and various ideas were suggested. During World War I the 83rd Division football team at Camp Sherman,

Chillicothe, O., had been rather successful financially and otherwise. With the end of the war the sprawling camp fell into disuse except as a mustering out place for returning soldiers. It was known that there was a sizeable sum in the Camp Sherman fund. At the March 21 meeting the board adopted a motion to name a committee "to see if the Camp Sherman fund could not be obtained toward a new stadium." Nothing came of this move.

In the end it developed that a stadium could be financed in only two ways: by public subscription and by profits from intercollegiate athletics, chiefly football. The plan for a stadium campaign which, in effect, would take the public into partnership began to take shape toward the end of 1919 after the close of a third highly successful football season. Public interest in Ohio State football reached unprecedented heights in Columbus and throughout Ohio for that matter. It was now quite clear that a much greater seating capacity than Ohio Field could ever afford along with much improved playing facilities were badly needed and this need must be met soon.

The resulting Stadium campaign, finally put on in the fall of 1920 after being postponed once, was the solution. The time was propitious seeing that Ohio State won its third Big Ten championship in 1920. The Stadium campaign capitalized on the enthusiasm generated by the great football successes achieved in 1916, 1917, 1919 and 1920.

It was not enough, however, merely to ask the public to contribute to a Stadium fund. It had to be given something in return for its money. Various schemes were devised to this end. As it worked out, $100 came to be the standard subscription from the alumni and public and $25 from students. In return, Stadium subscribers were guaranteed certain preferences as to football tickets in future years and there was talk of perpetuating their names on bronze tablets to be erected on the Stadium walls whenever finances permitted. In time it developed that this would cost something like $30,000 and the expanded athletic program, followed by the bleak depression that began with the stock market collapse of 1929, never permitted this luxury. But tablets identifying donors of $5000 or more were erected on individual Stadium boxes.

First plans for a Stadium campaign were announced in the winter of 1919-20. The original goal was $600,000. At the outset plans called for a stadium to seat at least 50,000 with the first games to be played in it in the fall of 1921. Lowry F. Sater, '95, Columbus attorney, was general chairman.

A Stadium Number of the *Alumni Monthly* in February, 1921 gave more details. The Stadium was to be horseshoe-shaped and around its perimeter and along the adjoining east bank of the Olentangy were to be twenty baseball diamonds, to the south of the Stadium six soccer and football fields, besides a running track, jumping pits and tennis courts. In addition, the Olentangy was to be straightened and diked to prevent flooding, and the plans called for a new bridge across the river to replace the old trestle north of the Stadium site, with a new east-west roadway, a new power plant, a new gymnasium, and even a new armory projected in the Stadium area.

The opening of the Stadium campaign finally was set for the week of October 18 to 23, 1920 centering in Columbus but including the entire state and major alumni centers elsewhere. The John Price Jones Corp., of New York City, was brought in to provide professional fund raising know-how. The Stadium Committee decided meanwhile that "a temporary delay would be wiser than too-suddenly sprung campaigning." The campaign and the Stadium Week observance were tied in with and followed the formal celebration that fall of the University's semi-centennial.

Samuel N. Summer, '05, Columbus industrialist, was chairman of the campaign executive committee and did yeoman service. In his job he had the help of six special committees headed by campus and civic leaders such as Prof. French, J. L. Morrill, '13, alumni secretary, Simon Lazarus, leading Columbus merchant, and others. Carl E. Steeb, University business manager, was treasurer.

Stadium Week in Columbus was marked by all the carefully planned hoopla and natural enthusiasm that the campus and the town could muster. There were pageants, demonstrations, parades and stunts. On Monday, the first day, there was a tremendous athletic pageant downtown with nearly 4000 students in athletic costume participating. It culminated, as the *Monthly* reported, in a "mammoth demonstration of physical education" on the north lawn of the Statehouse. It was estimated that a throng of nearly 100,000 saw the parade. On another day the campus infantry and artillery regiments paraded downtown with full equipment. On Friday afternoon still another parade downtown was made up of fifty-one floats representing fraternities, sororities and independent campus organizations.

Each noon and daily at 5 p.m. there were music, stunts and short "pep" talks from a stage on the west front of the Capitol grounds. The downtown newspapers carried reams of publicity. Billboards were used and a huge horseshoe with electric lights denoting the progress of the campaign was suspended in front of the Deshler Hotel. At nearby Gay St. a big transparency was stretched across High St., bearing the plea, "Boost Ohio Stadium. It's for Columbus." The response to the campaign enthusiasm was boosted by the fact that the 1920 football team had won another Western Conference title, its third in four seasons, not counting the "unofficial" 1918 season.

During the campaign a special play was made for large givers with subscriptions of from $1000 to $5000. Earlier, at its December 2, 1919 meeting, the Athletic Board voted that $100 be "the minimum subscription for Patron." It was voted also that patrons "be allowed the privilege of ten years' option on two seats and names to be inscribed in corridors [*sic*]" and that patrons "contributing over $1000 be given an option on four seats." Experience proved that the donors came to expect such preferential treatment, originally intended for a term of years, to be permanent. This helped to complicate the ticket distribution in later years.

Steps went forward, meanwhile, for the selection and engineering survey of a site for the Stadium. In effect, a deal was worked out whereby the Animal Husbandry Department agreed to surrender pasture land west of Neil Ave. bordering on the Olentangy in return for a promise of new buildings and other facilities west of the river. Like the Stadium itself, this was to take time but this was how it worked out.

An important move taken at the November 10, 1920 board meeting was the appointment of a 7-man Stadium construction committee. It consisted of President Thompson as chairman, Prof. French as vice chairman, Summer, Steeb, Prof. D. J. Kays, J. N. Bradford, University architect, and Director St. John.

On Ohio State Day, celebrated across the nation November 26, 1920, it was reported that subscriptions had reached $923,775. This was broken down as follows: alumni and citizens, $544,500; Ohio outside of Columbus, $144,948; from other states, $77,727; and campus—students and faculty—$156,600. The measure of enthusiasm can be gauged from the fact that earlier there was talk that $300,000 was the most that could be expected from Columbus, apart from the campus, while the actual response was nearly double that figure.

By January 20, 1921 the total figure stood at $1,001,071. The July, 1921 *Monthly* gave it as $1,042,689, divided as follows: Columbus, $565,980; campus, $156,969; Ohio, $196,127; and outside of Ohio, $120,887.

The contract was let presently to the E. H. Latham Co., of Columbus, on its bid of $1,341,017. The campaign itself was over but the books were still open as there was a gap of $300,000 between the contract price and the amount pledged. All expenses of the campaign were paid by the Athletic Department so that every campaign dollar pledged could go into the Stadium.

Ground was broken for the Stadium in formal ceremonies August 3, 1921. Governor Harry L. Davis wielded the first shovel, followed by President Thompson, Chairman Summer and a galaxy of official, campus and stadium committee dignitaries. A crowd of 2500 was present along with the regimental band, sparked by the national and University colors. The audience dutifully sang "America" and "Carmen Ohio."

Completion date for the Stadium was set for October 1, 1922. Concurrently with the erection of the Stadium the University let a contract for the new bridge and roadway over the Olentangy just north of the Stadium at a cost of $117,900. His unique design calling for a double-decked, horseshoe-shaped structure won for Architect Smith the gold medal of the American Institute of Architects for "excellence in public work."

The University trustees, meanwhile, at their April 25, 1921 meeting adopted an important resolution under which the Stadium was to be built and fixing the responsibility of the Athletic Board. By now the project was known officially as the Ohio Stadium. More than $1,000,000 having been raised, it was now up to the building committee to see the project to completion. It was stipulated, among other things, that the University itself was to incur no financial obligation in connection with the Stadium and that the cost of the structure was not to exceed $930,000. Before it was completed it was to cost twice that much.

The long trustees' resolution, after reviewing the background of the campaign and its successful conclusion, went on:

And whereas, the Board of Trustees of the Ohio State University has approved the project for the erection of a Stadium and has given its permission for the prosecution of the campaign upon certain conditions, to-wit,—

1. All matters pertaining to the location of the Stadium, the final choice of the Supervising Architect, and the adoption of plans and specifications, shall be subject to the approval of the Board of Trustees.
2. A clear title to all buildings and structures erected shall follow the land, divested of all claims of all persons whomsoever.
3. The interests of the University shall be so safeguarded that no financial obligation shall be incurred by it in connection with the erection or completion of the proposed Stadium structures.
4. A plan for the expenditure of the Fund shall be submitted to the Board for approval before the letting of any contracts, and all contracts shall be open for the inspection of the Board.

And has further approved the appointment and personnel of the committee for the purpose of planning and completing the construction of the Stadium; and has designated the site upon which the structure shall be erected.

And whereas, it is expedient that this board now declare its policy and recognize its responsibilities growing out of the foregoing facts; therefore be it

Resolved, by the Athletic Board of the Ohio State University, that this board hereby accepts the trust imposed upon it by the subscribers to and donors of the Ohio Stadium fund, recognizes the fact that said fund is in its possession subject to said trust, and declares its purpose to carry out the object of said trust by proceeding at once with the letting of the necessary contracts for the erection of the Ohio Stadium.

Resolved, that this board hereby ratifies and confirms all acts and agreements of the Campaign Committee, known as the Ohio Stadium Committee, including the designation of the treasurer of the fund; and all acts and agreements of the building committee heretofore referred to and known as the Ohio Stadium Building Committee; and all expenses heretofore incurred by said building committee are hereby approved as within the purposes of the trust imposed upon the fund.

Resolved, that this board hereby accepts all the conditions imposed by the Board of Trustees of the Ohio State University; declares its purpose to conform all future action in the discharge of the trust to the wishes and direction of said board of trustees and specifically directs its committee and all other agencies subject to its control to observe the directions and wishes of said board of trustees in all respects.

Resolved, that the Ohio Stadium Building Committee heretofore appointed, be and it is hereby authorized and directed to invite bids and enter into a contract or contracts properly secured, for the erection of the principal structure to be known as the Ohio Stadium in accordance with the plans and specifications heretofore adopted, or as hereafter modified at a cost not to exceed nine hundred and thirty thousand dollars ($930,000.00) and the preparation and drainage of the playing field therein and appurtenances thereof; such contract or contracts shall be made in the name of the Ohio Stadium Building Committee as agent of this board; all moneys now in the hands of the treasurer of the Ohio Stadium Fund or hereafter coming into his hands from the collection of subscriptions heretofore or hereafter made, or otherwise are hereby specifically appropriated to the discharge of such contract or contracts and the expense of administration incurred by said committee.

The University trustees formally approved the plans and specifications of the Stadium at their May 25, 1921 meeting. The building committee directed the engineers to submit plans to contractors for bids to be opened June 17. Letting of the contract to the Latham firm was approved July 7. The design finally adopted called for a double-decked, horseshoe-shaped structure on a north-south axis lying in the bottom lands bordering the

Olentangy River. Clyde T. Morris, '98, of the civil engineering department, was the engineer in charge, assisted by William S. Hindman, also of that department.

The Stadium was to have a seating capacity of 63,000 and was to be built of concrete. There was some difference of opinion over both the size and the materials to be used. Dr. T. C. Mendenhall, sole surviving member of the original faculty in 1873 and an influential trustee in 1921, was insistent that the seating capacity be held to 35,000. The argument was that a large stadium was not needed and would never be filled. There was also some argument on political grounds that brick be used instead of concrete.

The site chosen was so low it was subject to flooding from the Olentangy. To offset this it was necessary to make an earth fill to an average depth of 7 feet. In time also the river was straightened and a substantial dike was built along the east bank but this did not come about until the PWA period in the depression.

Various ideas were proposed in connection with the Stadium. There was even talk of its use with a sort of open air theater—this came about years later, but underneath the structure—and for public meeting purposes such as commencement. The original plan made no provision for a running track and this was one of the first things added. A petition was also presented to the Athletic Board to provide roque courts. This was referred to the Stadium engineer "with a recommendation that the courts be constructed in a suitable place."

Steady progress was made on the Stadium construction. Prof. French presented the report of the Stadium engineer at a January 19, 1922 board meeting. A motion was adopted that "the necessary steps be taken along the lines of the special committee of the Stadium Building Committee to insure completion of the Stadium by October 1, 1922."

To make the Stadium ready for actual use involved a lot of details, e.g., the purchase of 3000 chairs for the boxes, a flagpole at a cost of $381, the numbering of the seats, and 1200 identification badges for employees. A major item was the installation of cables for telegraph and telephone service. There was also need for a score board and for liability insurance. At its May 7, 1923 meeting the board approved the building of an outdoor cinder track at the Stadium and the erection of a fence across the open end of the horseshoe.

The Stadium engineer was authorized also to make plans for a new Varsity baseball field in the area northeast of the Stadium. Another recurring problem was the necessity of oiling the ground underneath the Stadium itself to settle the dust. Years later this was solved permanently by blacktopping it. On December 5, 1923 the board authorized the construction of a 6-lap track and straightaway under the west side of the Stadium together with tennis courts and the grading of the Varsity baseball field at a cost of $5650. It was not until May, 1926 that purchase of a canvas cover for the football playing field was approved.

Meanwhile early in 1922 a subcommittee named to consider the matter of financing the completed Stadium foresaw that with funds in hand and with anticipated collections on Stadium subscriptions between January and May construction expenses could not be met until the June 1 payment. On the basis of a 4-year statement of receipts and expenditures, with a similar estimate for the future, it was felt that "the loans could all be paid off by April 1, 1927." This proved highly optimistic. In any case, the subcommittee recommended to the Stadium Building Committee that it "recommend to the Athletic Board that the necessary steps be taken to secure loans of funds as may become necessary for the completion of the Stadium this year and that the Stadium Building Committee be authorized to proceed with the construction accordingly." The building committee approved the subcommittee report January 18 for transmittal to the Athletic Board.

The estimated schedule of expenses to complete the Stadium by October 1, 1922 totaled $1,488,168, of which $1,341,017 applied on the Latham contract. The remainder covered office expense, engineer payroll, and "grounds and extras"—the last in the amount of $81,290.

Stadium Fund subscriptions were shown at a face value of $1,078,114 of which $975,428 was paid. Athletic profits for 1921-22 came to $134,000, leaving loans to be negotiated in the amount of $378,740 from Columbus banks. Such borrowing was on unsecured personal notes signed by Athletic Board members and was divided unevenly between two major Columbus banks.

At the June 15, 1922 board meeting, Engineer Morris presented his final estimate of the cost of the completed Stadium. The total expense was now given as $1,491,761 and the amount to be borrowed as $386,000. Authority was given the treasurer to borrow "from time to time as the funds may be needed a sum not to exceed $386,000, on the best possible terms." But as of December 1, 1922 the cost of the Stadium was now estimated at $1,509,130.

Despite receipts which dwarfed the limited income of a decade earlier, the board felt pinched because of the heavy expenditures on the Stadium and the need for heavy borrowing. When the 1922-23 operating budget was presented the board after extended discussion adopted as the "sense of the meeting" that "Owing to the financial obligations incurred by the Board, through the completion of the Stadium at this time, . . . every possible effort be made not only to keep the operating expense for the year within the budget as approved but to effect all such savings as may be possible in any or all of the budgetary items." The inescapable fact was that the budget, too, had grown and as with any expanding operation was bound to grow still more.

From time to time the board explored ways and means of easing the financial burden incident to the Stadium debt. At a meeting in February, 1923 approval was given for the appointment of a committee "to investigate if possible for the transfer of the loans made by the local banks on the Stadium to some State fund." Nothing tangible came of this. Still later the possibility of funding the debt through a bond issue was investigated. The Huntington National Bank, after inquiry, informed the board that it had learned such bonds would be illegal unless authorized by the state legislature and therefore it could not undertake such financing.

At the April 6, 1923 meeting Chairman French reported on an interview with President Thompson "relative to the Stadium financial situation." Five days later, at a special meeting, "The Board parceled out the list of delinquent Stadium subscribers and discussed ways and means of collecting money due on such pledges." At the April 30 meeting, the treasurer reported borrowing an additional $50,000, bringing the total indebtedness to $457,000.

At a meeting June 29 at Summer's office he informed the board that the Huntington National Bank was agreeable to handling the proposed Stadium bond issue in the fall, the first bonds to mature a year later. Meanwhile the bank was willing to advance such further sums as the board might need for current expenses. The loan was to be for $500,000, at 96, the bonds to bear 6 per cent interest, with the principal payable in ten years "in blocks of $50,000 annually beginning in 1924." As it turned out this did not materialize because of questionable legality. The board was so notified at its January 17, 1924 meeting and the hope was expressed that the legislature would give its consent but this did not work out. The trustees had approved such a plan in October, 1923 on condition that neither they nor the University "assumes any responsibility for the payment of said debts."

At a meeting April 7, 1924 the Athletic Board took steps to relieve the Stadium Committee "from further duty" and directed that an audit of the Stadium treasurer's books be made. So the committee ended its work after four years of strenuous effort filled with problems and perplexities from the planning through the construction stage, and particularly with the financing of the gigantic structure. The names of this hardworking group which unselfishly devoted its time and talents to the project without pay should have been commemorated in bronze on the Stadium itself.

The Stadium Executive Committee and the Stadium Building Committee went out of existence June 30, 1924 at a joint meeting with the Athletic Board. By a resolution the attached report of the Stadium treasurer and the audit of the Stadium books were accepted and cash on hand and certain securities were ordered turned over to the Athletic Board treasurer. It directed also that books, records and cards of the Ohio Stadium Fund be turned over to the board and that Carl E. Steeb, Stadium Fund treasurer, "be released from any and all obligations and responsibilities" incident to the office, and that the committee adjourn *sine die*. These signatures were appended: Samuel N. Summer, chairman; Carl E. Steeb, Thomas E. French, W. A. Ireland, John A. Kelley, F. R. Huntington, J. L. Morrill, Simon Lazarus, C. F. Kettering, J. J. Munsell, and T. V. Taylor.

The treasurer's final report, submitted by Steeb and certified by George W. Eckelberry, C.P.A., showed total cash receipts as of June 30, 1924 of $1,557,185.75 and total disbursements of $1,548,634.75, leaving a cash balance of $8551. As of that time payments of $770,016.94 had been made on Stadium subscriptions and from profits and loans the Athletic Board had advanced $638,000. The remainder was accounted for by the sale of U. S. bonds ($123,274.74), and interest ($18,861.54), and the sale of Stadium stamps in student subscription books ($7032.53). The amount paid to the contractor was $1,423,527.18. A year later the indebtedness was $440,000, the sum of $100,500 having been paid off during the year.

After the completion of the Stadium outside interests made all sorts of requests for its use. It soon became apparent that the board would have to determine a policy and the matter was turned over to the field committee for recommendation. The first request for such use was transmitted through President Thompson on behalf of the opening of a Children's Hospital "drive" for the first Sunday in October, 1922. This was approved as was a request from the city schools for their annual field day in October, 1923.

A request from Capital University for use of the Stadium for its football game October 10, 1925 with Western Reserve was granted. Approval was given also for the use of the Stadium on September 26,

1925 "to the New York Central Lines for their national field meet." On November 22, 1926 permission was granted to Columbus North and East High Schools to play their annual game in the Stadium.

In 1927 a curious proposal developed over the use of the Stadium for a football game between Army and Georgetown. At the October 28, 1927 board meeting a letter was read from Secretary of War Davis thanking Director St. John for such use of the Stadium when, in fact, no such permission had been given. The business manager of the Army team, who was present, explained the intended arrangement whereby the Columbus Baby Camp would get 5 per cent of the proceeds, the local American Legion 15 per cent, and the two teams would divide the remainder. A board member made the point that "insofar as the Board has already refused other colleges the use of the Stadium, he could not see why an exception should be made in this case." The upshot was a suggestion that Army play a team of "Ohio All-Stars" but nothing came of this.

There was even talk late in 1929 of the possibility of staging the annual Army-Navy game in the Stadium "in the near future." At a December 23, 1929 board meeting Director St. John reported that a downtown committee had conferred with him relative to the use of the Stadium for such a purpose. The board authorized him to say that it would "look with favor upon the use of Ohio Stadium for such a game, under equitable financial arrangements."

At a September 23, 1932 meeting a request was presented on behalf of the Loyal Order of Moose to use the Stadium October 22 for a football game between two midget teams. The board voted that "the organization be informed that we have other use for the Stadium on that day." On November 21, 1939 the board gave permission for a "Buckeye Bowl" football game to be played in the Stadium on December 2, 1939 "between undefeated high school teams of the state." At a May 4, 1945 meeting the board granted the use of the Stadium for the staging of a pageant, "Here's Your Infantry," on May 30 in connection with the 7th war loan drive. Permission was given the Girl Scouts at the April 10, 1946 board meeting to use the Stadium for a city-wide folk dance festival. And Jehovah's Witnesses once used the Stadium on a Sunday, with about 40,000 present, in connection with a statewide rally.

As far back as 1931 the board was informed that a survey by Paul S. Cleland, of New York University, of sixty stadia in all parts of the country showed that "your report ranks second highest in the number of different activities held in stadia." At a board meeting April 14, 1942 a request from an American Legion group in Los Angeles sought the use of the Stadium for a July 4 fireworks celebration. Nothing came of the matter. One of the strangest requests for the use of the Stadium was presented to the board in the summer of 1944 by the advance agent of the Ringling Bros. circus. The board at a July 11 meeting declined the request. (This was after the circus had lost its main tent in a horrible fire at Hartford, Conn., in which many persons perished.)

As early as 1925 it was apparent that further improvements were needed to develop the Stadium and the surrounding site. The field committee was directed to present such a report so that the necessary work could be done before the next football season. In its report of March 13, the committee recommended various items: treatment of the ground under the Stadium to prevent dust and provide a clean dirt floor, paved approaches for foot traffic from the east and north, another for automobiles and trucks, a 25-foot paved walk entirely around the Stadium with steps at the north entrance, the erection of thirty-six bronze tablets for boxholding subscribers, and waterproofing at points where water was beginning to come through the seat banks. The work was authorized at a cost not to exceed $15,000.

On December 8, 1927 the Athletic Board took official steps to turn the Stadium over to the University. A resolution pointed out that the board had carried out its responsibility of developing a plan, obtaining the funds and constructing the plant. It pointed out that the plant now represented an investment of $1,900,000. Of this $900,000 was "the gift of alumni and friends," $800,000 had been paid from athletic receipts and the "early liquidation" of the remaining debt of about $235,000 was "assured from athletic receipts." The board resolved, therefore, to "turn over to the University to become the property of the State of Ohio, this practically completed athletic plant valued at $1,900,000" and further that beginning January 1, 1929 "the University assume the administration of all athletic funds on the same basis as all other similar activities of the University."

In essence, the University trustees agreed to this December 12, 1927, but with the express understanding that the Athletic Board was responsible for the remaining debt. The shift of administrative control over athletic funds put those funds under the same regulations and restrictions as other University funds and made them subject to state audit. The trustees' resolution accepted the Stadium "on behalf of the State of Ohio," and the administration of athletic funds as of January 1, 1928, "provided, however, that the Athletic Board retain the obligation to complete the payment of any indebtedness due on the Stadium, and that such indebtedness shall constitute a first lien upon athletic receipts until it is fully paid." The resolution also commended the Athletic Board for "their devotion to duty" and for "the successful way in which they have brought their task within sight of completion." The debt then stood at $234,948.33.

The November 1, 1928 Athletic Board meeting marked a red letter day in that as of September 30 Director St. John reported "all notes outstanding on the Stadium indebtedness had been paid. As of June 30 the sum of $924,998.97 had been paid on total Stadium subscriptions of $1,090,009.69, leaving $165,010.72 outstanding. Up to that time also the board had invested $726,726.01 in the Stadium out of football profits.

This was a financial achievement of real magnitude which justified the faith of the Stadium Committee, the University administration and the Athletic Board in the dream of a major stadium. In eight years from the time of the Stadium campaign of 1920 the great structure had been completed and paid for. In that time the board had paid off an indebtedness which at its peak reached some $500,000. During that period the Stadium facilities had been substantially increased and improved. The athletic management was now ready to begin meeting other pressing needs. It was estimated as of July 1 that Stadium subscribers would pay 47.4 per cent of the cost of the Stadium and athletic profits, mainly football, 52.6 per cent.

After sixteen years the remaining unpaid Stadium subscriptions, amounting to $166,229.75, less $2032.03 reserve for unredeemed Stadium stamps, were finally written off June 3, 1936 by the board. The reserve was in connection with student subscriptions.

An unexpected use of the Stadium in the depression days was the utilization of part of the space under the west side for low cost men's housing. This grew out of an idea coming from Business Manager Steeb and Dean of Men J. A. Park. As on other campuses the enrollment multiplied after World War II and housing was at a premium. To help relieve this situation the trustees authorized the construction of dormitories on both the east and west sides of the Stadium. As President Bevis told the board at its November 14, 1945 meeting the cost of such construction was estimated at only one-fourth to one-third of the cost of new construction.

Some objection was expressed by Director St. John who reviewed the history of the Tower Club idea and voiced the opinion that such housing was undesirable and a lower grade of accommodations than should be included in a permanent unit. In the end the Stadium dormitory facilities were greatly expanded to house a total of 700 men, but the expansion was confined to the west side of the Stadium.

It became evident in time that still further improvements were necessary at the Stadium. The matter came to a head early in 1946 when the board heard a report from the Stadium engineer and the architect. There were three major items: greater toilet facilities, an elevator, and enlargement of the press box.

At the January 23 meeting the board authorized an addition to the budget of $21,500 for additional toilet facilities and another $25,000 for the installation of an elevator for the convenience of newsmen, photographers, broadcasters and others. With the increased use of news reels and other coverage unknown in the early days of the Stadium it was necessary to carry much heavy equipment to the press box. An elevator would relieve the situation.

As to the press box, two ideas were advanced: the erection of a second story on the existing box or the building of a second box, chiefly for broadcasting, on the east side of the Stadium. Originally the Stadium had two press boxes—one on the west side of the upper deck for the working press and another on the east side for "observers." In time the west box was enlarged and enclosed while the other was removed. Director St. John emphasized the advantage of concentrating all of the "press" facilities in one location and ultimately this was done with the construction of an entirely new box.

A little later the idea of constructing bowling alleys under the Stadium was revived. The cost was estimated at $150,000. The justification was that bowling was one of the most popular sports on the indoor intramural program and High St. facilities for this purpose were limited. Several members expressed the opinion that primary attention should be given to a field house. At a March 13 meeting there was a passing revival, too, of the idea of housing for canoes in connection with boating on the Olentangy. Director St. John was authorized to explore the idea but nothing came of it.

XI
FOOTBALL

1. The Wilce Era
1913–1928

THE 1912 season marked the transition from the old to the new. Ohio State was in but not yet of the Western Conference as far as football participation was concerned since the 1912 schedule was made up before the University was admitted to the Conference. The brief regime of John R. Richards as coach-director, moreover, proved to be an interlude in the switch to the Conference and a prelude to the long reign of John W. Wilce as director of football.

Because of the lateness of choosing the new coach there was no spring football practice in 1912. But Richards kept in touch with individual players by mail during the summer. One immediate effect of Ohio State's becoming the "baby" member of the Conference was to raise the eligibility rules. Under Conference regulations a deficiency in a single subject made a player ineligible for competition.

Richards was described as "a born coach" who had "winning teams everywhere." He was called back to Wisconsin in 1910 when Badger athletic fortunes were down and achieved "a complete, almost miraculous reversal of form in all departments of athletics." That entire year, the record showed, Wisconsin lost only two contests to Conference opponents, one each in football and baseball. It won Conference titles in basketball and baseball, while "the showing of their crew was the best ever."

Following his arrival on the Ohio State campus he introduced a number of innovations. On the field he was described as "a driver with no sympathy for a loafer." He did away with secret practice. Any "secret" work was done at meetings with the squad at the Athletic House several evenings a week. One result of this was "that students as well as Columbus people have turned out in far greater numbers to watch evening practice than ever before."

Richards was quoted as saying that Ohio State athletics would be brought up to Western Conference standards but that there were a lot of changes to make and much to be done before this could be accomplished. The squad he inherited included seven of the previous year's regulars while the freshman team was described as "the richest in material that has ever been produced at State."

With the new setup enthusiasm reached a new peak on the campus that fall. The alumni magazine, now a monthly, declared that "Not in a decade has there been such a flurry of interest as has attended the inauguration of the football season at Ohio State. . . . Among the students, among alumni and within the ranks of the men who come up to the campus from downtown, a deeply entrenched feeling that State is going to do things this year seems to prevail. The thrill of confidence and enthusiasm is in the air . . ."

In its first game under the new regime the Varsity swamped Otterbein, 55 to 0, and Denison fell next, 20 to 0. But in the game with Michigan, the last for some time, the home team lost, 14 to 0. A crowd of 8500, the largest up to then on Ohio Field, saw the contest. In the fourth game of the season Ohio State defeated Cincinnati, 45 to 7. Another innovation was the use of "incandescent" lights on the field to enable the squad to continue practice after sundown. Conference rules prohibited an official training table but the squad took its meals at the same place.

Case, an old rival, was beaten soundly on its own field, 31 to 6. "Old scores were evened," the *Monthly* crowed, "and the Scientists got the worst beating in ten years from any conference eleven." In Columbus "a battalion of lusty-throated students waited for the train from Cleveland, but were disappointed in not finding the victors aboard." Not daunted, they donned "the flowing white robes of midnight and paraded the principal streets in celebration of the downfall of Case. It was a rollicking, roistering, riotous, rabble . . ."

Reaction to the defeat of Oberlin, 23 to 17, which gave Ohio State its first state title in six years, was similar: "The aftermath of bon-fires, night-shirt processions, mock funerals and undergraduate enthusiasm, made city people open their eyes and ears wide. There could be no doubt that the football championship of Ohio had come to Columbus to stay." Another sign of changing times was that the Athletic Board "banqueted" the team after the game.

In the game with Penn State the Easterners were favored since they had won every game to date, with Cornell and Washington & Jefferson among their victims. But no one expected the game to turn out as it did. With the score 37 to 0 in the visitors' favor and with 9 minutes to play in the fourth quarter, Richards took the home team off the field because of rough play and the failure of officials to enforce penalties early in the game or to call them later. The official result was a forfeit, 1 to 0.

On the way off the field, Richards stopped by the box occupied by

Athletic Board members who concurred in his action, which followed the alleged "roughing" of two players. According to the *Lantern* account, "It was the culmination of one of the roughest football games ever played on Ohio Field."

It is still something of a question whether, as the visitors' coach insisted, it was hard "Eastern football" or whether there was unnecessary roughness. The *Lantern* contended that "Had the umpire exercised his duty and banished the offenders from the game at this juncture [third quarter] the contest would have ended with members of both teams 'playing football.'" At that the paper conceded that "Penn State presented the best drilled team that appeared on Ohio Field in 1912 and it is small wonder they were able to run up 37 points on Ohio crippled as they were." The home team could not cope with the end runs and forward passes of the visitors.

To make a bad matter worse, Penn State's colors were burned on the south goal posts. President E. E. Sparks, of Penn State, an Ohio State alumnus, was in the stands. For burning the colors a Toledo freshman took the blame. A committee of alumni and others apologized to Dr. Sparks before his train left and a student apology was sent to Penn State.

Coaches Richards and St. John stood their grounds, however. To the former, who gave out a lengthy statement, the issue was "sportsmanship vs muckerism" and he insisted that Ohio State had made no mistake. Echoes of the unfortunate occurrence continued to be heard for some years. Richards' feelings were shown by this brief quote from his statement:

The Ohio State team may have been guilty of infractions of the rules but such infractions were passionate self defensive acts committed in the face of malicious calculating acts and not designed to maim or put a man out. The mucker playing was getting worse and worse and when I felt it was about to break into open riot I took Ohio State off the field.

It was not a "peevish" act or one of a coach who could not stand defeat. It was a protest of an exhibition that would harm the sport. It was not due to fear of anything except a fear of doing wrong. It is always harder and takes more nerve to take a team off the field than to leave them on.

In another statement, Prof. French as board chairman defended Richards' action. But he called the burning of Penn State's colors "an act of thoughtless impulse."

In the next to the last game of the season, Ohio Wesleyan was defeated, 36 to 6. But in what was to be the last Thanksgiving Day game, Ohio State lost to the Michigan Aggies [Michigan State], 35 to 20. Six Ohio State players "made" the All-Ohio after the season. Walter

Eckersall chose Capt. Don Barricklow, tackle, on his All-Western team. Financially the season was good and it was reported that the board closed the year with a $5000 balance.

In a surprising move near the end of the year, Richards resigned. His somewhat sudden departure left the athletic directorship and the head football and track coaching positions open. The board moved promptly to fill the gap. As noted elsewhere the directorship fell to L. W. St. John.

At first there was some talk of finding a man who, like Richards, would coach both football and track. The choice fell upon Carl J. Rothgeb but this did not work out and in the end Richards was replaced by separate coaches for football and track. For track coach Frank R. Castleman was brought from the University of Colorado where he had made a good record. He was to coach both track and cross country, help with football and for a brief spell coached soccer.

The football coaching job took more time to fill. As indicated, a hitch developed in the plan to hire Rothgeb and at a January 7, 1913 board meeting a motion was adopted that his "proposition be laid on the table." A committee was named "to investigate candidates for coaching positions."

Some time during the next month the appointment of John Schommer, a noted University of Chicago athlete, was approved for the football coaching post. Schommer was offered the place at $2250 a year, but "if the above is not satisfactory . . . that he receive $1500 and have the privilege of retiring at the end of the foot ball season." In effect, this opened the way for a return to a seasonal coach, at least temporarily. But for reasons not recorded the negotiations with Schommer came to nought.

The ultimate choice for football coach was John W. Wilce, Wisconsin '10, who taught and coached earlier at LaCrosse, Wis., high school. Wilce, who was not quite 25, was hired in the spring of 1913. Thus began a long and distinguished career at the University where he was director of football and of intramural athletics and later, until his retirement in 1958, director of the University Health Service. He was football coach from 1913 to 1928, inclusive, a span of sixteen seasons which brought Ohio State from relative obscurity to three Conference championships, its first Rose Bowl game, its first real All-Americans, and an outstanding over-all record. Wilce had been a 3-sport man at Wisconsin where he was All-Conference fullback, played basketball and was a stroke on the crew.

One innovation in football was a tournament as the climax to the spring training season. Various events were set up for which plaques were awarded for punting, passing, sprints, most improved player, and the like. This was continued for some years. With the opening of fall training, Wilce issued a call for more candidates for the team. "King" Brady had succeeded Farrell as trainer and "Doc" Welch continued in charge of the freshmen.

Although this was to be the first season for the Buckeyes in Western Conference football competition, the early sale of student season books was light. Through arrangement with the Military Department, the cadet regiment was used to step up the cheering. Early in the season the cadets went to Ohio Field for midweek cheering practice. In another development helpful to football the Military Department was persuaded to excuse Varsity players from the daily drill at 4 p.m.

The band had money troubles. Under prevailing Conference regulations the board could not send the band or cheerleaders to out-of-town games. So the device of "passing the bucket" at football games was used to raise the necessary funds. Under Conference rules, moreover, only thirty players could be taken on trips for out-of-town games.

For its first Conference season, Ohio State had a 7-game schedule with three Conference games. After a 0-to-0 tie with Oberlin, Indiana provided the opposition for Ohio State's official debut in Conference play. The game was preceded by a Friday afternoon "twilight" rally with a bonfire on Ohio Field at which "Prexy" Thompson and Wilce spoke. The *Lantern* reported that 800 students "snake-danced" around the bonfire. But on the morrow the home team lost, 7 to 6. In the next Conference game the Ohioans lost to Wisconsin, 12 to 0, at Madison. The band made the trip along with seventy-six loyal followers, four of whom said they went by "blind baggage" at a cost of 80c.

The new athletic and football regime began to pay real dividends, however, in the Northwestern game, the last of the season, in which the visitors were beaten, 58 to 0, to the great delight of the crowd which jammed Ohio Field. Receipts for the season, however, were less than expected.

In earlier games that fall the Varsity defeated Ohio Wesleyan, 58 to 0, Western Reserve, 14 to 8, and Case, 18 to 0. As a climax to the season a football banquet was held. Fifteen players were awarded the Varsity "O" and appreciative students gave Wilce a watch. Welch, the freshman coach, was hired for $100 that season, and George E. Little, an ex-Ohio Wesleyan captain, was engaged for such "services that he might be able to offer in coaching athletic teams this school year" for $200. Little, later Michigan coach, was taking graduate work.

"Secret" or closed football practice became an issue after Ohio State's admission to the Conference. At a meeting June 19, 1915 the Athletic Board voted two ways on the matter. One motion was passed, the minutes say, "to limit secret football practice to two nights a week." But in the next breath a different motion was adopted to the effect "that we do not approve limiting secret football practice to two nights a week."

Football scouting began to assume a more important part in the Varsity football picture. In Grant P. Ward and Walter J. Essman, assistant coaches, Ohio State a little later had two of the best scouts in the business. In the fall of 1916 when Ohio State was on its way to its first Conference championship—although the Conference did not officially recognize football titles in those days—the board approved a motion that "about $150 be appropriated as additional scouting expense." Former Varsity players were sometimes used for this purpose.

To anticipate, Ward, who was to join the staff later in a full-time capacity as assistant coach and as intramural athletic director, was offered $500 "for spring and fall football in 1917," according to the minutes. This was a small step but it was in the direction of the expanding football program. It reflected also the flush of Ohio State's first real successes in bigtime football.

The next eight football seasons were ones of almost unbelievable accomplishment for the "'baby" of the Conference. In that span Ohio State became a football power and the resulting enthusiasm not only made Ohio Field threaten to come apart at the seams but gave a boost to the athletic program generally. In that time, specifically, Ohio State won its first three Big Nine championships, missed the unofficial title by only one game in each of two other seasons, and had two top All-Americans in the peerless "Chic" Harley and "Pete" Stinchcomb. This was the golden age of Ohio State's first two decades in the Conference.

In each of the 1913, 1914, 1915 and 1916 seasons the team played seven games. In 1917 it played nine, but in 1918—regarded as unofficial because it was a war year—there were only six games. In the 1919, 1920 and 1921 seasons there were again seven regular games, the 1921 Rose Bowl game being extra, of course.

In that 9-year period under Wilce's skillful coaching, Ohio State won 50, tied 3 and lost only 12 games. Excluding the war year the record was 47-3-9. And against Big Ten competition during that period—Michigan having returned to the fold in 1918—the mark was 35 won, 1 tied, and only 10 lost. Not counting 1918, it was 25-1-7.

In 1914, Wilce's second season, the Varsity defeated three Ohio opponents and broke even in four Conference games. The Ohio victims were Ohio Wesleyan, 16 to 2; Oberlin, 39 to 0; and Case, 7 to 6. For the first time the team played four Conference games. Indiana was defeated, 13 to 3, but Illinois won, 37 to 0. Wisconsin edged the Buckeyes, 7 to 6, but Northwestern lost again, 27 to 0.*

A year later the showing was still better—five wins, one loss and one tie. By now it had become customary for Ohio Wesleyan to open the season, and it was defeated, 19 to 6. Oberlin was next, 25 to 0, and then Case, 14 to 0. Indiana was nosed out, 10 to 9. Then came the game with Illinois which was one of the early Conference thrillers on Ohio Field. The Illini had lost several key men by injuries but hardly anyone expected the home team to hold them to a 3-to-3 tie.

Next came Wisconsin at Madison and the Ohioans were all hopped up as a result of the Illinois game. There was a heavy fall of snow at Camp Randall, but in any case the invading Ohioans were outgunned, 21 to 0. In the final game, however, Northwestern was beaten for the third straight time, 34 to 0.

Ohio State football fortunes rose to a peak in 1916 when "Chic" Harley, a Columbus East High product, entered the picture as a sophomore. This success continued in 1917 and was resumed in 1919. Harley won All-American recognition all three years for his outstanding performance at halfback. He had the further distinction of captaining the 1918 and 1919 teams although he was away from the campus in military service the former season. By an odd coincidence, the Columbus East High teams on which he played lost only one game, his final high school game. And the only losing game in which he played in three Varsity seasons was the last game in 1919 in which Ohio State led 7 to 6 with only seconds to play but Illinois made a field goal in the closing moments to win 9 to 7 and shut Ohio State out of a third title. Harley was not only Ohio State's first recognized All-American but won his "O" in four sports. For a time he held the indoor 50-yard dash mark.

To open the 1916 season Ohio Wesleyan was disposed of, 20 to 0, and Oberlin was crushed, 128 to 0, the largest score ever made by Ohio

---

* A girl cheerleader, Clara Rutherford, appeared at one of the early games in the new era "decked out," she recalls, in the visiting team's colors. But on the Monday following she was called before the dean of women. That ended the innovation.

State against a football opponent. Case was shut out, 28 to 0. The going was somewhat tougher against Conference opponents: Indiana was beaten, 46 to 7, and then came a pair of "squeakers" with Illinois and Wisconsin. The former was edged, 7 to 6, and the latter, 14 to 13. The game against Illinois was the famous one in which Harley ran for a late touchdown in the mud at Urbana, and then calmly changed to a dry kicking shoe to boot the winning point after touchdown. Northwestern was beaten for the fourth straight time, 23 to 3, and the Ohions had their first Conference title of any kind. Wilce and the team were the heroes of the city and the state.

Athletic success in 1916 not only meant more business but more details. One outgrowth of this was the addition of George M. "Red" Trautman to the coaching staff. His appointment as basketball coach for 1917-18 followed. As an undergraduate Trautman was a 3-sport letter man in football, basketball and baseball. In the last he was the pitching half of a well known battery whose other member was John W. Bricker, '16, later governor, U. S. Senator and longtime University trustee. In time Trautman became assistant athletic director and in after years held a succession of important baseball positions.

More football success followed in 1917, only this time Ohio State won eight straight games and then tied Auburn in a post-season game at Montgomery, Ala., for the benefit of Ohioans training there in the 37th Division (Ohio National Guard). Except for the Auburn game none of the scores was very close: Ohio Wesleyan, 53 to 0; Denison, 67 to 0; Case, 49 to 0; Indiana, 26 to 3; Illinois, 13 to 0; Wisconsin, 16 to 3; and Northwestern, 40 to 0. In an extra game at home the Camp Sherman 83rd Division team from Chillicothe was defeated, 28 to 0. To the confident Ohioans the tie with Auburn was an upset.

In 1918 conditions were different. It was war time and the Conference approved a limited schedule which was more or less unofficial. Many of the previous year's players were in uniform and several were already casualties, including Fred Norton, a halfback on the 1916 team, whose plane was shot down over France, and Harold J. "Hap" Courtney, one of the two brothers who were tackles on the first championship team. Courtney went into the Navy where he died from pneumonia. Coach Wilce, who was studying medicine, was in uniform although he remained on the campus.

Under unusual conditions the 1918 team played six games, winning three from Ohio opponents but losing all three to Conference foes. The record: Ohio State, 41, Ohio Wesleyan, 0; Ohio State 34, Denison 0; Ohio State 56, Case 0; Ohio State 0, Michigan 14; Ohio State 0, Illinois 13; and Ohio State 3, Wisconsin 14.

But Ohio State was back in stride in the 1919, 1920 and 1921 seasons. It won its third football title in 1920 and barely missed in the next two years. The 1919 season was climactic, with Harley again in the starring role, aided by "Pete" Stinchcomb. Ohio Wesleyan succumbed, 38 to 0, Cincinnati, 46 to 0, and Kentucky, 49 to 0. In Conference games, Michigan was beaten for the first time in Ohio State history in a rousing game at Ann Arbor, 13 to 3. Wisconsin lost, 3 to 0, thanks to a field goal by Harley, and Purdue was defeated, 20 to 0. Then came the heartbreaker with Illinois which won by snatching victory from defeat in the closing seconds, 9 to 7. Players and fans streamed from the exits from Ohio Field disbelieving what they had seen. The *Lantern* showed unusual enterprise with a football "extra," but took a last minute chance and came off the press proclaiming an Ohio State victory, 7 to 6.

But 1920 was another year and again Ohio State not only won the mythical Conference title but a chance to play in the Rose Bowl game for the first time. During the regular season the team won seven straight games, only to lose to California in the climactic aftermath. Ohio Wesleyan and Oberlin were defeated, 55 to 0, and 37 to 0, respectively. Five Conference opponents were disposed of: Michigan, 14 to 0; Illinois, 7 to 0; Wisconsin, 13 to 7; Purdue, 17 to 0; and Chicago, 7 to 6. This was the second straight time Michigan was beaten and the first time the Ohioans met Chicago, then a Conference powerhouse coached by the famous A. A. Stagg.

The climax after winning the Conference crown for the third time in four regular seasons was the invitation to appear in the Rose Bowl game. In anticipation of such an opportunity the Athletic Board on November 24, 1920 authorized acceptance "in case the formal invitation is received." Spadework toward getting such an invitation was done on the coast by an alumni group headed by Merlin Cox, '11. The board instructed Prof. French to "see personally the Conference representatives relative to the Ohio State team being granted permission to go to Pasadena for the championship game." This was done and the Conference somewhat reluctantly gave the necessary permission.

Unlike the fabulous three trips of later years, the first Ohio State excursion to the Rose Bowl in 1920 was a shoe-string affair. In contrast with the situation years later a relatively small squad was taken, it traveled by regular train, one player was added after the squad left Columbus, and the Ohioans made several stops en route to limber up and to receive the greetings of local alumni. The Athletic Board bore the expense of about $10,000 as against many times that amount on later trips.

Ohio State made its first invasion of the West Coast with high hopes. It was also the first appearance of a Big Ten team in the Rose Bowl in nearly two decades after Michigan's trip there in 1902. California, under Coach Andy Smith, formerly of Purdue, was known to be a strong team. But the result, both in terms of the kind of game played and the one-sided score, was a shock and disappointment to Ohio State and its followers. This was, of course, long before the days of radio or television and reports of the 28-to-0 score by telephone that night in Columbus were received with disbelief and incredulity.

The question was, what happened? The answer was simple: California had too much deception and power and, instead of the bruising, crushing attack expected, took to Ohio State's open game that had been so successful during the Conference season, and did it more successfully. Even the *Alumni Monthly* in its account of the game conceded that California won "cleanly, fairly and by the superior execution of good football." It won, in brief, by dazzling use of the forward pass and the end run against which Ohio State could not get going.

The Bears scored their first touchdown in less than 7 minutes of play after recovering an Ohio State fumble. Halfback "Red" Blair stirred Ohio State hopes when he carried the ball shortly to the California 8-yard line where another fumble ruined the opportunity. In the second quarter Ohio State again reached the California 8-yard line but was unable to score. California tallied later on a double pass and again on a short end run. The third quarter was scoreless but the West Coast team added a fourth touchdown in the last quarter.

The game was always remembered for a spectacular pass thrown by "Brick" Muller, big California end. It was unexpected in that it was supposed Muller would be on the receiving rather than the throwing end of a pass. Legend persisted that the pass went 70 yards, but more accurate evidence was that the throw went about 58 yards and the receiver then carried it for another dozen yards.

On its part, Ohio State, with a fine passing record during the regular season, was able to complete only eleven of twenty-five passes attempted. There was some feeling that the 80-degree temperature at game time handicapped the vistors more than the West Coast team. And unquestionably Ohio State was below par much of the game after Quarterback "Hoge" Workman was hurt early in the contest, and "Pete"

Stinchcomb, its All American halfback, suffered an ankle injury. In actual play the game was not as one-sided as the score indicated but the outcome was a sore disappointment. The crowd numbered 42,000.

Strained relations with Wisconsin developed after the 1920 football season in which the Badgers were runners-up to the Ohioans. The situation grew out of remarks attributed to Coach John Richards, who had returned to Wisconsin. The ill feeling that resulted between the two schools was a major order of business at several Athletic Board meetings. It died out in time as such things have a way of doing. At a January 13, 1921 meeting Dr. Wilce was authorized to "shape up the statements" as to the "situation," and he and Prof. French were then to go to Wisconsin "and present them to the President of the University and the Athletic Board." A committee of three was also to draw up a resolution to "be taken to President Thompson to be addressed to Wisconsin's President and Athletic Board." There was mention of the issue in later board meetings and at the one of June 6 the reply of the Wisconsin Athletic Council was read but the minutes gave no details.

There were some repercussions also from the Rose Bowl game as a result of remarks attributed to Cach Smith, of California. The differences with Wisconsin, meanwhile, were not dead. Dr. Thompson discussed the matter at a December 21 board meeting. After discussion a motion was passed that "in view of the statements and charges made by John R. Richards of the University of Wisconsin while acting as their representative and published in the Wisconsin *Daily Cardinal* January 5, 1921, and in view of the reply made by the President of the University of Wisconsin and his Athletic Council, to the statement presented to the University of Wisconsin authorities by the Ohio State University, that the Ohio State University shall suspend all intercollegiate athletic relations with the University of Wisconsin until such time as the University of Wisconsin authorities shall make satisfactory representation and amends to the Ohio State University."

The 1921 season, meanwhile, was another good one in the main. It was marred by only two defeats, one at the hands of Oberlin and the other by Illinois. A scrappy Oberlin team defeated the home talent, 7 to 6, early in the season. This was the last time Ohio State lost to another Ohio team. But the defeat had its brighter side for a week later the Buckeyes rose up and whipped Minnesota in the first meeting between the two teams. The game was played on a muddy field and it was thought that the heavy going would favor the invading Gophers, but the stunning result proved otherwise.

In other games, Ohio State once more defeated Ohio Wesleyan, 28 to 0, and Michigan for the third straight time, 14 to 0. The Illinois game was the seventh straight in what had become a series of thrillers and in which the margin was never more than 13 points. This time the Illini won by the margin of a single touchdown, 7 to 0. In the other two games Purdue fell, 28 to 0, and Chicago, 7 to 0. The defeat by Illinois cost Ohio State another title.

A sort of postscript to the 1921 season was a charity game November 26 in the Stadium between the "Starbucks," made up of former Varsity players, and the "Rainbows," ex-stars from other campuses. The latter included two all-time All-Americans and seven All-Americans named by Walter Camp. The "Rainbows" won, 16 to 0, on a muddy field. In their ranks were "Pudge" Heffelfinger, the great Yale guard who, although 53, played part of the game. Jim Thorpe, the famous Carlisle Indian, was on hand but did not play because of an injury although he gave a kicking exhibition. Younger stars included "Bo" McMillin, of Centre, and Eddie Casey, of Harvard. The game was played for Columbus charity.

The football successes led to other things such as the dream of a stadium and a desire to widen the field of competition. In the fall of 1917 the idea of a Thanksgiving game with Army was broached but while the board passed a motion to this end nothing came of the proposal. When the 1922 schedule was approved there was serious discussion about the possibility of adding "name" opponents from outside the Conference such as Dartmouth, California and Cornell.

About the time the Stadium was building the making of football schedules began to shift from a year-to-year to a long range basis. In the process Ohio State began to get new opponents. It was regarded as a distinct feather in the hat of Director St. John that he was able to arrange 3- and 5-game series, especially with certain older members of the Conference, particularly Chicago. Games were arranged with Iowa for 1922, 1923 and 1924 and with Purdue in 1923 and 1924. Iowa was new on the schedule.

The seven seasons from 1922 through 1928, inclusive, saw something of a decline in Ohio State football fortunes. They also brought new opponents into the picture, especially a number of the better known Eastern teams. By contrast with the earlier period of the Wilce regime, in only three of those seven campaigns did the Varsity win more games than it lost and in one season it broke even.

For the entire period indicated the record showed 28 games won, 21 lost, and 6 tied. But against Conference competition it was 12 won,

16 lost and 2 tied. What particularly disturbed Ohio football fandom was that after defeating Michigan three straight times from 1919 through 1921, the Varsity lost five consecutive times from 1922 through 1926.

In the 1922 season, the first of the Stadium era, the team won three games and lost four. It defeated its old Ohio rivals, Ohio Wesleyan and Oberlin, 5 to 0, and 14 to 0, respectively. Then came the Stadium dedication game with Michigan which was lost, 19 to 0. Illinois was beaten, 6 to 3, but all of the other games were lost: Chicago, 9 to 14; Minnesota, 0 to 9; and Iowa, 9 to 12.

It was appropriate for Ohio Wesleyan, Ohio State's oldest football rival, to furnish the opposition in the first scheduled game in the Stadium. It was equally fitting that Michigan had the honor three weeks later of sharing in the formal dedication of the big concrete horseshoe. This was partly in return for the fact that Ohio State the year before had taken part similarly in the dedication of the enlarged Ferry Field at Ann Arbor.

The dedication game was played October 21 before a crowd estimated at 72,500 of which some 16,500 were Michigan adherents. By 1 p.m. the stands were pretty well filled. A canvas wall was erected behind the temporary bleachers at the south end of the field.

The 110-piece Ohio State band, headed by the colorful "Tubby" Essington, entered from one tower, sending out the "Buckeye Battle Cry." The 80-piece Michigan band followed from the other. In the procession were Eloise Fromme, of Urbana, the "Stadium Girl," Governor Harry L. Davis, Presidents M. L. Burton, of Michigan, and W. O. Thompson, of Ohio State, the mayor of Columbus, the deans of the colleges, alumni officers, student representatives, members of the Stadium committees, the Athletic Board, the Physical Education Department, former football captains and players, other Varsity "O" men, and others.

The procession marched the length of the field along the east side, then countermarched down the center to the flagpole. Dr. Thompson gave the brief dedicatory address, the other Big Ten schools were saluted, and the band played "Fight the Team Across the Field." Artillery pieces south of the Stadium fired a 21-gun salute.

As at Ann Arbor the year before, the game was a different story. Just as Ohio State won the Ferry Field dedication game, Michigan triumphed in the Ohio Stadium inaugural, 19 to 0. It scored in every quarter, with field goals in the first and final quarters, and touchdowns in the second and third. The game itself was a case of too much Kipke and too much Goebel. The latter was the Michigan right end and captain, while Kipke was the star halfback. Between them they made all of Michigan's points.

The first Michigan field goal followed a blocked punt. A subsequent Ohio State fumble resulted two plays later in a touchdown by Kipke. In the third quarter he intercepted an Ohio State pass and ran about 40 yards for another touchdown. In the fourth quarter he intercepted still another pass and this led to the second Michigan field goal. On the plus side, Ohio State had 11 first downs to 6 for Michigan. It penetrated in the third quarter to Michigan's 4-yard line but was unable to score. So for the first time in four years it lost to Michigan in football.

After the season there was a development of another sort. When John R. Richards again resigned at Wisconsin that university went after Coach Wilce. But early in 1923 he declined the offer from his alma mater. As the February, 1923 *Alumni Monthly* explained, the pressure on him from Wisconsin was offset "by countless expressions of confidence and respect and admiration which flooded Dr. Wilce in resolutions by many Ohio State University alumni associations and in personal letters from scores of individual alumni and friends." On his part Wilce said he believed "thoroughly" in the future of Ohio, of Columbus and the University, and that Ohioans would "increasingly appreciate that Ohio State University is their institution." And the April, 1923 *Monthly* reported that it was an "open secret" that Wisconsin would soon be back on Ohio State's schedule "probably in 1924, certainly in 1925." The way had been paved by Richards' resignation.

The next three seasons—1923, 1924 and 1925—on the record might be said to have been so-so. In 1923 Ohio State won 3, lost 4, and tied 1, the schedule having been increased to eight games. The next year it won 2, lost 3, and tied 3 games, and in 1925 the record was 4 wins, 3 losses, and 1 tie. There were mounting dissatisfaction and criticism over the fact that in this 3-year period the Varsity won only three Conference games, as against ten losses and two ties.

In 1923, Ohio Wesleyan and Denison were defeated, 24 to 7, and 42 to 0, respectively. But Michigan won, 23 to 0, Illinois, 9 to 0, Chicago, 17 to 3, and Iowa, 20 to 0. The lone Conference victory was over Purdue, 32 to 0, and there was a 23-to-23 thriller with Colgate.

The next season Ohio Wesleyan was beaten again, 10 to 0, but Wooster held the Varsity to a 7-to-7 tie. Michigan, Indiana and Illinois all won—16 to 6, 12 to 7, and 7 to 0. Purdue was again Ohio State's lone Conference victim, 7 to 0. The games with Chicago and Iowa ended in ties, 3 to 3, and 0 to 0.

On the whole the 1925 season was somewhat better, but not in Conference play. Ohio Wesleyan and Wooster succumbed, 10 to 3, and 17 to 0, respectively. But Michigan won again, 10 to 0, and Illinois overcame the Ohioans, 14 to 9. Iowa won also, 15 to 0, and the Chicago game for the second straight year ended in a 3-to-3 tie. Columbia, a new opponent, was defeated, 9 to 0, and Indiana was beaten, 7 to 0.

The 1926 season was another story. This looked like one of the earlier championship teams. It won seven out of eight for the season and three out of four in the Conference. In the last but one of the long series with Ohio Wesleyan, the Varsity won, 47 to 0, and defeated Wittenberg, 40 to 14. Then came one of the most thrilling games with Michigan which the home team lost, 17 to 16, before what was probably the largest Stadium crowd in history—before or since. This defeat was partly offset by a 7 to 6 victory over Illinois. The other victims were: Chicago, 18 to 0; Iowa, 23 to 6; Wilmington, 13 to 7; and Columbia, 32 to 7.

The November 20 game with Michigan remains one of the all-time "thrill" games in the Stadium. It was notable for a number of reasons: a record attendance, a thrilling game which Ohio State lost by one point as the result of a backfield man trying to pick up a rolling punt which Michigan recovered deep in Ohio State territory and on which it soon scored, and a series of accidents and mishaps of which the worst was the explosion of an aerial bomb in the lower rows of the temporary bleachers at the south end of the field.

Attendance for the game was announced as 90,437. But the actual attendance was never known because the crowd surged past the gates, climbed fences, stood in the aisles and occupied every square inch of space even including the slanting roofs of the two press boxes the Stadium then had. The figure given, which stood as a Conference record for some years until Michigan enlarged its new stadium, was chosen arbitrarily on the Sunday before the game at a session in Director St. John's office. (The writer was there.) The game even then was a sellout and in fact it was not far off the mark that 90,000 were present that day—some even thought the figure was closer to 100,000.

Broken arms and legs were suffered by youths trying to climb the steel fence, particularly at the south end, and in the press in the runways. Several persons were struck by bottles dropped or thrown from the upper deck. One result of this experience was that never again was standing room sold for a Stadium football game no matter how great the demand.

Ironically the aerial bomb was fired from a box in the field south of the Stadium under the direct supervision of the Military Department. The bombs exploding at a height above the Stadium were to release flags which were carried away by the wind. The first ones performed properly but a perverse down draft carried the last one to about the fourth or fifth row in the bleachers where it exploded at the feet of two Columbus sisters, one of whom was badly burned and spent some time in the hospital.

As a state agency it was a question of whether the University or the Athletic Board was legally liable. Under the law of the time the state itself was not suable and it was the opinion of competent attorneys that neither it nor the Athletic Board could be sued successfully. There were several precedents elsewhere in the Conference and with high schools which seemed to bear out this belief. The legal remedy, if any, appeared to lie with the state Sundry Claims Board.

At the same time, the Athletic Board had no disposition to evade its responsibility in these matters although it had no insurance protection. The question was discussed at several board meetings. At the December 1 meeting Director St. John reported "upon the progress of spectators injured" at the game and "submitted the legal opinion of Prof. Clarence D. Laylin, of the College of Law, relative to the board's liability in such matters." With her attorney, who insisted he was not in the case for a fee, the chief victim appeared before the board at two meetings. She was ultimately voted $5000 for personal injuries, plus additional sums for her hospital and medical expenses and damage to her clothing. She was to get complimentary tickets for life. At its May 6, 1917 meeting, the board appropriated $16,279.66 to meet operating deficits, including claims growing out of the Michigan game.

The 1927 and 1928 seasons, the last of the long Wilce era, were somewhat better than some of their immediate predecessors. In 1927 the Varsity broke even in an 8-game schedule, and the next year it won 5, lost 2 and tied 1. In those two seasons also it broke even in Conference play, winning 5 and losing 5.

For the first time in many years Ohio Wesleyan was off the schedule in 1927, but two other Ohio teams were defeated: Denison, 61 to 6, and Wittenberg, 31 to 0. The remaining games resulted as follows: Michigan 21, Ohio State 0; Illinois 13, Ohio State 0; Northwestern 19, Ohio State 13; Ohio State 13, Chicago 7; Ohio State 13, Iowa 6; and Princeton 20, Ohio State 0. The Princeton game was played in Palmer Stadium. Ohio State at times used a 5-man line which brought some criticism in view of the result but the formation was widely used in certain defensive situations in later years.

For 1928 the results were: Ohio State 41, Wittenberg 0; Ohio State 19, Michigan 7; Ohio State 39, Muskingum 0; Ohio State 13, Indiana 0; Illinois 8, Ohio State 0; Ohio State 10, Northwestern 0; Iowa 14, Ohio

State 7; and Ohio State 6, Princeton 6. The return game with Princeton was a thriller which had the big crowd on edge throughout. "Wes" Fesler, All-American end—and in later years, Varsity head coach—, was the Ohio State star.

Through a combination of circumstances much of the criticism growing out of the downturn in football fortunes fell upon Dr. Wilce. Much of this was unjustified, uninformed or prejudiced and largely vocal. It came from individual alumni, including former "O" men, from a few alumni groups—notably Toledo—, and especially from hostile newspapers. The Columbus Varsity "O" Association which met regularly for dinner on Monday evenings during the football season for a time at the Ohio Union was inclined to be critical not only of football but of the entire athletic operation. Its members heard detailed reports on the previous Saturday's game, asked searching questions, and at one stage even appointed an investigating committee.

Part of the difficulty undoubtedly arose from a sharp difference of opinion between the head coach and certain of his assistants, notably Grant P. Ward who was head scout, assistant line coach and intramural director. This impasse was finally solved to a degree by Ward's resignation. But Ward had quite a following, especially through his widely read newspaper column on football. He had studied law, was admitted to the bar, and became an influential member of the legislature where he was friendly to the University. He continued to be friendly also with Director St. John but his criticism of Dr. Wilce and his methods was unabated.

Inevitably this situation reached not only the Athletic Board but the University administration. It came before the board, for example, at its December 21, 1925 meeting. There was an utterly unfounded charge that Dr. Wilce had "spied" from a Stadium window on the Illinois team during its practice the day before the Ohio State-Illinois game. A national press association carried the story from coast to coast. It was strongly denied by Wilce and in this he was supported by Coach Robert C. Zuppke, of Illinois.

At the meeting referred to, the board adopted a resolution of confidence in Dr. Wilce. It read:

The Athletic Board expresses its full confidence in Dr. Wilce, both as to his professional qualifications as a coach, his ethical standards and his leadership. He has the entire support of this Board and merits the loyalty of all those who have the best interests of Ohio State football at heart.

At this same meeting Ward submitted his resignation, effective July 1 next. The board accepted it, but effective immediately. By a 5 to 3 vote he was given three months' salary in view of his long service. (By a coincidence Ward's close friend and associate, Walter J. Essman, was killed in an automobile accident a little earlier while en route to Toledo where he was taking Fred Grim, a Varsity halfback, for an alumni meeting. Grim was slightly hurt. The board authorized a bronze memorial tablet to Essman on the Stadium, but this was never done.)

In his letter of resignation, Ward said in part that it was not his desire "to embarrass in any way" Director St. John's administration of the Athletic Department and assured the latter that "I hold you in the highest esteem and am deeply appreciative of the many favors you have shown me." He added that he hoped "no act of mine will cause you to entertain any other feeling than that of friendship to me."

About this time the Toledo alumni were restive over the coaching situation and called for "an Alumni Conference on the athletic situation." Much of this discontent grew out of the four straight losses to Michigan from 1922 through 1925 despite the three earlier wins in 1919, 1920 and 1921. After extensive discussion at a January 5, 1926 board meeting a committee consisting of the chairman and the two alumni members was appointed "to confer with the Toledo alumni . . . relative to the athletic situation." At an April 7 meeting, Chairman French reported that the committee conferred March 12 with the Toledo alumni but no details were given.

As a partial solution to the football difficulties, two additions were made to the coaching staff at a January 13, 1926 board meeting. On Dr. Wilce's recommendation, Samuel S. Willaman, '14, was hired as assistant football coach and intramural director, and Andrew J. "Swede" Oberlander, Dartmouth '26, was engaged as assistant football coach. In effect, Willaman replaced Ward but Oberlander's position was new. The vacancy caused by Essman's death was filled by Harold S. Wood, Oberlin '22, who later became intramural director.

Willaman, a former Varsity player, had had a successful coaching record at Iowa State College. Oberlander was the star halfback and captain—and All-American—of Dartmouth's great 1925 football team. Willaman, in a word, brought added experience and Oberlander youth, enthusiasm and a familiarity with new forward passing developments. It was argued also that the additional help would relieve Dr. Wilce of administrative details so that he could give more time to coaching. In any case, the results in the following season—1926—were markedly better.

Despite a good season in 1926 and a fair one in 1927, the pressure against Dr. Wilce continued to mount. This was particularly true of the so-called "downtown coaches" and other vociferous critics. The matter came to a head at an unprecedented 8:30 a.m. Saturday board meeting June 2, 1928 when Dr. Wilce's resignation was read and accepted to take effect in June, 1929.

He declared his intention of entering "the active practice of medicine and to continue a degree of teaching." He also expressed his "full appreciation of the complete and cordial support of the board over my coaching period." The board, in turn, voiced "sincere regret" at the resignation. Its resolution went on:

The Board appreciates the long, faithful and conspicuous service he has rendered to The Ohio State University in particular and to intercollegiate athletics in general in the fifteen years he has been Director of Football here. The Board recognizes that Dr. Wilce has made a lasting contribution to the development of the University. It conveys to him its gratitude, acknowledges an enduring obligation to him for exemplary and devoted services, and is happy that he contemplates continuing his university teaching relationships.

At its November 20, 1928 meeting the board granted him leave of absence for the Winter, Spring and Summer Quarters, 1929, on the basis of accumulated leave. This was to enable him to continue his medical studies in the United States and abroad.

Lengthy discussion of "the problems involved in the selection of a football coach to succeed Dr. J. W. Wilce" occurred at the December 6, 1928 board meeting. What was not generally known at the time was that Director St. John was negotiating with Knute K. Rockne, the nationally known Notre Dame coach. It was St. John's strong impression that Rockne was interested if he could be released from his Notre Dame contract. At a December 21 meeting St. John "presented the names of various men as possibilities for the football coaching positions and expressed his belief that Mr. Willaman was best qualified for the position of head coach, but that he was not ready to make a final recommendation at this time." The board adjourned, after "much discussion," at 11:40 p.m. to meet the next day.

The following day St. John reported that "he had new information regarding the availability of a nationally known football coach and that he desired more time before making a final recommendation to the board." This reference was obviously to Rockne. It was the sense of the board that St. John should present to it "a complete survey of all men available and the terms on which they could be secured as head football coach. This the Director hoped to be able to do after the national football meeting in New Orleans."

St. John saw Rockne and others during the meetings. He always insisted afterward that Rockne left with him a definite impression that he was willing to come to Columbus if he could get away from his commitment at South Bend. This he reported later he was unable to do and the search turned elsewhere. Rockne was killed in an airplane crash in 1931.

Although the minutes do not show it, it was understood at the January 16, 1929 board meeting that Rockne was not available. St. John then made a detailed report on sixteen other possible names. In an accompanying letter he gave as his conclusion that "the best solution for our present football coaching problem lies in making Samuel S. Willaman head football coach." He cited Willaman's "many superior qualifications" and expressed the belief "that he will acquit himself in a most creditable manner." An accompanying recommendation was that George Hauser, the Minnesota line coach, and Don Miller, one of the Notre Dame "Four Horsemen," be employed as assistant coaches. The board approved both recommendations.

The community shortly gave an appreciation dinner at a downtown hotel for Dr. and Mrs. Wilce along with a new automobile. So ended the 16-year Wilce era of Ohio State football. Over that long span Ohio State teams he coached ran up the impressive record of 78 games won, only 33 lost, and 9 tied for a percentage of .703. It also included three Conference championships and near titles in three other seasons. Dr. Wilce set high standards for himself and for the squads he coached and proved that a man could be a gentleman and a bigtime college football coach at the same time. In the development and use of the forward pass as well as in other ways it was well said that he was ahead of his time. He added greatly to the stature of Ohio State athletics, especially football, and he left town and gown—the city, the state and the campus—heavily in his debt. His over-all record was unmatched until the later years of the Hayes regime, a quarter of a century afterward.

2. WILLAMAN AND SCHMIDT
1929–1940

It would be hard to find two more contrasting regimes that those of Sam Willaman, who had charge of Ohio State football fortunes from 1929 through 1933, and of Francis Schmidt, who reigned colorfully from 1934 through the 1940 season. On the surface, Willaman was successful

Early Campus Playing Fields

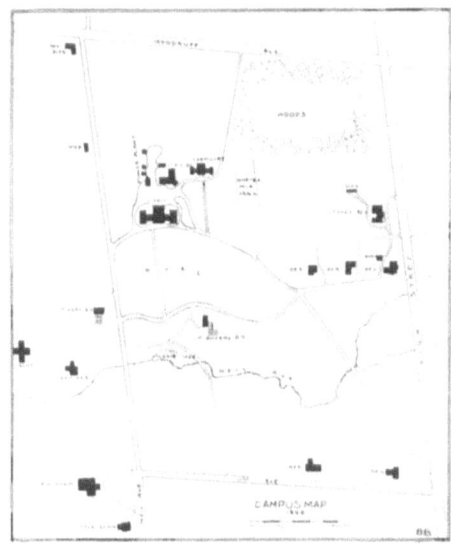

Running track north of Oval, about 1888

Varsity field adjoining North Dorm, about 1892

Faculty-Senior baseball game, 1892(?)

Track meet at Columbus Driving Park, 1895

Dash, Big Six meet, Ohio Field, 1915

Dash, Ohio Relays, 1924

First football squad at campus spring

John Sigrist, killed in 1901 game with Western Reserve

Pile-up in Denison game, Recreation Park, 1891

Squad after muddy game, 1891

Early football game on University (later Ohio) Field; note tallyho and buggies

Dedication, Ohio Stadium, 1922

Winning place kick in 1958 Rose Bowl game

(Courtesy AP Wirephoto)

The "perfect" play—Harley carrying ball against Northwestern, every man carrying out blocking assignment

The 1917 champion backfield—kneeling, Yerges, qb.; standing, l. to r., Harley, hb., Boesel, fb., and Stinchcomb, hb.

Other All-Time "Greats"

"Wes" Fesler (1928-29-30)

Les Horvath (1942-43-44), first Heisman trophy winner from Ohio State

Howard "Hopalong" Cassady, (1953-54-55), Heisman trophy winner

Vic Janowicz, (1948-49-50), also a Heisman trophy winner

Ohio State Olympians

Clement C. Cooke,
Stockholm, 1912

Garnett Wikoff,
Stockholm, 1912

Harry Steel, 1924,
heavyweight champion

Perry Martter, 1924, welterweight, with teammate

The incomparable Jesse Owens, in the broad jump; record still on books in 1959

Olympic Champions

Coach Larry Snyder and "My boy Jesse"

Glenn Davis, winner of 400-meter hurdles at Melbourne; Sullivan Award winner

Mal Whitfield, 800-meter winner in 1948 and 1952 Olympics; Sullivan Award winner

Olympic Swim Champions

Bill Smith, 1948, free style

Ford Konno, 1952 and 1956, freestyle

Yoshi Oyakawa, 1952 and 1956, back stroke

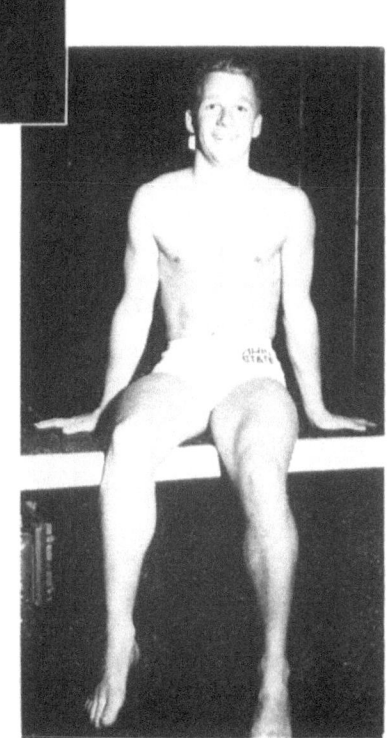

Bruce Harlan, 1948, diver

Bob Clotworthy, 1956, diver

Notable Football Coaches

Dr. J. W. Wilce, 1913-1928

Dr. J. B. C. Eckstorm, 1899-1901

Francis Schmidt, 1934-1940

Alexander Spinning Lilley, the first coach

Wayne W. "Woody" Hayes, 1951-

Other Veterans

Bob Kepler, golf, 1938-

Mike Peppe, swimming, 1931-

H. G. "Oley" Olsen, basketball, 1922-46

Leo Staley, intramurals, 1937-

Tony Aquila, groundskeeper extraordinary

Dr. H. Shindle Wingert, 1907-12

Richard C. "Dick" Larkins, 1947-

Athletic Directors

John R. Richards, 1912

Lynn W. St. John, 1913-47

Vernon H. Davis   George W. Rightmire   W. C. Mills

Graduate Managers—Early 1900s

Conference Representatives

Thomas E. French, 1912-44   James E. Pollard, 1944-47   Wendell D. Postle, 1947-

Harry E. "Mother" Ewing

"Tubby" Essington and the Band

Early Cheerleaders and a Drum Major

"Pink" Tenney, "Hub" Atkinson and Bob Sigafoos

Armory and Gymnasium, torn down 1959

Scenes of Action

Main entrance, Ohio Field

Ohio Stadium, new Gymnasium upper left

Clubhouse, Golf Course

Later Physical Plant

Natatorium

French Field House and St. John Arena

in that his teams won 26, lost 10, and tied 5, for an over-all percentage of .722. But against bigtime competition—the Conference—the record was a little less favorable. It showed 14 games won, 8 lost and 4 ties, for a percentage of .636.

Five years after Willaman took over, Schmidt burst onto the campus from the Southwest where he had spectacular success coaching the teams of Texas Christian. He brought with him the "razzle-dazzle" then prevalent in that league. "Schmidtty" was colorful in more ways than one. In World War I he had been a tough bayonet instructor and his vocabulary was in keeping with his calling.

Even at the moment he came some question was raised on this score and a telegram was sent to the president of Texas Christian. Back came the reply: "Any time you don't want him, we'll be glad to have him back"—or words to that effect. So Schmidt was hired on the usual 1-year contract with the understanding that the engagement was for longer if things worked out, i.e., if he succeeded. To him football was an obsession and he cut a wide swath until the opposing teams—and his critics—began to catch up with him.

To return to Willaman, his first Varsity team had only fair success. It won 4, lost 3, and tied 1. In Conference play it won 2, lost 2, and tied 1. Kenyon was beaten, 54 to 0, and Wittenberg, 19 to 0. In one of the high spots of the season Michigan was beaten also, 7 to 0, but the Indiana game resulted in a 0-to-0 tie. For the rest, Illinois won, 27 to 0, and Northwestern likewise, 18 to 6. Iowa was edged, 7 to 6, but Pittsburgh won, 18 to 2, in the first game with that opponent.

The 1930 season was somewhat better and Ohio State won 5, lost 2, and 1 tie. The outcome of the Michigan and Illinois games was the reverse of that of the preceding year: Michigan won this time, 13 to 0, but Illinois lost, 12 to 9. Indiana was defeated, 23 to 0, but the Wisconsin game ended in a scoreless tie. In the other Conference game, Northwestern won, 19 to 2. Mt. Union was defeated easily, 59 to 0, and Pittsburgh lost, 16 to 7. A high spot of the year was the opening of a home-and-home series with Navy, which was beaten, 27 to 0.

In Willaman's third season in 1931 the team played nine games, winning 6 and losing 3. In the Conference, the record was 4 wins to 2 losses. Cincinnati was beaten, 67 to 6, and Michigan was defeated for the second time in three years, 20 to 7. Illinois and Indiana were also disposed of, 13 to 6, and 40 to 0, respectively. But Vanderbilt in its first appearance as an Ohio State opponent won a colorful game, 26 to 21.

Wisconsin was defeated, 6 to 0, but Northwestern won, 10 to 0. Ohio

State took the return game with Navy, 20 to 0. And in a post-season game with Minnesota, at Minneapolis, the Ohioans lost, 19 to 7. The extra game was played for charity.

Early in 1932 a further reorganization of the football coaching staff was made necessary with the return of George Hauser, line coach, to Minnesota. Don Miller, backfield coach, who wished to devote more time to his law practice, was re-employed on a seasonal basis. Ernie Godfrey, '15, former coach at Wittenberg, continued to have charge of freshman coaching with additional responsibility for Varsity line coaching. Floyd Stahl had general charge of the Reserve squad and assisted with backfield coaching. Wes Fesler, '32, All-American end and 3-sport star, was to assist Godfrey. Dick Larkins, a teammate of Fesler, was to have actual charge of freshman coaching under Godfrey's direction. Years later, Fesler was to become head coach and Larkins athletic director.

In their next to last season under Willaman, the Buckeyes won 4, lost only 1, but tied 3 games. In the Conference the record was 2 wins, 1 loss, and 2 ties. Ohio Wesleyan was back on the schedule for the last time and lost, 34 to 7. But Michigan won, 14 to 0, Indiana was tied, 7 to 7, and Illinois lost, 3 to 0. The Wisconsin game resulted in a 7-to-7 tie. Northwestern was beaten, 20 to 6, the Pittsburgh game ended in a 0-to-0 tie, and Pennsylvania, a new opponent, was beaten, 19 to 0.

On the face of it, Willaman's last year was his best. The 1933 team won seven out of eight games and, in the Conference, four out of five. Michigan was the only opponent to win, 13 to 0. The other foes were disposed of as follows: Indiana, 21 to 0; Illinois, 7 to 6; Vanderbilt, 20 to 0; Wisconsin, 6 to 0; Northwestern, 2 to 0; Pennsylvania, 20 to 7; and Virginia, 75 to 0.

In the face of his over-all record it might seem strange in retrospect that Willaman resigned. Actually his resignation was because of a number of reasons. There was some vocal criticism over his handling of his squads and, particularly, over his style of play. His critics wanted "to see an Ohio boy run with the ball."

The "situation" was discussed at a December 17, 1933 board meeting but no action was taken except an agreement to meet again on or before January 15 for further discussion "of this matter." There was more than appeared on the surface, however, because at a meeting January 24, 1934, Director St. John reported having conferred with Willaman "concerning the latter's plans for the future, pursuant to the informal understanding of the board at its meeting on December 17, 1933." The director was instructed "to advise Mr. Willaman that, in view of the lapse of time, the board must be apprised of his plans by February 4, 1934, as definite arrangements for next year cannot be safely postponed beyond that date."

Action now came rapidly because at another meeting January 31 a letter of that date from Willaman was presented saying that he was resigning to take effect at the close of the school year. The resignation was accepted and a committee was appointed "to advise with the Director in canvassing the situation and recommending to the board a successor for Mr. Willaman." Temperament was a contributing factor in the situation leading to his resignation.

The search for a successor was relatively short. Only thirty days elapsed from the time Willaman's resignation was presented until his relief was named. Willaman presently went to Western Reserve in the dual capacity of athletic director and head coach. There was talk of Earl "Red" Blaik, of West Point, as Willaman's successor but this came to nought.

At a March 2 board meeting, the special committee supported St. John's recommendation that Francis A. Schmidt, of Texas Christian University, be named head coach at $7500 a year. This was approved unanimously with the understanding that the appointment was for three years. And so began one of the most colorful periods of Ohio State football. Schmidt was an exponent of open football and ushered in an era of "razzle-dazzle" play in the Stadium and on opponents' fields which attracted wide attention and greatly increased the interest in football. Schmidt himself was equally colorful.

To say that the Schmidt era of Ohio State football was "different" is putting it mildly. It was different in many ways—in the man himself, in his handling of players, in the imagination of the offense he produced, and in the drama of the games played in those seven years. Schmidt in street clothing hardly looked the part of a bigtime football coach. He wore bow ties and looked more like a successful businessman than the head coach of a major varsity team.

He made a hit almost from the outset with his unorthodox ways and his habit of getting to the point. A favorite example was his pungent comment when the Michigan "menace" was first mentioned. In the sixteen seasons preceding his arrival Michigan had won ten games to six for Ohio and nine of the last twelve. But Schmidt, sure of himself and confident of his methods, raised a quizzical eyebrow and demanded, "Well, they put their pants on one leg at a time the same as anyone else, don't they?"

Out of this offhand remark the Michigan Pants Club was born. It consists of alumni and downtown businessmen who still stage a special dinner after the close of any season in which Ohio State defeats Michigan in football. The Varsity squad and coaches are guests and they are presented with miniature gold football pants to commemorate the occasion. That Schmidt knew whereof he spoke was borne out by the fact that his teams beat Michigan four straight times after he came to the campus.

His over-all record was amazing, especially his first four seasons. During his seven seasons on the campus his teams won 39, lost 16 and tied one game for a percentage of .722. In the Conference, the record was 30 won, 9 lost, and one tie, for a .769 rating. The Varsity won its first Big Ten title in fifteen years in his second season at the helm, repeated this in his sixth season, and narrowly missed in two others.

In 1934, his first season, Ohio State won seven and lost only one game. The lone defeat was a 14 to 13 victory by Illinois. As it turned out this was the only time in his seven years that the Buckeyes bowed to the Illini. Other opponents during the 1934 season were disposed of as follows: Western Reserve, 76 to 0; Michigan, 34 to 0; Indiana, 33 to 0; Northwestern, 28 to 7; Chicago, 33 to 0; Iowa, 40 to 7; and Colgate, 10 to 7.

But the 1935 season was the real thriller. This was the year Ohio State won its fourth title, and it was the year of the memorable game with Notre Dame, one of the all-time thrillers in Varsity history or in U.S. intercollegiate history, for that matter. Kentucky was disposed of, 19 to 6; Michigan was shut out, 38 to 0; and Indiana was polished off, 28 to 6. Illinois was edged, 6 to 0, Northwestern was beaten, 28 to 7, and Chicago succumbed, 20 to 13, to make a clean sweep in the Conference. Drake was swamped, 85 to 7.

But Notre Dame, in the first meeting between the two elevens, was something else. Ohio State completely dominated the play in the first half while Notre Dame had the upper hand in the second. It was still unbelievable in that despite the shift in play Ohio State, with less than four minutes to play, still led and seemed to have the game well in hand only to lose. But Notre Dame then scored three times in the hectic final quarter—twice in the last two minutes.

Two intercepted passes in the first quarter resulted in home team touchdowns. One of them, tied in with a lateral—a favorite Schmidt play—, went for 70 yards. But in the second half the visitors kept the Buckeyes pretty well bottled up. In the closing moments of the third quarter, Notre Dame kicked out of bounds on Ohio State's 8-yard line. Ohio State promptly fumbled but recovered on its 3-yard line. It then punted and Notre Dame returned to Ohio State's 12-yard line as the quarter ended. When play was resumed a pass put Notre Dame on Ohio State's 1-yard line and the visitors scored on the next play, but the attempted place kick hit the cross bar and left the score 13 to 6.

After the kickoff Ohio State was unable to gain and finally punted to Notre Dame's 46-yard line. A pass interference ruling then put the ball on Ohio State's 8-yard line. (Movies of the game showed later that instead of interfering the Ohio State defender was held by an opposing player as he batted the ball down.) The situation was saved for the moment when Notre Dame fumbled on Ohio State's 1-yard line and a defending lineman recovered. With less than four minutes left Ohio State moved the ball nearly to mid-field and punted to Notre Dame on its 21-yard line.

Notre Dame promptly took to the air. A pass from Pilney carried to Ohio State's 38-yard line, another netted 9 yards more, a third took the ball to Ohio State's 15-yard line, and a fourth yielded a touchdown. But this time the place kick was wide and the score stood at 13 to 12.

Notre Dame then tried an onside kick but Ohio State recovered on its 46-yard line. A substitute carried in word to freeze the ball, but somehow this was ignored and on the first play an Ohio State halfback fumbled and Notre Dame recovered on the home team's 49-yard line. Pilney fell back to pass but ran instead to Ohio State's 19-yard line. An Ohio State defender had the next pass in his hands only to drop the ball. With time running out a pass from Shakespeare brought a touchdown—with defeat for Ohio State and delirium for Notre Dame.

Both teams went into the game unbeaten, although Ohio State was a 7 to 5 favorite. A capacity throng of 81,018 sat in on the spectacle. How the game seesawed was shown by the fact that in the first half Ohio State had 9 first downs to 2 for Notre Dame, but in the second half Notre Dame had 11 and Ohio State only one. The next *Alumni Monthly* called the game "the most stunning upset in Ohio State football history." For thrills it was likened to the 17-to-16 game with Michigan in 1926.

The 1935 team tied with Minnesota for the Conference title, neither being defeated in five games in the league. In recognition of this achievement the board voted the award of gold footballs emblematic of the title to the team and the coaches. And so great was the demand for a showing of movies of the Notre Dame game the board voted also to buy a new projector for football films and "a new copy" of the Notre Dame film.

The 1936 team slipped a bit, winning five games and losing three, but won four out of five in Conference play. The one Conference loss was to Northwestern, 14 to 13. But the team lost to Notre Dame in a return game at South Bend, 7 to 2. There was satisfaction, however, in a third straight whitewash of Michigan, 21 to 0, in beating Indiana, 7 to 0, Illinois, 13 to 0, and Chicago, 44 to 0. A new opponent on the schedule was New York University which was overwhelmed, 60 to 0. But Pittsburgh won a tight game, 6 to 0.

Then there was Notre Dame again. This time with five minutes to play Notre Dame led, 7 to 2, having scored a touchdown to a safety for Ohio State, resulting from a blocked punt. In the closing minutes Ohio State moved the ball from its own 29-yard line to Notre Dame's 12. After two passes failed, Notre Dame took over and did what Ohio State should have done the year before—it froze the ball, the gun went off, and Notre Dame had won again.

The 1936 season marked the close of the 3-year agreement under which Schmidt came to the campus. In those three seasons the team had won fourteen and lost only two in Conference competition, and had an over-all record in that time of nineteen won and five lost. In that period also it tied with Minnesota for the Conference title in 1935 and was runnerup in 1934 and 1936.

The Athletic Board was so pleased with Schmidt's showing that at its November 23, 1936 meeting it voted an expression of its appreciation of his services and the hope that he would extend the "gentleman's agreement" to include 1937, 1938 and 1939. The minutes said: "He has measured up to all our expectations as a gentleman and as a coach. His services have been eminently satisfactory." And because "so convincing has been his performance during the last three years," the desire for an extension of his contract for another three was in order.

The 1937 record was a shade better, the team winning six and losing three games. Michigan was defeated again, 21 to 0, but Indiana won, 10 to 0, while Illinois lost for the third straight time, 19 to 0. Northwestern, Purdue and Chicago were beaten by scores of 7 to 0, 13 to 0, and 30 to 0, respectively. A pair of games with newcomers to the schedule was divided —Texas Christian, Schmidt's old school, was beaten, 14 to 0, but Southern California won a squeaker, 13 to 12.

Things were somewhat different in 1938, the team winning four, losing three and tieing one game. Michigan finally won for the first time in five seasons against Schmidt, 18 to 0, but Indiana was defeated, 6 to 0, and Illinois, 32 to 14. The Northwestern game was a scoreless tie, Purdue won, 12 to 0, and hapless Chicago was beaten, 42 to 7. New York University was disposed of, 32 to 0, but Southern California won again, 14 to 7.

The picture was brighter in 1939, the Varsity winning six and losing only two games and capturing its second Conference title under Schmidt. The two losses were to Michigan again, 21 to 14, and to Cornell, a newcomer on the schedule, 23 to 14, in a game which at first seemed to have been sewed up by the home team. Except for Minnesota, which was defeated, 23 to 20, the other opponents were held scoreless: Indiana, 24 to 0; Illinois, 21 to 0; Northwestern, 13 to 0; Chicago, in the last game with the Maroons who were abandoning football as a varsity sport, 61 to 0; and Missouri, another newcomer on the schedule, 19 to 0.

In Schmidt's final season on the campus the Varsity broke even in eight games. It lost to Michigan, for the third straight time, 40 to 0, to Northwestern, 6 to 3, to Minnesota, 13 to 7, and again to Cornell, 21 to 7. This last game, played at Ithaca, was not only a disappointment but led to unfortunate charges after the game of coaching from the Cornell bench which hurt relations between the two schools. For the rest, Ohio State defeated Indiana, 21 to 6, Illinois, 14 to 6, Purdue, 17 to 14, and Pittsburgh, 30 to 7.

The 1940 season marked the end of the road for Schmidt on the campus. There had been mounting criticism of some of his coaching methods, particularly in his handling of the men. There was a feeling that the parade had caught up with his "razzle-dazzle" offense. So he gave way to Paul Brown who, if anything, was even more of a perfectionist than Schmidt. But for years Schmidt was remembered as one of the most colorful figures ever identified with Ohio State football. It is a singular fact that while he was best known as an offensive coach, his teams had a stout defense. In the fifty-six games during his seven seasons the opposition went scoreless in twenty-five games to six times for Ohio State.

As had happened with earlier coaches there were rumblings over the football situation in the late 'Thirties. There was some dissatisfaction after the 1938 season and although things were better in 1939 when the team won the championship the situation soured again during the 1940 season when Ohio State tied for fourth in the Conference. Not only had the opposition caught up with Schmidt's open style of play but there were personal factors which helped to worsen the situation such as his relations with individual players and his actions on the practice field. To a public fed on victories the record of the last three years, despite the 1939 title, was unsatisfactory: 11 wins, 6 lossses and one tie in the Conference, and 14 won, 9 lost and one tie in over-all competition.

The situation came before the board officially for the first time at its December 9, 1940 meeting when Director St. John recommended the appointment of a committee "to consider the general football situation."

A 3-man committee, with the chairman and the director as ex officio members, was instructed to report its findings "as soon as practicable."

The matter came to a head quickly with the submission of the resignations of Schmidt and four assistant coaches effective at the end of the fiscal year. These were accepted unanimously and Schmidt was given leave of absence with pay for the Winter and Spring Quarters. As it turned out, two of the assistant coaches, Ernie Godfrey and John R. Blickle, stayed on. Another, Gomer Jones, in time became the successful line coach at Oklahoma. Still another, Sid Gillman, later made an enviable record as head coach at Miami and Cincinnati before turning to the "pro" coaching field.

3. Brown Through Fesler
1941–1950

For some years the legend persisted that Ohio State was the "graveyard" of football coaches. But a closer examination of the facts showed that this was not true. From Wilce's first season, 1913, through Hayes' first year, 1951, the University had eight head football coaches in a span of thirty-eight years. But counting Schmidt's last year, 1940, and the first Hayes year, 1951, there were six head coaches in that period. This was due in part to wartime conditions.

Schmidt left after seven years and Paul Brown, who followed, remained for three and then left to go eventually into professional football where he was highly successful. Carroll Widdoes, his first assistant, was top man for two years, and Paul Bixler for one but both quit voluntarily. Widdoes later became athletic director and head coach at Ohio University and Bixler, after several years as head coach at Colgate, returned to Brown's staff. Wesley Fesler then came on for four years, after having been head coach at Wesleyan University and at Pittsburgh. He, too, left of his own free will. Then came "Woody" Hayes who was still head coach as this was written in 1959.

So in the forty-six seasons in which Ohio State competed in the Big Ten between 1913 and 1958 it had eight head football coaches. Wilce served longest with sixteen seasons and Hayes, the last of these, had completed his eighth season. The average tenure, even counting the World II period, was nearly six years.

With the resignation of Schmidt and his assistants, Director St. John pressed the search for a succcessor. At an Athletic Board meeting January 14, 1941 he recommended the appointment of Paul E. Brown, highly successful coach of Massillon High School, as head coach. The day before the University trustees voted their approval in advance of any appointee acceptable to H. S. Atkinson, chairman of the trustees and their representative on the Athletic Board, and President Bevis.

Brown was hired on a 3-year "gentleman's agreement," with a salary scale of $6500, $7000 and $7500, with the privilege of naming his assistants. It was understood also that he would have "complete freedom . . . in the conduct of the football coaching job." His appointment marked the first time the University had hired a head football coach directly from the high school coaching ranks. The new coaching staff was completed February 6 when the board approved the hiring of six assistants for Brown: Hugh S. McGranahan, Paul Bixler, Carroll C. Widdoes, Frederick C. Mackey, Trevor Rees, and Frederick Heisler.

The new coach was a perfectionist who made a fetish of condition. During a time out in a game, for example, he would not permit players to relax by sitting down. He insisted upon speed and precision and his system got results.

He came to the campus a few months before active U. S. involvement in World War II. He had spectacular success in his first two seasons. But the 1943 season, by which time most of the available men had been siphoned off into the Armed Forces or to other campuses such as Michigan and Wisconsin where there were special service programs, was less successful from the won-lost standpoint. By another season Brown himself had gone into service to coach at Great Lakes and, as it turned out, not to return to the campus although he was on leave.

In his first Ohio State season the team won six, lost one and tied one game. In Conference competition, the record was three won, one lost and one tied. After three straight losses to Michigan a 20-to-20 tie with that opponent was a welcome change. Illinois was defeated, 12 to 7, Wisconsin was "taken" in a free scoring game, 46 to 34, but Northwestern won, 14 to 7. Purdue was edged, 16 to 14, and Pittsburgh succumbed, 21 to 14. Ohio State defeated Southern California for the first time, 33 to 0, and Misouri lost, 12 to 7.

The 1942 team won another Big Ten title, the sixth for Ohio State, and lost only to Wisconsin. The over-all record was nine won to one lost, and in the Conference it was five won plus the Wisconsin defeat. Michigan was beaten, 21 to 7, Indiana, 32 to 21, Illinois, 44 to 20, Northwestern, 20 to 6, and Purdue, 26 to 0. Pittsburgh was swamped, 59 to 19.

Two games were played also with service teams. Ft. Knox was defeated, 59 to 0, and the Iowa Seahawks lost, 41 to 12. The season was notable for its heavy scoring, Ohio State tallying more than 30 points in 5 of the 10 games. This reflected the fact that while the defense was good, Brown was offense-minded.

The 1943 season was something else. The manpower was depleted to the extent that, under Conference rules, freshmen were permitted to play on Varsity squads. The 1943 team played 9 games of which it won only 3 and lost 6. A majority of the games were on the free scoring order.

Michigan won, 45 to 7, the widest margin of Wolverine victory in any game with Ohio State since 1935. Indiana won also, 20 to 14, but Illinois was beaten, 29 to 26, in a game that ended on an unusual note. Northwestern won, 13 to 0, and Purdue, 30 to 7, but Pittsburgh succumbed again, 46 to 6, and Southern California, 27 to 6. The Iowa Seahawks won, 28 to 13, and Great Lakes, which Brown was to coach the following year, won also, 13 to 6.

At the end of 60 minutes of play in the Illinois game, the score was a tie, 26 to 26, in what had been a thriller. A last moment Ohio State pass failed, the two squads left the field and the crowd thought the game was over. But Illinois had been called offside. The teams were brought back and the crowd halted in its tracks. John Stungis, a freshman quarterback, kicked the goal and Ohio State won after all, 29 to 26, as a result of what became known as the "Fifth quarter" field goal. A network radio announcer was so excited at the unexpected outcome, he cried over the air, "The --- -- - --- made it!"

There were other high spots to the season even in games the Buckeyes lost. The game with Purdue, for example, was played in the Cleveland Municipal Stadium. The "home" team led, 7 to 0, for the first half. But in the second half of the rain-drenched game, Purdue scored five touchdowns. And in the game with Indiana, Ohio State was ahead, 14 to 13, up to 39 seconds before the end of the game when Hoernschmeyer, the star Hoosier back, flipped a 20-yard pass to a teammate in the end zone and there was the ball game.

Despite the over-all record in 1943 the feeling was that Brown had done a commendable job under the circumstances. This was recognized at the November 22 board meeting at which Director St. John paid tribute to Brown and the coaching staff "for the wonderful job of teaching which has been effected during the season just closed." The board concurred in the testimonial.

Before another season rolled around, Brown had accepted a Navy commission and was stationed at Great Lakes. At the April 14, 1944 board meeting, Carroll C. Widdoes was named acting head coach with "the hearty approval of all members remaining on the coaching staff," a number of others having gone into service. The 3-year record under Brown showed 18 wins, 8 losses and one tie for a .692 percentage. In the Conference the tally was 9 victories to 6 defeats for a percentage of .600.

As one of Brown's chief assistants, it was more or less natural for Widdoes to take over the top coaching job when Brown went into the Navy. This was on the expectation that this was only an interim arrangement and that Brown would take up where he left off when he returned from service. But it turned out otherwise.

In Widdoes' two seasons at the helm, Ohio State had remarkable success. The 1944 team was undefeated in eight games and that of the following year won 7 out of 9. For the two years the over-all record was 15 won as against 2 losses, for a percentage of .882. In the Conference the corresponding showing was 11 wins to 2 losses for an .846 percentage. Despite its brevity this was one of the best showings in Ohio State football over a 2-year period under any Buckeye coach.

It was inevitable some would say that in his first year Widdoes, in effect, was cashing in on the legacy left by Brown. This was true to a degree, but Widdoes himself, with the help of a sound staff, contributed much to this success.

The 1944 team, indeed, some might argue, rose to as great heights as any Ohio State eleven before or since. It won the undisputed Conference title. It was recognized generally as the mythical national civilian champion. In Les Horvath, an unusually fine back, it had not only another All-American but the top player of the year.

More specifically, in the 1944 season, the Buckeyes overcame these opponents: Michigan, 18 to 14; Indiana, 21 to 7; Illinois, 26 to 12; Wisconsin, 20 to 7; Minnesota, 34 to 13; Iowa, 34 to 0; Pittsburgh, 54 to 19; Missouri, 54 to 0; and Great Lakes, coached by Brown, 26 to 6.

Quarterback Horvath made one of the greatest records ever made by an Ohio State football player. He was All-Conference and All-American, and won the Heisman Trophy as the college player of the year. Scarlet Key, undergraduate managers' group, proposed that his playing number, 22, be "retired" in honor of his achievements. After discussion the board laid the matter on the table "with the understanding that some kind of a definite program should be set up to honor all of our superlative team members." This was not done.

The only fly in the ointment of this unusual team success was the refusal of the Big Ten faculty representatives to let the team go to the Rose Bowl. There was some hope that the Conference might make an exception on this point. The day after the final game of the season in which Michigan was defeated, 18 to 14, and which clinched the title, a special meeting of the faculty representatives was held in Chicago. California, the Pacific Coast winner, had issued an informal bid to Ohio State on the optimistic feeling that the Western Conference might give the necessary permission. (The Big Ten had withdrawn its approval after the 1921 defeat of Ohio State by California in the Rose Bowl.)

But Ohio State's hopes were dashed at the meeting. The arguments pro and con were heard. When the matter was put to a vote only Indiana and Iowa supported the Ohio State proposal. So the Buckeyes had to be content with their unofficial Conference title and with their mythical national honors.

A formal resignation from Paul Brown was reported at the February 13, 1945 board meeting. It was accompanied by a personal letter "of explanation, appreciation and regret." The resignation was accepted and Prof. J. R. Hopkins, board chairman, was authorized to acknowledge the resignation and extend to Brown the board's appreciation "for a job well done" and good wishes for the future. At a February 20 meeting, Widdoes was named head coach in his own right with Bixler and Godfrey as assistant coaches.

The record for the 1945 season under Widdoes was: Michigan 7, Ohio State 3; Ohio State 27, Illinois 2; Ohio State 12, Wisconsin 0; Ohio State 16, Northwestern 14; Purdue 35, Ohio State 13; Ohio State 20, Minnesota 7; Ohio State 42, Iowa 0; Ohio State 14, Pittsburgh 0; and Ohio State 47, Missouri 6.

On the heels of the unbeaten season of 1944, Ohio State thus made another fine showing in 1945, winning five and losing two in the Conference and seven of nine games for the season. But there were rumblings of discontent and Widdoes came to the conclusion that he desired to be relieved of the head coaching position. This came about formally January 2, 1946 when his resignation was presented. At this same meeting a recommendation that Bixler be made head coach with Widdoes as assistant coach was approved. The Bixler appointment was for two years.

In his letter of resignation, Widdoes emphasized that his action was "entirely a voluntary one." He expressed his appreciation for the cooperation he had had and for the "loyalty and cooperation" of all the members of the coaching staff. But he said that the position of head coach was one "'to which I had never aspired" and he had reached the conclusion that "I was better satisfied as an Assistant than I have been as Head Coach."

As it turned out, Bixler had the shortest tenure of any head football coach on the campus since 1912. He stepped up from the ranks when Widdoes stepped down, but at the end of the 1946 season he, too, relinquished the reins to go to Colgate as head coach.

The 1946 team won 4, lost 3 and tied 2 games. In the Conference the record was 2 wins, 3 defeats and a tie. The team lost to Michigan, 58 to 6, the second most lopsided score piled up by the Wolverines against Ohio State since 1902. For the others, Illinois won, 17 to 6, and Wisconsin, 20 to 7, but Northwestern was beaten, 39 to 27, the game with Purdue resulted in a 14-to-14 tie, and Minnesota was beaten, 39 to 9, as were Pittsburgh, 20 to 13, and Southern California, 21 to 0, while Missouri earned a 13-to-13 tie.

Bixler's desire to step down was fairly well known and his resignation was formally presented at a board meeting February 14, 1947. Director St. John, knowing of the impending move, had negotiated with Wes Fesler, who as an undergraduate had won nine Varsity "O's" and had made one of the best all-around records in Ohio State athletic history. He had tried his hand briefly in professional baseball and had been on the coaching staffs at Wesleyan, Harvard and Princeton and was currently head football coach at Pittsburgh.

At the same meeting at which Bixler's resignation was accepted, the Fesler appointment was approved, subject to trustee confirmation. Fesler brought with him Lyal Clark as line coach and Dick Fisher, former Varsity halfback, as backfield coach. A 5-year "gentleman's agreement" was entered into with Fesler whereby he was to receive $12,500 his first year with increases of $500 for each of the next two years and $13,500 for the last two years. The appointment was effective March 1.

Fesler was a "natural" to succeed Bixler. He was thoroughly familiar with the campus, he was one of Ohio State's all-time athletic "greats," he had had a varied and, on the whole, successful coaching career. Although he had no particular desire to leave Pittsburgh, where he was well regarded, Director St. John had little difficulty in persuading him to return to the scene of his undergraduate triumphs. He remained for four seasons.

Between 1947 and 1950, inclusive, Fesler-coached teams won 21, lost 13 and tied 2 for a percentage of .618. In the Conference the record was 13 wins, 10 losses and 2 ties for a percentage of .565. Fesler resigned after the close of the 1950 season, not entirely unexpectedly, to go into business.

His first season, that of 1947, was somewhat disappointing. Of its 9-game schedule, the team won 2, lost 6 and tied 1, and in the Conference the record stood at a single victory, 1 tie and 4 defeats. Michigan, Indiana and Illinois all won from the Buckeyes by scores of 21 to 0, 7 to 0, and

28 to 7, respectively. Northwestern was edged, 7 to 6, but Purdue won 24 to 20, and Iowa was tied, 13 to 13. For the first time in eight seasons, however, Pittsburgh won from Ohio State, 12 to 0. Southern California also won, 32 to 0, but Missouri was defeated, 13 to 7.

At the close of the 1947 season the board, at a meeting November 24, adopted this resolution commending:

Wesley E. Fesler, the Coaching Staff, the Squad, the Student Body, the Alumni, the Press, and the University Community, upon the fine spirit of cooperation and loyalty, which has developed out of the disappointments and joys of the Football Season. The fine influence of Wesley E. Fesler upon the Squad, and their intense loyalty to him, have caught the admiration of all who watched it develop. To the development of such values, the Athletic Board gives hearty support.

The second season under Fesler was distinctly better, the team winning 6 and losing 3 games, although in the Conference the record was 3 wins as against 3 losses. Michigan won again, 13 to 3, but Indiana and Illinois were beaten by scores of 17 to 0, and 34 to 7, respectively. In a free scoring game Wisconsin was edged, 34 to 32, but Northwestern and Iowa won by scores of 21 to 7, and 14 to 7, respectively. Pittsburgh was buried, 31 to 0, Southern California was whitewashed, 20 to 0, and Missouri was defeated, 21 to 7.

Early in 1949 a number of changes took place on the football coaching staff. Widdoes, former head coach, resigned as assistant coach, effective February 28, to go to Ohio University as head coach. Dick Fisher was moved up from freshman to Varsity backfield coach. Harry L. Strobel was hired as freshman coach and Gene Fekete, former Varsity fullback, as assistant freshman coach.

Next came another Conference championship, shared with Michigan. The season showed 7 wins as against 1 loss and 2 ties. This was climaxed by the 1950 Rose Bowl game in which Ohio State defeated California, 17 to 14, and partly evened old scores with the Bears, representing the Pacific Coast Conference.

It was the 7-to-7 tie with Michigan which had brought Ohio State a share of the Big Ten title and opened the way for it to play in the Rose Bowl game. (Michigan had played in the 1948 Rose Bowl game and thus, under the Conference rule, was ineligible to go.) The only Conference game the team lost that season was to Minnesota, 27 to 0. The other tie game was with Southern California, 13 to 13, but in the opening game the Buckeyes had a narrow escape with Missouri, winning, 35 to 34. Along the way they defeated Indiana, 46 to 7, Illinois, 30 to 17, Wisconsin, 21 to 0, Northwestern, 24 to 7, and Pittsburgh, 14 to 10.

The Rose Bowl game was a thriller. The first quarter was scoreless. In the second an Ohio State touchdown was nullified by a holding penalty. A fumble was recovered by California which then went 74 yards in five plays, one of them a forward pass good for 54 yards, to score. The Bears kicked goal and the score stood at 7 to 0 at the half.

In the third quarter, Vic Janowicz intercepted a California pass on his own 25-yard line and returned it to the California 30. Morrison, the Ohio State fullback voted later the outstanding player in the game, scored a touchdown and End Jimmy Hague tied the score with the point after touchdown. In a matter of minutes, Trautwein, a big Ohio State tackle, blocked a California kick on the Bears' 20. Krall soon scored and, with the goal after touchdown, it was Ohio State 14, California 7. In two minutes, California tied the score, going 58 yards in five plays. At the end of the third quarter the score was 14 to 14.

Ohio State got its break late in the fourth quarter. The California quarterback took a bad pass from center and tried to punt it on the run. The ball squirted out of bounds on the Bears' 13-yard line. Several plays were run after which Hague made a place kick. After it got the ball California was unable to get into scoring position and surrendered the ball. Ohio State then ran out the clock to win, 17 to 14.

On the ground, Ohio State had the edge, 221 to 133 yards. California gained 106 yards by passing to 34 for Ohio State which had 19 first downs to 12 for California. The game was played before a crowd of 100,963, the largest up to then to see an Ohio State football game. It was the fourth straight win in the Rose Bowl for Western Conference teams. The Ohio State Marching Band gave a memorable performance both in the Tournament of Roses parade and in the bowl.

Even while the team was on the coast there were rumors that Fesler would resign as coach. There was no confirmation of this when the squad returned to the campus. President Bevis pointed out that Fesler's agreement still had two years to run. In a statement the president said the University had "never been advised that Mr. Fesler intends to resign. We hope he will not."

The Athletic Board, at its January 9 meeting, drafted a letter of commendation to Fesler. In reaffirming its confidence and support, the board said it
joins with a host of others in congratulating you and your associates upon a

successful football season, climaxed by the great victory in the Rose Bowl. Because you and your staff exemplify so fully the type of coaching leadership under which we desire the young men in this University to train in competitive sport, the Board is deeply gratified at your decision to remain as part of the University community. That you would remain as Head Football Coach has, as you know, at all times been our earnest hope; in this hope, the Board had at no time authorized, and consequently the Director of Athletics had not undertaken any consideration whatsoever of a possible successor. . . .

It developed that Fesler had entertained the idea of getting out of coaching and into a line of activity where the pressure was less severe. When this became known every effort was made to persuade him to remain. A determining factor at the time was official assurance on the part of the trustees and the administration that as long as he cared to remain he would have tenure and if he ever decided to give up coaching he could be assured of a lifetime position in the Physical Education Department.

So Fesler came to his fourth and, as it proved, final season on the campus. Here the record was good although not up to that of the previous year. In the regular 1950 season the team won 6 and lost 3 games, with a 5-won-2-lost record in the Conference. The two Conference losses were to Michigan, 9 to 3, in the now famous "Snow Bowl" game, and to Illinois, 14 to 7. Outside of Conference play the Buckeyes lost a 32-to-27 thriller to Southern Methodist in the first meeting between the two schools. Otherwise Ohio State defeated Indiana, 26 to 14, Wisconsin, 19 to 14, Northwestern, 32 to 0, Minnesota, 48 to 0, Iowa, 83 to 21, and Pittsburgh, 41 to 7. The Iowa score was the largest Ohio State has ever run up on a Big Ten opponent.

In many respects the 1950 "Snow Bowl" game with Michigan was perhaps the most unique in the long history of Ohio State football. The contest, with at least a share of the Conference title at stake, was played under almost impossible weather conditions. The game had been a virtual sellout since August, but many stayed away at the last minute or were unable to get to the Stadium. Even so, 50,503 hardy souls sat through most of the game. They were garbed in all sorts of outlandish costumes and combinations to ward off the snow. Some in the "A" Deck sat huddled with cardboard cartons, with peepholes cut in them, over their heads. Many cars were marooned in the parking lots for days after the game and hundreds were stalled en route home.

Almost up to game time, it was a question whether the game would be played. The two coaches, Fesler and Oosterbaan, favored canceling the game. But this would have been unfair to the thousands who braved the elements to get to the Stadium. It might also have given Ohio State the questionable honor of "backing" into the championship. In the end, Director Larkins made the decision to play the game.

At game time there were 5 inches of snow on the ground, more was falling steadily, and a 28-mile-an-hour gale blew out of the northwest. It was the worst blizzard in thirty-seven years in Columbus. A crew of several hundred, mostly volunteers, were 2 hours and 20 minutes in getting the worst of the snow off the playing field. The field cover in many places was frozen to the ground.

The game turned quickly into a punting duel in which Michigan had the advantage. The Wolverines won, in fact, without making a single first down as against 3 for Ohio State. All told, Michigan punted 24 times during the game and kept Ohio State in the hole. The home team kicked 21 times but had 4 punts blocked. At that Ohio State scored first when a Michigan attempt at a quick kick was blocked. Not long afterward Michigan kicked out of bounds on Ohio State's 4-yard line where it blocked an Ohio punt and scored a safety to make the score 3 to 2.

The only Michigan touchdown came in the last minute of the first half. This time Michigan kicked out of bounds on Ohio State's 9-yard line. On third down, with 47 seconds to go, Michigan took time out. Instructions were to punt when play was resumed but the Ohio State kick was blocked, a Michigan player fell on the ball in the end zone, and the conversion was good.

Regular cleats were of little use during the first half, so Ohio State switched to tennis shoes for the last two quarters. But the Buckeyes could not get going and the score remained 9 to 3. The outcome gave Michigan the title with a 4-1-1 record in the Conference. It also provided food for argument for months as to "what might have been" or "what should have been."

The "Snow Bowl" game was played November 25. Fourteen days later Fesler's resignation as head coach was announced. With others he was attending the Conference meetings in Chicago. In a 400-word statement explaining his action, he gave two reasons for resigning. One was a business opportunity, but the other—and more important one—was that "the tension brought about by the tremendous desire to win football games for Ohio State" was beginning to affect his health. Thus the efforts to reassure him less than a year earlier after his return from the 1950 Rose Bowl trip came to nought.

The Athletic Board at a meeting December 15 adopted a resolution of regret at Fesler's leaving, adding that it "joins thousands of other well-wishers in hoping for you satisfying success and happiness." Chairman Frank Strong at this same meeting named a 6-man committee, with Director Larkins as ex officio chairman, to look for a new coach. It was agreed also in respect to publicity that "no information be divulged to anyone unless official approval has been given through the proper channels."

The screening committee reported at the January 17 board meeting that it had held three meetings, had examined some thirty candidates, and had reduced the list to six but no names were mentioned. To the surprise of everyone, meanwhile, Fesler early in the winter accepted the head coaching job at the University of Minnesota, taking with him Lyal Clark, line coach, and Dick Fisher, backfield coach. In the meantime, too, there was considerable clamor in the press and from other quarters for the reappointment of Paul Brown, former coach, who was head coach of the Cleveland Browns.

The screening committee set up a detailed list of qualifications for the position under personal, professional and University. It was concerned that the appointee "be a man of both intellectual and moral integrity," that he "be suited by temperament, interest and background for productive work with young men, for cooperative advancement of the present sports program of the Department of Physical Education and Athletics, and for professorial membership in the University Faculty," and that he be "by proven capacity and experience, skilled in football technique, in the effective teaching of the game, and in the organization and direction of a staff."

In the minutes there followed a list of forty "active and proposed" candidates, several of them marked "confidential" and including many of the best known names in U.S. college football. At least three well known "pro" coaches were listed, besides many college coaches whose names were household words, and a scattering of high school coaches. Also listed were five from other Big Ten schools and two members of the Ohio State staff.

The committee held personal interviews on January 19, 20, 26 and 27. One of those it interviewed on the 27th was Paul Brown for whom there was a demonstration in front of the Faculty Club on his arrival. On February 3, W. Woodrow "Woody" Hayes, upon whom the choice finally fell, was interviewed. He had coached successfully at Denison and at Miami.

At a board meeting on the morning of February 12 in the office of Vice President Stradley, the screening committee presented a unanimous recommendation for the appointment of Hayes. Director Larkins proposed a 5-year agreement with him at a starting salary of $12,500 with the possibility of a $500-a-year increase until $15,000 was reached. The two recommendations were approved subject to confirmation by the University administration and by the trustees. At a special meeting of the trustees at 4 p.m., Sunday, February 18 the appointment of Hayes was confirmed.

4. THE HAYES PHASE
1951–

What turned out to be the longest football regime at Ohio State except for that of Dr. Wilce began when "Woody" Hayes took over the reins in the late winter of 1951. Like his immediate predecessors, he was under a 1-year contract but with a "gentleman's agreement" that the engagement was for five years with the likelihood of an extension. In mid-1959 Hayes was still going strong after a remarkable record for eight seasons of play that brought three Confernce titles, two Rose Bowl games, one season in which the team was unbeaten in ten games and another with only one loss in ten games.

Hayes, who served in the Navy in World War II, had attracted attention by his success on two other Ohio campuses. He had done well at Denison University, his alma mater, and perhaps even more so at Miami University. Soon after he and Mrs. Hayes came to the campus they were introduced at a Faculty Club dance. He expressed appreciation for the warm welcome, adding pointedly, "We expect to be around quite a while." And so it proved.

As with his predecessors he had the privilege of naming his own assistants. Ernie Godfrey stayed on as did Strobel, but the others who were new to the campus had worked with Hayes elsewhere. He brought in his own system which stressed fundamentals, a stout defense and more of a ground than an aerial attack which steadily chewed out gains and seldom resorted to the spectacular. Hayes, too, was essentially a perfectionist.

His first Ohio State team, that of 1951, had only a fair record. This was perhaps understandable in that the squad had to adjust to the new system. For the season it had a record of 4 wins, 3 losses and 2 ties. In the Conference, it was 2 wins, 2 losses and 2 ties. The ties were with Illinois, 0 to 0, and with Wisconsin, 6 to 6.

The three losses were to Michigan, 7 to 0, to Indiana, 32 to 10, and to Michigan State, 24 to 20, in a thriller. (This was the first game with

Michigan State, the newest member of the Conference, since 1912.) On the winning side, the Buckeyes edged Northwestern, 3 to 0, and defeated Iowa, 47 to 21, Pittsburgh, 16 to 14, and Southern Methodist, 7 to 0.

At the close of the season the Student Senate unanimously recommended to the Athletic Board that 31, the number worn by Vic Janowicz, star halfback, All-American, winner of the Heisman Trophy, be retired in tribute to Janowicz as "the outstanding college football player." This kind of suggestion, understandably sentimental, had come up in connection with other playing numbers. At the November 26 meeting a motion to approve the recommendation was lost. A further motion established this policy: "Resolved, that it is the sense of this Board that we establish a policy of being opposed to the retirement of any athlete's number." This, too, was understandable as a practical matter.

The next two seasons, 1952 and 1953, had identical marks of 6 wins as against 3 losses. In the former season, Ohio State lost to Purdue, 21 to 14, to Pittsburgh, 21 to 14, and to Iowa, 8 to 0. The other games resulted as follows: Ohio State 27, Michigan 7; Ohio State 33, Indiana 13; Ohio State 27, Illinois 7; Ohio State 23, Wisconsin 14; Ohio State 24, Northwestern 21; and Ohio State 35, Washington State 5.

Michigan, Illinois and Michigan State upset Ohio State hopes in the 1953 season. The Wolverines won, 20 to 0, the Illini were on the long end of a 41 to 20 score, and Michigan State again emerged victor, 28 to 13. The scores of the other games were: Ohio State 36, Indiana 12; Ohio State 20, Wisconsin 19; Ohio State 27, Northwestern 13; Ohio State 21, Purdue 6; Ohio State 33, California 19; and Ohio State 12, Pennsylvania 6.

But 1954 was quite another story. It was, indeed, one of the high spots in more than sixty years of football on the campus. The team won all seven of its games in the Conference for an undisputed title. It polished off two non-Big Ten opponents and climaxed the campaign by winning the Rose Bowl game with Southern California as the opponent. Howard "Hopalong" Cassady, its star halfback, was a general choice for All-American and won the Heisman Trophy as the outstanding player of the year.

The team won most of its games impressively. Its ten opponents scored a combined total of only 75 points against a stout defense and no opponent scored more than twice. Offensively the team was a crowd pleaser with Cassady's long sweeps and with enough forward passing to keep opponents off balance. The regular season non-Conference opponents, Pittsburgh and California, were defeated, 26 to 0, and 21 to 13, respectively. The other victories were as follows: Ohio State 21, Michigan

7; Ohio State 28, Indiana 0; Ohio State 40; Illinois 7; Ohio State 31, Wisconsin 14; Ohio State 14, Northwestern 7; Ohio State 28, Purdue 6; and Ohio State 20, Iowa 14. It was the first time the team had played seven Conference games.

Winning the championship and being chosen as the Big Ten's representative in the 1955 Rose Bowl game immediately created problems, especially as to the allocation of tickets. Ohio State's share was 12,800 tickets for general distribution. It was decided that the tickets, with rare exceptions, would be delivered to the recipients upon identification in Los Angeles. Ticket Director George Staten and other staff members went ahead to set up the necessary machinery.

Arrangements were made to take the entire playing squad, the Marching Band, the top University administration, the Athletic Board, the Board of Trustees, and other officials. There were six special trains as well as special plane flights and numerous private planes. Each of three student trains was in charge of faculty personnel, plus a physician and a chaplain. There was also a special band train, one sponsored by the Alumni Association, and one by the Columbus *Dispatch*.

The University declined commercial sponsorship to send the Marching Band. The task of raising funds for this purpose was taken over by the Alumni Association but the response was inadequate. The balance was made up from other University funds.

At its November 22 meeting the Athletic Board authorized this letter of commendation to the squad and members of the football coaching staff:

In recognition of the prestige brought to The Ohio State University, the Athletic Board wishes to commend the members of the football squad, their coaches, trainers, and administrative staff of the Athletic Department for a job well done.

The excellent team performance, exemplary conduct, on and off the field, and the outstanding team spirit has been an inspiration to the student body, the faculty, alumni and friends of The Ohio State University.

Just as the 1950 Michigan game went into the records as the "Snow Bowl" game, the 1955 Rose Bowl game will be remembered as the "Mud Bowl" game. By mid-morning the "Oregon mist" had turned to a steady rain and the playing field, which had not been covered, soon resembled a quagmire. Bad as it was, this condition was made worse by the formations staged by the two bands between halves—an activity protested unsuccessfully by Coach Hayes.

By the *Alumni Monthly* account, the game was played "under the worst conditions of all time, and the first rain in the last 20 years of Rose

Bowl history." Ohio State won without too much difficulty by the score of 20 to 7. Its superiority was shown by the fact that it did not fumble once, made 22 first downs and gained 370 yards net. Despite the rain, Quarterback Dave Leggett handled the ball 80 times without a miscue and completed 6 of 11 pass attempts. Southern California, by contrast, fumbled 7 times and made only 6 first downs.

After missing on its first two opportunities to score, Ohio State cashed in on a Southern California fumble and went 69 yards to register its first touchdown. Three plays later it recovered another Southern California fumble on a pitchout and tallied a second touchdown. The Pacific Coast team made its only touchdown on a fine 86-yard punt return. There was no scoring in the third quarter, but Ohio State added a third tally in the final quarter. The game was a sellout but the crowd of 89,191 was some 11,000 below capacity. The 1954 team thus won its tenth straight victory and was the first Ohio State team to win that many games in a season. Some hailed it as "the greatest ever to represent the University."

In terms of games won and lost the 1955 season was not quite as good as the previous one, but it produced another Conference title for the Buckeyes. This time, under the Conference rule limiting the appearance of any team in the Rose Bowl to once in three years, Ohio State was unable to return to Pasadena. The Ohioans had to wait another two years for this.

In Conference play that fall, Ohio State won 6 and lost none. For the season the record was 7 wins and 2 losses. The two defeats were to opponents from opposite ends of the country. The Buckeyes lost a sluggish game to Stanford (there), 6 to 0. And they dropped a thriller to a fine passing team from Duke, 20 to 14. Against Conference opponents the scores were: Ohio State 17, Michigan 0; Ohio State 20, Indiana 13; Ohio State 27, Illinois 12; Ohio State 26, Wisconsin 16; Ohio State 49, Northwestern 0; Ohio State 20, Iowa 10; and Ohio State 28, Nebraska 20. The climax was the smashing defeat of Michigan on its own field in a game in which the Wolverines were thoroughly outplayed.

The Varsity did not fare quite so well in 1956 when it won 6 and lost 3 and its Conference record was 4 wins and 2 losses. In non-Conference play it trounced Nebraska, 34 to 7, evened matters with Stanford, 32 to 20, but lost to Penn State, 7 to 6. In the Conference, Indiana, Illinois, Wisconsin and Northwestern were defeated by scores of 35 to 14, 26 to 6, 21 to 0, and 6 to 2, respectively. But Michigan won, 19 to 0, and Iowa did likewise, 6 to 0.

But 1957 again was quite a different story. Pre-season guesses had Ohio State as a promising but not an outstanding contender. Some of the doubt deepened when it lost the opener to Texas Christian, 18 to 14. Then things began to happen and the Buckeyes found themselves and went on to win eight straight games, the Conference title, and a return trip to the Rose Bowl where they defeated Oregon, 10 to 7.

En route to Pasadena, although the trip was not assured until it defeated Michigan in the final game, Ohio State disposed of Indiana, 56 to 0, Illinois, 21 to 7, Wisconsin, 16 to 13, Northwestern, 47 to 6, Purdue, 20 to 7, Iowa, 17 to 13, Washington State, 35 to 7, and Michigan, 31 to 14. The Wisconsin, Purdue and Iowa games were even closer than the scores indicated, and until late in the game the annual encounter with Michigan was not as one-sided as the final score might suggest. In five major games, in fact—those with Wisconsin, Purdue, Iowa, Michigan and, finally, with Orgon—the Buckeyes came from behind to win.

The season also brought the Hayes record to new heights. In seven years he produced three Big Ten championship teams and two Rose Bowl teams. In the last four seasons the Buckeyes won 26 of 28 Conference games and until the Iowa defeat in 1956 had a record of 17 straight wins in the league. The 1957 Wisconsin game was probably the turning point of the season. Ohio State overcame a 2-touchdown deficit in the first quarter to win. This seemed to give the squad the extra confidence it needed to go on from there.

For their fourth appearance in the Rose Bowl, the Ohioans were heavy pre-game favorites over Oregon. But the Pacific Coast Conference representative held the heavier Buckeyes at bay. The Ohioans scored first in relatively easy fashion, but after that it was touch and go. Ohio State was favored to win by as much as 20 points but Oregon evidently had not read the predictions. Nationally Ohio State was ranked first (with Auburn) as against seventeenth for Oregon. Ohio State was the undisputed Big Ten champion where Oregon was only co-champion in its league.

But the Western team more than made up in speed, fight and aggressiveness whatever it might have lacked in other ways. Ohio State scored early on a 79-yard march, but after that it was a different story. Oregon scored early in the second quarter, going 80 yards in 10 plays. Late in the third quarter Oregon missed a field goal try on fourth down from the Ohio State 18-yard line. On the next series of plays Ohio State drove to the Oregon 18-yard line early in the final quarter. On fourth down Sutherin kicked a field goal that was nearly blocked. Then it took a couple of "saves" by alert Ohio defenders to hold off Oregon.

One explanation, offered by Sutherin, was that "We just couldn't get ourselvs up for this one." Coach Hayes' comment was: "It's a good team that wins on its bad day and this was ours. Taking nothing from Oregon—they played a fine game—we certainly have played better ball." Before the game, incidentally, he kept insisting that the predictions of a one-sided Ohio State victory were "unrealistic."

To climax the season, apart from the Rose Bowl game, Ohio State was given the No. 1 national ranking by two of the three top groups making this selection annually. The United Press and International News Service made the award, but the Associated Press poll put Ohio State second to Auburn. On two earlier occasions Hayes was among the leaders in the coach-of-the-year balloting, but this time he was ranked first by his fellow coaches. He was the second Ohio State coach to win this distinction, Carroll Widdoes being the first in 1944. And Right Guard Aurelius Thomas was named to three top All-American teams.

Another large contingent followed the team to the bowl game. Some drove and many went by air. But the majority traveled by train—an alumni "official" train, three "Ohio Stater" trains, and a Columbus *Dispatch* train. The Marching Band went on a de luxe train under the sponsorship of the Oldsmobile division of General Motors and paraded in Dallas, Phoenix and San Francisco en route.

The 1958 season was somewhat paradoxical. It began, as noted, with the 10 to 7 victory over Oregon in the Rose Bowl. It ended eleven months later with a 20-to-14 win over a fired-up Michigan team. In the closing moments of the game the home team won after a Michigan fumble on the Ohio State 6-yard line on fourth down with a yard to go.

At the start of the season, Ohio State was generally rated Number One in the nation. Such a rating was not deserved, as Coach Hayes and others pointed out. Ohio State won the opener against Southern Methodist, 23 to 20. Next it won another "squeaker," this time against Washington, 12 to 7. Illinois was then subdued, 19 to 13, on its own field, and Indiana fell, 49 to 8, in the Stadium.

Then came a tie, a defeat and another tie. The first tie was with Wisconsin, 7 to 7. Next a "hot" Northwestern team won, 21 to 0, on its own field. Actually the game was close for three quarters, but Ohio State got behind, gambled and lost. The 14-to-14 tie with Purdue followed. Oddly the only Buckeye scores against Purdue were made by tackle Jim Marshall on a blocked punt and a blocked pass which he turned into touchdowns.

Ohio State was at its season's best against Iowa. Up to this point the Iowans were unbeaten, but the invading Ohioans won, 38 to 28, sparked by touchdown runs of 37 yards by Clark and 71 yards by White.

Despite the fact that Ohio State's string of wins was stopped at 13 (by Northwestern), and despite the over-all record of 6 wins, 1 loss, and 2 ties (4 wins, 2 ties and 1 loss in the Conference), the season will long be remembered—and debated. It was featured by new successive attendance records (83,481 at the Purdue game) and during the early games by a running controversy between Coach Hayes and game officials over what he called lax officiating. Total at-home attendance, a record for six games, was 499,119. Three Ohio State players made various All-American teams—Houston at end, White at fullback, and Marshall at tackle. White set Conference records of 218 "carries" in all games, a total of 859 yards gained, and was not thrown once for a loss. Against Iowe he carried the ball on 11 of 14 straight plays.

To sum up, in forty-seven years as a member of the Western Conference, Ohio State had become a consistent football power. In that time its teams had been to the Rose Bowl four times and won or shared ten Conference championships. In 380 games against all opponents from 1913 through 1958 it won 254, lost 102 and tied 24 for a percentage of .713. In Conference play over that period, it won 155 games, lost 74 and tied 15 for a percentage of .677.

The record by coaches was as follows:

	ALL GAMES			CONFERENCE GAMES		
Coach	Won	Lost	Tied	Won	Lost	Tied
Wilce	78	33	9	37	26	3
Willaman	26	10	5	14	8	4
Schmidt	39	16	1	30	9	1
Brown	18	8	1	9	6	0
Widdoes	15	2	0	11	2	0
Bixler	4	3	2	2	3	1
Fesler	21	13	2	13	10	2
Hayes	53	17	4	39	10	4

For the twenty-six seasons through 1957, Ohio State stood seventh among the major teams in the country as follows:

Team	Won	Lost	Tied	Percentage
Notre Dame	184	49	14	.789
Tennessee	191	56	12	.773
Oklahoma	186	55	17	.772
Duke	175	60	13	.749
Michigan State	158	54	12	.745
Army	167	59	14	.739
Ohio State	156	59	12	.726
Michigan	157	65	7	.707
Princeton	133	65	11	.671

So many All-American teams are chosen each year by various agencies —newspaper and other—it is difficult to keep track. The list generally recognized as authoritative is that compiled for the Official N.C.A.A. Football Guide. By this reckoning, Ohio State has had 37 men so honored. Two of them, "Chic" Harley and Wes Fesler, each won this honor three times. By positions, the list follows:

Ends

Charles Bolen	1917
Wesley Fesler	1928, 1929, 1930
Merle Wendt	1935
Esco Sarkkinen	1939
Robert Shaw	1942
Jack Dugger	1944
Dean Dugger	1954
James Houston	1958

Guards

Iolas Huffman	1920
Edwin Hess	1925, 1926
Joseph Gailus	1932
Regis Monahan	1934
Inwood Smith	1935
Gust Zarnas	1937
Lindell Houston	1942
William Hackett	1944
Warren Amling	1945
Robert Momsen	1950
Mike Takacs	1952
James Parker	1955, 1956
Aurelius Thomas	1957

Tackles

Robert Karch	1916
Iolas Huffman	1921
Leo Raskowski	1927
Charles Csuri	1942
William Willis	1944
Warren Amling	1946

Centers

Gomer Jones	1935
Robert McCullough	1950

Backs

Chas. Harley	1916, 1917, 1919
Gaylord Stinchomb	1920
Martin Karow	1926
Donald Scott	1939
Leslie Horvath	1944
Victor Janowicz	1950
Howard Cassady	1954, 1955
Robert White	1958

Similarly, three Ohio Staters, Harley, Fesler and former Coach Jack Wilce, have been elected to the College Football Hall of Fame. Fesler and Wilce were chosen in 1954 and Harley in 1951, one of the first group so honored.

XII
OTHER SPORTS

BESIDES football, a dozen or more other sports—as well as the extensive and important intramural program—have been part of the intercollegiate athletics picture at Ohio State over the years. Only two sports have been self-sustaining and they, in fact, have made it possible to carry on the others. These are football and basketball, with the former paying most of the athletic freight.

Because of space limitations and because a detailed record of the thousands of contests involved would be outside the scope of this account, only a summary can be given of the other sports in the Varsity program. The pattern followed is to give the essential facts in each case with certain highlights of particular sports.

Before going into Ohio State's showing in the Big Ten a brief summary of its part in N.C.A.A. competition is in order. National intercollegiate championships in various individual sports go back a good many decades, in tennis, for example, to 1883. Drawing these various activities together under the National Collegiate Athletic Association is an accomplishment of more recent years. As of 1957 the N.C.A.A. conducted or recognized annual championship meets in thirteen sports: baseball, basketball, boxing, cross country, fencing, golf, gymnastics, ice hockey, skiing, swimming, tennis, track and field, and wrestling.

Considering that Ohio State has never sponsored three of these—boxing, ice hockey and skiing—and has rarely entered teams or individual athletes in several others such as cross country, fencing, gymnastics and tennis—its over-all showing has been among the best in the country. Specifically, according to the 1959 N.C.A.A. record book, Ohio State was in sixth place in total team championships with 13. Southern California was first with 26 (20 in track), Yale was second with 25 (21 in golf), Oklahoma State was third with 23 (20 in wrestling), Michigan fourth with 19, and Illinois fifth with 15.

Ten of Ohio State's team titles were in swimming, as will be described below, with one each in fencing, golf, and track. Illinois similarly won 8 team titles in gymnastics, 5 in track and 2 in fencing.

But Ohio State, as 1959 began, was first in individual titles with 131, followed by Michigan with 128, Illinois with 85, Southern California with 84 and Yale with 82. The Ohio State individual titles were divided as follows: swimming, 87; track, 36; golf, 3; wrestling, 2; gymnastics, 2; and fencing, 1.

BASEBALL

Baseball, probably the oldest sport on the campus, has had its ups and downs over the years but has made its best over-all showing since 1951 when Marty Karow, a former Varsity star, returned to take charge. Between 1913 and 1959 the Varsity had six coaches, one of whom served two "hitches" in that post. They were L. W. St. John, 1913-1928; Wayne Wright, an alumnus, 1929-1932; Floyd Stahl, 1933-1938 and 1947-1950; Fritz Mackey, also an alumnus, 1939-1944; Lowell Wrigley, another alumnus, 1945-1946; and Karow, 1951 to date.

For a good many years, before as well as after Ohio State's admission to the Big Ten, Varsity games were played in the northwest corner of Ohio Field. This site was inadequate, both as to seating facilities which were limited, and as to playing conditions since the outfield encroached on the practice football field in one direction and the running track in the other. For several seasons another diamond was used along W. Eleventh Ave. where, in the late 'Fifties, the new men's dormitory group was built. This, too, was inadequate since the outfield was uneven and only temporary bleachers could be used.

With the building of the Stadium the baseball scene also shifted to that section of the campus. For some years the Varsity diamond lay to the northeast of that structure and later to a corresponding site just northwest of the big horseshoe. Still later a new diamond was built in the low land to the southwest of the Stadium and it is in this area that a permanent baseball plant is projected. As of 1959 its construction was postponed until a more favorable time.

Of the head coaches listed above, a number had professional baseball experience. St. John, for example, had been an umpire at one time (under the assumed name of "Mr. Jacks" in summers while he was athletic director and coach at Wooster College); Wright in the American League and American Association; and Wrigley and Karow in minor league ball.

The over-all record for the 47-year period covered was spotty but the Buckeyes generally finished in the upper half of the Big Ten more often than not. But they were Conference champions only four times—in 1917, 1943, 1951 and 1955. (They missed one in 1924 because of a tie game, although in games won and lost they were tied with Michigan with an 8-2 record.) Including ties for position, they finished second in the Conference 7 times, third 8 times, fourth 5, fifth 5, sixth 5, seventh 3, eighth 3, ninth 3, and tenth 4 times. For the 47-year span, Conference games only, the record showed 252 games won to 218 lost for a percentage of .536.

There were games, of course, with many other teams—pre-Conference season games with Ohio college teams, games with teams from outside conferences or even from Japan. There was one notable game with Notre Dame, for example, on the field northeast of the Stadium. At the end of the top half of the ninth inning the visitors were ahead 9 to 0. But the home team got a rally going and, incredibly, scored 10 runs to win in the bottom of the ninth.

In the early 'Twenties the practice was begun of sending the squad south during the Spring vacation to hasten its preparation for the regular season by a series of a half dozen or so games with Southern teams such as Georgia, Georgia Tech, Oglethorpe or with teams en route such as Maryville or Eastern Kentucky. This practice was dropped during the depression and war years but was revived after World War II. In more recent years it has taken the form of a kind of round-robin tournament in Texas or Florida. To save time the later squads have flown to the scene where the earlier ones went by train.

The spring trip was justified on the ground a) that it speeded up the spring training and gave the squad needed competition; b) many other college teams, including those in the Western Conference did it; and c) not to do so would retard the training and put the squad at a disadvantage with opponents on the regular schedule. But there was some doubt in the Athletic Board on this. In the Spring of 1928 a modified pre-season program was approved "in lieu of the usual southern trip." In 1929, similarly, a spring training trip of a week in Kentucky was arranged.

On two occasions in late years Ohio State has figured in the N.C.A.A. playoffs for the national title. By rule the team winning the Big Ten championship qualifies automatically for these playoffs in District 4. In 1951 the Buckeyes got to the "nationals" at Omaha but were eliminated by losing to Oklahoma and to Texas A.&.M. In 1955 the team qualified again but lost two out of three to Western Michigan in the district finals.

The 1955 squad, however, had a reward such as no other Buckeye baseball team ever enjoyed. Besides winning the Conference title and getting into the N.C.A.A. competition, it was flown to Japan for a series of games with U. S. service and Japanese teams.

In recapitulation, the over-all Conference baseball record, 1913 through 1959, was:

Coach	Year	Won	Lost	Coach	Year	Won	Lost
St. John	1913	0	4	Mackey	1939	2	10
	14	2	3		40	3	5
	15	4	4		41	5	7
	16	4	2		42	7	5
	17	6	1		43	6	1
	18	3	2		44	5	5
	19	2	2			—	—
	20	8	2			28	33
	21	6	4				
	22	3	4	Wrigley	1945	4	5
	23	8	2		46	3	8
	24	8	2			—	—
	25	8	4			7	13
	26	3	5				
	27	6	6	Stahl	1947	9	5
	28	6	5		48	9	5
		—	—		49	6	6
		77	52		50	6	5
						—	—
						30	21
Wright	1929	4	6				
	30	4	4				
	31	4	3	Karow	1951	10	2
	32	3	6		52	7	7
		—	—		53	9	4
		15	19		54	10	5
					55	9	3
Stahl	1933	0	7		56	9	3
	34	5	6		57	4	5
	35	7	3		58	9	6
	36	1	10		59	5	10
	37	5	4			—	—
	38	5	5			72	45
		—	—				
		23	35				

Like other leading college baseball teams, Ohio State has had a fair quota of players who have gone into professional baseball. The number has tended to increase in recent years. One of the later ones was Fred Taylor, '50, onetime first baseman, who in 1958 became Varsity basketball coach. He was for several years the property of Washington, played in the minors and had two trials with the Senators but finally gave up "pro" baseball to go into college coaching. Wes Fesler, in his time a 3-sport star, also had a brief fling at "pro" baseball but gave it up for coaching.

Several of the more recent players were so-called "bonus babies." Perhaps the most outstanding of these was Frank "Chico" Howard, basketball and baseball star from 1956 to 1958. Howard was signed at the end of the '58 basketball season by the Los Angeles Dodgers to a fat bonus. A teammate on the '57 squad who also went into "pro" baseball was Pitcher Galen Cisco.

The Big Ten Records Book (1957–1958) credits a number of records to Ohio State players. Catcher Jack Gannon, of the 1952 team, in a game May 10 that year against Wisconsin scored the most runs by one player —5. The year before on May 5, Leftfielder Elbert Gutzweiler similarly had the most runs batted in—8. Also in 1951, on May 25, Second Baseman Bill Zimmer had the distinction in a game against Michigan of tieing the Conference record for the most assists—8.

Pete Perini, star pitcher on the 1948 team, had a double achievement —he pitched the most innings—62—and he scored the most victories—6. He was one of four Ohio State pitchers who led the league—he in 1948 with a 6-1 record, Ed Bohnslav in 1951 with 3-0, Paul Ebert in 1952 with 5-0, and Cisco in 1956 also with 5-0. In 1951, Third Baseman Bob Montebello led the Conference in hitting with a mark of .467. Ebert declined a "pro" baseball career to go into medicine.

In 1924, Frank D. Potter, w'97, of New York, in his day a Varsity player, established the Potter Runmaker Cup. This trophy is awarded annually to the player who makes the best record in producing runs during a season. His name is engraved on a permanent trophy and he gets a replica as a personal award.

Track and Cross Country

Along with baseball and perhaps tennis, track and field sports are the oldest competitive athletics on the campus. But with occasional exceptions, as in baseball and basketball, the over-all record has been good rather than outstanding although it has been studded with many brilliant individual performers. The number of team championships has been comparatively small. There have been many individual stars, including several world champions, and between 1912 and 1956 Ohio State provided eleven members of U. S. Olympic track and field teams, and half a dozen others who came close.

Track and field sports, except on a few occcasions, have never commanded the attention in Ohio that they have in some other states. There are also so many colleges and universities in the state that the available talent has been spread rather thin so that at times even the smaller colleges have had outstanding teams or individual stars, e.g., Oberlin and Baldwin-Wallace. In the case of Ohio State, it was not until 1957 with the dedication of the French Field House that it had indoor track facilities worthy the name.

The indoor running track in the old Armory was never adequate and with the removal of men's physical education to the new building in 1931 facilities for indoor practice were virtually non-existent or at an absolute minimum. As noted elsewhere, for some years a makeshift track was used underneath the west seat bank of the Stadium, with canvas to cut off the wintry winds. For a time also other "ersatz" facilities were tried in a building at the State Fair Grounds but these, too, were found wanting.

During all the years Ohio State has been in the Big Ten it has had only three head track coaches. This does not include John R. Richards, who was athletic director and football and track coach during the first year Ohio State was in the Conference but who resigned before the indoor track season began. To succeed him, Frank R. Castleman came in the winter of 1913 from the University of Colorado and coached until 1931. He had been a star athlete at Colgate and an intercollegiate dash and hurdle champion in his undergraduate days.

He was followed by Laurence N. Snyder, who has been coach ever since except for the period 1943-45 when he was in the Navy during World War II and George Haney substituted for him. Snyder had been a star athlete under Castleman and for several years was assistant coach before taking over the reins. Like Castleman, he was an outstanding hurdler in his time.

Ohio State has never had as strong a tradition in track as some other Conference schools, notably Michigan, Illinois and Chicago, have had at one time or another. In its earlier years in the Conference, therefore, the record was somewhat spotty. But in more recent years, while the team championships have been few, the record has shown more second, third and fourth team places in the Big Ten title meets, both indoors and outdoors.

Three times the Buckeyes have won the indoor crown—in 1942, in 1948 and in 1950—and in 1949 they tied with Wisconsin for first. Five times they have been runners-up, including 1957 and 1958. Both of these squads won the indoor as well as the outdoor crowns. Outdoors the Ohioans were runners-up in 1929, 1932, 1936 (tie), 1946, 1949, and 1957. The only cross country championship was won by the 1923 team. For the rest, indoors Ohio State has finished third twice, fourth 10 times, and fifth 5 times.

Yet some of the best individual marks in the Big Ten Records Book are to the credit of Ohio State athletes. Some of these, like those made by the incomparable Jesse Owens in the mid-'Thirties, have stood for years while others, such as those hung up by the matchless Glenn Davis, are as recent as the 1958 spring campaign. Four Ohio State athletes share in "best winning performances of Big Ten athletes as undergraduates" indoors as listed in the 1957-58 Big Ten Records Book as follows:

70-yd. high hurdles	Jack Keller	8.4 sec.	2/12/32 at Indiana
	Lloyd Duff	8.4 sec.	3/13/48 Conf. Meet
70-yd. low hurdles	Jesse Owens	7.6 sec.	2/8/35 at Indiana
High jump	Mel Walker	6' 9¾"	3/20/37 Butler Relays
Broad jump	Jesse Owens	25' 9"	2/23/35 Natl. A.A.U.
	Jesse Owens	25' 2"	1935 at Illinois

Five Buckeye athletes and a relay quartet are credited with eight marks in outdoor competition as follows:

220-yd. dash (one turn)			
	Jesse Owens	20.3 sec.	5/25/35 Conf. meet
880-yd. run (four turns)			
	Mal Whitfield	1 min. 50.3 sec.	6/19/49 N.C.A.A.
220-yd. low hurdles			
	Jesse Owens	22.6 sec.	5/25/35 Conf. meet
220-yd. low hurdles (one turn)			
	Jack Keller	23.5 sec.	5/20/33 Conf. meet
High jump			
	Mel Walker	6' 10¼"	8/12/37 Malmo, Sweden
	Dave Albritton	6' 9¾"	6/12/36 Olympic trials
Broad jump			
	Jesse Owens	26' 8¼"	5/25/35 Conf. meet
880-relay	Owen, Collins, Wright, Hammond	1 min. 25.9 sec.	4/25/42 Drake Relays

Of the fourteen indoor and outdoor marks listed above, six are to the credit of Jesse Owens, by common consent one of the greatest track men the world has ever known. Owens starred on the 1933, 1934 and 1935 Ohio State teams and on the 1936 U. S. Olympic team where he made history by winning four gold medals and by the further fact that

Hitler, who was present in the Berlin stadium, refused to shake hands with him. Owens, a Cleveland high school product, set Ohio interscholastic marks before entering Ohio State.

On May 25, 1935 at Ann Arbor, Mich., in the Big Ten outdoor championships of that year, Owens had one of the greatest days any track athlete ever had. In the space of a little more than two hours he set three world records and tied a fourth. (Some wondered facetiously what was wrong with him in the fourth event—the 100 yd. dash—in which he merely equaled the world record of 9.4 sec.) It is a tribute to his remarkable prowess that the other three marks stood for more than two decades. The track that day was just right, the weather conditions perfect and Owens was at the peak of his form.

Earlier, for special individual achievements during that season, the Athletic Board on June 4, 1931 authorized the purchase of gold shoes for the following track men: Rupert R. Beetham, Jesse Fazekas, Jack A. Keller, Paul F. Strother and Lloyd S. Wise. All but Keller were members of the sprint medley relay team which set a world record of 3 min., 27.6 sec. Keller had set a new Ohio State and unofficial world record of 14.3 sec. in the high hurdles.

The winter and spring of 1935 were the golden age of Ohio State track accomplishments up to that time because of the feats of Owens and a brilliant supporting cast. In recognition of their achievements the board on June 7, 1935 authorized these special awards for Owens: a gold track shoe charm with a diamond in the toe of the shoe; a silvered shoe trophy made with a pair of shoes worn by Owens in the Big Ten championships when he broke three world records and tied a fourth. Additional gold track shoe awards were authorized to: Charles J. Beetham, in the 880-yd. run; George V. Neal, shot put; Dominic P. Renda, mile run; and John W. Wonsowitz, pole vault. In 1936 a gold shoe with diamond chip was authorized for Dave Albritton, high jumper, and gold shoes for Paul E. Benner, 2-mile run; Thomas E. Sexton, mile run; and Mel Walker, high jumper.

Although Ohio State has had eleven track Olympians—two each in 1912, 1924, 1932, 1936 and 1952 and one each in the 1948 and 1956 games—only one other Buckeye has paralleled Owens' performance. This was Glenn Davis, the "one-man gang" of the 1957 and 1958 track teams. In the 1956 Olympics at Melbourne, Davis set an Olympic mark of 50.1 sec. in the 400-meter low hurdles, with an earlier mark of 49.5 at Los Angeles. In the spring of 1958 he hung up a mark of 51.6 for the 440-yd. low hurdles. And in the Big Ten championships that spring he set a new world mark of 45.7 sec. for the 440-yd. dash and coasted to the finish because no one was close. Like Owens, Davis was an Ohio high school product—from Barberton.

For his world record in the 440-yd. dash the board awarded him a gold track shoe with a diamond. At the close of the 1958 season the board also granted gold track shoes to Jim Marshall, shot putter, for a new Varsity mark of 54' 6", another to him for a new discus mark of 172' 1", and one to Stan Lyons for raising the pole vault record to 14' 9".

Davis climaxed his earlier achievements by a series of remarkable performances as a member of a U.S. team which competed successively against the Russians in Moscow, the Poles in Warsaw, the Hungarians and Czechs in Budapest, and the Greeks in Athens in the summer of 1958. In the space of fourteen days he won nine out of ten races against Red Europe's best in his events, and set another world record. At Budapest he set a new world mark of 49.2 sec. in the 400-meter low hurdles. George Eastment, coach of the U.S. team, declared as the tour neared its end that "Davis is the most versatile runner alive today." In Moscow Davis won the 400-meter run and the 400-meter hurdles and ran on the winning U.S. 400-meter and 1600-meter relay teams. Larry Snyder was one of the other U.S. coaches on the trip. At Budapest after his new world mark the crowd of 40,000 gave Davis an ovation, demanding that he run an honor lap.

With one quarter of eligibility left, Davis climaxed his career by winning the Amateur Athletic Union's James E. Sullivan Memorial Trophy. The award, announced December 31, 1958, is given annually to "the amateur athlete who, by performance, example and good influence did the most to advance the cause of good sportsmanship during the year." In the nationwide voting for the honor Davis won by a narrow margin over Rafer Johnson, world decathlon record holder. Davis was the second Ohio State track man to win this top award. Mal Whitfield, also an Olympic champion, won it in 1954.

As indicated, Ohio State has had eleven men in the track events of seven Olympiads as follows:

1912 (Stockholm)—Clement C. Cooke, sprinter, and Garnett Wikoff, middle distance runner.

1924 (Paris)—Russell Payne, 3000-meter steeplechase, and George P. Guthrie, high hurdler.

1932 (Los Angeles)—George Simpson, sprinter, and Jack Keller, low hurdler.

1936 (Berlin)—Jesse Owens, sprinter and broad jumper, and Dave Albritton, high jumper.

1948 (London)—Mal Whitfield, 800-meter run.

1952 (Helsinki)—Mal Whitfield, 800-meter run, and Gene Cole, 400-meter dash and 1600-meter relay

1956 (Melbourne)—Glenn Davis, 400-meter hurdles.

Their individual performances are summarized as follows:

1912—Cooke reached the semi-finals of his dash event, but Wikoff developed a lameness on ship board on the way over and was unable to finish.

1924—Guthrie finished third in the 110-meter hurdles, but Payne did not place in the steeplechase.

1932—Simpson, kept out of the 1928 games by a pulled tendon, got a measure of reward when he placed second in the 200-meter dash in 1932. Keller was fourth in the 110-meter hurdles.

1936—Owens was the outstanding star of the track and field games, winning four gold medals. He set a world record of 10.2 sec. for the 100-meter dash in the trial heats but this was disallowed because of a helping wind, and he won the final in 10.3 sec. In the 200-meter trials he set a record of 21.1 sec. and broke that in the finals with a mark of 20.7 sec. In the broad jump he made his best mark on his third leap with 26' 5½". He capped this by running the first leg for the U.S. in the 400-meter relay in which a new mark of 38 sec. was set. Albritton, his teammate, was second in the high jump.

On his return to this country Owens had a tumultuous reception in New York and in Columbus. He was the first American to win four gold medals in the Olympics and only the third athlete of any nation to do so in the entire history of the games.

1948—Whitfield set a new record of 1 min. 49.2 sec. in the 800-meter run, finished third in the 400-meter dash, and anchored the winning U.S. 1600-meter relay team.

1952—As he had at London four years earlier, Whitfield again won the 800-meter run and was sixth in the 400-meter dash. He and Cole, his teammate, were on the U.S. 1600-meter relay team which placed second in that event.

1956—Davis set a new Olympic mark of 50.1 sec. in the 400-meter hurdles.

Across the years Ohio State had a number of other star track men who just missed qualifying for the U.S. Olympic squad or who suffered last minute injuries which kept them out of the final tryouts. Among these were Snyder, in the high hurdles, in 1924; Black, high hurdler,

1932; Walker, a high jumper, and Charlie Beetham, who had set a new U.S. mark in the 880-yd. run, in 1936; Lloyd Duff, a pole vaulter, who was second in the U.S. decathlon, in 1948; Len Truex, a miler, in the 1500-meter, in 1952; and Jerry Welbourn, pole vaulter. One man, for example, placed fourth in three events in the U.S. final tryouts when a third in any one of them would have qualified him.

As related, it remained for Davis in the 1958 season to bring back memories of Jesse Owens' exploits of two decades earlier. Davis was a one-man track team himself in dual and Conference meets. Besides setting the earlier world mark of 49.5 sec. for the 400-meter hurdles at Los Angeles, he capped his intercollegiate career by setting two more world marks in the spring of 1958. In the N.C.A.A. meet, as noted, he set a new record of 45.7 sec. for the 440-yd. dash and another of 49.9 for the national A.A.U 440-yd. low hurdle event. As described, he was the star member of the 44-man U.S. team which competed behind the Iron Curtain in the summer of 1958. In the Quantico Relays in April, 1958 he won five gold medals. All told, it was said he won more than 300 medals.

To turn to the N.C.A.A. track championships, which began in 1921, Ohio State won only one team title, in 1929, and was runner-up 6 times—in 1928, 1931, 1932, 1935, 1936 and 1942—but over the years it was second only to Southern California with individual champions. In this respect the standing, according to the 1957 N.C.A.A. record book was U.S.C., 53; Ohio State, 34; Illinois, 31; and Michigan and Stanford, each 26.

Jesse Owens, after more than two decades, still led all the others with eight titles—four each in 1935 and 1936. Bob Wright, hurdler, was tied with seven others with four titles, in the high and low hurdles in 1941 and 1942, and Dave Albritton was one of a score with three titles—the high jump crown in 1936, 1937 and 1938.

By events, the N.C.A.A. champions from Ohio State over the years were:

100-yd. dash—George Simpson, 1929; Jesse Owens, 1935, 1936.

220-yd. dash—Simpson, 1929, 1930; Jesse Owens, 1935, 1936.

440-yd. dash—Glenn Davis, 1958.

880-yd. run—Charlie Beetham, 1936; Bill Clifford, 1947; Mal Whitfield, 1948, 1949.

120-yd. high hurdles—George Guthrie, 1926; Dick Rockaway, 1929; Jack Keller, 1931; Bob Wright, 1941, 1942.

220-yd. low hurdles—Keller, 1931, 1932; Owens, 1935, 1936; Wright, 1941, 1942.

400-meter hurdles—Davis, 1958.
Pole vault—John Schmidt, 1944 (tie).
Broad jump—Gaylord Stinchcomb, 1921; Owens, 1935, 1936; Dallas Dupre, 1942; Ralph Tyler, 1944.
High jump—Dave Albritton and Mel Walker, 1936 (tie); Albritton, 1937 and 1938 (tie).
Hammer throw—Ray Bunker, 1925.
Discus throw—Pete Rasmus, 1929.

The Ohio Relays were added to the athletic program in 1924 and were a feature of the early spring track season for some years until the depression caused their abandonment. They were revived in 1952. A proposal for the inauguration of the Relays, similar to the Penn, Drake and Kansas Relays, was approved by the Athletic Board on December 15, 1923. The first Ohio Relays were held April 19, 1924. After World War II a series of quadrangular meets was arranged and after several years this was expanded into a revival of the Relays.

Although cross country running had been part of the Varsity program for several years it was not until later that it was made a separate sport. At its April 3, 1913 meeting the board set up a committee to "consider the matter of granting a cross country 'O.' " Some question arose later as to the place of cross country. At a board meeting June 19, 1915 a motion was carried "that the faculty make investigation of the hygenic [sic] effects of cross-country." Except for 1918, 1935 and 1937 there has been a Varsity cross country team regularly since 1912. Only the 1923 squad, however, won a Big Ten title.

BASKETBALL

Of all of the major sports other than football, basketball over the years has had the greatest crowd appeal in the modern (post-1912) period at Ohio State. Soon after the close of World War I the gymnasium was outgrown and Varsity games were moved, as noted elsewhere, to the Coliseum at the State Fair Grounds. With the postwar bulge in enrollment, the Coliseum was outgrown and this need was met finally with the shift to the new St. John Arena during the 1956-57 season.

Since its admission to the Big Ten, Ohio State has had only six head basketball coaches, including Fred Taylor, the latest, who was named in June, 1958. Director St. John was coach during the eight formative seasons from 1913 to 1920, inclusive. He was succeeded for two seasons by George M. "Red" Trautman, who had been assistant coach. In 1923

Harold G. "Oley" Olsen came from Ripon College to concentrate on basketball coaching and to help with football and, for a time, golf. His 24-year tenure ended at the close of the 1946 season when he went into "pro" basketball. For four years, from 1947 through 1950, W. H. H. "Tippy" Dye, who had played under Olsen, was head coach. Floyd Stahl, who from 1933 through 1938 had been baseball coach, returned to the campus to take charge of the cagers for eight seasons. At the close of the '58 season he asked to be relieved of the coaching chores to devote his time to his other duties as assistant athletic director. After a canvass of possibilities, the choice fell upon Taylor who had played under Stahl and was chief scout and freshman coach.

Over the 47-year period from 1913 through 1959, Ohio State basketball has had moderate success. In that time its teams played 570 Conference games of which they won 274 and lost 296 for an over-all percentage of .481. In all games for those years the record was 505 won as against 425 lost for a percentage of .543.

In Conference play there were six championship teams—those of 1925, 1933 (tied with Northwestern), 1939, 1944, 1946, and 1950. In the nearly half century span, Buckeye cage teams finished or tied for second, twice; third, 5 times; fourth, 5; fifth, 5; sixth, 6; seventh, 6; eighth, 3; ninth, 7; and tenth, twice.

The contrast with later day conditions is afforded by a brief look at Ohio State's first Big Ten cage team. It made a trip during the 1912 holiday season in the course of which it met six amateur teams and defeated five of them. The jaunt began at Toledo and wound up at Pittsburgh. The Buckeyes began their first Western Conference season by losing to Northwestern, 30 to 22, before 1800 spectators. On their first Conference road trip they defeated Indiana at Bloomington, 34 to 22. They lost the next game to Wisconsin at Madison, 22 to 11. This was said to be the longest trip ever taken up to that time by any Ohio State team.

When it came to making up the 1913-14 cage schedule, Ohio State had some difficulty in completing its schedule. It was able to get only six Conference games. Prof. T. E. French, the Conference representative, said he would fight for enforcement of the rotation rule so as to get more games.

The 1925 team, captained by George D. "Jake" Cameron, was a scrappy one. By later standards it was a small team. Johnny Miner, the first of the great Buckeye basketball players, was undersized but he more than made up for it by his speed and a sharp shooting eye. In his day basketball scoring was still relatively low so that the records made then have long since been erased by the faster, heavier scoring play of the later period. But the 1925 team won all of its 12-game Conference schedule and all but 2 of 16 for the season for its first Conference title.

It was not until 1932-33 that Ohio State again had a championship contender on the hard court. That season the team tied with Northwestern for the title. It won 10 of its 12 Conference games and 17 out of 20 for the season. Then the Buckeye basketball fortunes ebbed again.

In 1937-38 the Ohioans tied for third place and the next year rose once more to championship heights, winning 12 in the Conference, 16 out of 23 for the season, and going all the way to the finals of the N.C.A.A. tournament where they lost to Oregon for the national title. This season marked the climax of the playing career of Jimmy Hull, one of the all-time "greats" in Western Conference basketball if not nationally. The next year the Buckeyes finished an undisputed third but the following season, 1940-41, they tied with two other teams for third.

Apart from the usual award of gold basketballs to a championship cage team, the Athletic Board went farther March 1, 1939 with an "award for spirit" to the "present outstanding basketball squad" captained by Hull. Its resolution, drafted by J. L. Morrill, read:

> Desiring to express by some special mark of appreciation the universal sentiment of all loyal to the Ohio State University, the Athletic Board hereby grants and bestows upon the captain and members of the 1939 basketball team its first formal "Award for Spirit" in the history of the University.
>
> Called upon to carry the colors of the University in intercollegiate competition, the members of the basketball team have responded not only with highly creditable performance, but more especially with an individual loyalty and an indomitable team spirit which will set high example for all accountable for the good name and fame of the University . . .

For three seasons, beginning in 1943-44, the Buckeyes were outstanding in the Conference, winning the title in '44 and '46 and narrowly missing it in '45. In 1943-44 the Ohioans won 10 of 12 in the Conference and 14 of 21 for the season. The corresponding record for the following year was 10 out of 12 in the Big Ten and 15 out of 20 for the season. For 1945-46 the Conference record was 10 out of 12 and 16 out of 21 for the season.

A somewhat unexpected development in the early fall of 1946 was the resignation of Coach Olsen. He had been a valued member of the staff since 1923 and some of his friends had hoped that he might be made athletic director to succeed Director St. John upon the latter's retirement. Olsen resigned as of September 30 and the board accepted the resignation "with regret and with appreciation of his long services to the University." Olsen resigned to become coach of a Chicago professional basketball team.

In his place the board appointed "Tippy" Dye, who had starred under Olsen and who not long before had returned as assistant coach. Another appointee at the time was Floyd S. Stahl, a former member of the staff, who had gone to Harvard. Stahl was named head baseball coach. Four years later he succeeded Dye in basketball when the latter went to the University of Washington. Fred Taylor, an alumnus, became head coach with the 1958-59 season.

In 1946-47 and 1947-48 the best Varsity could do were ties for sixth place in the Conference followed by a tie for fourth in 1948-49. But 1949-50 was another championship year and the Buckeyes won all but one of their 12 Conference games and 22 of 26 for the season. Since then the best they have done were ties for third in both the 1955-56 and 1956-57 seasons.

Unlike football, intercollegiate basketball has not had a recognized All-American team until recent years. The one generally acccepted is that sponsored by the Helms Foundation. For example, Johnny Miner, star of the first championship team in '25, and Jimmy Hull, star of the championship '39 squad which he captained, played too early for this particular recognition. Four later players, however, were accorded this honor. They were Dick Schnittker, forward, in 1950; Paul Ebert, center, in 1954; Robin Freeman, guard, in 1956; and Frank Howard, forward, in 1957.

Of these, Schnittker went into "pro" basketball and Howard into professional baseball. But Hull still has one distinction apart from the others: he is the only Varsity basketball player whose name is perpetuated in the campus grove of buckeye trees dedicated to outstanding athletes of the past.

The Big Ten Records Book (1957-1958) is full of records made by Ohio State basketball players. Most of these, although labeled as "all-time records," have been made in recent years because of the more open style of play and the resulting heavier scoring. Most of these credited to Ohio State men were made by the players listed above. In the 1956 season, for example, the incomparable Robin Freeman tallied 46 points in a game against Michigan State and 43 in one with Illinois. That season also he averaged 32.5 points per game in the Conference. In each of two games against Michigan State that season he sank 16 field goals, and for the season had 163 field goals in 14 games.

In 1950, Schnittker set a Varsity record by making good on 91 free throw attempts in 12 Conference games. Based on 100 or more attempts, John Miller, of the 1950 team, set a similar record in field goal attempts by "canning" 93 out of 193 for a percentage of .482. Schnittker and Ebert, in the 1950 and 1954 seasons, respectively, each sank 13 free throw attempts without a miss. And for the season, Max Gecowets, of the 1942 team, made 33 of 38 free throw attempts for an .868 percentage.

Teamwise over the years, Ohio State made a pretty fair all-around showing in scoring. The 1956 squad, for example, amassed 1192 points in 14 games for an average of 85.1 points. That squad also made 376 free throws during the season for an average of 26.9 per game, and had one of the best Big Ten team free throw shooting averages that season with a percentage of .739.

The 1957 team had two similar marks: in a game with Wisconsin it made good on 26 out of 49 field goal attempts for a .531 percentage, and ended the season with a percentage of .431 with 418 goals from 969 attempts. For individual scoring, Ebert had a total of 1027 for the 1952-53-54 seasons, the second highest in Conference history. Schlundt, of Indiana, had 1451 points, but these were made over a stretch of four seasons to three for Ebert.

In individual scoring in the Conference, Hull was first in 1939 with 169 points; and Freeman led in 1957 with 455 points. Hull's record was made in a 12-game Conference schedule, and Freeman's in 14 games. Hull, likewise in 1939, tallied the most free throws in Conference play with 66. Dick Fisher led in 1942 with 62, Ebert in 1953 with 145, and Freeman in 1956 with 163.

Ohio State players have led the Conference twice in free throws, Schnittker in 1950 with 91, and Freeman in 1956 with 129. Three times Ohioans have had the best field goal shooting average in the Big Ten: Schnittker in 1948, Donham in 1950, and Miller in 1955. Four Buckeyes have had the Conference's best free throw shooting average: Gecowets in 1942, Bowen in 1944, Huston in 1945, and Freeman in 1955.

In the forty-seven seasons between 1913, the first year Ohio State competed officially in the Big Ten in basketball, and 1959 its teams have played more than 900 basketball games. (Early in this period there were occasional games with local amateur teams. e.g., the Toledo Y.M.C.A.) By years and coaching periods, the record was:

Expansion and Competition

Coach	Year	Big Ten Won	Big Ten Lost	All Games Won	All Games Lost
St. John	1912-13	5	4	12	7
	14	5	1	10	4
	15	3	9	6	10
	16	2	8	10	12
	17	3	9	15	11
	18	5	5	12	7
	19	2	6	7	12
	20	3	9	17	10
		28	51	89	73
Trautman	1920-21	2	10	4	13
	22	5	7	8	10
		7	17	12	23
Olsen	1922-23	1	11	4	11
	24	7	5	12	5
	25	11	1	14	2
	26	6	6	10	7
	27	6	6	11	6
	28	3	9	5	12
	29	6	6	9	8
	30	1	9	4	11
	31	3	9	4	13
	32	5	7	9	9
	33	10	2	17	3
	34	4	8	8	12
	35	8	4	14	6
	36	5	7	12	8
	37	7	5	13	7
	38	7	5	12	8
	39	10	2	16	7
	40	8	4	13	7
	41	7	5	10	10
	42	4	11	6	14
	43	5	7	8	9
	44	10	2	14	7
	45	10	2	15	5
	46	10	2	16	5
		154	135	256	192
Dye	1946-47	5	7	7	13
	48	5	7	10	10
	49	6	6	14	7
	50	11	1	22	4
		27	21	53	34

Stahl	1950-51	3	11	6	16
	52	6	8	8	14
	53	7	11	10	12
	54	5	9	11	11
	55	4	10	10	12
	56	9	5	16	6
	57	9	5	14	8
	58	8	6	9	13
		51	65	84	92
Taylor	59	7	7	11	11

Ohio State has figured in the N.C.A.A. basketball championships four times. The best the Buckeyes did, however, was in 1939 when they were runners-up in the finals, losing to Oregon, 46 to 43. That year they were the champions, however, of the Eastern division. Three years running also—1944, 1945 and 1946—they were runners-up in the Eastern division. In 1939, too, Hull was the high scorer with 58 points in three games. Ohio State was also a contender in 1950 but did not place, losing to C.C.N.Y. by one point—56 to 55—in the first round.

SWIMMING

More than any other Varsity sport, the story of swimming at Ohio State University is the story of one man: Mike Peppe. In the long ago days where there was no swimming except that in the smelly little pool in the old Gymnasium which all men students, unless excused for good cause, had to be able to navigate before graduation. This pool, only 30 x 18½ feet, was not suitable for competitive swimming. There was a similar pool for women on their side of the Gymnasium. Both pools were filled in later.

But there was a hint of competitive swimming as far back as 1917. The Athletic Board at its January 17 meeting that year voted to "support a swimming team (to the extent of about $50.)" The Columbus Athletic Club offered the use of its pool. In a meet March 9 with Ohio Wesleyan, the "team," coached by H. C. Ohlson, of the physical education staff, lost, 50 to 18.

It was not until 1931 when the new Natatorium, with its three pools, was dedicated and put to use that the dream of swimming as a Varsity sport came true. (The governor who helped to dedicate the building insisted in his dedicatory remarks upon calling it the "natatarium.) Peppe was the first Varsity swimming coach and after twenty-eight seasons he was still going strong in 1959.

Howard Dwight Smith, University architect, at a July 10, 1930 board meeting, made a preliminary report on plans and estimates of cost for the Natatorium, with sketches and models of the building. The tabulation of bids was presented at a trustees' meeting July 15. A minor complication arose over whether the new men's physical education building and the Natatorium were to be built as a unit. One contractor sought to withdraw his bid when he learned that separate contracts might be let. He reported also that he had made an error of $25,000 in his estimates.

Another contractor emphasized his readiness to complete the Natatorium four months ahead of time and argued since he was the low bidder on the gymnasium that "the only practical way to build the two buildings" was by "the same organization." It was recommended nevertheless that the Natatorium contract be awarded separately and this was approved. The total contract came to $307,697.

In his more than a quarter of a century as head coach, Peppe produced a long string of team and individual champions. The total record, in fact, was unsurpassed by any other swimming coach or swimming teams anywhere else. Peppe was particularly strong with his divers and produced a large number of U.S. Olympic team members, divers as well as others.

Except for Michigan, where swimming was a varsity sport for some years before Ohio State made its entry into Big Ten and N.C.A.A. competition, the Buckeyes had the most impressive record in the Conference. Where Michigan had a near monopoly on team titles in the 'Thirties, Ohio State had an unbroken string, except for 1948, that ran from 1946 through 1956.

Statistics can be boring but they are also impressive. The over-all record under Peppe from 1931 through 1956 showed a dozen Big Ten team titles, 10 N.C.A.A. crowns—6 indoors and 4 outdoors. In team meets the Buckeyes were undefeated for 11 straight seasons.

In dual meets, through the 1958 season, Ohio State won 145 and lost only 32 for a percentage of .819. Although its string of ten consecutive Big Ten titles was broken in 1957 by Michigan State, Ohio State edged the Spartans 59 to 42 in a dual meet that year.

On the individual side, 1931 through 1959, Ohio State swimmers won 289 individual titles—95 in the Big Ten, 82 in the N.C.A.A. championships, 64 in national A.A.U. indoor meets and 48 in national A.A.U. outdoor meets. Emphasizing Peppe's particular proficiency with divers,

121 of the 289 individual titles were in diving events. In 22 of 23 seasons, divers coached by Peppe won Big Ten titles, in 19 of 21 years in the N.C.A.A., and 19 of 22 in A.A.U. championship meets.

As a result of this outstanding record, Peppe became a world figure as a swimming coach. He was twice the diving coach for the U.S. Olympic team. In 1956 Olympics in Australia, Bob Clotworthy, a Peppe product, won the springboard title, with Don Harper, another Buckeye, second, and Glen Whitten, a third Ohio Stater, fourth.

The team championship record under Peppe from 1931 through 1958 was as follows:

Big Ten—1938, 1943, 1946, 1947, 1949, 1950, 1951, 1952, 1953, 1954, 1955, 1956.

N.C.A.A.—1943, 1945, 1946, 1947, 1949, 1950, 1952, 1954, 1955, 1956.

A.A.U. (indoor)—1938, 1939, 1943, 1946, 1947, 1948.

A.A.U. (outdoor)—1938, 1942, 1947, 1952.

For the four Ohio State athletes, three swimmers and a runner, who starred in the 1948 Olympics, and for Peppe as the U.S. diving coach, the Athletic Board in September, 1948 formally expressed its "great pride" and hailed them as "among the most skillful of the University's sons." The runner was Mal Whitfield and the swimmers were Miller Anderson, Bruce Harlan, and Bill Smith. And following the 1952 Olympics the board similarly adopted resolutions commending Track Coach Larry Snyder on his appointment as assistant coach of the U.S. team and Peppe as diving coach for the U.S. squad.

Varsity swimming had a small beginning, however, before the new Natatorium was finished. In his first year as coach, Peppe coached a squad which used the Columbus Y.M.C.A. pool. The sport, even with the impetus of the new facilities—a beginners' pool, a practice pool, and one of the finest exhibition or Varsity pools in the country—was slow to take hold. But once it caught on and once good material began to come to the campus the impressive record was under way.

On the personal side, Peppe was a home product. His family moved to Columbus when Mike was 10 and he attended the University where he received his degree in 1927. Peppe got his M.A. at Columbia in 1928 and that fall joined the physical education staff and has been on the campus ever since.

The 1931 team, Peppe's first, won 3 and lost 2 dual meets. But the next season, the first in the Natatorium, produced an augury of what was to come for the team was undefeated in 8 dual meets. The 1933 depression-year squad won all 3 of its meets. In the next 4 seasons, 1934 through 1937, Ohio State won 18 and lost only 7 dual meets. In 1938 it rose to championship heights for the first time, winning all 5 dual meets and the Big Ten and indoor and outdoor A.A.U. crowns. In 1939 the team was again undefeated in dual competition.

The 1940 season was one of only two seasons in which an Ohio State team lost more dual swimming meets than it won. That year it took only one of 4 meets and in 1944, toward the end of the war when available men were pretty well drained from the campus, it lost all 4 dual meets. But the Buckeyes had spotless seasons in 1946, 1947, 1950, 1951, 1952, 1954 and 1956 in dual competition, lost only one dual meet each in the 1941, 1948, 1949 and 1955 seasons, and 2 in 1953.

At its March 8, 1954 meeting the Athletic Board authorized a letter to Peppe to congratulate him on the fact that the team had again won the Conference championship. "The regularity with which your teams have been establishing records and winning championships," the letter said in part, "speaks for itself as to your inspiration, leadership and exceptionally fine coaching." A letter of commendation also went to Coach Stahl, of the basketball team. Although the final standings, it commented, "did not show your team up in the winner's position, on the basis of good conduct and the finest in sportsmanship, you and your team were champions all the way."

The roster of individual champions produced by Peppe reads like a Who's Who of swimming. Forty-one swimmers shared the 289 individual titles referred to above. Twelve of them each won 10 or more titles in Varsity competition. Another, Bob Clotworthy, was close with 9. The twelve were:

	Big Ten	NCAA	AAU (ind.)	AAU (out.)	Total
Ford Konno	9	6	8	8	31
Yoshi Oyakawa	6	7	4	5	22
Al Patnik	3	5	8	4	20
Keo Nakama	6	4	3	6	19
Bruce Harlan	5	5	4	4	18
Bill Smith	3	7	6	1	17
Miller Anderson	3	5	7	1	16
Jack Taylor	8	4	2	0	14
Don Harper	5	3	3	1	12
Dick Cleveland	3	3	2	3	11
Al Wiggins	4	2	2	3	11
Earl Clark	1	3	2	4	10

Endless records have been made by Ohio State swimmers, while others have been made by swimmers from other schools in meets held in the Ohio State pool. Some of these marks were for the Conference only, but others were world, intercollegiate or American records at the time. The marks to the credit of Ohio State swimmers follow:

50-yd. free style—21.9 sec., Dick Cleveland, 1954, U.S.
440-yd. free style—4 min., 28.4 sec., Ford Konno, 1955, intercollegiate.
100-yd. back stroke—55.7 sec., Yoshi Oyakawa, 1954, world.
200-yd. back stroke—2 min., 5.1 sec., Oyakawa, 1953, U.S. and intercollegiate.
100-yd. butterfly stroke—54.4 sec., Al Wiggins, 1956, world.
150-yd. individual medley—1 min., 24.3 sec., Wiggins, 1955, U.S. and intercollegiate.
200-yd. medley relay—1 min., 44.2 sec., Oyakawa, Hoffman, Wiggins, Kimmel, 1956, world.

One other record set in the Varsity pool by an outside swimmer, other than for the pool itself, was for the 220-yd. free style. This was a world record in 1955 by Jack Wardrop, of Michigan, in 2 min., 3.4 sec.

Oddly, the first Ohio State swimmers to attain national recognition were two co-ed sisters, the "Smith twins." They were Ruth and Eleanor Smith, w'25. They competed under Ohio State colors in the 1922 indoor A.A.U. meet, winning first and second in the breast stroke. Because of their prowess and achievements there was some advocacy of Varsity "O's" for them but this came to nought because of the longstanding board rule limiting the "O" to men.

In all, 21 Ohio State swimmers have taken part in various Olympic games starting in 1936, 16 of them under the colors of the United States, 4 for Canada, and one for Cuba. Among them, they accounted for 7 gold medals as first place winners, 5 silver medals (second), and 2 bronze (third). One, the great Ford Konno, was a triple winner, with two gold medals and one silver at Helsinki in 1952 where thirteen Ohio State swimmers took part. Two others, Bill Smith and Bruce Harlan, were double winners at the London Olympics in 1948. Smith won 2 firsts and Harlan a first and a second. Five Ohio State swimmers—Anderson, Clotworthy, Konno, Oyakawa, and Silverio—each competed in two Olympics.

The Buckeye Olympic swimming roster through the 1956 games follows:

1936 (Berlin)— John Higgins, breast stroke
Ralph Gilman, freestyle

1948 (London)— Bill Smith, free style
Bruce Harlan, springboard and platform dive
Miller Anderson, springboard and platform dive
(Peppe was U.S. diving coach for these games.)

1952 (Helsinki)— Ford Konno, freestyle
Dick Cleveland, freestyle
Yoshi Oyakawa, back stroke
Frank Dooley, freestyle
Jack Taylor, back stroke
Jerry Holan, breast stroke
Miller Anderson, springboard dive
Robert Clotworthy, springboard dive
Jack Calhoun, platform dive
Leo Portelance, breast stroke (Canada)
Gerry McNamee, free style (Canada)
Lucien Beaumont, freestyle (Canada)
Nicholas Silverio, freestyle (Cuba)
(Peppe again U.S. diving coach)

1956 (Melbourne)—Ford Konno, freestyle
Yoshi Oyakawa, back stroke
Al Wiggins, back stroke
Robert Clotworthy, springboard dive
Donald Harper, springboard dive
Glen Whitten, springboard dive
Nicholas Silverio, freestyle (Cuba)

In addition, Buckeye swimmers have cut a swath in the Pan-American Games which were begun in 1951 and which are held quadriennally the year before the Olympic events. In the 1951 games, held in Buenos Aires, Peppe was the U.S. swimming coach, and two Ohioans figured in the medals. Cleveland won two gold medals and Anderson earned a silver and a bronze medal. In the 1955 games in Mexico City, Clotworthy won a gold medal and Harper, a diver, won the trampoline title in gymnastics.

Evidence of how Ohio State in late years dominated the N.C.A.A. swimming championships is shown by such facts as: the most individual championships in one year, 9 (1954), 8 (1955), 7 (1946), 6 (1953), 5 each (1943, 1947, 1949, 1950 and 1952), 4 each (1940, 1945, and 1948), 3 each (1939 and 1956), and 2 each (1937, 1938, 1941, 1942, 1944, and 1951).

On the individual side, Jack Hill, of the 1944 team, won 3 titles that year: 220-yd. freestyle, 440-yd. freestyle, and 200-yd. breast stroke. Yoshi Oyakawa and Bill Smith tied for runner-up with the most individual titles in their Varsity careers with 7 each, Oyakawa in the 100-yd. back stroke in 1953, 1954 and 1955, and the 200-yd. back stroke in 1952, 1953,

1954 and 1955; and Smith in the 220-yd. freestyle in 1943, 1947, 1948 and 1949, and the 440-yd. freestyle in 1947, 1948 and 1949. (Only Jack Medica, of Washington, surpassed this with 9 individual titles.)

Repeat Ohio State individual champions in N.C.A.A. competition were numerous: Oyakawa was a 4-time winner in the 200-yd. back stroke in 1952, 1953, 1954 and 1955; Smith, similarly, in the 220-yd. freestyle in 1943, 1947, 1948 and 1949; three times—Bruce Harlan, 1-meter diving, 1948, 1949 and 1950, and 3-meter diving those same years; Konno— 1500-meter freestyle, 1952, 1954 and 1955, and 400-yd. freestyle those same years; Al Patnik, 3-meter diving, 1938 and 1939, and 1-meter diving, 1938, 1939 and 1940.

Don Harper, of the '56 squad, set a unique N.C.A.A. record unmatched by any other college athlete except in track and cross country. He won the trampoline title in the gymnastics meet at North Carolina and the next week won the 3-meter diving title in the swimming championships at Yale, the first time anyone ever won N.C.A.A. titles in separate sports the same year. (Track and cross country men accounted for similar records five times.) Harper repeated this feat in 1958.

GOLF

Efforts to add golf to the list of campus sports occurred even prior to 1900. "A start has been made towards golf at the University," the April 28, 1897 *Lantern* told its readers. "Friday afternoon about a dozen of those interested in the sport met informally and arranged for the immediate laying out of a course on the campus. The links have already been constructed, and play began this week . . ." The site of the "course" was not indicated but the paper added that a golf club was to be organized. It was to be open to all students, faculty members and adult members of their families.

A real move toward the establishment of golf as a Varsity sport was made at an Athletic Board meeting March 21, 1916. The record shows that "Mr. Wilce moved that the Athletic Board go on record as willing to do all in their power as far as practical at the present time toward promoting the formation of a University golf team and signify its favor of the existence of a 'varsity team as soon as it should become practical." In a further move, Prof. M. B. Evans, of the board, was named a committee of one to "make arrangements with the Arlington Club for University teams." Varsity teams later used this club, located in Marble Cliff, for several years.

For a time a 9-hole "course" of sorts was laid out west of High St. in the area between W. Eleventh Ave. and the buildings on the south side of the Oval, and generally east of the old Ohio Union. On the recommendation of Asst. Director Trautman, the board on February 25, 1921 appropriated $200 to "repair and put in condition nine golf greens on the campus."

It was still a long way off but at a board meeting February 5, 1926 a 3-man committee was named to "inquire into the proposition of a Varsity golf course." A decade later, Director St. John was to be instrumental in seeing this dream come to reality in not one but two fine 18-hole courses, the Scarlet and the Gray, owned and operated by the department. Their development is dealt with elsewhere in this account.

Mike Godman, a well known Columbus amateur of the time, was coach from 1921 to 1923, although the records indicate that no "O's" were granted in golf until 1923. Godman was followed by George W. Eckelberry, a member of the accounting department faculty and later assistant to President Rightmire. Eckelberry served in 1924 and 1925. The coaching chore was taken over then by George Sargent, "pro" at the Scioto Country Club and a former National Open champion. Sargent was coach from 1926 to 1931, and was followed in 1932 by Francis Marzolf, another Columbus "pro." In the depression years from 1933 through 1937 the golf coaching was handled by Harold G. Olsen in addition to his duties as head basketball coach.

In 1938, with the new courses ready for use, the long reign of Bob Kepler began. "Kep" was a star Varsity player, blossomed into a fine "pro," and proceeded to make Ohio State a power in golf. He was still at the helm in 1959.

Ohio State won its first Big Ten team title in golf in 1928. The tournament that year was played at Scioto, then the Buckeyes' home course, which may have helped. The winning team score was 1323. The first championship team was composed of Alan B. Loop, Howard C. Park, Alfred G. Sargent, and Wolford M. Shane. For their prowess they were awarded "major" Varsity "O's."

The first Ohio Stater to win the individual crown was Billy Gilbert, in 1940, with a 298 total. Before the 'Forties were out, three other Buckeyes had done likewise; Howard Baker and John Lorms, in 1945, and Howard B. Saunders, co-champion in 1947. Ohio State again won the team title in 1945 with a total of 603, again in 1951 with a total of 1528, and once more in 1954 with a 1527 total. Ohio State was again host to the Big Ten championships in 1940, 1950 and 1958.

In intercollegiate golf the N.C.A.A. meet, established in 1939, is the high point of the golf season. For nearly two decades the Ohio State squad has invariably taken part in this tournament which three times—in 1945, 1951 and 1956—was held on the Varsity course. Invariably, too, teams coached by Kepler have been contenders in the N.C.A.A. competition.

In the 1945 tournament the Buckeyes scored a double victory. They won the team title with a gross score of 603 and Johnny Lorms won the individual crown. By a coincidence in each of the other years Ohio State was host to the tournament a member of its team won individual honors—Tom Nieporte in 1951, and Rich Jones in 1956. (Nieporte later turned "pro.") In 1951 the Buckeyes lost the team championship by one stroke to North Texas State.

OTHER SPORTS

Over the years various other sports have sought or been given Varsity recognition, either temporary or permanent. Several such sports have been part of the Ohio State program with some intercollegiate competition although they were not officially part of the Western Conference program. Some sports such as tennis, gymnastics, wrestling and fencing have been carried on for years as part of the Varsity program.

Tennis, for example, ranks with baseball as the oldest sport on the campus. There were teams in the earliest days and there were both matches that would now be considered on the intramural level and matches with city teams. As noted, there was an early tennis court on the site of the Thompson Memorial Library, there were other courts in the vicinity of Neil and Eleventh Aves., and there was a sizeable number of courts just north of the old Armory and Gymnasium where the later Mershon parking lot was located.

Tennis was a sort of athletic stepchild in the early days. For lack of adequate facilities on the campus, Varsity matches were played for a time at Indianola Park, no longer in existence. This was some distance from the campus. Only a seasonal coach was employed. In the fall of 1913 the Athletic Board began to take steps to remedy this situation. It authorized the appointment of a committee "to see about building two tennis courts so that intercollegiate tennis matches" could be held on the campus. Charles Farber, a Columbus enthusiast, was seasonal tennis coach in the pre-World War I period.

The Western Conference Records Book (1957-58) shows T. H. Connell as the Varsity coach in 1921, followed by R. L. Grismer in 1922-24, and then by the long reign of Herman Wirthwein from 1926 to 1957 when ill health compelled him to give up this activity. Wirthwein was followed by John W. Hendrix. For a time an "old English," i.e., a script, "O" was awarded to tennis players as against the block or oval "O" in other sports.

With a few exceptions, Varsity tennis never created much of a stir on the campus. But as far back as 1915, Charles A. Carran, '16, later for many years city manager of Lakewood, Ohio, was Western Conference singles champion. His feat was not duplicated by an Ohio State player until 1937 when Robert Nihousen was Conference singles titlist, and again in 1945 when Aris Franklin did likewise.

But there were three years in a row when Ohio State supplied the Conference doubles winner. This was in 1943, 1944 and 1945 when the titlists were Wasserman and Sampson, Aris Franklin and Mitchell, and the brother duo of Aris and Alex Franklin.

Gymnastics, golf, wrestling and fencing were slow to develop as Varsity sports. Formal recognition of golf, wrestling and gymnastics as "minor" sports was given December 14, 1920 by the Athletic Board. It was pointed out that these three sports had been carried on for several years on the campus as part of the work in physical education and the student response had been good. At a recent meeting of Conference schools, the board was told, "there was a lot of enthusiasm over the future development of these activities" and the group had gone on record "as favoring the establishment of these activities as a part of the Intercollegiate sport program."

For Ohio State it was recommended that "minor" sport letters should be awarded to members of any of the three teams representing the University in the annual Western Conference meet, with "major" sport letters for the members of any of these teams winning a Conference championship or to any individual champion in wrestling or the "All around Championship winner" in gymnastics.

The official Conference records show only three Ohio State gymnastics coaches in the long period from 1923 to 1958. But there were gymnasts and gymnastics teams, at least under men's physical education, in the early years after the old Gymnasium came into use in 1898 and in the early 1900s. At any rate, Glenn Alexander, also a pole vaulter, was gymnastics coach in 1923, when he was succeeded by Leo Staley from 1924 to 1932, and Joe Hewlett from 1947. The sport was abandoned in the intervening years.

Gymnastics was never a sport to attract the multitudes and Varsity gymnasts often had a hard row to hoe to keep the sport alive. An outstanding example of this was Sam Manos who in the winter of 1947 made his own way to the Big Ten meet at Illinois where he won an individual championship. At the April 16, 1947 meeting the Athletic Board voted to award him a Varsity "O" and to reimburse him for his expenses.

The introduction of the trampoline added a more spectacular element to gymnastics competition and exhibitions. In this event Ohio State had several outstanding performers. The most notable was Don Harper, also one of Mike Peppe's star divers, as noted. In 1956 and again in 1958 Harper was N.C.A.A. champion in the trampoline event.

Soccer, a very old athletic activity, is another sport not in the official Western Conference calendar. Yet it was a sport on the Ohio State campus in the first years after its admission to the Conference. There were matches with Oberlin and other nearby Ohio colleges. After various ups and downs—more of the latter than the former—the sport was revived on a Varsity basis in 1953 under Bruce Bennett.

The introduction of soccer as a Varsity sport probably owed as much to Prof. J. A. Leighton, a board member, as to any one else. Dr. Leighton had played the game as an undergraduate. At a board meeting January 7, 1913 his motion that "soccer foot ball be started at Ohio State in the near future" was passed. Track Coach Frank R. Castleman and Allison W. Marsh, of the men's Physical Education Department, were the first coaches.

Over the years interest in soccer lagged and it was abandoned as a Varsity sport. On December 8, 1927, on a request from Leo G. Staley, the coach, soccer was again recognized as a "minor" sport and letters were awarded to three players and a student manager. Interest later receded again but in the spring of 1953 a Soccer Club request to the board to grant the sport Varsity status the next season was approved. Howard G. Knuttgen was coach for several years and was succeeded in 1958 by Walter F. Ersing.

Wrestling is another Varsity sport with an uncertain record over the years. There have been a few seasons when the sport attracted a good deal of attention on the campus but these were the exception rather than the rule. As the Big Ten Records Book explains it, "From 1912 through 1921 team championships were determined in the 'Western Intercollegiate Wrestling, Gymnastics and Fencing Association,' which was an open meet. From 1922 through 1933 team championships were based on dual meet records. In 1926 the Conference sponsored its own meet, but individual champions only were named until 1934, when a point system was adopted to name a team champion in that event."

Al Haft, a well known professional wrestler and later a successful wrestling promoter, was the first specialized wrestling coach on the campus, although Henry C. Ohlson, of the men's physical education staff, had done some coaching earlier. Haft served through 1925 and was followed by Bernard F. "Spike" Mooney, from 1926 to 1942. In the spring of 1928 a proposal was offered to recognize wrestling as a "major" sport. Lawrence Hicks was coach in 1943 and 1944, followed by Mooney again from 1945 to 1947, and then by Casey Fredericks, formerly of Purdue, since 1948.

The Big Ten Records Book shows that Ohio State was co-champion in the Conference in 1923 and won the title again in 1951. Two of the earlier wrestlers stood out—Perry Martter, a welterweight, and Harry Steel, a heavyweight. Both were members of the 1924 U.S. Olympic team. Steel, in fact, won the Olympic title. Efforts were made to persuade him to turn professional after his return to the United States but he declined.

What "Chic" Harley was to Ohio State football, Martter was to Varsity wrestling on a smaller scale in the early 'Twenties. In twenty bouts in three Varsity seasons he lost only one. In that one he went into a heavier class and was "so badly injured he had to be taken to University Hospital." Martter was a natural welterweight but often went out of his class to defeat middleweights and even heavyweights. He twice won the Conferenec welterweight title.

Between 1929 and 1956, as shown by the official records book, Ohio State cut only a fair figure in N.C.A.A. wrestling. In only eight of those years did its entries score. In the individual competition of the last thirty years, two Ohio State entrants won championships. Both were heavyweights. George Downes won the crown in that division in 1940, and George Bollas, a 300-pounder, won similarly in 1946.

Fencing is another sport which has long been a part of the Varsity picture but has never had much crowd appeal. Its beginnings antedate World War I but the first Varsity coach listed by the Big Ten Records Book (1957-58) is L. A. Kunzig from 1922 to 1924. Kunzig was followed by Dr. Frank A. Riebel, a former Varsity star, in 1925 and 1926, then by Ted Lorber in 1927. Dr. Riebel resumed coaching in 1928 and stayed on in that post until 1944. The 1927 team composed of Captain Edward R. Stephens, Theodore Lorber (sabre champion), Charles S. Fox, Victor R. Brombeck and Benjamin F. Wills won the Big Ten title.

Ohio State was host to the first N.C.A.A. fencing championships in 1941. The bouts had 76 contestants from 19 colleges and universities. The following year Ohio State won the N.C.A.A. championship at Washington University (St. Louis) with 34 points, edging St. John's with $33\frac{1}{2}$ points. Dr. Riebel was coach. The Buckeyes had one individual N.C.A.A. title holder in Ben Burtt in epee. Between 1941 and 1956, except for the war years, Ohio State took part in the N.C.A.A. championships eleven times occasionally finishing in the upper division, e.g., 1941—6th, 1942—1st, 1947—10th, 1949—11th, 1955—8th, and 1956—7th.

A rifle team was recognized as a "minor" sport team by board action March 8, 1922. This activity was really sponsored by the Military Department and its recognition was largely a matter of good relations with that department. There was always some question, however, as to its legitimacy as a Varsity sport since there was no actual man-to-man or team-to-team competition as in other sports and the results of the competition were exchanged by telegraph. This issue came up at a May 14, 1925 board meeting but at another meeting November 30, 1925 it was reported that "the military department had agreed to conduct that team on the same basis as other varsity teams."

The question of Varsity "O" awards for the rifle team arose again in the spring of 1930. The rifle team of that year had made an outstanding record, among other things winning the Fifth Corps match and the Western Conference title. The board at its April 24 meeting approved a recommendation to grant the team members "O's" under the provision for "meritorious service in athletic competition or outstanding accomplishment made in competition." This was with the stipulation, however, that "this award involved no commitment by the Board" as to the future policy in this regard. The records show there were rifle teams from 1922 through 1933, then there was some interruption, but with teams again from 1938 through 1943.

This activity continued after World War II when efforts were made to have it supported and again recognized as a Varsity sport. The objection was that it was not a team sport in the accepted sense. At a September 22, 1948 board meeting the then commandant asked the board to "authorize and support" a University pistol club. The board granted $25 a month to pay a noncommissioned officer as coach but with the express stipulation "that recognition as a Varsity sport and seasonal awards be withheld."

The addition of polo as a recognized sport on the campus also came up through the Military Department. At a December 8, 1927 board meeting $400 was appropriated for its support and polo was made part of the intramural program. Col. G. L. Townsend, commandant, pointed out that a Polo Club had been functioning for two years and during the 1927 Fall Quarter had six teams of six players playing regularly five days a week and on Thanksgiving Day played a match with a Zanesville club. In June, 1928 the board appropriated $500 to improve the polo field, located south of the Stadium.

At a June 3, 1929 meeting the board voted to recognize polo as a Varsity sport. It approved the Varsity "O" award for eleven men on the squad. The polo coach was Lieut. John P. Eckert, of the Military Department. There was a polo team thereafter through 1943 but the sport was not revived after World War II.

From time to time advocates of other sports have sought to promote them to the level of a Varsity activity. These have usually died from lack of facilities or lack of sufficient interest on the part of enough people to persuade the board to grant such a recognition. One of these was hockey for which no rink was available on the campus. A more recent one was weight lifting.

Lacrosse was another sport that reached the Varsity stage in the mid-'Fifties. Although it was not on the official Big Ten schedule a Varsity team was organized and a schedule arranged with Ed Baker, of physical education, as coach. Howard Knuttgen later took over the coaching chores. Fred Keller, mid-fielder on the '57 team, was an All-American in the sport.

Back in 1948 it was reported to the board that the office of the Dean of Men had officially recognized the Lacrosse Club which had arranged matches with Oberlin and Kenyon. The board authorized the club to represent the University "on an informal basis" in these matches, but with the understanding that the action "did not establish Lacrosse as an intercollegiate sport and that Varsity letters would not be awarded for competition in these matches." On June 7, 1951 the board approved a suggestion that the certificate of merit award be used for participation in soccer and lacrosse.

In the spring of 1952, however, members of the lacrosse team and their coaches petitioned the board to grant the Varsity "O" in this sport. The board approved the request, the first such awards to be made in 1953. In the spring of 1956 the squad had a spring vacation trip, playing the University of Baltimore and Dickinson College. The regular schedule called for eleven games, five of them away from home.

Now and then advocates of boxing have sought to have that sport recognized as part of the intercollegiate program. It became an intramural sport for a time but not an intercollegiate one. A petition was presented to the board May 28, 1930 from the Ohio State Boxing Club urging that "boxing be recognized, financed and promoted as an intercollegiate varsity sport at the Ohio State University" or that the board permit the club to use campus facilities "to stage intercollegiate matches." Instead, the board adopted a resolution "That in view of the scarcity of available intercollegiate competition in boxing and in view of the present financial obligations and commitments," it was "unable to approve or to undertake the establishment of intercollegiate boxing at the Ohio State University at this time."

Also over a long period of years there was talk of adding rowing to the list of Varsity sports. This occurred as far back as 1904 after the completion of the Griggs Dam on the Scioto River. It was pictured again as a possibility when the Ohio Stadium was built, this time with the Olentangy as a possible site. For a combination of reasons nothing ever came of these moves partly for lack of genuine interest, partly because neither of the sites was really suitable for this purpose, partly for lack of nearby competition, and partly because of the expense involved.

INTRAMURAL ATHLETICS

By a later day definition the first athletic activities on the campus would have been regarded as intramural except that they were unorganized and haphazard. Later there were interfraternity sports, baseball in particular, and interclass and intercollege contests. For this purpose there were for years three baseball diamonds on the Oval itself, but these were moved elsewhere about 1912 or 1913. There was a natural expansion of intramural activities after the Armory-Gymnasium was completed and especially after "gym" was made compulsory for everyone. But non-Varsity sports were still incidental and without much direction and lacked financial support.

In the period immediately preceding Ohio State's admission to the Conference this kind of activity was referred to as "recreative" sports. With the coming of the Richards-St. John regime the idea of organized intramural athletics began to take firmer shape. In the spring of 1913 there were intra-college and interfraternity baseball schedules. But a *Lantern* editorial of April 30 pointed out that while the University was well provided with athletic facilities, the "recreative" sports were yet to be given their proper attention.

The real seed for what came in time to be one of the leading college intramural programs in the country was laid at a September 24, 1913 Athletic Board meeting. On motion, members of the Athletic Department were directed to "investigate the question of intra-mural sports and report at the next meeting." Intramurals date officially from January 9, 1914.

It remained for Dr. John W. Wilce to give the initial impetus to the extensive intramural program along with his duties as director of football. For a number of years the indoor intramurals had their climax in the annual intramural festival staged in the old Armory with a combination of relay and individual events. For a time, for example, there was great rivalry among relay teams made up of fraternity men who wore the colors of various sororities, e.g., the combination of Phi Gamma Delta and Phi Mu.

But when the first of the championship football teams took more and more of Dr. Wilce's time he yielded the intramural reins and responsibility to others. For a brief time George M. Trautman, assistant to Director St. John, had charge of this activity. Then Grant P. Ward, chief football scout and assistant line coach, ran the intramural show from 1920-21 until his resignation at the end of 1925.

Next Sam S. Willaman, assistant football coach, had charge until the middle of the school year 1928-29. When he was made head football coach, Harold S. Wood was brought back from the University of Michigan to take over the intramural program. Wood, captain of the 1921 Oberlin football team that defeated Ohio State, had previously been an assistant. He remained until the end of the 1936-37 school year when he resigned to become athletic director at Wesleyan University. He was followed by Leo Staley who has been in charge ever since.

A dog-eared copy of the "Constitution of the Intra-Mural Athletic Association" in the Athletic Department files shows that it was organized in 1913. At the time the document was printed in 1919-20, Trautman was shown as director. The object of the association was "the organization, promotion and conduct of Intra-Mural athletic activity for the student body, exclusive of members of intercollegiate teams or squads." In other words, it was athletics for the masses of men and women on the campus. As of that time the "intercollegiate" division of the association (inter-college), was composed of agriculture, veterinary medicine, law, arts, pharmacy, commerce and journalism, dentistry, medicine, and mechanical, electrical, chemical, architectural and civil engineering. Varsity "O" men could participate but only in sports in which they had not won their letters. Sports on the 1919-20 program were soccer, cross country, basketball or indoor baseball, baseball, and the indoor and outdoor track and field meets.

The over-all program, changed from time to time and expanded as the University grew, was naturally and necessarily designed to appeal to the masses of students. There was an intramural program for women as well as the one for men. From year to year thousands of students took part in this form of competition, particularly fraternity teams. An innovation during the 1957-58 season was a revival of the indoor intramural track meet. This was made possible by the completion of the French Field House and its availability for such a purpose. Mrs. Dorothy Sumption Wirthwein was in charge of the women's program.

As a measure of participation, by the end of the depression (1937-38), the men's intramural program included 21 sports or activities with 10,182 participants. In ten team sports there were 909 teams. On the women's side there were 14 sports with 1076 participants. That same year the Varsity program, by comparison, consisted of 13 sports in which 162 contests were played with 1209 men students participating.

Because of space limitations and because this account is concerned primarily with intercollegiate athletics a brief summary of the intramural program must suffice. By 1940-41 the Athletic Department no longer financed the program which was underwritten out of student fees although the Athletic Board retained general supervision of the policies. The faculty athletic committee report of that year, the last before World War II, to the general faculty showed that as against 180 contests in the 13-sport intercollegiate program with 1186 participants, including duplicates, there were 1064 men's intramural *teams* in 18 sports with 11,147 participants. Similarly, there were 1662 women participants that year in 16 sports or activities.

For some unexplained reason there was a decline in 1950-51 in both intercollegiate and intramural sports. In a dozen intercollegiate and two "semi-intercollegiate" sports that year there were 1165 participants as against 1296 the year before. In intramurals, although there were more teams, there were only 9036 participants, a decrease of 700. But what were labeled as "free play," i.e., individual, activities such as golf, swimming and tennis showed an estimated participation of 15,300 students. Among intramural team sports the most popular were basketball with 294 teams and 2521 participants, softball with 192 teams and 2202 participants, touch football with 133 teams and 1715 participants, and volleyball with 150 teams and 1162 participants.

In 1954-55 the men's program consisted of 16 sports or activities: Autumn—touch football, volleyball and bowling; Winter—basketball, bowling, wrestling, handball, squash, weight lifting; Spring—softball, tennis, golf, badminton, track, swimming, archery and fencing. All of this activity filled a real need on the campus and gave a broad organized outlet for student energies, both individual and team.

PART III

ATHLETIC ADMINISTRATION
1912–1959

XIII
THE PHYSICAL PLANT

INTERCOLLEGIATE athletics generally has a strong tendency to feed upon itself. The more it grows the more it requires. In this respect it is a kind of Frankenstein for which the great majority of colleges and universities seem to have no ultimate solution. This is particularly true of the physical plant and other facilities necessary for anything like a complete sports program.

In the case of Ohio State it was a long jump from the primitive conditions of the late 'Seventies and 'Eighties to the Stadium era which ushered in a period of mounting bigness. In the next third of a century these major facilities were added: the Natatorium, two 18-hole golf courses, the French Field House, and the St. John Arena. The Stadium itself was "stretched" and improved. Each of these facilities meant more maintenance and more upkeep until, as of mid-1958, the athletic budget was stretched to the utmost and it became a serious question whether the limit of foreseeable revenues had not been reached.

1. THE COLISEUM

While it did not keep pace with football, basketball also began to have growing pains after Ohio State became a member of the Big Nine. With increased interest in the sport and with a rapidly growing enrollment, the old Gymnasium was soon outgrown. The solution was to move basketball to the Coliseum at the State Fair Grounds. At its January 25, 1918 meeting the Athletic Board approved a recommendation to do so.

Varsity basketball entered a new era with this move but the change was not an unmixed blessing. It was necessary to design and provide a sectional floor and special baskets. The Athletic Department had to pay maintenance costs, including the installation of heating equipment. The building was never intended for winter use and proved hard to heat. From time to time there was damage to shrubbery and light standards at the Fair Grounds and the state billed the University for such things although the responsibility was sometimes in doubt. It was expected that the Coliseum would be used only until the University had its own facility, but this proved to be a long run and Varsity basketball was played there through 1955-56.

As early as 1918 the board began to consider ways and means of meeting the need for a field house. At its February 27, 1918 meeting a committee was named to "lay the matter of a field house before the Board of Trustees." Nothing tangible came of this for a good many years and Ohio State was one of the last of the country's large universities to build a field house. This came about finally in 1955-56 when the St. John Arena was built.

The University meanwhile had used the Coliseum for a variety of purposes. This was chiefly for basketball but also for the intramural festival and, for some years, for commencement until the place got too small. This was always by arrangement with the state department of agriculture. Such arrangements were common between state departments and agencies. The University, in turn, performed services or loaned facilities or even personnel to other state departments, including agriculture.

There was never any question of paying rent for the use of the Coliseum, however, until July, 1951 when the board was informed that the agriculture department was now seeking to be paid. The agriculture director, oddly, was a former Varsity athlete. At the July 26 board meeting Director Larkins was authorized to proceed with negotiations in the hope that no rental would be necessary in view of the University's multiple counter-services to the agriculture department.

At the October 3, 1951 meeting Larkins reported further on the matter. The agriculture department's chief argument was that it had continuous applications from other sources for use of the structure and felt that it was losing considerable revenue as long as the University was using it during the winter months. Larkins submitted figures showing that it had cost the Athletic Department $77,000.89 to operate the Coliseum from 1946-47 through 1950-51. Including the comparable expenses from 1936 to 1942, total expenditures for the period were $119,897.86. By contrast Varsity basketball had been played for two years in the Columbus Auditorium at a cost of $4440.42 and in the men's gymnasium for two years at a cost of $991.53. Larkins was empowered to negotiate further with the department in the matter.

At the November 21 meeting he reported again on the situation. The state agriculture director, he said, emphasized the necessity of offsetting the loss of revenue to the state by some rental from the Athletic Department. Estimated costs for operating the structure during the winter season were put at $9600 and, on request, Larkins submitted a proposed rental fee of $1500. One alumni board member, a former attorney general, objected on the grounds that "the University furnishes to the State, without charge, many services and much equipment for the State Fair and on other occasions. It is generally considered unusual for one State Department or Division of government to charge another for services." The board nevertheless authorized payment of a fee of $1500 for the season. This was increased later to $3250.

2. THE GOLF COURSE

The ultimate need for a University golf course was recognized fairly early in the Stadium era. At the June 12, 1928 board meeting a letter was read from John K. Kennedy, '09, "concerning a site for a golf course." This was referred to the golf committee. It had to do with a possible site on Kenny Rd. and consisted largely of a farm owned by Mr. Kennedy's parents which had been in the family for many years, along with certain adjacent parcels. In time a deal was worked out whereby the board took an option on acreage which led ultimately, after some modifications, to the construction of two 18-hole courses, the Scarlet and the Gray, on a site west of Tremont and Kenny Rds. and south of McCoy Rd., about three miles from the campus.

Action on developing the site soon followed. The board on August 9, 1928 authorized Assistant Director Trautman "to communicate with Mr. Donald Ross relative to coming to Columbus to survey the proposed golf sites" and to pay his fee in this connection. On September 18 the board approved Trautman's report of a study "on proposed locations for a golf course, together with a recommendation for a particular site." The recommendation for the site, described above, was approved also. The board also designated a committee to confer with President Rightmire "on the questions involved in the purchase of a golf site." Presumably these had to do with questions of policy, especially that of increasing the athletic debt if the new venture was undertaken.

At a November 1 meeting the special committee reported that Dr. Rightmire had given his approval to proceed in the matter of a site for the golf courses and the board authorized the committee to obtain options on the proposed site. Options on the various parcels needed were obtained by Kennedy. At a March 12, 1929 meeting the board approved the purchase of the site under the contracts presented by Kennedy, subject to the approval of President Rightmire. Nine parcels were involved, amounting to 296.22 acres at a cost of $155,714 or a little more than $502 per acre. The largest single parcel was about 131 acres and the next 72.

On October 7, 1929 the board authorized the employment of Dr. Alister MacKenzie, noted golf architect, to lay out the golf course for a fee of $6000 for an 18-hole course or $10,000 for two.

Acquisition of the land for the golf course was only the first step in realizing this dream. The course or courses had to be laid out, a water supply assured, drainage provided for along with a clubhouse and shelter houses, planting and sanitary facilities. The Works Projects Administration which was in full swing in the mid-'Thirties as a depression relief agency provided much of the manpower necessary to prepare the site. It put hundreds of men to work at pick-and-shovel jobs to this end.

This labor possibility, which proved of great value in expediting the early completion of the course, was brought before the board at its August 22, 1935 meeting when the golf course commitee was authorized "to proceed with the proposal relative to initiating a W.P.A. project of starting construction on the golf course." To this end an appropriation of $3000 was approved. At the October 11 meeting the board authorized the payment of $11,700 to exercise its option on a tract which was part of the site. This was increased by $2700 at the October 30 meeting when the heir of one of the original owners objected that the amount proposed was "insufficient."

It soon developed that the $3000 voted for construction of the golf course was only a start. The board at a November 15 meeting voted an additional $8000 "for materials and professional services." But this was with the further understanding that the commitment was for a 27-hole course. Before the matter was ended the board went ahead with the entire 36 holes, giving the University two fine 18-hole courses.

About the time the first Franklin D. Roosevelt administration came into office with the nation's economy stalled, it was felt that renegotiation of the contracts for the purchase of the golf course site was in order. At the April 17, 1933 board meeting a communication was presented from Kennedy as to modifications of the existing contract with a tentative plan for payments in the near future. The proposal was referred to the golf committee for study and report. At the May 11 meeting the committee reported that it could not see its way to accept the new terms proposed and the board supported this.

At a November 27, 1933 meeting the golf course committee, after consulting with the finance committee, reported that it could not recommend the acceptance of Kennedy's proposal to pay the principal of about $100,000 in three years. A suggestion was made that perhaps the board could get a release from the contracts and lease the land at a lower charge with an option to purchase it later. The committee was authorized to negotiate on this basis.

A solution to this problem was reached at the May 2, 1934 meeting when the golf committee reported that Kennedy had obtained agreement from all but one of the owners of the golf course site "for reductions of principal and interest." The aggregate reduction in the contract cost was $28,421 while the annual carrying charge was to be approximately $1800 a year as against $6491.87 under the former contracts. The new schedule was approved.

Further items for the development of the golf course were authorized at the April 15, 1938 board meeting in the amount of $16,000. These included additional construction, development of the clubhouse parking area, and furnishings for the clubhouse. W.P.A. proposals were presented also for the installation of a water line, for tiling and rough grading of the last nine holes, and construction and maintenance of the first 27 holes to June 30. At a December 16, 1938 meeting the board authorized the erection of two shelter houses.

Earlier a start on a clubhouse for the golf course was made at the October 26, 1936 meeting when the board voted to ask the University cabinet to authorize Howard Dwight Smith, University architect, to begin work on plans. Further discussion followed at the April 6 meeting concerning plans for the clubhouse and related buildings.

Previously at a January 31, 1936 meeting the board took several further actions as to the golf course. It named John S. McCoy superintendent and voted to "commit itself to the minimum amount necessary to be contributed to the present W.P.A. project and to preserve the results of the same." To this end it asked the golf course committee to prepare an estimate of these expenditures to be submitted to the finance committee for approval.

A further step was taken May 1, 1937 when the board approved a budget of $30,500 for the completion of 27 holes of the golf course. There were reports also on proposed golf course buildings, of sewage and water disposal units, and on a 6-inch well on the property. The drilling of the well at an approximate cost of $1000 was approved. At a meeting May 31 the board voted to appropriate $60,000 to be expended during the fiscal year 1937-38 for buildings and building equipment at the golf course. The board adopted a resolution of intent with respect to the golf course at its July 21, 1937 meeting similar to those adopted earlier regarding the Stadium and the Natatorium. In this case it declared its intention of ultimately turning the course over to the University trustees "free and clear of all claims and liens whatsoever."

At a September 14, 1937 meeting the board was informed of the possibility of a new W.P.A. project to complete the labor on the golf course up to 36 holes. For the moment the board was unwilling to commit itself beyond the 27 holes authorized but was willing to have W.P.A. authorities approached to see whether they wished to start a new project on the golf course. The board also approved the letting of a contract for the clubhouse, amounting to $48,374 additional.

Another necessary step was taken in the development of the golf program at the January 5, 1938 board meeting with the appointment of Robert Kepler as golf instructor and coach. Many persons took a hand in the over-all development of the golf course and program. Director St. John reported at the March 17, 1938 board meeting that in addition to the regular sources he had the help of an informal committee consisting of George M. Trautman, Harold M. Gardiner, Hazard Okey and Samuel N. Summer on construction problems as well as generous legal help from John K. Kennedy and Clarence D. Laylin.

In answer to some critical comments from certain state officials to the University administration questioning the wisdom of the golf course from a financial standpoint, a report was prepared on the use of the course during 1940. This was presented at the June 6, 1941 board meeting. It showed a total of 13,074 rounds of golf by students plus 570 tournament rounds during the state high school, Ohio intercollegiate and Western Conference championships held on the course. Other activities there included archery, golf, student dances and organized picnics.

The completed course, a useful byproduct of the depression years, was finally—and officially—presented to the trustees by board action of June 1, 1949, two decades after the start. At that time Director Larkins called the golf course "a most important part" of the physical education facilities and "a valuable addition" to the University's recreational program. The amount represented by W.P.A. assistance had not been determined, he added, but the cost out of athletic receipts was $363,617.36, of which $133,030 was for land, $137,389.80 for construction, and $93,197.56 for buildings. Final payment on the golf course indebtedness was made in April, 1949 so that the way was now clear to transfer the title to the University as had been done earlier with the Stadium and with the Natatorium. This was done as a matter of record.

3. THE NATATORIUM AND MEN'S GYMNASIUM

Earlier, with the Stadium paid for, a plan began to take shape for the further development of the athletic plant. There was still pressing need for such major items as a natatorium, a field house and a golf course. There was even some speculation as to the architectural possibility of a temporary roof over the Stadium or the enclosure of part of it during the winter season for basketball and other purposes. From time to time also there was talk of providing other facilities such as an indoor hockey rink and bowling alleys.

At the November 1, 1928 board meeting the committee on the development of the athletic plant reported at length on architectural studies of the proposed development. Chairman H. S. Atkinson, a trustee, also explained the plans and air views submitted by the architect, Howard Dwight Smith. The drawings had been presented previously to the board of trustees which had "approved the preliminary plans and authorized the Athletic Board to proceed with plans for their consideration and approval."

The general plans Smith submitted envisaged these major items: a men's gymnasium, a natatorium, an intramural sports building, a men's field house or cage, and a women's field house. There were three "co-related requirements": a military science building and drill hall, an aviation building and hangars, and a boat house. All of these or equivalent buildings came into being save the boat house, but it took the next quarter of a century to accomplish the program.

The men's gymnasium was built in 1931 from state funds at a cost of some $500,000. The Natatorium, to which it was joined, was built the same year as an obligation of the Athletic Board at a cost of $314,353.47. A small field house for women, built in 1927 at a cost of $26,800, burned early in 1958. A military science shop and storage building was built in 1941 at a cost of $111,000 from Federal funds but by then the R.O.T.C. program had grown so large a drill hall was impractical. Similarly, Don Scott Field, named for a former Varsity athlete killed in service, was added in 1943, with hangars and shops, seven miles north of the campus.

Construction of a field house, one of the last two major items, did not get under way until late in 1954. This was designated, appropriately, as the St. John Arena. It cost $3,710,344.70. It was intended for basketball and other uses such as indoor commencements, Farm and Home Week, and other large campus gatherings. In the spring of 1955 a contract was let to the same general contractor for the erection of a field house adjoining the Arena for indoor track and baseball and other uses. This was named, likewise appropriately, after Prof. French. The Arena and the Field House were financed partly by accumulated football profits and the remainder was met by the issuance of bonds to be paid off out of future athletic profits. This was made possible by a state law permitting the construction of self-liquidating projects such as dormitories and other facilities. No such law was on the books when the Stadium was built. The Field House cost $1,024,103.50 and the Arena and Field House together cost two and a half times as much as the Stadium. This was an index of how costs had risen.

In his preliminary report and survey in the fall of 1928 Architect Smith emphasized the need 1) for keeping the Stadium field and the main north and south axis "entirely open and unencumbered to King Avenue"; 2) to keep the new physical education buildings "as close to existing campus activities as possible"; and 3) to study the new buildings "as far as possible" in a group to "fit in with existing conditions, having in mind harmony with present architecture, and economy of construction." In essence this came about.

The men's physical education building and the Natatorium were located on the main approach to and southeast of the Stadium, adjacent also to the new tennis courts and playing fields. The north-south axis was preserved and the entire area south to King Ave. was used for a variety of purposes, especially intramural and recreational. The Arena and the adjoining Field House were erected just north of the Stadium, between the north campus roadway and Lane Ave. This gave compactness and unity to the total facilities except for golf. As of 1958 the total athletic facilities, including the golf course, represented a gross investment of about $8,500,000. Of this amount all but the men's gymnasium came from athletic funds or anticipated receipts. This plant could not have been duplicated for considerably more than it cost. Bonds in the amount of $2,400,000 were issued on the Arena and Field House alone.

At its February 28, 1930 meeting the board adopted a declaration of intent "to construct an addition to the physical education building containing aquatic and other facilities," i.e., a natatorium, subject to the permission of the trustees. The later gave permission to proceed with the financing and construction of the natatorium March 11.

The Natatorium was badly needed. When built it was perhaps the finest structure of its kind in the country. It gave Varsity swimming a boost and made it possible for Ohio State to become—and remain—

a power in intercollegiate swimming under the long reign of Coach Mike Peppe. The natatorium contains three pools—a beginners' pool, a practice pool, and the exhibition pool. The last, with under water lighting, is one of the finest indoor pools in the country. There are seating accommodations for about 1500.

While the new men's gymnasium and the Natatorium added badly needed facilities for important parts of the athletic program, other sports were still unprovided for. At a January 13, 1937 board meeting the pressing needs of the track, baseball and tennis teams were presented. As a temporary solution it was suggested that the cattle building at the State Fair Grounds could be adapted for part of this purpose. For a brief period this was done but it was a makeshift arrangement at best.

4. The Arena and Field House

Somewhat earlier an athletic building program was presented looking to the financing as well as the construction of additional sports facilities. These included a glass enclosure of the lower part of the Stadium, construction of locker rooms, and a start on the acquision of a golf site. The program projected anticipated receipts and outgo for the period July 1, 1929 through June 30, 1937.

In that time estimated receipts, despite the onset of the depression, were put at $1,400,000 with offsetting expenditures of $1,348,815. In that period, it was thought that these new major facilities could be provided: locker room, $25,000; glass enclosure of Stadium, $35,000; golf site, $215,000; natatorium, $300,000; and field house, $500,000. It was also the committee's belief that "the estimates on income have been sufficiently low and the estimates of outgo sufficiently high to permit the construction of the Golf Course or the Baseball-Football Wing of the Field House."

At a May 13, 1929 board meeting a report of the field committee on the details of the foregoing building program was approved. The enclosure of the Stadium—"at least the west half"—was justified on the ground of providing "indoor" facilities for the winter months pending the construction of a field house. Also contemplated were additional lecture rooms and locker space in the Stadium for intramurals. Several ideas for relocating the press boxes were considered: to "hang" them under the projecting edge of the "C" deck or to put them in the central bay of the "B" section. It was agreed finally to retain the original location and to enclose the front of the west box with glass. Other items included resurfacing of the running track, repainting the Stadium steelwork, and checking the leakage of water in the aisles and runways. The total cost was estimated at $87,610.

With the depression under way, the board at its May 28, 1930 meeting adopted a report of the development committee bearing on the expansion program. The committee was "of the opinion that it would be unwise to project plans very far into the future, because of rapidly changing conditions." It considered, therefore, only "the immediate pressing needs of the Department." The urgent need was for a field house and there was talk that the legislature might be interested in a plan for one which would combine the features of an auditorium. Nothing came of this, particularly since the general situation in Ohio and elsewhere became worse. The committee pointed out that the department was obligated to exercise its option for the purchase of land for the golf course site on or before April 1, 1935 amounting to $137,000. Its belief was that "if a plan of finance can be worked out which will in no way retard the promotion and construction of the proposed Field House, that the golf course be developed coincidentally with the Field House development." Specifically it recommended that "the next major dvelopment be that of a Field House, to be located south of the proposed Gymnasium" as part of a proposed quadrangular group.

At a December 16, 1938 board meeting Director St. John reported on "some recent developments pointing to an early possibility for the construction of a field house." Actually the addition of this facility was still a long way off. There was extended discussion of a field house at the April 7, 1939 meeting but the deterring factor was the "present bank indebtedness," i.e., hanging over from the Natatorium and golf course construction. But at a May 17, 1939 meeting the appointment of a special field house committee was authorized.

After this there was frequent discussion of this project in one form or other for several years until war priorities as to steel and critical building materials put an end to it for the time being. For a while discussion of a site centered on a location south of the men's gymnasium. Still later there was again serious consideration of a combination field house and auditorium. About the end of World War II there was a proposal for a structure that would be a memorial to the University's war dead. Hope was still expressed that the legislature might help with a structure to serve other University purposes.

At the November 1, 1940 board meeting, Prof. Clyde T. Morris, as chairman of the field house committee, reported that "definite activity" in preparing field house designs and plans was under way. At the December 9 board meeting the special committee made a long report. After considering a number of locations it was voted to recommend one "immediately north of the Stadium" which, after many delays, ultimately became the site of the St. John Arena. The report envisaged a field house-auditorium with a maximum seating capacity of 15,300 to cost from $1,200,000 to $1,500,000.

The committee made a further report on January 24, 1941. Its studies, based partly on existing field houses on other campuses, had reached the preliminary blue print stage. As of the moment the plans contemplated a 3-part structure: the main section including an exhibition floor and track, plus two dirt-floor areas for practice and indoor sports. The main auditorium would be in the form of a circle 344 feet in diameter with two appended playing areas 130 x 180 feet. The seating capacity would be 12,002 but for large assemblies this could be increased to 14,068. The University cabinet subsequently gave its approval to the choice of location and the general plans for the field house.

The field house-auditorium proposal was brought up again at the May 31, 1944 board meeting. The talk was in terms of a University auditorium seating not less than 15,000. This was conceived as "a University project and that it might well be planned and built so as to accommodate large audiences and, also, to provide facilities for necessary indoor sports during the Winter season," especially Varsity basketball.

The matter came up again at the July 11 meeting when Hugh E. Nesbitt, as chairman of the finance committee and of the committee to consider a memorial coliseum and/or field house, made a further report. He submitted "a financial picture of the last twenty-two years," and pointed out that the contemplated action was "very much involved with the University program for new buildings and that teamwork between the administration and the Board was quite necessary." He called attention also to the problems incident to sharing expense and authority in a structure representing a joint project between the University and the Athletic Department.

University Architect Smith made a further report on the memorial coliseum idea. If it materialized such a structure was to bear the name of "The Ohio Memorial Coliseum." It would be located north of the Stadium as agreed upon in 1941, would have a maximum seating capacity of 20,000, but would have no running track. In further discussion at a May 21, 1945 board meeting, Director St. John reported on possible changes in the plans "to include a Memorial Coliseum at the north end of the Stadium and a single Field House type of building, to be erected as a separate unit."

There was further discussion of the project at the October 10, 1945 meeting. St. John felt that two buildings were needed, a field house for sports activities such as track, baseball, indoor football practice, and even tennis. The other would be on the order of a coliseum with a seating capacity of from 15,000 to 20,000 for basketball and for general University purposes. The entire question, including Stadium repairs and additions, came up again at another meeting November 28.

The architect concurred in the idea of two buildings rather than one. But he pointed out the rise in costs, estimating that the one building which a year earlier would have cost between $1 million and $1½ million would now cost between $2 and $3 million. The parking problems incident to a structure seating up to 20,000 persons were also pointed out. It was agreed informally that an octagonal coliseum north of the closed end of the Stadium was most desirable for that structure, with further study of a field house location where parking was less important.

The discussion was continued at the December 19 board meeting at which the architect presented a campus layout showing the location of existing buildings in relation to models of the two proposed structures. There was further discussion at the January 23, 1946 meeting. At the April 10 meeting it was reported that no progress had been made because "of the impossibility of securing materials," but the architect informed the board that plans were being drawn for a structure 400 x 175 by 40 feet.

In the late 'Forties the field house project continued to simmer. At a June 16, 1948 meeting Director Larkins explained that while a field house for participants and a coliseum for spectators "could not be combined to make an ideal solution, he felt that we would be forced by practical considerations to make such a combination as other schools have." Plot plans and preliminary designs were shown to the board.

In the meantime the board was laying up a "kitty" toward the day when such a structure would take form. At the September 28, 1948 meeting it authorized an increase in the reserve for a field house from $610,00 to $700,000.

The project began to come to a definite head once more at a March 10, 1949 meeting when the board approved a Larkins recommendation that it request the trustees to declare the field house a University project. This was because the structure would be financed from "money now held in reserve" by the department, plus money to be borrowed, plus administration help. Larkins put the total from these sources at $2,500,000. The idea was that by making the field house a formal project, "it would be the hope that the Athletic Department would be able to move forward on the construction plans and further investigate methods of financing."

Still another step was taken at the January 9, 1949 meeting when a special committee of eight was named to proceed "with this project as rapidly as possible." This action followed a letter of December 20 to President Bevis and Vice President Jacob B. Taylor which recommended that the structure be designed to accommodate basketball, track, baseball, football (bad weather practice area), tennis, and golf. It was recommended further that the basketball area have a minimum of 15,000 permanent seats for spectators, besides press, radio, television and other facilities.

In the spring of 1953 the discussions on the field house group began to take final form with the end decisions dependent upon financing and the grouping of facilities. It came down ultimately to whether to undertake two or three structures. In the end two were decided upon and built.

At the April 13 meeting the board was brought up to date on the over-all project. At that time the third set of plans was being developed, the two earlier ones having been abandoned because of "discovered limitations and inadequacies." As a matter of fact five sets of drawings were needed for each structure. As then contemplated the field house group would consist of three structures, an arena for basketball and other activities, a baseball house, and a track shed. An alternative, finally adopted, was to combine the last two.

The matter came up again at the October 19, 1953 meeting when Director Larkins presented a letter from Vice President Taylor to President Bevis which pointed out that the time was near when the director, the board, the University administration and the trustees "must decide the nature of the first step to be taken in the construction program and the precise instant of time when the start should be made." After reviewing current trends and long range prospects, the letter observed that "it does not seem wise now to contemplate a large debt." Taylor went on to say he was inclined to agree with the opinion of Director Larkins that "the most sensible and most desirable first step lies in the construction of the track house and the adjoining baseball house," delaying the so-called arena until later.

Exhibit I, a comparative balance sheet attached, showed that the Athletic Department between June 30, 1944 and June 30, 1953 had increased its assets from $160,236.57 to $1,557,633.98. Of this latter figure,

$1,331,492.51 was in investments which represented the "kitty" toward construction of the field house group. Under physical plant, similarly, the department's assets in those years had increased from $2,638,600.69 to $3,215,583.88 and the total liabilities and net worth from $2,798,837.26 to $4,773,217.86. It was estimated that the net profit for 1953-54 would be $200,000 so that as of the anticipated first bid on a unit or units of the field house group about $1,700,000 would be available without any borrowing. After extended discussion the board recommended proceeding with the construction of the track house and the adjoining baseball house at a cost fo $2,450,000. This was conveyed to President Bevis in a letter dated October 23.

But at a March 4, 1954 board meeting the field house group project took another turn when Director Larkins reported the receipt of a copy of another letter from Vice President Taylor to President Bevis and the trustees relative to the construction of the Arena. This followed a series of conferences among the interested parties. Cost of the Arena was now estimated at $3,633,198. The director recommended approval of the University cabinet's recommendation to proceed with construction of the Arena and this was done.

As it turned out, much more favorable bids were received for building the Arena than had been anticipated. In view of this development, Director Larkins recommended at a May 17 board meeting that the baseball house be eliminated in future plans for the group and that locker and shower facilities be approved for the Arena. Their elimination from the proposed track building would make room in the latter for baseball. He recommended also that "in the light of present developments relative to increased revenue and a more favorable bidding on the Arena than anticipated" that construction of the proposed building for track be recommended to the University administration. The board unanimously approved this.

The board also approved a motion that as soon as it was financially feasible it should consider "as the next item of development for the athletic program, the construction of a Baseball Stadium in connection with the new baseball field which is to be ready for use next year." As it developed, however, this project was delayed further.

At its May 17 meeting the board adopted a resolution urging that the administration approve naming the new structure in memory of Director St. John. The idea was advanced originally by the 1913 basketball team, the first Western Conference team St. John coached, in a resolution presented to the board in September, 1952. This was done presently although for the Arena and not for a field house as first proposed.

Director Larkins informed the board at its June 4, 1954 meeting that on the basis of a restudy of the project by the University architect the cost of the track-baseball structure as an additional unit would be $1,200,000 instead of the earlier figure of $800,000. The board unanimously reaffirmed its recommendation to the University administration to proceed with the construction.

The matter of a baseball stadium continued to come up. At an April 15, 1955 meeting Director Larkins reported that plans were "in process" in the University architect's office. The estimated cost was put at $100,000 but no plans had been developed for financing such a project. The proposal came up again at a June 3 meeting when the board was informed that the University business office was "quite anxious" to proceed with the baseball stadium. The board still felt, however, that while it would like to see this improvement its first obligation was to retire the debt on the Arena and the Field House.

But the idea was revived in the spring of 1956. Including site improvement, the cost was now estimated at $274,000. Plans were approved by the University trustees but the bids, when received, outran the estimates by $45,000 so that the project was again delayed until the plans could be revised and new bids obtained.

Another necessary improvement was the landscaping and blacktopping of the area surrounding the new Arena and Field House. This was authorized in March, 1956 at a cost of $248,000. The parking was expected to provide space for about 1600 cars.

Completion of the Arena in the fall of 1956 created a new problem in respect to basketball ticket allocation. The board anticipated this, however, at its April 27, 1956 meeting. At that time it approved a plan under which the majority of seats were to be allocated in this order: students, faculty and administration, general public. Seats available for public sale were fixed at a maximum of 3000.

5. Stadium Improvements

After twenty-five years of use, the Stadium began to show some signs of weathering in spots so that the Athletic Board embarked upon a program of gradual repair, maintenance and replacement where necessary. From time to time the exposed structural steel had to be repainted, the ground floor under the east side, which got the heaviest traffic, was blacktopped and that under the west side was treated to settle the dust. It, too, was blacktopped later.

At a September 23, 1947 board meeting it was reported that a new field cover had arrived. Remodeling was also approved to provide a new lecture room. To meet the signs of deterioration of the Stadium concrete it was recommended that several waterproofing compounds be tried out on small sections. This was done and in succeeding years, several sections at a time were treated so that the entire Stadium was ultimately waterproofed. Wooden risers on the seat banks were gradually replaced with aluminum I-beam supports and the original oak seat banks gave way to weather-resistant redwood.

Press facilities when Ohio State joined the Big Nine bordered on the primitive. From personal experience dating from 1913 when he was campus correspondent for the *Dispatch* the writer can testify that at Ohio Field they were little more than planks laid lengthwise across trestles at the front of the student bleachers. Folding wooden chairs served as seats. From this vantage (?) point, only a little above ground level, play-by-play reports of home football games were telephoned to the downtown papers.

With the growth and success of football, particularly after the 1916 and 1917 championship years, better facilities were required. These took the form of a new press box at the top of the student bleachers. For this purpose the Athletic Board on December 6, 1917 approved the expenditure of $368.

The Stadium, as noted, originally had two press boxes, both open in front. After these gave way to a single enlarged box on the west side of the upper deck it was not many years until the latter was outgrown. A makeshift solution for a while was to erect temporary booths for the accommodation of some radio broadcasters and others. For practical reasons there was a longstanding rule against women in the press box. This created an issue when the *Lantern* had a woman sports editor during World War II, but this was solved by assigning her to one of the extra booths adjoining the press box.

By the close of the 1948 football season it was apparent that something must be done to remedy the Stadium press and radio facilities. Director Larkins outlined the inadequacies of the existing box at a November 17 meeting, along with a preliminary sketch and estimate by the University architect for the new facilities, including an elevator. The estimated cost was $182,000. Larkins recommended that a new box be built and the board authorized the transfer of $200,000 from the field house reserve for the purpose.

Work on the project was postponed until the close of the 1949 season. A meeting was held with press and radio representatives to discuss the plans for the new box. One long overdue facility added in time for the 1949 season was the elevator at the north end of the Stadium. Its use was limited to top University administrative personnel, special guests, and press, radio, television and motion picture personnel and equipment, and Athletic Department personnel. At the October 10 meeting it was reported that bids for construction of the new box totaled $216,263 or $57,000 more than the amount authorized. This was met by transferring additional cash from reserve funds.

After World War II the operation of a public address system as part of the Stadium facilities, especially for football, was taken for granted. But this was a long time in coming. The Student Senate presented a request at a November 6, 1929 meeting of the board for "favorable action" on the purchase and installation in the Stadium "of an amplifier megaphone system, over which appropriate announcements and a running account of football games might be broadcast to the spectators." It was reported that a trial installation for the impending game with Illinois could be had for $350 or a permanent installation for $4600. But the Senate was informed that "in view of the expense involved and the very short time remaining in the present football season, the Board felt unable to authorize the necessary expense, but would be glad to reconsider the question at a later time."

On September 29, 1931, however, the board authorized the installation in the Stadium "for experiment and try-out" of the public address system used by the Columbus Baseball Co. This was on the understanding that if the system proved satisfactory a rental of $400 for the season would be authorized. Purchase of a public address system for the Stadium was finally authorized January 13, 1932 at a cost of $2160.

In the early years of the Stadium the width of individual seats was figured at 20 inches. This was a bit more generous than was to be found in most big college stadia. But after the close of World War II when space was at a premium in the Stadium, it was decided to fix the width at 17 inches and, except for Sections 1 to 6, all of the Stadium seats were renumbered at a cost of $2500. By so doing the seating capacity was increased by 4000 seats. Upon recommendation the board subsequently authorized the renumbering of seats at the north end of the Stadium also, "no seat to be less than 17 inches in width."

The 1947 season marked the start of the second quarter century of Stadium use. At the September 27 board meeting it was suggested that the twenty-fifth anniversary of the opening be observed with a between-halves ceremony and by placing a bronze tablet containing the names of the men who were responsible for building the Stadium, including the architect, the engineer, the contractor, the president of the University, the athletic director and members of the board, and the Stadium campaign chairman. The chair was authorized to name a committee for this purpose but nothing came of the proposal.

XIV
THE ADMINISTRATIVE SIDE

A STRONG feature of Ohio State's athletic program under Director St. John and later was its operation along with physical education under a single head. The success of such a joint program, making common or joint use of facilities and personnel, depends to a considerable degree upon the director. On the whole, "Saint" was remarkably successful in accomplishing this as was Richard C. Larkins who followed him. This merger came about early in 1914.

About a decade later, however, a strong movement developed to set off women's physical education as a separate activity. This divorce was desired by a number of alumnae and had influential support in the Board of Trustees. The issue reached the point in 1922 that St. John declared he would resign rather than be a party to the separation proposed. This created a tense situation for a while but in the end the status quo was maintained.

With the active involvement of the United States in World War I manpower on the campus was greatly depleted and it was necessary to curtail the athletic program. The 1918 football schedule, for example, was regarded as unofficial although a reduced schedule was played. Basketball and baseball were also in question. When the shooting war ended November 11 it was too late to arrange a regular basketball schedule. At a December 4, 1919 meeting the board expressed itself as "opposed to dropping basket ball" and favored "the continuation of baseball." Coach Wilce was in uniform and Assistant Director George M. Trautman was athletic officer of the 37th (Ohio National Guard) Division at Camp Sheridan, Montgomery, Ala.

Some time after the war the board, in a move to de-emphasize excessive participation in Varsity sports, adopted a resolution June 1, 1921 that the Athletic Department "continue and strengthen its present administrative policy. First—To encourage sound, universal participation, not overindulgence, by the student in athletics. Second—To discourage intercollegiate participation by any individual in more than two major or minor sports activities during any one collegiate year."

In the fifteen years between 1912 and 1927 tremendous changes had occurred in Ohio State athletics. From a comparative unknown the University had become a force in intercollegiate athletics, especially in football, basketball and track. What had been a more or less incidental campus activity had mushroomed into permanent big business. This was doubtless an inevitable byproduct of the pre- and postwar football successes and particularly the Stadium fund raising campaign which, in effect, took the public into partnership in the athletic venture.

Specifically, the actual business spiraled from a little under $20,000 in the year 1912-13 to nearly $650,000 in 1927-28. The Stadium was nearly paid for and already there was talk of expanding the physical facilities to meet other needs. Yet the machinery for handling so large a volume of business had not kept pace with the needs and some laxity had developed in spending. There was never any hint of wrongdoing but both in the board and on the part of the University administration there was a growing feeling of a need for tighter controls and better accounting.

This came to a head in the summer of 1927 when a downtown accounting firm made a report on an audit of the Athletic Department for the year 1926-27, with recommendations for suggested changes. The accountant in question was retained as an advisor for a year. The report was under discussion at four board meetings in the unprecedented space of twelve days between July 28 and August 9, 1927.

In effect, the audit analyzed departmental operations, called attention to loose methods of doing business that had crept in, and made numerous specific recommendations to improve the system and eliminate the laxity. The report also cited an apparent shortage of some $5700 in the Stadium Fund. A recheck disclosed, however, that only $43.75 was "unaccounted for."

The auditing report was taken up at a board meeting August 4 and at a 5-hour session the next day. Various actions emerged from these meetings: that a copy of the audit and recommendations be sent to President Rightmire; that the 1927-28 budget be reconsidered; that salary warrants be paid on the last day of the month only—a practice had developed of drawing pay checks early; that only board members, the director and assistant director and treasurer attend board meetings, with others "present only on the invitation of the board." The operating budget was approved "with the hope that, by careful administration during the year 1927-28, the budget will show a credit balance at the end of the fiscal year."

The accounting rules and regulations adopted filled four and a half single-space typewritten pages. In effect, they were only what good business practice required, especially as to expenditures and a proper accounting therefor. Because of the absence of Director St. John on vacation a number of questions raised by the audit were deferred until his return.

At the October 31, 1927 board meeting attention was called to a 5-page, single-space typewritten letter from President Rightmire to the board concerning the special audit and the resulting recommendations. The president had discussed these with Chairman French and with St. John. "We discussed generally," the president wrote, "the conditions surrounding the growth of the athletic activities here and the rapid expansion in the financial transactions through the last ten years, and the methods generally that have been projected into this rapidly expanding period but which were adapted to a smaller organization and a less extensive field of operation."

In his responsibility for the entire University, Dr. Rightmire cited the need for his being familiar with athletic matters. Because of the rapid growth, he commented, "there has come a quickened appreciation of this work all over Ohio, and more or less curiosity about the manner of dealing with the large incomes which the years have been producing, and the occasions for expense which are necessarily numerous and many of them calling for very large outlay."

On the matter of "some disagreement with reference to the paid Stadium subscriptions," growing out of the auditor's report, he made it clear where he stood. "Knowing the integrity of the persons who have dealt with this matter," he said, "I have no doubt that the disagreement is already explained or is in the process of explanation. However, until it is adjusted, it gives a rather damaging look to that page of the report."

Dr. Rightmire was anxious to have the remaining debt on the Stadium paid off as rapidly as conditions permitted because of the "hold" such obligations might seem to give to those to whom the board was in debt to the extent of $335,000. On this point he wrote that:

the financial obligation to parties who have no relationship with the educational institution should be liquidated as fast as it is possible so that the Athletic Board may feel itself absolutely free from any outside contacts or possible sources of suggestion or influence. I beg the liberty to suggest that the liquidation of these note obligations is one of the most important of the things which has the interest of the Athletic Board, and I believe that this is more important than almost any suggestions for further expansion in our facilities. Much has been heard in the last decade of "commercialized" athletics and it is at this point that the charge can continue to be made against us with the nearest approach to justification. Our very bigness is both strength and weakness . . . .

On the score of the procedural changes recommended which the board had adopted the president was confident that these would "adequately take care of all such matters, and consequently hereafter the business procedure dealing with the management of athletics will be carried on in a well organized and highly efficient manenr." But he emphasized that "deviations from these rules of procedure should be permitted only in cases of the greatest emergency where an explanation would at once strike reasonable persons as justifiable. In the matter of travel expense, which the auditor made the subject of a special exhibit, he observed that the "figures present rather large individual items and a large total for many kinds of travel occasions" and to him they seemed "to present some questions of importance."

He had some concern also for another special exhibit in the report relating to advertising for the State Fair for which the Athletic Board had been paying. This grew out of the use of the Fair Grounds Coliseum for basketball and other University purposes. An arrangement had developed by agreement, but apparently never specifically authorized, whereby full pages of advertising in the downtown papers for the annual State Fair were paid for out of athletic funds. In this connection, Dr. Rightmire wondered "whether for the use of the Coliseum the State Department of Agriculture is expecting considerable revenue. If so, it seems that this is a situation which might be adjusted. At least if this sum is called for on our part for permission to use the Coliseum for basketball, it looks like an effort on the part of the State to take to itself a portion of our athletic receipts in an indirect fashion. Any movement on the part of the State to participate in athletic receipts or the management thereof, or any movement which would have for its purpose legislative or State Department accounting for athletic receipts and control of expenditures in the manner that prevails in the State Departments, would clearly lead to much discomfort here and inconvenience in carrying on our athletic activities. . . ."

He closed with a further reference to his ultimate responsibility in all University matters and his need to be "constantly in a position where I can furnish all information" necessary to defend against "any sort of attack or suggestion of innuendo . . . ."

Various items noted in the accountant's report came up at later board meetings. There was extended discussion of some of these matters at the November 18, 1927 session. On the Stadium debt it was reported that the $75,000 currently budgeted for that purpose had been paid but on November 28 an additional $25,000 was ordered paid. On the question of paying for State Fair advertising in lieu of rent for the use of the Coliseum it was reported that the use of such facilities had been "provided for at a conference with the Governor."

Other items reported on and clarified included football game expenses, the handling of ticket sales with an accounting of student and complimentary tickets, pre-season and pre-game meals for the football squad, and the hiring of W. D. Richardson, a New York *Times* sports writer, for special publicity in connection with the Columbia game. One item questioned was the outlay of $633.21 in connection with the 1926 Army-Navy game at Chicago attended by thirteen in the Ohio State party. Another similar item was one of $1115.79 for "scouting Michigan."

Further steps were taken at a special board meeting November 21. One issue here was a "surprise" audit of the athletic ticket office by the accounting consultant. The board was unanimous that his retention "did not contemplate such surprise visit." Audits were requested as of January 1, April 1 and July 1, 1928 "and that, prior to the next football season, the Ticket Office be so equipped, manned and organized as will permit of a surprise audit at any time." At another special meeting November 28, attended by President Rightmire, the special accounting report was explored further. And at a December 8 meeting a special committee disposed of the remaining items to which the accountant had called attention. Its opinion was that "the expense incurred at the Army-Navy game was excessive," that the expense of "scouting Michigan" was also excessive, and it recommended that any future employment of "special publicity agents" be made only with prior board approval.

The Mahoning County Alumni Association, among others, took note meanwhile of "serious charges of inefficiency and of neglect of duty made by Mr. A. W. Raymond and others, against the present heads of our Athletic Association." The Youngstown alumni adopted a resolution asking President Rightmire for an investigation of athletics on the campus. They also pledged the president "our loyal support in whatever action you may see fit to pursue." The president assured them that "all matters relating to athletic conduct here are constantly under careful consideration and that we shall appreciate your sympathetic thought and encouragement in the future as we have in the past."

Early in 1927 when the legislature convened for its biennial session there was some talk of creating a state athletic commission which, among other things, would have control of University athletics. The issue never came into the open as far as the University was concerned, but reasons were advanced why such a commission or agency, even if created, should not be given authority over Ohio State athletics since they were already under state control through the Board of Trustees which was answerable to the governor.

With the transfer of athletic funds to the University at the end of 1927, R. M. Royer, longtime treasurer of the Athletic Association, was out of that job since the funds would now be under the University treasurer. The board at its December 22, 1927 meeting took note of this fact and voted the payment of the outgoing treasurer's salary for one year from July 1, 1927. It was reported also that substantial savings in expenditures had been made since June below budget estimates made at that time. President Rightmire in a letter to Chairman French expressed confidence that the board and the athletic administration would adhere to "the new business procedure in both letter and spirit."

With minor amendments the board adopted a new constitution for the Athletic Association at its November 10, 1927 meeting. The object of the association was "to promote all the legitimate athletic interests of the Ohio State University." Active members were to consist of voting members of the board and associate members were to include the athletic director, assistant director, treasurer and other persons. The instrument spelled out the duties and responsibilities of the director and committees, use of the Stadium, major and minor sports, and letter awards.

It specified that with the consent of the board the Stadium could be used by other University organizations "insofar as such does not interfere with the Varsity teams." It could also be used "by city, state, national and religious organizations for purposes" approved by the president of the University and the board. As to athletic participation it provided that "No individual, team or organization may represent the Ohio State University, or any class thereof, nor may any man use the name of the Ohio State University in athletic competition, except with the authority of the Athletic Board, which may withdraw this authority at its discretion." It recognized football, baseball, basketball, track and field athletics and cross country as major sports, with tennis, swimming, wrestling, gymnastics, golf, rifle shooting "and such other sports as may be added" as minor sports. The bases for letter awards were substantially as before.

Still another constitution was presented at the May 28, 1930 board meeting, the old one having "become obsolete." The new one was designed "with a view to expressing herein the relationships and principles now actually existing." The name was the same as before, The Ohio State University Athletic Association.

The association's object was "to plan, finance and execute such policies as are deemed advisable to promote wider knowledge of and interest in intercollegiate athletics on the part of the students of the University, the officials and trustees of the University, the alumni of the University—including in the phrase 'alumni' those who have enrolled at the University but have withdrawn before enough academic credit has been earned for the granting of a degree—the secondary schools, particularly of the state of Ohio, and the general public, as well as a general participation in intramural athletics among the students of the University. It shall also be the object of this Association to promote an effective and inclusive plan of general recreation among its members."

Membership was to fall into four groups—the president and trustees, all students, all faculty and administrative staff members, and all alumni as defined above. Control was to be vested, as before, in the board, subject to such regulations as might be prescribed from time to time by the University trustees—five from the faculty, two from students, two alumni, and one trustee. The two students were to be chosen by the Student Senate and the two alumni from the Ohio State University Association.

In the fall of 1930 a new method of electing team captains was discussed. At the October 1 board meeting a special committee reported on the basis of about sixty letters sent out to "representative" athletes as to the method to be followed, but only twenty-five replies were received. The committee recommended that Varsity team captains be "elected by their service team-mates during the week preceding the first Western Conference contest." Twenty of the twenty-five replies received favored this plan. Director St. John was instructed to make a further canvass and to report later. At a meeting October 30 a highly detailed system of selecting Varsity managers was approved with a view to encouraging "the finest men in the University to participate in the management of Ohio State athletic teams."

A report on a revised method of electing team captains was adopted May 11, 1931. Under this plan nominations should be made by a committee consisting of two sophomores, a senior and the coach. The committee was to nominate two or more men for captain. The election was to be held "at the close of the season," instead of just before the first Conference game under the earlier plan.

For a long period after the 1912 reorganization there were comparatively few changes in the faculty membership on the board. During most of the next fifteen years Prof. French was both chairman of the board and the University's representative in the Western Conference.

In the fall of 1929, however, a partial reorganization of the board was accomplished when President Rightmire replaced French, Dean O. V. Brumley and Prof. D. J. Kays with Junior Dean J. L. Morrill and Profs. Harold E. Burtt and Clarence D. Laylin. French was continued as Conference representative, a position that was made a separate appointment. At its November 6, 1929 meeting the board elected Prof. Clyde T. Morris chairman.

A change in the alumni representation occurred in the spring of 1933 when Ralph W. Hoyer, '06, gave way to Hugh E. Nesbitt, '14. Hoyer, a former football captain and assistant coach, had been a member for two decades. At its June 9 meeting the board expressed its "deepest appreciation for this long, continued service." A corresponding faculty change occurred that fall when Prof. Morris gave way to Col. G. L. Townsend, commandant. The board took recognition of Prof. Morris' long service both as a member and as Stadium engineer. Another stalwart to leave the board was Samuel N. Summer, '05, who had been Stadium Committee chairman and the chief reliance of the board in financial matters. In the alumni election of 1934 he gave way to Robert E. "Heinie" Heekin, w'06, of Cincinnati.

An unusual step was taken at the December 17, 1941 meeting when President Bevis joined the board as a regular member, replacing Vice President Morrill who was leaving the campus. Never before had a president of the University sat as an active board member although Presidents Thompson and Rightmire had sat occasionally with the board. To quote the minutes: "Dr. Bevis stated that this was a field in which he had no intimate acquaintance and, therefore, he hoped to get some insight on this particular subject to make himself a more valuable executive." There was some mild criticism since he was already an ex officio board member on the ground that he was depriving a faculty member of a place on the board. He remained an active member for some years.

Three new members joined the board at its November 19, 1947 meeting. Dr. Bevis, in answer to questions, described these changes as "routine." His place on the board was taken by Vice President Bland L. Stradley. That of Prof. James E. Pollard as Conference representative was taken by Dean Wendell D. Postle, of the College of Dentistry. The third new member was Dean Frank Strong, of the College of Law. Dean Postle thus became the University's third Conference representative.

Meanwhile the effects of the depression had continued to be felt in the mid-'Thirties. At its January 30, 1935 meeting the board authorized its finance committee and the director to review the budget for 1934-35 and to consider prospects for 1935-36 with a view to the indebtedness to Columbus banks. At this meeting the winter and spring sports schedules were approved except for a pair of baseball games at Iowa, the N.C.A.A. swimming championships at Harvard, and the Penn Relays. These items were reserved for future consideration but participation in the Penn Relays was finally approved. At a further report at the March 13, 1935 meeting things looked somewhat brighter for 1935-36 chiefly because of the impending football game with Notre Dame which, as it turned out, was a sellout.

Prof. Laylin and Summer appeared before the Board of Trustees February 11, 1935 with reference to the Athletic Board's indebtedness to the banks for the construction of the Natatorium and the fact that the depression "greatly affected athletic receipts." As a result the board had not been able to "make payments on this indebtedness to the extent originally intended." The trustees said they stood "ready to cooperate with the Athletic Board in finding ways and means of meeting this indebtedness in case the net receipts of next year's operations do not materialize as anticipated." The 1935-36 budget, subject to changes, was adopted June 7, 1935. It called for expenditures of $184,766.63 and total income of $279,000, leaving some $94,000 for possible reduction on the indebtedness.

The board continued to tighten its belt against the depression not only to enable the department to stay within its income but to continue to reduce its indebtedness. The experience of those years varied and estimates did not always come up to expectations. In June, 1932 the annual budget as presented showed anticipated income for the next year as $273,000 as against operating expenses of $226,650. Even then polo, rifle and pistol, and fencing were "temporarily provided for in an Intramural way." Contracts with individual staff members were on the basis that if necessary the board would reconsider them after December 1. After the close of the 1932 football season the board took another look at the athletic budget which it revised January 17, 1933 since total receipts were only $147,380.08 as against disbursements of $175,811.00 through June 30, not including anything against the debt. A policy was adopted that for the half year beginning January 1, 1933 all sports except basketball and track were to be run on an intramural basis and that the track schedule "be drastically curtailed." Additional pay reductions were put into effect.

Through no wish of its own the University in the fall and winter of 1935-36 got into an unhappy and unproductive controversy with Governor Martin L. Davey. The issue arose originally over budget matters but was expanded to other items including athletics. The governor's charge that most of the 1935 Varsity football squad were on the state payroll, with overtones of subsidizing and professionalism, got nationwide attention.

As to the charges concerning the football squad, these were flatly denied as far as subsidizing and professionalism were concerned. It was admitted freely that quite a number of players were working part-time for the state, but it was emphasized that they had not obtained their employment through the University, and that they were actually working for the wages they received. In any case the charges were referred to Major John L. Griffith, the Conference commissioner, for an impartial investigation of the situation. His exhaustive report some time later completely cleared the University of Davey's malicious and unfounded charges. The board at its October 30, 1935 meeting had requested Griffith to look into the charges and pledged "its complete cooperation with your office, promising unreservedly any assistance that you may require."

Griffith lost no time in complying. The inquiry made by Griffith was checked carefully by Profs. W. J. Moenkhaus, of Indiana University, and Alfred C. Callen, of the University of Illinois. The result of their report, in sum, was a complete exoneration of the Ohio State athletic administration and fifteen athletes, all members of the football squad, of the Davey charges. The Griffith report, dated January 14, 1936, was presented at the January 31 board meeting.

The inquiry developed that of some fifty students employed in the legislature as pages or clerks, four were Varsity football players. Of twenty students on a part-time basis in the public works department, six were athletes. It was also shown that students from other Ohio colleges and even from Wisconsin and Purdue were employed similarly. In its conclusions the report emphasized that Ohio State athletes were so employed, that the work they did was "the same as that performed by other employes," and there was no evidence of "made" jobs, that they were paid on the same basis as non-athletes so employed, that athletes so employed were in the minority, and that those listed "received their appointments by and through friends or friends of the family" and not through the Athletic Department, nor was there any proof of collusion.

Profs. Moenkhaus and Callen met January 4 to consider the Griffith report. They had this to say: "The Committee feels that Major Griffith has made a thorough investigation. The evidence shows that these much-publicized state jobs are given to non-athletes as well as to athletes, and the committee does not feel that this evidence indicates that athletes have been unduly favored. The Committee finds no evidence that either the Athletic Department or other University authorities were in any way instrumental in securing the appointments to these jobs."

During the depression, meanwhile, University staff members took a total of three pay cuts imposed by the trustees in line with prevailing state policy and to stay within available revenues. Because Athletic Department salaries were not paid out of state funds a question arose whether similar cuts should be applied to the athletic budget. Director St. John argued that they should not as long as funds were available. The 1931-32 budget was adopted by the board and approved by the trustees before the cut imposed that summer took effect. But the trustees at their August 6 meeting instructed President Rightmire to return the athletic budget "with the request that said budget be revised in accordance with the plan adopted by the Trustees." H. S. Atkinson, trustee member of the Athletic Board, was asked to request the trustees to reconsider their action. In time a compromise was worked out whereby that portion of athletic staff members' salaries paid from state funds was reduced in line with the general University cut but not salaries or portions thereof paid from athletic funds.

A general policy against "passing the hat" at football games and other contests for whatever purpose was followed after the completion of the Stadium. But a partial exception was made at the game with Navy in 1931 in connection with a nationwide campaign for a memorial to the late Knute K. Rockne, Notre Dame football coach. At its October 29, 1931 meeting the board approved the distribution of "literature" relative to the memorial but outside of the seating area, a 1-minute announcement over the public address system between halves, and for some plan for the collection of money or pledge cards from contributors "provided that buckets were not passed or individual solicitation made."

During the early years of the depression various efforts were made to schedule extra intercollegiate football games for charity purposes. Ohio State was no except to this pressure. At a board meeting November 6, 1930 President Rightmire read a telegram from Governor Fred Green, of Michigan, to Governor Myers Y. Cooper, of Ohio, urging the latter to use his influence through the president to get the board to rescind any rules "which might prevent the scheduling of football games for charity." Governor Cooper merely referred the matter to him, Dr. Rightmire explained. He then asked the board to advise him on two questions: whether it desired to relax its own or Conference rules to permit the scheduling of such games, and whether it had "any disposition or plan to aid charities and public relief." After discussion the board adopted a motion that it was "inexpedient and unwise to instruct the University's Faculty Representative . . . to vote for any suspension or relaxation of Conference rules covering the scheduling and conduct of intercollegiate contests."

It was brought out also that "the present football season will produce net receipts little more than sufficient, if indeed sufficient, to operate the present budget and that these receipts will fall far short of amounts which had been anticipated and budgeted in advance for payments on the construction of the Natatorium." On some belief that various colleges, especially the larger state universities, were making large profits from football, various proposals had been advanced in the press for the donation of athletic receipts to the Red Cross, to state agencies, and to community chests. A budgetary analysis reported at the January 16, 1931 board meeting showed an anticipated deficit for the year of $58,410.44.

The question of a charity football game came up again early in November, 1931 when a Cleveland delegation, including former Governor Harry L. Davis, appeared before the board. The project this time was for a post-season charity game in Cleveland, preferably with Notre Dame, with part of the proceeds to go to the School Children's Dollar Fund for the relief of some 40,000 pupils there suffering from undernourishment. It was argued that the great emergency in Cleveland would justify waiving any University or Conference rules to make such a game possible. It was reported that Notre Dame was willing to schedule such a game.

Prof. French explained the action of the Conference in authorizing the playing of extra games for such purposes. Dr. Rightmire reviewed the situation of a year earlier when pressure had been exerted to permit such games. He expressed a willingness to approve a shift of the Ohio State charity game, if any, to Cleveland if the board cared to authorize it with Conference permission. The board then adopted a resolution appreciating the need presented by the Cleveland committee and desiring "to be as helpful in the present emergency as its responsibilities and relationships will permit."

As it worked out, however, an extra game for charity purposes was finally scheduled with Minnesota. Ohio State traveled to Minneapolis and lost. A story of the time was that the train carrying the squad stopped somewhere en route and a number of players got off and ate green apples which made them sick at game time and this, in turn, probably cost Ohio State the game. Minnesota won, 19 to 7.

A comprehensive financial statement going back to 1927-28 was presented at the April 27, 1936 board meeting. It was prepared by Charles A. Kuntz, University comptroller. Figures in the statement as of March 31, 1936 emphasized how far athletics had become big business since Ohio State's admission to the Conference in 1912. The balance sheet showed assets of $2,348,967.80 with an indebtedness of $282,671. The fixed assets were as follows:

Stadium	$1,803,596.01
Natatorium	314,353.47
Golf course	155,266.92
Equipment	69,533.34

Of the indebtedness, $86,671 was due on land contracts in connection with the golf course site. The remainder consisted of notes due the downtown banks, mostly for the construction of the Natatorium.

The contrast between the lush years of the 'Twenties and the effects of the depression in terms of income and expenditures was shown as follows:

	Receipts	Expenditures
1927-28	$674,895.85	$675,080.49
1928-29	821,632.93	823,881.48
1929-30	691,981.76	682,248.66
1930-31	727,928.27	737,944.44
1931-32	608,878.35	608,610.38
1932-33	253,436.46	250,549.55
1933-34	251,543.39	255,216.11
1934-35	358,300.15	357,336.44

Figures for expenditures included payments on notes and for capital outlay.

The remarkable showing of the football team, meanwhile, in the first three years of the Schmidt regime enabled the board to resume or increase payments on the principal of its indebtedness and to begin to enlarge the sports program again. At the December 23, 1936 meeting it voted to add modest sums to the budget for pistol shooting, $200, rifle shooting, $610, polo, $800, and fencing, $300.

Thanks to improved economic conditions in the late 'Thirties and the continuing enthusiasm reflected in increased football attendance during the first years of the Schmidt era, the board was enabled to pay off its indebtedness more rapidly than had been anticipated. At the

November 1, 1940 meeting Director St. John told the board that all indebtedness to the banks had been discharged and all payments then due for the golf course land had been made. For the moment the board was out of debt except for some $60,000 yet to be paid on the land contracts for the golf course site.

Faculty regulations called for an annual report from the Athletic Board but for years this was honored more in the breach than in observance. Such a report was prepared, however, for 1937-36. Among other things it emphasized that "the application of eligibility standards to all students engaged in every form of extra curricular activity, following the pattern set by the Athletic Department, has been a most important factor in raising standards of scholarship throughout the entire student body. The Athletic Board points with pride to this as one more contribution which intercollegiate sport has made to the general welfare of the Ohio State University."

In terms of intercollegiate competition, it listed 13 sports, showing a total of 162 contests and gross participation by 1209 students. The intramural program for men, similarly, showed 21 sports with 909 teams and 10,182 participants. For women the corresponding figures showed 14 sports and 1076 participants.

The onset of World War II quickly affected college campuses all over the nation. Athletic schedules were curtailed, wartime regulations had to be met, and manpower was at a minimum. Many universities, including Ohio State, had thousands of men in uniform on the campus. But they were there for purposes related to the war and the Army and Air Force forbade their participation in sports. The Navy was more lenient and this gave an advantage to certain universities. There was also talk of Conference action permitting freshmen to compete and this was done ultimately.

Coaching staffs were also depleted as many of the younger men received commissions in the armed services. At the February 13, 1942 board meeting Director St. John reported on the economies made possible by this development and said that as far as possible resignations or leaves of absence would be met by remaining members of the staff.

To cope with the war situation the Conference representatives meeting March 7, 1942 in Chicago adopted certain waivers of Conference regulations. These were reported to the board at its March 13 meeting. The actions "were taken to meet changing conditions attendant upon accelerated college programs and in response to definite requests for games with service teams of the Army and Navy." The actions included:

1) permission to play ten football games of which two must be with service teams; 2) to permit freshman teams to compete, except that in football "the number of games with other freshman teams, with service teams, and with varsity teams of other colleges be limited to three"; 3) to permit competition with other universities not observing Conference rules.

Substantial contributions were made from football receipts during the later war years to service funds, particularly Army and Navy relief funds. A board meeting was called May 8, 1942 to discuss such participation. The contracts with the two service teams on the 1942 football schedule called for a 50-50 division of the gross receipts but the comment was made that "wisdom seems to point to a more widespread contribution from the whole schedule." The board authorized a contribution to the Army and Navy Relief Fund of 10 per cent of the gross receipts from all sources for the year "or any adjusted schedule of contribution which would approximate the same amount of money."

Another result of the war was that military authorities took over the State Fair Grounds, including the Coliseum, so that other arrangements had to be made for Varsity basketball. Another consequence of the wartime situation was the shifting of certain football games away from the home field of the host team. This, too, required special Conference approval. Two games in which Ohio State was involved were moved. One was the Ohio State-Illinois game of 1942 to the Cleveland Municipal Stadium, and the other was the transfer of the Purdue-Ohio State game to the same site in 1943. At the board meeting of June 10, 1942 permission was given to shift the Illinois game to Cleveland, at the request of Illinois, with the further provision that 10 per cent of the gross receipts were to go to the Army and Navy Relief Fund.

A number of members of the coaching staff went into military service. One of the first to go with Coach Laurence N. Snyder, of the track team. Two others who went in the early months of the war were Tucker P. Smith, trainer, and Robert Williams, assistant greenskeeper at the golf course. Their "resignations" were accepted at the June 10, 1942 meeting with the understanding that they would be regarded as leaves of absence.

Since wartime travel was on a priority basis travel incident to athletics was limited and often uncertain. Under the circumstances the usual band trips to out-of-town football games were out of the question. At its October 8, 1942 meeting the board faced the question of whether the band should be sent to the Illinois-Ohio State game in Cleveland. Director

St. John reported that the Conference athletic directors had "clearly indicated that no band travel would be underwritten for this current football season." The board concurred. Three freshman football games were scheduled that fall: with Pittsburgh and Michigan in Columbus, and with Indiana at Bloomington.

At the July 19, 1943 meeting the board was informed of the adoption at the Conference meeting of June 23 of a resolution taking further recognition of the war situation. This was to the effect that since it was "obvious that for the duration of the war intercollegiate athletic programs are to be essentially activities of the armed services," competition during the war period "sponsored by any college or university shall not be deemed 'intercollegiate' as such term is used in the Conference rules and regulations." This was on the understanding, however, that no eligibility rules were waived as regards bona fide enrollment as a student and preservation of the amateur status.

Even the matter of broadcasting football games was tied in with the problems growing out of the war. Divided opinion was expressed at the September 22, 1943 board meeting when the broadcasting committee report was presented which called for the broadcasting of all games. Director St. John spoke in favor of a "considerably reduced" program, reminding the board that "the financial picture of the present fiscal year was not at all bright." The question was resolved by approving the report after deleting the Great Lakes and Pittsburgh games. As of the spring of 1944 when the war was beginning to enter its final stages seven members of the Varsity coaching staff were on leave for active duty with the armed forces.

At the May 31, 1944 meeting Director St. John informed the board that the withdrawal of Chicago from Conference competition was, as far as he knew, "a temporary step due to war conditions." As a matter of fact Chicago remained in the Conference for another two years but finally withdrew completely.

A letter was read at the March 15, 1945 meeting from President Bevis to the effect that at the Board of Trustees meeting on March 5 "considerable concern was manifested by a number of members over the practice of publicizing the actions of the Athletic Board, prior to consideration, by the Board of Trustees, of matters within its cognizance." This was based on the fact that final authority lay with the trustees in such matters as appointments. The letter pointed out that "the possibility of embarrassment growing out of premature publicity is evident."

At this meeting Trustee Donald C. Power, '22, was introduced as the alternate trustee member of the board, vice H. S. Atkinson, '13, who could no longer attend because of ill health.

To bring the Athletic Board and the Athletic Department operations in line with those elsewhere in the University, the trustees at a November 1, 1948 meeting adopted certain amendments to faculty rules and regulations. The two major items concerned staff appointments and the annual budget. To be effective such appointments must have trustee approval and the athletic budget similarly must have final trustee approval. On the latter point, all athletic expenditures were to be "accomplished in accordance with University procedures under the general supervision of the Business Manager." The effect of these changes was to bring both matters under closer University control and to lessen Athletic Board authority in such matters. This was in keeping with similar moves in other areas but was also a further reflection of the fact that intercollegiate athletics had become big business.

After thirty-four years of devoted and farseeing service to the University, Athletic Director St. John approached retirement age in mid-1946. Several months earlier the board began to canvass possibilities for his successor. St. John himself was not a party to these discussions and refrained from making any suggestions. Possible candidates were considered both from on and from off the campus.

The matter came to a head at a board meeting July 6, 1946 when a special committee unanimously recommended the appointment of Richard C. Larkins, '31, associate professor of physical education and since 1933 a member of the athletic and physical education staffs. Larkins was also the preference of a "large majority" of the members of the physical education staff for the joint position of athletic director and chairman of the Physical Education Department. He had won his "O" in football and basketball and had returned to the campus after wartime service in the Navy. Larkins was elected unanimously, subject to trustee approval.

The arrangement was that Larkins would "sit in" for the year 1946-47 while Director St. John completed his service. Larkins was then to take over as of July 1, 1947. At the June 25, 1947 meeting the board adopted the following resolution concerning St. John:

Since Mr. Lynn Wilbur St. John retires from his position as Director of Athletics and Physical Education on July First, the Athletic Board wishes to express officially its enthusiastic appreciation of his long years of distinguished service and his outstanding contribution to athletics at this University, over the State of Ohio, and throughout the nation. His record of unselfish consecration to the interests of The Ohio State University is unsurpassed, and the Athletic Board considers itself fortunate to be associated with an administration which has been so eminently successful.

The department lost another of its veterans with the retirement in June, 1947 of Henry D. Taylor, '09, longtime director of ticket sales. "Hen," as he was known to thousands of alumni and others, came into the department with the Stadium era. He chose to retire voluntarily after he reached the age of 60. In addition to handling tickets, he served also as freshman baseball coach and in other ways in the department. He was a former Varsity basketball captain. His job in the ticket office called for vast patience, which he had in abundance, and for skill in dealing with people who were sometimes unreasonable in their demands and expectations. After twenty-five years in this troubled business, "Hen" got out to spend his remaining years in leisure. He was followed successively by Oscar L. Thomas, '26, 1947-49; H. Wade Kraner, 1949-50; J. Ed Weaver, 1950-1953; and George R. Staten, 1953 to date.

Under state law retirement from University employment is mandatory at 70. On rare occasions an extra year may be granted. This was done in the spring of 1946 for Tony Aquila, long a familiar part of the athletic picture as Stadium groundskeeper. It was reported at the May 5, 1946 board meeting that the trustees had granted an extension of service for Tony for a year beyond the normal retirement age.

Radio and Television

In the early 'Thirties the question of broadcasting football and basketball games was before the board a number of times. At the July 8, 1931 meeting the chief topic centered around a discussion of future policy as to broadcasting over WEAO (later WOSU), the campus station. Some felt strongly that broadcasting hurt attendance and gate receipts. Others felt that, given a chance, broadcasting would increase attendance and interest.

R. C. Higgy, WEAO director, urged continuance of broadcasting on the ground that football radiocasts attracted more listener interest for the station than any other program feature, that there was no proof that broadcasting cut down attendance, and that there would be an unfortunate public reaction if the broadcasts were discontinued. The possibility of the board selling the service to other stations was broached. For the time being the board postponed a decision.

It took up the matter again at a July 13 meeting when Higgy recommended that it make "a definite arrangement" for WEAO and that "arrangements with the out-of-town commercial stations be made in the best manner possible with a view to reducing the cost of our own broadcasting." He estimated expenses for WEAO alone as $2110. This was tentatively approved as the basis for negotiations with outside stations. The current budget had an item of $1500 for broadcasting.

The question of whether to broadcast basketball came up in connection with the 1931-32 season. At its November 23, 1931 meeting the board once more discussed the policy involved. At its December 18 meeting it authorized WEAO "to broadcast such basketball games as its time will permit during 1932, with the further provision that President Rightmire's Committee on Public Relations be invited to utilize these broadcasts in whatever way it may desire."

The broadcast issue continued to bob up during the depression. On November 27, 1934 the board voted to continue the practice of not broadcasting basketball games during the coming season. On March 13, 1935 it voted to "approve the policy of selling broadcasting rights to a commercial sponsor, with appropriate safeguards as to the kind of sponsor, the type of commercial announcement, and the continuance of broadcasting privileges for WOSU," and to empower its committee on programs, concessions and publicity "to negotiate further and enter into the appropriate contract." In the spring of 1935 at a Conference meeting at Ann Arbor the broadcasting issue was discussed. The faculty representatives and athletic directors went on record as favoring a cooperative broadcasting program for the Conference but two Conference university presidents, unnamed, were opposed.

A detailed report with recommendations as to broadcasting brought in at the June 10, 1936 board meeting was adopted with minor changes. The report dealt with certain "implied assumptions" growing out of a Conference study of the problem. One of these was that the Conference "apparently does not feel it wise or possible to recommend that football broadcasting be discontinued and prohibited." On its part, the board, acting for the University, adopted ten rules:

1. Not to permit sponsored broadcasting of football games except as provided in Item 9 below.
2. Through WOSU to conduct a broadcast of all games played in the Stadium and of such games away from home as can be financed and arranged for.
3. Any reputable U.S. radio station which desires to pick up the WOSU broadcast of any game . . . could be given permission to do so . . . on certain conditions . . . at a fee of $50 a game, etc.

4. Any reputable Ohio station which desired to carry the WOSU story of the game by simple rebroadcast from its own receiving set might get permission to do so on certain conditions.
5. Any reputable Ohio station desiring to broadcast direct from the Stadium might get permission to do so, subject to the limits of available facilities, on certain conditions . . .
6. The athletic administration reserved the right to grant or decline the requests of broadcasting chains . . .
7. The University assumed no obligation to get football broadcasting privileges for privately owned stations at foreign fields.
8. But the athletic administration would seek to get for WOSU the privilege of broadcasting games away from home.
9. The University would also permit any visiting school playing in the Stadium one broadcasting station of its choice outside of Ohio and to grant such station Stadium broadcasting privileges under certain conditions.
10. The University "should present to the Faculty Conference the question of the right of athletic staff members to undertake sponsored broadcasting for personal compensation—and should . . . request a Conference ruling or regulation or recommendation as to policy in this matter."

A further report on the broadcasting of football games was made at the June 10, 1937 board meeting by J. L. Morrill, broadcasting committee chairman. This had to do with the results of an experiment with unsponsored broadcasts. This policy, he reported, "had resulted in a great deal of dissatisfaction among our followers, the criticism arising principally from poor coverage and mediocre broadcasting." Other members expressed the opinion that "more had been lost than gained in public relations through our unsponsored program of last football season."

Full details of a new policy were presented at a July 21, 1937 meeting. The broadcasting rights for five home games were offered for sale but the department reserved the right to reject any or all sponsors or to discontinue the broadcasting of any station any time a previous broadcast was considered "incompatible with good taste or the best educational propriety of the University." Commercial announcements were limited in time and in no case would "advertising comparing or connecting the University, the games, the players or any activity within the Stadium with the sponsor or sponsor's product be permitted." WOSU meanwhile would continue to give an unsponsored broadcast of all home games and other stations could arrange for the "WOSU description" on an unsponsored basis. The new plan worked better and its continuance was authorized March 17, 1938. WOSU was also given permission to broadcast basketball games in 1938 and 1939.

By the early 'Forties the smaller colleges began to feel the pinch on football attendance as a result of the broadcasting of big college games. Director St. John reported at the December 17, 1941 board meeting that he had a letter from L. C. Boles, athletic director at the College of Wooster, as to the sentiment of a group of smaller colleges "requesting serious consideration of the abandonment of broadcasting football games" on the ground that nationwide broadcasting of the larger games was having "a very serious, if not fatal effect on the attendance at football games between smaller colleges and universities."

As with broadcasting earlier, the question of televising football games began to come to the fore early in 1948. At the March 17 board meeting the broadcasting, programs and publicity committee reported that it had conferred with representatives of WLW, Cincinnati, regarding the telecasting of the 1948 football games. The committee recommended that the board agree to the telecasting of two games, probably those with Pittsburgh and Michigan, under the joint sponsorship of the University and the station, but without a commercial sponsor, and "with the Station assuming all direct 'out of pocket' expenses." The report was approved.

At a meeting April 20, 1949 Prof. Strong reviewed the problems incident to the telecasting of football games. He informed the board that a group of persons who would probably be connected with television on the campus had met recently to formulate University policies concerning television. Further developments were reported at the September 21, 1949 meeting. The board was informed that WLW-C would probably have its installation ready in time for three games at $1500 a game, that Philco would photograph home games at $1000 for the season for television films, and that the Ford Motor Co. would sponsor a Conference television show with the proceeds going to the Conference office. To meet these needs six new radio booths had been added at the Stadium. There was also a proposal from a motion picture theater owner in the campus neighborhood to "pipe" television pictures to the theater. The director was authorized to enter into a 1-year agreement.

In the fall of 1949 the television question arose in connection with the impending basketball season. A committee recommendation was that the director be authorized to negotiate with local stations on the basis of not less than $200 a game. The committee referred also to earlier regulations which distinguished between sustaining and sponsored programs. It now felt this provision to "be unwise" and recommended its deletion. This was done.

All of the Conference schools were faced by problems growing out of the rapid development of television. Director Larkins reported that the matter had been discussed at length by the Conference athletic directors. The discussion took the line that "live television was a very dangerous thing," and resulted in a recommendation that live telecasting of football be banned during the 1950 season. But the matter was to be reconsidered at a later meeting. One proposal was to permit the taking of pictures for televising but not to release them until Sunday or Monday following the game. On the home front the matter came up in respect to a request from a Cincinnati station to televise the spring practice football game. Director Larkins was authorized to negotiate on a minimum basis of $200 for the game.

The television question was brought up at a joint meeting April 30, 1950 in Chicago of the presidents and faculty representatives of the ten Conference schools. It was the majority feeling "that they did not favor having the games on live television." At the May 9 board meeting, when this was reported, Director Larkins said that at their April 15 meeting the Conference athletic directors voted 8 to 2 "in favor of the policy of banning live television for this one season."

At the May 9 meeting there was extended discussion of the television problem and the policy involved. The television committee recommended that live television be banned for the 1950 season, but Trustee Power reported that the Board of Trustees, sensitive to the public relations involved, was "almost unanimously against" the athletic directors' April 15 action against live television of 1950 games.

In the middle of the 1950 season the board came back to the over-all issue of televising football games. At its October 26 meeting it recommended "the disapproval of a ban on 'live' television for its own sake. But because of concern for the safeguarding of Athletic Revenues, the Board recommends that television be authorized provided there is adequate protection of the sports program."

As possible solutions, it recommended consideration of these:

1. "Live" television of all football games, provided the University protect, from legislative appropriations, an adequate and expanding program . . . .
2. "Live" television locally of out-of-town games, under whatever mechanical and financial arrangements are found to be possible.
3. National "live" television of selected games of the week, Ohio State to share in receipts from the sale of television rights when one of the teams is in participation.
4. "Live" television of all football games for which the sale of tickets

has attained ninety per cent (90%) of the proceeds realized on the average for comparable games in the five years immediately preceding the advent of telecasting.

Two related questions were involved. One was the necessity of safeguarding the paid attendance so that the support of the expanding athletic program would not suffer by reason of loss of athletic revenue. The other implication was that the University administration would see to it that the state, through the legislature, would not lessen its support of the University by offsetting the athletic receipts. There had been some talk of this although not from responsible sources.

The issue also continued to come up in the Conference. At the December 15, 1950 meeting Dean Postle reported that faculty representatives on December 8-9 in Chicago voted 9 to 1 against live televising of football games. He reported further that theater telecasts were "deemed a successful venture, but a bad public relations project."

During the 1951 session of the legislature several bills were introduced which in effect would have made the telecasting of football games and other athletic events on the campus mandatory. Nothing came of these since it was felt that this was a policy matter best left to the trustees and the administration. But at the March 28, 1951 board meeting it was pionted out that Ohio State was the only Conference school to favor lifting the ban on live television and that not enough publicity had been given to this fact.

As conditions in the rapidly expanding television industry changed the board from time to time was faced with new problems incident to the telecasting of athletic events, particularly football, or the necessity of changing rules and policies to meet new conditions. At a September 25, 1951 meeting, Director Larkins informed the board that the Western Conference had been notified that the radio and television rights for the Rose Bowl football games for 1952, 1953 and 1954 had been sold to the National Broadcasting Company for $1,510,000. This would materially increase the "take" of the two Conferences and the participating schools.

A distinction continued to be made between live telecasts and telecasts by film the day after the game. At the October 17, 1951 meeting Director Larkins presented the matter of local television stations requesting a consideration of contracts on games to be televised. Their original consideration for film showing was based on no live telecasting taking place at any of the games. A reduction in rates for telecasting football games was approved at the May 21, 1952 meeting for movies of Ohio State games which had been the subject of live television.

The Conference continued somewhat at odds with the N.C.A.A. meanwhile on the television issue. On May 21, 1952 Director Larkins reported that the Conference had objected to the current N.C.A.A. proposal and had asked for Conference or regional control of live telecasting. When it developed that Ohio State charges for broadcasting were higher than those shown in the Standard Rate & Data Book, the rate "bible" for the advertising industry, Larkins recommended that the rates be brought in line and this was approved. A revised rate schedule for post-game television films was approved February 24, 1953 with a substantial reduction in some items.

In respect to radio broadcasting a policy was adopted whereby if an Ohio originating station should be deprived of the privilege of broadcasting an out-of-town Ohio State game because of lack of booth space, the facilities of WOSU were to be made available to such a station for "pickup" purposes. But the "pickup" station was to pay the host school the usual broadcasting fee without further responsibility to Ohio State or to the Athletic Department.

The extent to which the televising of football games quickly became big business was illustrated by the fact that on October 24, 1954 Larkins reported to the board that the contract with A.B.C. for broadcasting the Ohio State-Michigan game called for a minimum guarantee of $140,000. This would be augmented as additional stations joined the network for this game. This meant a substantial increase in revenue from a new source to meet current expenses and paying for the new arena and field house group. The game was an early sell-out.

The over-all policy as to televising foootball games continued to be a matter of extensive debate in college circles. At the December 9-10, 1954 Conference meeting in Detroit there was unanimous disapproval of the prevailing N.C.A.A. plan along with a preference for one of three other plans. On whether the Conference would participate if a plan unacceptable to it was adopted by the N.C.A.A., the vote was 9 to 1 in the negative. All of this was reported at its December 16 meeting when the board supported the position taken by Director Larkins and Dean Postle at the Conference meeting. The Conference committee declared that the N.C.A.A. policy in operation during the 1954 season was "entirely unacceptable to the Big Ten" and reaffirmed its belief in "a program of nationally controlled regional television" as the most suitable plan for N.C.A.A. controls.

Larkins reported at a February 18, 1955 meeting that the N.C.A.A. television committee had been charged with the responsibility of developing a program for 1955. Members of the Big Ten television committee could not agree on a program and were reported as being "vitally concerned over the Western Conference withdrawing" from the N.C.A.A. program. Larkins added that there was no desire to cause a rift within the N.C.A.A. but it was felt that "the Big Ten should be allowed freedom of negotiations on the television program."

The Big Ten suggested that the rule should be one telecast of a game at home and one away from home. The proposed schedule called for a 12-week schedule with eight national and four regional programs sold to one sponsor. The catch was that any proposed N.C.A.A. program would be voted on by the 435 member schools of which 350 were small ones. Under the tentative N.C.A.A. television program for the 1955 season as finally adopted, the Stanford-Ohio State game was one of those scheduled. At the April 15 board meeting, however, Larkins reported that the schedule was unsatisfactory to the sponsors who now wanted to schedule another game instead.

XV
PROBLEMS AND POLICIES

FROM time to time questions under discussion in the Western Conference were reflected in the Athletic Board minutes. The same was true in a lesser degree of the N.C.A.A. in which Ohio State men played leading roles. As far back as 1914 Dr. Wingert was chairman of the N.C.A.A. intercollegiate and recreative sport committee. In time Director St. John became chairman of the basketball rules committee, a post he held for years, and Prof. French similarly headed the important committee on committees. In 1958 Director Larkins was elected a member of the executive committee.

At a November 30, 1915 board meeting a motion carried to the effect that "Ohio State support the amateur principle in its present form until some better administration of the principle is proposed, the delegate to the Western Conference to be so instructed." About that time the Conference abolished baseball as a Big Nine sport. At a December 15, 1915 meeting the board moved to "enter a protest on the action of the Western Conference in abolishing baseball."

A decade later football was under close scrutiny in the Conference. At a May 7, 1926 board meeting Chairman French read a letter from Prof. J. F. A. Pyre, of Wisconsin, concerning suggested changes in the conduct of football in the Conference. The board directed French to inform Pyre that "it was the sense of the Board that football as administered in the Western Conference is in a satisfactory condition, that the Board does not favor any substantial changes in its administration, and that any fault is to be found with the things that surround football rather than with the game itself."

At a June 10, 1932 meeting a new Conference rule as to migratory athletes was accepted. This provided that an athlete who followed any member of the athletic or coaching staff from any other college to a Conference university should be ineligible for intercollegiate athletics.

Until after World War I no organized effort was made to publicize Ohio State athletics or the University itself, for that matter. But by the fall of 1919 some mimeographed material began to issue from the old Athletic House. Some of this was to satisfy press inquiries and requests for information but it reflected also the mounting interest in Ohio State football and other sports.

A publicity office was part of the Stadium fund raising campaign in 1920. This activity was continued on a permanent basis after the campaign was over. The first publicity man was William P. "Scoop" Dumont, '18, former *Lantern* editor. The office thus set up, in the Ohio Union, served the entire University for publicity purposes although the Athletic Department footed the modest bills. When Dumont left he was succeeded March 1, 1923 by James E. Pollard, '16. By 1927 the work had grown so that an additional man was hired. He was William D. "Bill" Griffith, a former track captain. He served also as assistant track coach. James B. Reston, later a Pulitzer prize winner and New York *Times* bureau chief in Washington, was an assistant during the 1933 football season. Griffith was succeeded in 1934 by James L. Renick who served for a decade. He was followed by Wilbur E. Snypp, '23.

Drinking, betting on games and other questionable conduct cast their shadows on intercollegiate football during the 'Twenties. Prohibition was still in effect but liquor was to be had for a price. In the summer of 1926 the Conference athletic directors drew up a statement on conduct at football games. The Athletic Board on July 23 authorized its use in connection with tickets orders in the fall. The statement was reproduced on the letterhead of the Athletic Department. It read in part:

... objection has been taken to making big football games the occasion for mass violation of the prohibition laws, for gambling and betting on the games, and for ticket scalping. These lapses seem to be most in evidence at "Homecoming" and other important contests involving the travel of considerable numbers of followers of one or both teams . . . .

It goes almost without saying that no genuinely loyal follower of Western Conference football would consciously do anything to injure the prestige it has rightfully enjoyed, and the Conference, on its part, is anxious to do everything in its power to maintain the high standards it has set, and to improve them where possible.

Appeal is being made, therefore, by the ten Directors of Athletics on behalf of the Western Conference and all that it stands for that the hundreds of thousands of loyal followers of its football and other sports will see their opportunity to help keep intercollegiate athletics on the highest possible plane . . . .

In January, 1927 a "Big Sixty Committee" met in Chicago to "deal with problems confronting the Western Conference." It was made up of six representatives from each of the Conference universities. At a January 27, 1930 board meeting Director St. John presented a detailed statement by Commissioner Griffith "covering a survey and investigation of 'recruiting and proselyting' in the Western Conference," but the minutes gave no details.

In the winter of 1931 the North Central Association of Colleges and Secondary Schools had interested itself in intercollegiate athletics in the Conference and was conducting an investigation. There was strong objection in the Conference to this activity and attitude on the part of the regional accrediting agency. President Rightmire brought the matter before the board February 27, 1931. President Walter Dill Scott, of Northwestern, meanwhile had called for a joint meeting of presidents, faculty representatives and athletic directors in Chicago to discuss the relation of the Conference with the association.

The matter came up again March 17, 1931 when a memorandum was presented from Major Griffith. Dr. Rightmire reported also to the board his correspondence with the president of the North Central with reference to a suggested investigation of athletic administration at Ohio State. Dr. Rightmire said he had approved such an inquiry but agreed to instruct the University's representatives at the North Central meeting March 17-19 "to withhold for the present any Ohio State University voting support for North Central Association athletic proposals."

Director St. John very early began to make his influence felt in Conference circles. For three decades until his retirement in 1947 he was a leader in the formulation of Conference policy, especially among the athletic directors. This was shown in 1922 when he was one of three members of a committee which recommended the appointment of Griffith as the first Conference commissioner. It was shown again in 1945 when he was influential in the appointment of K. L. "Tug" Wilson to the commissionership following Griffith's death.

The appointment of a commissioner was brought up at the annual Conference meeting in June, 1922 at Iowa City. This was approved by the faculty representatives. The Ohio State board gave its approval to the arrangements in July. In a statement of the time, the "main object" of the commissioner's office was to be "to sell the idea of the amateur principles in this territory, in its broadest sense, to high schools, colleges, students, alumni and the general public." It was also to carry on "research work in athletic problems" and to "assist in the enforcement of the amateur rules."

On the eve of World War II proposals began to be revived that the annual Rose Bowl football game in Pasadena be held between teams representing the Western Conference and the Pacific Coast Conference. At the December 1, 1940 board meeting Prof. French gave a digest of the Conference proceedings to this end and asked for instructions. Upon the death of French early in November, 1944 after thirty-two years as

Ohio State's representative, President Bevis appointed Prof. James E. Pollard to that post. The latter's first major task was to present Ohio State's request to have the Big Ten rule against post-season games waived so that the champion Buckeyes could play in the 1945 Rose Bowl game. The matter came up at a special Conference meeting November 26, 1944 in Chicago but the vote was 7 to 3 in the negative.

But in September, 1946 the Conference entered into a 5-year agreement with the Pacific Coast Conference to participate in the Rose Bowl. The vote was 7 to 3. This was renewed in May, 1951 for three years with the understanding that no Big Ten team could compete more often than once in two years. A financial statement on the Ohio State-California Rose Bowl game in 1950 was reported at the May 31, 1950 Athletic Board meeting. The Big Ten share, after expenses, was $128,954.84 which was to be divided into eleven shares. The competing school was to receive two shares and the commissioner's office one. Ohio State's "distributive share" was given as $23,446.34, plus $16,507.45 in contributions to send the band.

When the 1951 renewal of the Rose Bowl agreement was up for discussion there was some dissatisfaction over the allotment of seats. At its April 18 meeting the board instructed its representative before voting for renewal "to see that a satisfactory adjustment of tickets be effected." At the Conference meeting Director Larkins was named one of the Big Ten representatives on the Rose Bowl negotiating committee. When Dean Postle reported at the January 21, 1953 meeting that the Pacific Coast Conference had invited the Western Conference to renew the agreement for another three years, the board again favored renewal "provided there is some agreement in the allocation of tickets among the participating schools and some improvements in the price of tickets."

The Rose Bowl agreement came up again in the spring of 1959 although what had been the Pacific Coast Conference had split meantime into two groups. In the Athletic Council the vote was 9 to 1 in favor of extending the agreement. In the face of this the Faculty Council by a strong majority instructed Ohio State's faculty representative to vote in the negative. Upon recommendation of President Fawcett, the trustees approved this stand by a 5 to 0 vote, one member abstaining. At the Conference meeting at Ann Arbor in May the vote for renewal was 5 to 5 and it was thereby lost. But by the same division of votes a provision in the Conference rules under which individual members of the Big Ten could participate in the Rose Bowl game remained in force.

Earlier Director Larkins discussed overemphasis in intercollegiate athletics, particularly football, at an October 2, 1951 board meeting. He proposed that some portion of athletic funds be set aside for general University scholarship purposes, especially in view of the anticipated increase in revenue from the Rose Bowl contract through the sale of radio and television rights. It was agreed to appropriate $15,000 for the purpose. The University trustees approved the board's action on October 15.

In common with other Conference schools the board opened the way to provide for a limited number of Ohio State athletic scholarships at its September 25, 1953 meeting. This was made possible by a change in the Conference rule on scholarships. It was a matter also of competing with other Conference schools which had already established such scholarships.

It was the consensus of the board that "1) we agree in principle and endorse the scholarship proposal and the matter of securing funds for deserving athletes, 2) the Board is favorably inclined to appropriate some funds to an athletic scholarship funds subject to agreements already made in reference to financing the Field House and allied projects, and 3) the Board requests a full report of the conference between the University administration, the alumni group, and the Director at its October meeting." Director Larkins reported November 18, 1953 that the trustees had approved the recommendations for athletic scholarships. He presented a report covering the first year for the athletic scholarship program at the October 20, 1954 meeting. There was discussion of the "inadequacy of available funds to continue this program," and a committee was authorized to study the problem and present it to President Bevis "as to what procedure should be followed to provide the necessary funds for future continuation."

In January, 1955 the board authorized setting aside $15,000 for athletic scholarships for 1955-56. It was estimated that $11,000 would be needed to support students then in the program. Director Larkins reported that by the fourth year of operation the amount needed might be from $50,000 to $60,000 a year.

There were two unusual developments during the 1955-56 school year involving the conduct and control of the University's athletic program. One originated on the campus and the other resulted from Conference action. The former grew out of a motion adopted by the Faculty Council, the campus legislative body, at its June, 1955 meeting for the election of a special committee to study the campus athletic situation. The other arose in an investigation by Conference Commissioner K. L. Wilson's office into irregularities involving jobs held by and loans to Ohio State football players.

At its October 24, 1955 meeting the Athletic Board formally indicated its willingness to cooperate with the Faculty Council committee. A number of meetings were held during the year with the committee of which Dean James F. Fullington, of the College of Arts & Sciences, was chairman. A special Athletic Board committee, headed by Dean Walter R. Krill, met with President Bevis and the Faculty Council committee.

At a special meeting January 22, 1956 the board met with Director Larkins and Coach Hayes for a discussion of "plans, procedures, and problems of administering the intercollegiate football program," but took no action. Part of the difficulty with the Conference arose from the fact that Hayes personally had advanced small sums of money to individual players for immediate needs. He freely admitted what he had done, insisted that it was a personal matter and at first refused to identify the players or disclose the individual amounts. But after the Conference penalized the University he gave Commissioner Wilson this information.

The other issue which contributed to the difficulty with the Conference was the charge that Varsity players received pay for jobs and for employment without doing or completing the work for which they were hired. About thirty players were involved. This, too, was cleared up before the 1956 football season began by having the men involved do or complete the work. In the meantime, however, the Conference put Ohio State on probation for the time being and made it ineligible for participation in the Rose Bowl even if it should win the 1956 Conference title. The N.C.A.A. also took up the matter of loans to athletes and its decision —and penalty—came later.

Commissioner Wilson announced the penalties against Ohio State in April, 1956 based on the irregularities described. The matter was still subject to review by the N.C.A.A. but at a mid-summer meeting in Denver it was put over until later.

At its April 27, 1956 meeting, meanwhile, the Athletic Board discussed the Wilson report. To quote the minutes: "Unanimous opinion was expressed that the Board should make every attempt to develop ways and means of strengthening our athletic program to coincide with the regulations of the Big Ten." Director Larkins outlined proposals to strengthen the program. From President Bevis, Larkins and the Athletic Board down it was a matter of widespread comment that Ohio State took its punishment without protest. Many felt, however, that the irregularities were minor and that what had occurred was going on elsewhere but only Ohio State was investigated and found guilty.

Another sign of the times was that with sellout crowds the Stadium was outgrown with no feasible way to enlarge it to any degree. Some kept urging that the open end of the horseshoe be enclosed but this was undesirable architecturally. There was some talk of utilizing the space occupied by the running track but this, too, was doubtful. One solution was to televise all home games but this was under strict control of the N.C.A.A. which would not permit such a telecast if another college game was scheduled within 50 miles.

To illustrate, the Ohio State-Stanford game of 1956 was an early sellout. Ohio State's plea to telecast the game over WOSU-TV, the campus station, was turned down because of a game that same afternoon at Springfield (Wittenberg), 45 miles distant, although WOSU-TV "carried" only 35 miles.

At the spring meeting of the Conference in May, 1956 a proposal was discussed, long advocated in some quarters, for a continuing round robin football schedule under which each Big Ten team would play every other team during the season. A 10-game schedule would be permitted so that each member could play an outside opponent if desired. The tentative plan was to start with a 7-game round robin for 1959 and 1960, an 8-game round robin in 1961, and finally increasing to a full round. But at its June 1, 1956 meeting the Athletic Board went on record against a 10-game schedule.

At this same meeting Dean Krill reported on the scholarship and loan plan. Under Conference rules a student must carry a minimum of 12 academic hours. Subject to draft board requirements, the board moved to have Ohio State conform to this rule. It voted also to set up $10,000 as a loan fund for student athletes to be available on a long time repayment plan.

Under the terms of Ohio State's probation in the Conference, meanwhile, all athletes who were involved in irregularities in the work program in the fall of 1955 had to repay fully in services the wages they had received. All of them, including some who were graduating, did so before the 1956 football training began. The N.C.A.A. infractions committee pointed out that Ohio State "was in error" in Coach Hayes' gifts and loans to players and in a basketball case involving the transfer of a player to another Ohio college. The board in August authorized a statement of the situation and an outline of the steps taken to correct it.

The year 1956-57 was another momentous one in Ohio State athletics. It was marked by such diverse developments as: the end of a football winning streak after seventeen straight Conference victories—a Conference record, the lifting of the probation imposed by the Conference, the dedication of the St. John Arena and the French Field House, the use of the former for a full Varsity basketball season and for the state high school championships, the use of the latter for the indoor Conference track meet which Ohio State nearly won, by the trip to Japan by the baseball team, and by the inauguration of the controversial grants-in-aid program for athletes sanctioned by the Conference—on which it split 6 to 4. And as a followup to the earlier Conference action on the aid to football players and the basketball transfer case, the N.C.A.A. barred Ohio State teams from N.C.A.A. championships for a year.

As always there was increased clamor for football tickets. Some modifications were made in the ticket distribution system but while this made for somewhat more equitable distribution it did not satisfy the demand. One solution, particularly for the Michigan game which again was an early sellout, was for a closed circuit telecast in the St. John Arena. This was finally done for three games at some financial loss and with indifferent acceptance by the public. The rotation plan for ticket allotments for alumni was increased materially but this was partly—and inevitably— at the expense of persons previously able to get tickets.

With the completion of the Arena and the Field House, Ohio State for the first time in years was on a footing comparable with the best in the country in respect to physical facilities. The Arena, seating about 13,400, was well filled during most of the Varsity season and was used also for the University's December convocation and in April, 1957 for the inauguration of President Novice G. Fawcett. The Field House, with a seating capacity of some 4000, had a full house for the Conference indoor meet and surprisingly good turnouts for individual meets. The only major physical plant item left was a baseball stadium but this was held in abeyance. The athletic ticket office was moved to the Arena followed by the Athletic Department offices in the summer of 1958.

The N.C.A.A. action referred to above occasioned no surprise. Except in the case of the swimming team, as it turned out, the N.C.A.A. ban worked no hardship on any of the squads. There was a feeling meanwhile that while Ohio State had offended it was a relatively mild offense and, in particular, that it had "come clean" in the matter.

An unusual feature of the year was the preparation of a Blue Paper on the interim report of the Western Conference on the issue of direct subsidy for athletes. The paper, prepared by faculty members of the board, was presented at the November 5, 1956 board meeting. With amendments it was adopted in principle and was ordered distributed to other Conference schools.

In essence it supported the minority view in the Conference which opposed the direct subsidy idea. Its tone may be judged by the opening statement which declared that the Conference report, adopted later by a 6 to 4 vote, "presents an unwieldly, inoperable proposition completely unworthy of the Western Conference however laudable may be the intent of its writers. The general overtone simulates an attitude of bureaucracy and greater concentration of powers, both of which we inalterably oppose as a matter of principle." The paper conceded the soundness of the report's premise, namely, to recognize a student's athletic ability on a par with scientific, music or art ability, for example. But it took exception to the "illusion" surrounding the premise and called other features of the report "equally preposterous."

To offset these objections the paper offered a counter-proposal modifying the proposed Conference plan. It took the position that "the present Western Conference rules may be changed to make possible a workable program of financial aids to the student-athlete in intercollegiate athletics." It held that financial aid to the student-athlete was "not inherently objectionable in the light of established educational policy." It proposed that each institution "operating within its own rules, be permitted to offer any eligible student-athlete scholarship or financial support up to the cost of attending that institution," that all "unearned aid shall be administered by that institution," that all such aid be based upon "satisfactory academic progress," and that any aid over the amounts indicated "shall be considered a violation" of Conference rules. A student-athlete would not be barred from employment beyond direct aid but it must be "useful" work, with no pay advanced and at "the going rate of pay" for a similar work in the locality. But if a student-athlete received full direct aid he could not accept employment during the season of athletic participation. To make the proposal effective, pledges must be had from institutional and athletic heads, and staff members not to tender or arrange for any other form of aid.

Gross athletic receipts passed the $1 million mark for the first time in 1951-52 when the total was $1,073,417 as against operating expenses of $782,259, leaving a surplus of $262,623. With an increase in ticket prices, the anticipated receipts for 1956-57, however, were $1,510,000 as against operating expenses of $1,164,640. Average yearly payments of principal and interest on the $2,400,000 Arena bonds were put at $128,000. Net operating revenue for the next few years was calculated at about $400,000, leaving some $247,000 available for other capital improvements or other new expenses such as the grants-in-aid program for athletes. Besides the projected baseball facility, continued renovation and protection of the Stadium were in prospect along with replacement of the south bleachers which had been in use for twenty-one years.

The revised plan of football ticket sales inaugurated in 1956 was continued for 1957. The board approved holding the season book sale, accounting for about 33,000 seats, before the sale of individual game tickets. This was in addition to about 10,000 faculty and 21,000 student season books, leaving only 14,700 individual game tickets available.

President Fawcett, who took office August 1, 1956, was a special guest at the March 12, 1957 board meeting at which he outlined his views on athletics. (He had sat previously with the board.) He pointed out the responsibility of coaches in furthering University relations. He emphasized that students come to the University primarily for an education and that sports and other activities are a part of but only incidental to gaining an education. He stressed that the University's goals are long range and that an institution is strong only through the strength of its total program. He added that there was need for unity of purpose and that this was a time "for every part of the University to re-examine its own objectives and moral responsibilities in the long range view." He said that the University's athletic program must be based on honesty, dignity and quality.

On the new Conference grants-in-aid program it was his opinion that the cost was "totally unrealistic in light of the over-all needs of the entire University," that its administration was "next to impossible," that a work program to be effective should be one that encourages "work," and that material rewards should be related to intellectual competence. But since the Conference had adopted the program it was also his view that the University should support it "and honestly," that it should adjust its financial support of the program consistent with other needs and commitments, that its support of the program should not be on the basis of asking for tax support from the legislature or a "touch" from outsiders, and that success of the program would be a test of the University's real integrity.

The grants-in-aid program presented continuing problems, chiefly financial. The board gave a further look at this at its March 25, 1957 meeting on the basis of a lengthy letter from Director Larkins which outlined various ways of meeting the added financial burden and of implementing the program. Basically it involved the maintenance of the student-athletes then in school on scholarships, members of the current football squad, the recruitment of thirty outstanding freshman football men and twenty other sports men. Specifically it involved the allocation of $119,000 in the 1957-58 athletic budget for the financial aids plan. This meant an actual increase, however, of only $29,000 over the amount previously committed for aid to athletes.

At its May 28, 1957 meeting the board employed J. Edward Weaver as associate athletic director. He had been in the department and more recently served as assistant to Vice President Taylor. He was to be responsible for the grants-in-aid program. A new alumni member of the board introduced at this meeting was Robin A. Bell, '28, former Varsity athlete. He succeeded Fred C. Mackey who had served for ten years.

The Fullington Committee, in a report presented November 12, 1957, urged the Faculty Council to abandon the traditional concept of the amateur athlete and to accept "a more realistic view of the problem of amateurism" in the Western Conference. It said that in the larger universities, including Ohio State, "there has evolved new justification of subsidy in athletics which those in charge would be reluctant to call professional and yet which hardly can be called amateur. This has bred an unintentional hypocrisy which presents a difficult problem today." It urged the faculty to "take a hard and realistic look at this situation and be prepared to accept some realities of the modern age."

The 39-page report was months in preparation. It contained twenty-one specific recommendations dealing not only with the amateur status of athletes, but also with a variety of other subjects ranging from academic tutoring of team members to reorganization of the Athletic Board. While the report was critical of certain aspects of athletics in the University, the committee was "pleased to report that the present administration of the university, acting independently of the Committee, has taken some steps, which are in full accord with several recommendations of the Committee." The report commended Director Larkins for "a capable and thoroughly honest job" and expressed "admiration" for the way he had "dealt with his many difficult problems."

Besides its remarks and recommendations on amateurism, which covered more than ten pages, the committee touched upon three other broad areas—faculty control of athletics, welfare of students, and athletics and the educational program. Capsule summaries of these follow:

Amateurism

A study of the Olympic code and practices in various conferences revealed a wide range of athletic subsidy plans. The report noted that "amateurism is being modified in our society today because of discernible changes in the economic and social setting out of which the original concepts of the amateur grew" and that "skill in any form is marketable in our society."

Because of this and because "college sport as we know it here is a $2 million a year enterprise, whether we like it or not, it is foolish to expect that the program can continue at that level without letting the athlete in for some portion of the gain, either as an inducement to come or as aid to him as a resident student. We should realize that it is no longer shameful *not* to be an amateur and that a college athlete *can* be a gentleman and a scholar and at the same time receive aid *because* of his athletic activity. The shame involved is only in the pretense we develop when we try to claim that college athletics are strictly amateur when actually many of them are not . . . .

"The committee is of the opinion that it is no longer possible or reasonable to conduct college sports at the Conference level where we play them on an amateur basis; and to labor through a maze of hypocritical statements, tongue-in-cheek cynicism, and an occasional instance of outright deception is far more destructive to the welfare of the student than to admit freely that amateurism is no longer a workable concept for college athletics."

The committee recommended that the athletic director devise a "workable plan" for financial aid to athletes; abolition or minimizing of the job program for athletes; and steps to insure against the "kind of incidents" which resulted in Ohio State's 1956 penalties by the Conference and the N.C.A.A. In its prefatory note, however, the committee pointed out that since May, 1957 the Conference had adopted the principle of grants-in-aid, the N.C.A.A. had lifted its suspension of Ohio State, and that President Fawcett had received from the coaching staff pledges of full compliance with the spirit and letter of N.C.A.A., Conference, University and department regulations.

The note also quoted a letter from the president which described changes effected in the past few months in administration of the job program and scholarships. The committee commended Dr. Fawcett "for attacking these problems with vigor and dispatch."

FACULTY CONTROL

The faculty, the report said, has "gradually and perhaps unknowingly relinquished much of its regulatory and policy-making privilege to the university administration and trustees, with the result that . . . there may be some question as to the eligibility of the university for Conference membership." The committee recommended establishment of a 10-member "Athletic Council," subject to Faculty Council jurisdiction, to replace the 9-member Athletic Board, with six faculty members to be elected from nominations made by the president. The Athletic Council would elect one of its faculty members to serve as faculty representative to the Western Conference. For years the five faculty members of the board, including the Conference representative, had been named by presidential appointment.

On athletic participation the report remarked, "It must be realized by the faculty as a whole that participation in athletics is in itself a worth-while experience. It has much to recommend it, and most athletes are willing to make reasonable sacrifices for the privilege of participating." On expenditures it noted "what seems to be extravagant expenditures in connection with the 1955 Rose Bowl trip and other entertainments which are of doubtful value to the University." On de-emphasis the committee believed "we would find insufficient support to warrant making any proposals for major de-emphasis." On sports in education, it recognized "It is desirable to include both instruction and competition in sports as a part of the educational program of the university." And on public appearances, it observed, "The off-season demands upon star athletes are unbelievably heavy. . . . Coaches, and other university officials, who have radio, television and other forms of public appearances to make, should keep the participation of student-athletes on the programs to an absolute minimum."

In February, 1958 the Faculty Council overwhelmingly approved two recommendations of the Fullington Committee report that reaffirmed faculty control of athletic policies. The new legislation would establish a 10-member Athletic Council—six faculty, two students and two alumni —replacing the old Athletic Board. Its faculty members instead of being appointed by the University president would be elected by the Faculty Council from nominations submitted by him. The new council, in turn, would choose one of its members as faculty representative in the Conference for a 3-year term subject to re-election. It was recommended that the new council report at least twice a year to the Faculty Council "on its problems and decisions."

The Faculty Council also "approved in principle" thirteen other Fullington Committee recommendations ranging from "invasion of student time" by athletics to the status and activities of members of the coaching staff. The committee was reactivated later to consider changes and the recommendations, with slight modifications, went to the rules committee for submission to the University trustees.

The divided decision—6 to 4—of the Conference in 1957 to adopt what in effect was a play-for-pay policy was one of the most important ever taken by the Conference. Realistically it was perhaps the correct—and only—decision since it legalized and brought into the open what had been going on in one form or other on many campuses. There were those, of course, who decried it as a surrender to commercialism or professionalism in college athletics. But a more realistic view was that the new policy was a factual and legal recognition of a situation that had long existed and, in form at least, put the policies of all ten Conference members on the same basis—on top of the table. This view was, in effect, borne out by the Fullington Committee report.

But while it may have provided solutions to some of the problems incident to large scale intercollegiate athletics the new policy created others, especially on the financial side. Where Ohio State, for example, had provided $15,000 as a start on athletic scholarships, the amount permitted under the Conference policy immediately jumped to about $130,000 initially and promised to run as much as $250,000 annually once the program was in full swing after four years and thereafter. This was a major addition to the athletic budget already strained about to the limit.

In 1957, the first year of its operation, Ohio State sent out eighty-nine scholarship "tenders" to high school athletes under the new aid-to-athletes program. Of these seventy-nine gave their acceptance and sixty-five actually enrolled on the campus. A year later the number of offers of aid was eighty-one with sixty acceptances, with $170,000 budgeted for the purpose.

There were two kinds of "tenders" or offers: one of full aid to a boy in the upper one-fourth of his high school graduating class who maintained a similar standing in the University, and aid on the basis of need, covering tuition, board, room and books, less whatever help his family was able to give. These subsidies, therefore, varied with the boy and his status, the college within the University in which he was enrolled, and whether he was from Ohio or from out of state. They ranged from around $1000 to $1600 each.

From time to time across the years other kinds of policy matters called for the attention of the athletic administration. These included such things as the award of the Varsity "O", ticket problems and priorities, football scheduling, cheering and cheerleaders, the band, the Harley Fund, and miscellaneous items. Each of these is dealt with below.

The Varsity "O"

As early as 1903 Varsity "O" men organized an association to help improve Ohio State athletics. George W. Rightmire, then graduate manager of athletics, is said have instigated this move. James R. Marker, football captain, was the first president. He was followed by Robert G. Paterson.

In the years just before Ohio State's admission to the Conference there was a growing feeling that the right to wear the "O" should be limited to Varsity athletes so recognized by the Athletic Board. As noted, there was a so-called Military "O" and a dispute on this came to a head in the spring of 1911. There was talk also of awarding an "O" to Varsity debaters on the ground that they, too, represented the University in intercollegiate competition.

For some time after the 1912 reorganization nothing was done about awarding the "O" to members of earlier athletic teams. At various board meetings, however, suggestions were made to this end. Steps were taken also to control the award of the letters. Under a resolution adopted November 13, 1912 the "O" was to be granted for merit only in intercollegiate competition. The board was also to approve the form of the letters.

An early move toward some recognition of former Varsity athletes came at a June 15, 1914 board meeting when Director St. John was authorized "to get further information" on such names and to report at the next meeting. At that meeting, undated, "The matter of giving passes to old Varsity 'O' men was discussed but not acted upon."

At a Student Council meeting in March, 1916 it was moved that the council "go on record as favoring the limiting of the granting of the letter 'O' to University Inter-collegiate Athletics." This was followed by Athletic Board action March 28, 1916 asking President Thompson "to give the Athletic Board the sole right of awarding the 'O'." In time this came about.

Another step toward recognizing former athletes was taken at a December 6, 1916 meeting when a committee was authorized "to make recommendations for the granting of the 'O' to former members of teams." According to the minutes, the first retroactive granting of a letter was authorized April 11, 1917 to Lear H. Van Buskirk, '08, "for services rendered while in school." Two others followed at the June 4 meeting. In March, 1923 one was awarded to David F. Snyder, w'83, winner of the Franklin Medal in the 1883 Field Day and president of the Athletic Association in 1884-85. The first "Medic" so honored was Dr. W. E. Lloyd who played on O.M.U. teams in 1902-03-04.

In the next few years the "O" was granted rather freely to former athletes of the earlier period. As noted, the recognition was extended to onetime players on the old O.M.U., and Starling-Ohio Medical College teams. This was on the basis of the absorption in 1914 of Starling-Ohio by the University. Of special interest also was the granting of the "O" to surviving members of the 1890 football team, the first on the campus. This was done in September, 1924.

A new policy or method "for the awarding of the regular Varsity 'O'" was adopted May 10, 1922 by the board. It recognized football, baseball, basketball, track and cross country as major sports, and tennis, wrestling, gymnastics and rifle shooting as minor sports. The "O" was to be awarded in football to any player participating in the homecoming or the final game of the season "or who shall take part with credit in any two Western Conference games." In basketball and baseball it was for all team members taking "part with credit in one-half of the scheduled Western Conference games." But members of minor sports teams who won a Conference championship or in individual cases or, in rare cases, "because of merited service" could win the major "O." Besides the minor (smaller) sports awards, there was provision also for an "OAA" award in football, for example, for players who had played two full games or "less than a quarter in one of the two most important games," or in other sports to men who "have satisfied one-half the requirements for the Varsity 'O'." The major letter was to be 8 x 6 ins. in size and the minor sport letters "a plain round letter" 7 ins. in diameter.

The bylaws with respect to the award of the Varsity "O" were amended again by board action April 9, 1930. The "O" was to be awarded to eligible members of Varsity squads for intercollegiate competition "as a recognition of athletic ability." But athletes who turned "pro" were not to get the award. In football, basketball and baseball to win the "O" an athlete must play in at least half the regularly scheduled games for at least one-fourth of the total playing time, although a football player must qualify by playing "in one full quarter of either the homecoming or final game of the season." At the April 24, 1930 meeting some dissatisfaction was reported on the part of coaches and others as to the new provisions, especially as to track.

James R. Hull, captain of the '39 basketball team, appeared before the board April 23, 1940 relative to the establishment of a Varsity "O" club. The earlier undergraduate Varsity "O" group had been inactive for some years. Objectives of the new group included these: "to improve the standards of athletic participation ... and through other requirements designed to improve ideals, loyalty and athletic proficiency of members of the University athletic teams." Membership was to be limited to juniors and seniors. The board approved the plan described and agreed to buy gold watch chain keys for those elected to membership and to set aside the use of a Stadium tower room for the club.

From time to time an effort was made to get the board to reward the drum major of the band with a Varsity "O." Such a proposal was made at the June 1, 1928 meeting by Col. C. L. Townsend, commandant. The argument was that the drum major won his position by competition and rendered as much service as the head cheerleaders who qualified for a letter. The board on May 31, 1934, on recommendation of the Student Senate, approved of the award of a Varsity "O" with "Drum Major" worked into the letter for James H. McCreary, 1933 drum major. On November 21, 1939 a drum major's "O" was finally awarded to G. Edwin "Tubby" Essington, the inspiring drum major of the early 'Twenties. This was on alumni recommendation. By board action March 13, 1942 the "O" was granted to these other former drum majors and cheerleaders: Augustus Hall, Robert Hines, William Knepper, C. W. Pettegrew, and H. S. Warwick. Warwick was of the pre-Big Ten era.

On at least two occasions women students have been proposed as a member of a Varsity team or for the award of the "O." Helen Jenkins, a sophomore, appealed to Prof. French in the fall of 1940 for permission to compete for the rifle team. The board decided that intercollegiate competition was basically "between teams composed of men students" but that "when and if a program for national collegiate competition among women student is organized and in full effect" the board would consider the matter further. Earlier award of the "O" was proposed for Eleanor and Ruth Smith, sister swimmers, who, as noted elsewhere, were the first to represent Ohio State in competition.

Honorary "O's" were rarely granted. One was voted to President Thompson on his retirement in November, 1925. Another was voted in January, 1927 to Elliott Nugent, '19, actor and playwright, "in recognition of his services to the University." Actually this was in recognition of his hit play, "The Poor Nut" in which he starred and which featured a track scene on a Midwestern campus, obviously that of Ohio State.

One was granted similarly in November, 1936 to Prof. Eugene J. Weigel, of the School of Music, for his "splendid service and untiring efforts" in connection with the Marching Band. Another recipient in February, 1937 was Col. Townsend, board chairman, who was retiring as commandant of cadets. "Tony" Aquila, long a familiar figure in the athletic scene, was another recipient in 1939 as were "Bill" North, longtime campus police chief, and J. L. Morrill, vice president of the University and former board chairman, on leaving the campus in 1941.

Still other recipients of the honorary "O" were: Mike Peppe, swimming coach, in February, 1947; Bernard F. "Spike" Mooney, in January, 1948 upon petition of Varsity "O" men in recognition of twenty-five years as wrestling coach; Manley R. Whitcomb, former director of the Marching Band and Elvin F. Donaldson, first director of the band; Dr. John B. C. Eckstorm, football coach, 1899-1901, in 1949; H. G. "Oley" Olsen, longtime former basketball coach, in November, 1952; and Dr. Walter E. Duffee, longtime team physician, in January, 1943. Cold-weather jackets with an "O" replaced the traditional sweaters in 1958.

Tickets and Priorities

In its last years the capacity of Ohio Field was taxed, especially in the 1919, 1920 and 1921 seasons. But with the Stadium in use starting in 1922, it was thought that this problem was settled. During the depression years, in fact, Stadium crowds shrank to as low as 12,000.

Basketball, too, had seating problems and, in time, so did swimming. First the old gymnasium was outgrown and years later the Coliseum was inadequate. The Natatorium necessarily had a limited seating capacity. And there were signs in 1958 that it would not be many years before the St. John Arena would not be adequate even with its 13,400 seats.

All of this meant a continuing ticket problem. The ticket priority promised at the time of the Stadium campaign was in force for many years. Year after year, especially after the World War II, the board, special committees, and the University administration pondered the problems of ticket priorities and tried to work out equitable solutions. Another troublesome problem was the matter of complimentary tickets.

Students had a first priority along with the faculty and alumni. But a state university is beholden to many publics, including state and local officials, the legislature and others. There were also "benefactors" of the University, the press and other groups to take into consideration. And in football, in particular, the visiting school had to be provided for. Michigan for years got an allotment of 16,000 seats every other year but in 1956 this was cut considerably. The heavy sale of season tickets in the 'Fifties was another factor.

Unlike many colleges and universities, Ohio State has never had a blanket athletic fee for Varsity and recreative athletics. But such a proposal has come up a number of times. As far back as May, 1914 a "monster student petition" advocated such a fee. This was referred to the trustees at their June, 1914 meeting but neither then nor later did they give their approval. The central idea was discussed anew at a May, 1939 Athletic Board meeting and again in June and September of that year after a Student Senate resolution sought to replace the sale of student athletic books by a student athletic fee. Nothing came of the matter.

Back in 1928 the Athletic Department had taken note of the rapidly growing demand for football and other tickets by setting up a ticket distribution system recognizing certain priorities. Certain preferences were worked out for students, faculty, alumni, Varsity "O" men, and Stadium subscribers. Upon recommendation these were now made more detailed and specific. From time to time the ticket distribution scheme was changed but first preference was given to the University community. After the University Development Fund came into being contributors to it as well as members of the Ohio State University Association received recognition.

After World War II when the enrollment exceeded 20,000 the proportion of seats for general use became smaller. One difficulty was that despite certain advantages in the horseshoe design of the Stadium, only 29,175 of the actual 79,658 seats were between the goal lines.

By action taken at a June 20, 1928 board meeting three groups were set up for ticket distribution. Group 1 consisted of Stadium subscribers, Group 2 of executive officers of the University and certain others, Group 3 alumni and the public. By this action also "The custom of selling block orders either to individuals or groups" was discontinued.

As a protection to bona fide student season ticket purchasers it was ordered May 28, 1930 that photographs of students be affixed to the ticket book for purposes of identification. It was also provided that Sections 9, 11, 13 and 15 A and B be regarded as the student section in the Stadium except for six rows at the top of 15A.

In the spring of 1931 a committee was named to consider the matter of preference in football ticket distribution "with special reference to the expiration of Stadium subscriber options." A resolution presented at the February 22, 1932 board meeting pointed out that the board had fulfilled its pledge in granting the priority for ten years but to continue it "on the same basis any longer seems likely to render the possibility of abandoning it more difficult." It recommended that priorities be established in this order: 1, students, faculty, Varsity "O" and visiting team supporters; 2, Alumni Association members; 3, Stadium subscribers not otherwise classified and members of the public who had bought tickets for the two preceding years; and 4, the public at large and non-member alumni. In May the board approved a request from the Varsity "O" Association requiring membership in that association as a requisite for free tickets to athletic contests for former athletes.

Taxation was another problem affecting tickets. Since Western Conference football, except for Chicago and Northwestern, was operated by state universities which were regarded as state agencies, there was some question whether the Federal tax on admissions was constitutional when applied to such an activity. It was proposed to bring up a test case in the Conference. The board agreed in October, 1932 to support such a movement but with the understanding that it would not "consent to the use of our institution" for the purpose.

After further study and discussion of the tax situation the board in May, 1937 approved the action of the administration in declining "to collect or pay admissions tax on and with respect to athletic events commencing with the football season of 1936." It had on deposit $36,000.04 of impounded money and took steps to create "proper reserves to cover contingent tax liabilities." It also authorized investment of the impounded money pending the ultimate settlement of the issue.

But the matter was far from settled. The Internal Revenue Collector notified the department October 1, 1937 that an assessment for unpaid Federal admissions taxes had been levied against the University, plus interest and penalty. Various conferences followed and the situation was brought before the board at its December 1 meeting. Since the assessments were levied against the University rather than the Athletic Department the matter also came before the trustees at their November 8 meeting. The latter ordered the assessment paid and this was done.

Although the payment was made, the University, through President Rightmire, petitioned the government for a remission of the penalties and it was understood that the University would file claims for a refund of the taxes should it be authorized.

Further refinements in the football ticket distribution system were made in the adoption of a ticket committee report by the board in April, 1947. Ticket allocations were made to these five groups, in order: students, faculty and employes, visiting school, Alumni Association members and benefactors, and general public. This plan was based on the necessity for recognized priorities, especially students, faculty and Alumni Association members and benefactors of the University. As a policy statement pointed out, "It seems evident that tickets should not be served on a first-come, first-served basis, but that certain groups are entitled to privileges which cannot be accorded to all." Students and faculty alone accounted by now for 28,000 tickets.

A further complication was the growing number of tickets needed each year for complimentary purposes. This was in part an outgrowth of the Stadium campaign, but it reflected also the University's place as a state agency dealing with state, county and local departments and officials. In a further report in June, 1947 the ticket committee presented a breakdown of these needs which showed an estimated total of 4388 complimentary tickets needed, of which 500 were for the press and 57 for radio.

For big football games, and especially for sellouts, tickets were greatly in demand and it was inevitable that some student tickets would find their way into the hands of outsiders. The athletic administration took every means to prevent this. At the 1948 Ohio State-Michigan game some sixty student books were "taken up from persons obviously not students," the board was informed at its November 22 meeting. It was agreed that these tickets would be held and the students concerned deprived of ticket privileges for the remainder of the year.

Early in 1949 the board took another look at the athletic ticket distribution setup. This was after a Student Senate ticket committee had recommended that separate ticket books be sold for the football season and that no sections in the Stadium be reserved for blocks. At its January 19 meeting the board adopted a motion that annual books covering all sports be used in 1949-50. It was the board's opinion that the annual book, adopted the year before, had "not had sufficient trial." It was also of the opinion that such a book helped to foster "interest for all sports within the student body," including "minor sports which in the past have commanded little interest from the majority of students."

The matter of policy on complimentary tickets, especially for football, became more and more complicated in the post-war years. The board policy, adopted in 1947, was reviewed late in 1951. As a matter of cold fact the problem involved the University as a whole and was one of both economics and of public relations. At the November 21 meeting Chairman Strong reported that Chairman Carlton Dargusch, of the trustees, was desirous of the reaction of Athletic Board members to a report on complimentary tickets prepared by the trustees' committee on athletics.

Behind this was a Conference rule that complimentary tickets were not to exceed 4 per cent of the paid attendance. In practice, however, after deducting proper game expenses any complimentary tickets in excess of the 4 per cent limitation were charged to the host school at half the face value of the tickets. The cost to the home school was offset in part by a "service" charge on complimentary tickets. Specifically, the board's auditor pointed out that, in round numbers, complimentary tickets were costing $78,000 offset to the extent of $16,000 by the "service" charge. This made the net cost $62,000 of which Ohio State's share was $31,000.

The board at a December 19 meeting unanimously adopted a 3-part report presented by the complimentary tickets subcommittee. It agreed that "the number of complimentary tickets should be held to a minimum consistent with the best interests of the University's public relations and the proper conduct of the athletic program." After reviewing the existing schedule, it suggested that "the minimum per game average of complimentary tickets consistent with the best public relations and conduct of athletic program is approximately 3650." It pointed out that "The discreet distribution of complimentary tickets in the interest of the University and the athletic program may be the most economical means of achieving useful objectives of the University." Finally it voiced the belief that the handling of complimentary ticket distribution was "a function which properly should be exercised in the Athletic Department responsible and reporting to the President."

In the spring of 1954 the Federal government, by act of Congress, finally removed the Federal tax on admissions to college athletic events. In line with the anticipated action by other Conference members, the board at its April 2 meeting approved the recommendation of Director

Larkins that the selling price of tickets be retained. This meant, in effect, that the department would increase its revenue by that much to be used against the cost of the field house group.

With virtually a sellout for each home football game, with a growing body of alumni and with steadily increasing enrollment the problem of an equitable ticket distribution became still more acute in the mid-1950s. After extensive study by the board's ticket committee and approval by the trustees, a revised plan took effect with the 1956 football season. It took account of several factors. It cut down, for example, the number of tickets allocated to Michigan for the 1956 game in the Stadium. Where Michigan formerly received up to 16,000 seats it was now to get only 8852 of which only 3000 were in preferred sections.

An important phase of the new plan was to change the sale of season books to alumni from a lottery to a rotation plan. In effect this meant that an order from an alumnus who was a member of the Alumni Association would "rotate in location from field-of-play seats, (i.e., between the goal lines) to seats in less desirable location and over a 3 to 4-year period would complete the cycle, returning to field-of-play location." But continuous purchase of tickets and continuing membership in the Alumni Association were required for participation in the rotation plan. Groupings were to be alphabetical. Most paying customers, incidentally, were deaf to the arguments of experts like former Coach John W. Wilce that the best place in the Stadium to see a football game was high up in the closed north end of the horseshoe.

Football Scheduling

Over the years, following its admission to the Conference, Ohio State was fortunate in its football schedules especially after the return of Michigan to the fold. The series with Illinois produced a steady stream of thrillers as did games with Chicago while it was still a power in the Conference and usually those with Iowa and Wisconsin.

In the late 'Twenties when Pittsburgh was a football power, Ohio State alumni there began to urge an exchange of games with Pitt which was added to the schedule for 1929. The relationship continued fairly regularly for a time. For some years, especially after the withdrawal of Chicago from the Conference, Pitt was anxious for a place in the Conference. Because of the relationship that had sprung up, Ohio State generally supported this desire although in the end Michigan State was admitted in 1949 to round out the Big Ten once more.

With the opening of football relations with Princeton, sentiment began to develop for entering into limited competition with other leading Eastern teams. In September, 1928 the board "expressed a desire to schedule the Navy for an exchange of dates." Navy was scheduled for a game in 1929 but at its request this was canceled with the understanding that the teams would meet at Annapolis in 1930 and in the Stadium 1931. The former game was transferred finally to Baltimore.

Where schedules in the early days had sometimes been completed at the last minute they now began to be made up several years ahead. At the June 8, 1931 board meeting, for example, schedule possibilities for the 1933 and 1934 seasons were discussed. There was hope of a renewal of the series with Princeton but this never materialized.

In 1931 for the first time Director St. John reported that Notre Dame was desirous of a 2-game series but no action was taken at the time. At a January 17, 1933 meeting his recommendation of home-and-home games with Notre Dame in 1935 (Columbus) and 1936 (South Bend) was approved. Despite the excitement it produced this series was never renewed. Southern California, a fairly frequent opponent in the next twenty years, first came into the picture in 1933 when St. John reported that a home-and-home arrangement was under discussion for 1936 at Columbus and 1937 at Los Angeles.

Another newcomer on the schedule was New York University which was still a football power although it later abandoned football as a varsity sport. The board in December, 1935 authorized the scheduling of NYU for a game in the Stadium in 1936 with a return game in New York City which was played at the Polo Grounds. Still another new opponent was Texas Christian, Coach Schmidt's former school, which was scheduled for the opening game of the 1936 season.

In the early 'Thirties it was suggested that the annual game with Michigan be scheduled as the last one of the season. The board took no action at a meeting in May, 1932 but there was general agreement on these points: at some Ohio Conference meeting Director St. John was to "present our point of view as to the desirability of occasional games with Ohio teams, but the difficulties encountered in securing such games"; to give "serious consideration" to the Michigan game as the last one of the season, but it was questionable for 1933.

In time it became increasingly necessary to make up football schedules well in advance and, in particular, to schedule certain games with new opponents several years ahead. In January, 1939, for example, Director St. John spoke at some length on football games possible for the 1941, 1942, 1943 and 1944 schedules besides the Conference games already arranged.

In the early 'Forties the Conference approved the addition of a ninth football game to the regular schedules. In February, 1942 St. John reported that this might make it possible to schedule one of the service teams for the extra game. As it turned out in the next three seasons a number of service teams were played: Ft. Knox, the Iowa Seahawks, and Great Lakes.

Policies involved in arranging football schedules were discussed at a March 30, 1950 board meeting. In the Conference the policy was for a minimum of six with member schools. In the case of Ohio State, because of the tremendous drawing power, the minimum was never a question. In scheduling outside conference schools the board asked Director Larkins to schedule opponents on these bases: schools with high academic standards, schools with good drawing power, schools that respected the Purity Code, and Pacific Coast and Ivy League schools if the Conference representatives set up such a recommendation.

At the same time the board approved the revised Rose Bowl agreement with the Pacific Coast Conference. This matter was also on the agenda for an unusual meeting April 30 in Chicago of the presidents and faculty representatives of the ten Conference schools. The schools stood 8 to 2 in favor of renewing the agreement.

In the early 'Fifties games were scheduled with new opponents such as Stanford and Washington. Still other schools were Duke, Penn State and Texas Christian. By 1958 the schedules were made up four years in advance with both Conference and outside opponents.

Cheerleaders

In the pre-Western Conference days the cheerleader was known as a cheermaster or yellmaster. For a time only one was chosen "from the list of candidates posted on the class ballots," that is, by student election. At first there was only the one but about 1909 two were chosen, the second man to act as assistant. He was then to become cheermaster in his own right the following year.

Since the early Varsity cheerleaders were elected they were not under the control of the Athletic Department. Among them were Fred A. Cornell, author of "Carmen Ohio," and H. S. "Dave" Warwick. One of the best known of the early cheerleaders was Harry E. "Mother" Ewing who functioned in 1907-08-09. One of the best cheerleaders during the first years Ohio State was in the Conference was Gerald E. "Pink" Tenney, '15, of Toledo. It was some years before the cheerleaders were rewarded with the Varsity "O." A later arrangement was for the Boost Ohio Committee, a joint student-faculty group, to make recommendations to the board for the appointment of the head cheerleaders.

But in 1928 the board approved a Student Senate proposal for the election of the Varsity cheerleader. Under this plan the Senate president each fall was to name a cheerleader committee to observe the work of the various candidates during the football and basketball seasons. After the basketball season began the committee was to make a recommendation for head cheerleader and alternates. The Senate would then make a selection to be sent to the Athletic Board for approval. The appointee was to receive a cheerleader's Varsity "O." But he was subject to removal by the board and must stay eligible scholastically.

In keeping with the trend elsewhere during the postwar years, the question of women cheerleaders came before the board in February, 1947. The chairman read various letters pro and con "relative to the acceptance of women cheerleaders at various games, particularly football," but a motion favoring women cheerleaders was withdrawn. Instead, the board adopted a resolution giving the opinion that "there is no regulation existing which would prevent any woman from becoming a cheerleader at The Ohio State University." It was not long before the presence of women cheerleaders at major sports events on the campus was taken for granted.

At a May, 1931 board meeting it was reported that a movement was on foot "for the establishment of a cheering section; the only required uniform for this will be a freshman cap." This move, centering in freshmen, was a start toward the Block "O" section of later years.

In the fall of 1934 student members of the board received from the Student Senate a protest against the use of cadets to form the block cheering at football games. At the November 27 board meeting this was referred for study and report. Such a report, no details given, was made at a January 30, 1935 meeting and was ordered filed. But at the June 7 meeting the board approved a motion that "in the light of the past year's experience, the cadet cheering section be discontinued for 1935-36." The board in December, 1938 approved the award of a Varsity cheerleader's "O" to the manager of the block cheering section.

THE MARCHING BAND

In Ohio State's first Conference football championship year the band began to be a more important part of the football pageant. In connection with the Case game at Cleveland late that season the board at a November 15, 1916 meeting approved spending $100 "toward sending the band to Cleveland, provided at least forty members make the trip."

In the fall of 1917 the band accompanied the team to Indianapolis for the game with Indiana. In so doing it incurred a deficit which was met later by the Athletic Board. A decade later steps were taken to put the band on a more solid footing. At a June 11, 1926 board meeting the Boost Ohio Committee urged the addition of 50c to the price of the student book starting with the next year. The increased was approved, making the price of the book $8.50.

In connection with the football game with Columbia in New York City in the fall of 1926 the board at its October 6 meeting gave permission for the band to go "provided the necessary funds are obtained and provided that the band be subject to the joint control and supervision of the Athletic Board and the Military Department." This was done and the band made the trip in a special train. The trip was financed by a band fund, New York alumni subscriptions, campus subscriptions, and the Columbia and Ohio State athletic departments each of which contributed $1137.94 for the purpose.

Dean George F. Arps, of the College of Education, and Prof. Royal D. Hughes, of the music department, appeared before the board August 20, 1929 in support of the music department's recommendation "for an appropriation for much needed band instruments." In response the board appropriated $3991 for the purpose and later an additional $4000. Prof. Eugene J. Weigel, of the music department, appeared before the board July 10, 1930 to present the need for additional funds "to bring the band and its facilities to a reasonable perfection." In September, 1932 Pittsburgh's proposal that the cost of taking the band to the game there be handled as game expense was approved.

The question of band trips in connection with football games away from home continued to come under discussion, for example, at a September, 1938 board meeting when it was "discussed thoroughly." Subject to approval of the dean of men, the board voted to send the band to the NYU game October 29 in New York City and to the Northwestern game at Evanston.

Once in a while there were matters involving visiting bands. One such incident occurred at the 1938 Michigan game when, it was alleged, the Michigan band suffered some mistreatment during its visit. J. L. Morrill, board chairman, took up the matter by correspondence and reported at the December 16 meeting that the apparent misunderstanding "had been ironed out to the satisfaction of both parties." On one occasion the Michigan band aroused some criticism by spelling out the name of its sponsor, "B-U-I-C-K," during its between-halves show in the Stadium in the face of a longstanding policy against "commercials."

In the 1939-40 athletic budget provision was made for band trips to Chicago and Michigan. But at a September 19 meeting the board authorized a trip to Minneapolis for the Minnesota game instead of to Chicago and added $1500 to the budget for the purpose. The policy was pretty well established of two band trips a year to out-of-town games. And the band went with the team to the 1950, 1955 and 1958 Rose Bowl games, participating also in the Tournament of Roses parade the morning of the game.

Following the close of the 1948 season the board at its November 22 meeting adopted the following resolution in praise of the Marching Band which had become an integral party of the football pageantry:

> A successful football season is dependent upon a number of factors. At the Ohio State University, one of these is our great All-American 120-piece band, developed down through the years by the combined efforts of its leaders—Donaldson, Weigel, and Whitcomb—with the cooperation of every man who has ever been a member of this outstanding organization.
>
> The Ohio State University Band, which has long been a leader among university bands throughout the country, has been responsible for the introduction of floating formations, the quick step, the quick break, the brass-wind band, script writing, and the appropriate use of modern music. Every university is interested in developing peaks of excellence. Without question, the Ohio State University has achieved a high peak of excellence in the Ohio State University band.
>
> The organization of a band is not unlike the development of a football team. It requires creative thinking, the development and execution of formations, showmanship, precision, hours of drill, and devotion.
>
> Tonight as we honor the football team upon the completion of a successful season, the Athletic Board desires to express its deep appreciation to the Ohio State University Band, the Director and Drum Major, for the Band's contribution to this successful season.

In the next decade the band continued to be a major part of the football picture, coming under the capable directorship of Jack O. Evans. Its half-time shows were among the best in the country. Competition for places in the band was as keen as that for the football team. And membership in the band, with recognition at the annual football banquet, was a matter of individual pride and prestige.

MISCELLANY

In the fall of 1951 the immortal "Chic" Harley became the first Ohio State man to be inducted into the National Football Hall of Fame. In 1954 the honor was accorded to Dr. John W. Wilce "in recognition of his long years of service as Head Coach and Director of Football at The Ohio State University from 1913 to 1928." He also was awarded an honorary Varsity "O." Wesley E. Fesler, former All-American and former football coach, was similarly honored in 1954.

Because of his ill health and from a desire to recognize in a tangible away all that he had done for Ohio State athletics, the Varsity "O" Alumni Association undertook a financial program for Harley which came to a head early in 1927 when the board approved it. This was implemented that fall when a benefit game was played in the Stadium. Under the plan Harley was to be assured of a minimum of $100 a month for life. For many years he was a patient in the Veterans Facility at Danville, Ill., but from time to time came to Columbus. In later years he was sufficiently recovered to be released from the facility.

In connection with the retirement of Dr. Wilce as football director a Wilce Appreciation Fund was undertaken. In July, 1929 the board accepted this fund, amounting to $2541.27 and directed that "a study of the Harley Fund be made to ascertain the possibility of placing this new amount in that fund." This was done ultimately. In November, 1934 R. M. Royer, treasurer, asked to be relieved of the custody of the Harley Fund. His accompanying report showed that the principal was $9221.94. The board asked him to continue as custodian but transfer of the funds to the Athletic Department was authorized as of June 30, 1939. In May, 1948 the board authorized transfer of the entire Harley Fund, consisting of $9500 in bonds and $1146.78 in cash, to the trustees to be deposited with the State Treasurer as part of the University's permanent endowment funds.

One of the finer traditions that grew up around Ohio State football is the Captain's Breakfast. By custom this is always held on the Sunday following the last game of the season. All living former football captains are invited. The high spot of the breakfast comes when the outgoing captain is welcomed into the ranks of the former captains. By custom the "tab" is usually picked up by an alumnus or other friend of the University. The breakfast was initiated in 1934 with Walter Jeffrey, of Columbus, as host.

The foregoing tradition belongs in the same category as the planting of a tree in the Buckeye Grove for each new Ohio State football All-American, the ringing of the Victory Bell put up in 1953 in the southeast Stadium tower, and other customs. The grove is located on the far side of the drive north of the men's gymnasium to the southeast of the Stadium. Each tree has a small stone with a bronze tablet carrying the name of the athlete and the year. The Victory Bell idea was discussed as early as March, 1943 but it was a decade in coming. By custom it is rung immediately after each victory in the Stadium for the home team.

Milton Caniff, '30, widely known artist and cartoonist, was responsible for designing a University emblem embodying buckeyes and buckeye leaves. The board approved the idea in September, 1950 and recommended the use of the emblem wherever appropriate in connection with athletics—for use on uniforms and for stencilling baggage equipment. It is also used by the band.

So at the end of some seventy-five years the athletic program had of itself grown to be big business. This was the hard fact. It was the result primarily of a football following almost unmatched anywhere else in the nation. Football crowds averaged 80,000 as a matter of course and gross athletic receipts were in the neighborhood of $1,500,000 a year. But because of the sheer necessity for the expansion of physical facilities, notably the Arena, the adjacent Field House, and land for the golf course, besides the grants-in-aid program, expenditures were close to outrunning income.

This was in sharp contrast with the 1890s and early 1900s when it was a struggle to meet the barest necessities and a football season which netted $5000 was cause for rejoicing. Even limited television, under strict N.C.A.A. control, yielded Ohio State about $60,000 for the year 1955-56. It was estimated that the 1955 Stanford game with Ohio State was viewed by an audience of 9,000,000 and the 1958 Rose Bowl game with Oregon by perhaps even more.

Football was still the principal source of revenue. For the 1956 season the board approved a further increase in ticket prices in line with increases already in effect elsewhere. It was estimated that this increase would yield an additional $191,000. But expenses were going up at the same time, including maintenance and repair of the Stadium and policing the games. The latter item alone went up $9000 in one year. Even the scoreboards, which were non-existent in the early Ohio Field days, cost $13,000 in 1956 to renovate the two at the south end of the Stadium and to install a new one at the closed end. And in the summer of 1958 a charge was added for football game parking to offset the cost of maintenance and policing. The complimentary ticket policy was further tightened in the summer of 1958.

After nearly fifty years in the Conference the University had an athletic operation that was inevitably big business and that continually involved major aspects of University policy and relations with all kinds of publics. Frankenstein or no, there was no escaping these facts. The policy over-all was as sane, sensible and realistic as the situation permitted. There was hope, too, in the strengthening of faculty control growing out of the recommendations of the Fullington Committee and the implementing of other phases of its report. On the whole the total record was good and there was no denying the fact that athletics had contributed to improving the standing of the University by the company it kept in the Conference and elsewhere in educational councils as well as on playing fields.

CALENDAR
(Numbers in parentheses indicate page)

1879
Baseball "team" plays Acme team (26)

1880
Baseball team meets Anderson club on Barracks grounds (26)

1881
Lantern makes plea for spring sports (4)
Football played at North Dorm (5)
Athletic Association organized (5)
Athletic grounds provided (6)
First annual Field Day run off (5, 30)
Class Day "exercises" held (30)

1882
Second annual Field Day held (6)
Baseball played in fall as well as spring (7, 8, 26, 27)
Baseball Association separate from Athletic Association (7)
Class Day meet held during commencement season (30, 31)
Ohio Intercollegiate Athletic Association in existence (8)

1883
Space taken from first athletic grounds for other purposes (23)
Mishaps and weather mar Field Day (31)

1884
First Ohio Intercollegiate Athletic Association meet held May 31 on campus (17)
Field Day held in November (31)

1885
Professor Lazenby recommends provision for athletic grounds (11)
Second Ohio Intercollegiate meet scheduled at Wooster (17, 18)
Baseball team again plays fall schedule (26)

1886
Professor Lazenby urges spending $150 on athletic grounds (11)

1887
Football "team" organized; game played with downtown team (36)

1888
"Pronouncing bee" held for benefit of athletics (9)
Professor Lazenby renews plea for money for better facilities (11)

1889
New chemistry building displaces tennis courts (11)
Professor Lazenby estimates $50 "would keep the ball grounds in fairly good order" (11)
Football begins to take root on the campus (38)

1890

State Field Day held (18)
Baseball team makes "tour" to play three games (11)
President Scott sees dangers and need for athletic control (11, 12)
Students petition trustees for $200 to help athletics (12)
Faculty committee recommends new athletic field near North Dorm (13)
Tennis team wins intercollegiate tournament (29)
First Varsity football played May 3 against Ohio Wesleyan (38–41)
Football resumed in fall, Kenyon first Thanksgiving opponent (41)

1891

Baseball team plays again in fall (27)
Ohio intercollegiate football schedule drawn up (42–43)

1892

Athletic stock company in existence (8)
Legislature passes law to require physical education (14)
Baseball team wins championship (27)
"Jack" Ryder coaches football team (44)
Trustees approve building fence and grandstand for field (13)

1893

Football and baseball squads excused from military drill (15)
Faculty tightens rules on athletic eligibility (14, 15)
Band appears at football game (45)
Crowd tears down fence at Thanksgiving Day game (45)

1894

Ed French wins 7 events in annual Field Day (32)
M. C. Lilley football coach (46)
Football games played during State Fair (46)

1895

Ohio college presidents draft athletic code to counteract professionalism (18–19)
Baseball team plays Michigan, game ends in "rhubarb" (27–28)
Football team plays three games in eight days (47)

1896

Athletic association deeply in debt (10)
Student representatives from 8 Ohio colleges draw up regulations (19, 20)
Ohio college presidents renew discussion of athletics (21)
Part-time baseball coach hired (28)
Annual Field Day held at Westerville (34)
Ohio State plays Otterbein in football at Canton as part of McKinley front-porch campaign (48–49)
Sid Farrar, interim football coach, followed by C. D. Hickey (49)

1897

Concert given as athletic benefit (10)
Faculty adopts new rules for activities, including athletics (15, 16)

Athletic Administration

President Canfield attends meeting at Madison, Wis., which deals with athletic problem (20, 21)
Ohio College Association discusses athletic problems (21, 22)
Golf "club" organized on campus (200)
Baseball team beats Michigan (28)
First football game with Michigan (52)
David F. Edwards new football coach (52)

1898

Armory and gymnasium completed and dedicated (54, 59, 61)
Revised student activity regulations adopted, 6 for athletics (54)
Recommendation made to relocate athletic grounds (17)
Ohio College Association again takes up athletic problems (22)
Dr. C. P. Linhart named director of physical training (15, 54)
Baseball in difficulty (55, 101)
Cross country run scheduled (94)
New athletic field used for first time (34)
Varsity basketball team makes appearance (97–98)
Campus athletics reorganized with board of control (57–58)

1899

J. B. C. Eckstorm hired as football coach (74)
Football team wins state title, Eckstorm rehired (77)

1900

Football team holds Michigan to 0–0 tie, (77, 78–79)
Squabble over game with Ohio Medics (78)
New grandstand in use (79)

1901

John Sigrist, Varsity center, dies from injuries in Western Reserve game (80)
Move to cancel remainder of schedule defeated (81)

1902

Perry Hale serves as football coach (81)
No Varsity basketball, track team disbanded (81)
Michigan beats Varsity 86 to 0, but Illinois is held to tie (82)

1903

Request presented for new site for athletic field (60)
Big Six track meet inaugurated (94)

1904

E. R. Sweetland heads football, first all-year coach (82)
Field north of power plant surveyed as possible site for new athletic field (61)
New bleachers built on east side of Ohio Field (82)
Vernon H. Davis graduate manager of athletics (83)

1905

Basketball team claims state title (99)
Tennis association absorbed by Athletic Association (62)
President Thompson in annual report comments at length on athletics (62–63)

Running track authorized near Eleventh Ave. (94)
Requirements for Varsity "O" modified (73)
Athletic relations with Denison broken after forfeiture of game (85)
"Carmen Ohio" written (85)
Prof. G. W. Rightmire as graduate manager of athletics (64)

1906

Ohio Conference tightens rules, so does Big Nine (63)
Carnival of sports held for benefit of athletics (64)
Al Herrnstein football coach (86)
Disorder marks game at Oberlin (87)
Football team wins 8 games and loses one, goal line uncrossed (87)
Basketball team wins state title (99)
Dr. H. Shindle Wingert hired as director of physical education and athletics (62, 63, 82)

1907

Athletic relations resumed with Ohio Wesleyan and Denison but are broken with Kenyon (88)
George Corneal named track coach (95)

1908

Improvements made to University Field, renamed "Ohio Field" (64–65, 66)
Ohio State runners compete in Penn Relays (95)
Gymnastic team makes appearance (99)
Baseball suspended temporarily as Varsity sport (67, 102)
W. J. McCarty named track coach (95)
Tony Aquila comes into athletic picture (88)
"Mother" Ewing declines cheerleader "O" (88)
Millard Gibson first Ohio State player mentioned by Camp as All-American possibility (89)

1909

Tryouts announced for fencing team (73)
Riley new track coach, plans for relay carnival announced (95)

1910

Howard Jones, of Yale, hired as seasonal football coach (68, 90)
Spring football practice held (90)
Basketball team again state champions (100)
Varsity baseball dropped again (102)
Rightmire raises question of Ohio State joining Big Nine (69)
Amended Ohio Conference rules put athletics under faculty control (70)
Steve Farrell hired as trainer and track coach (90, 95–96)
Football team in 3 to 3 tie with Michigan (91)
Tom Kibler basketball and baseball coach (100)

1911

Rightmire again points out desirability of joining Western Conference (71–72)
Controversy over award of Varsity "O" (73)
Howard Vaughn last of seasonal football coaches, Welch freshman coach (92)
Athletic Association finally out of debt (93)

New bleachers built on west side of Ohio Field (72–73)
Only one basketball "O" granted (100)

1912
Cooke and Wikoff on U. S. Olympic team (96–97)
"Sox" Raymond basketball coach, "Red" Baird baseball coach (101, 102)
Athletic Board reorganized under faculty control (107–108)
Year-round coaches hired with faculty status (108)
University admitted to Western Conference, Rightmire presents Ohio State's case (107, 112)
John R. Richards new athletic director, football and track coach (111–112)
L. W. St. John returns to campus to begin notable career (105, 112)
Football team wins first state title in six seasons (132)
New coach takes team off field in Penn State game (132–133)
Ohio State loses final Thanksgiving game (133)

1913
John W. Wilce engaged as football coach and F. R. Castleman as track coach after Richards resigns (115, 134)
Soccer added to list of sports (115, 204)
St. John becomes athletic director (114)
Varsity engages in first Western Conference competition in baseball, track, and football (115)
Steps taken to provide for tennis as sport, C. H. Farber coach (202)
Intra-Mural Athletic Association organized (209)

1914
Organized intramural program replaces "recreative" sports (209)
Athletics and physical education put under one head (233)

1915
Carran wins Conference tennis singles title (203)
Board contradicts itself on secret football practice (136)

1916
Ohio State wins its first mythical Western Conference football title (138)
"Chic" Harley first Ohio State player on Camp All-American (137)
George M. Trautman joins athletic staff (138)

1917
Football team wins second Conference crown (138)
Baseball team wins Conference title (178)
Athletic Board votes to support swimming team (194)
First talk of a stadium (117)

1918
Fred Norton and "Hap" Courtney war casualties (138)
Coach Wilce in uniform (138)
Football team breaks even in 6 games (138–139)
Move made to shift Varsity basketball to State Fair grounds (213)
Board discusses plans for new athletic field and stadium (117)

1919
Ohio State loses to Illinois in last 9 seconds, but beats Michigan for first time in football (139)
Stadium campaign begins to shape up (118)

1920
Ohio State wins third Big Ten football crown (139)
Ohio Stadium campaign takes public into partnership (118–120)
Strained relations develop with Wisconsin (141)
Golf, wrestling and gymnastics recognized as lesser sports (203)

1921
Football team loses to California in first Rose Bowl appearance (139–144)
Ohio Stadium begins to take shape, double deck plan unique (122)
Amount pledged for Stadium passes $1,000,000 (120)
Football season, last on Ohio Feld, successful except for losses to Oberlin and Illinois (141–142)
Post-season charity football game played (142)
Trautman head basketball coach, Godman first golf coach, Connell tennis coach (188, 201, 202)

1922
New baseball diamond provided (178)
Stadium project runs to about $1,500,000—$457,000 borrowed (124–125)
Decline begins in Ohio State football fortunes (142)
Ohio Wesleyan opponent in first game in Stadium (143)
Michigan wins Stadium dedication game (143–144)
Smith twins (co-eds) compete for Ohio State in AAU meet (198)
Grismer tennis coach, Kunzig fencing coach (202, 205)
Rifle shooting recognized as "minor" sport (206)

1923
Wilce declines Wisconsin offer (144)
Cross country team wins Conference title (183)
Olsen comes as head basketball coach, Alexander gymnastics coach (189, 203)
Ohio State co-Big Ten wrestling champion (205)

1924
Stadium Committee relieved of further duty (125, 126)
Potter Runmaker Cup established as baseball trophy (181)
Payne and Guthrie on U. S. Olympic team (track), and Steel and Martter on wrestling team; Steel wins title (185, 205)
Ohio Relays added to athletic program (188)
Eckelberry serves as golf coach, Staley as gymnastics coach (201, 203)

1925
Stadium improvements authorized (125)
Athletic Board voices confidence in Dr. Wilce, Grant Ward resigns (147)
Basketball team wins first Big Ten title (189–190)
Al Haft wrestling coach, Riebel coaches fencers (205)

ATHLETIC ADMINISTRATION

1926

Michigan wins 17 to 16 thriller before record crowd (145–146)
Athletic Board faces claims for injuries from bomb explosion, &c (146)
Toledo alumni restive over football situation (145, 148)
Willaman and Oberlander added to football coaching staff (148)
Sargent, Scioto Club "pro," serves as golf coach (201)
Wirthwein begins long stretch as tennis coach, Mooney as wrestling coach (203, 205)
Athletic Board takes stand on drinking, betting and ticket scalping (259)

1927

Football pressure mounts (148)
Soccer again recognized as Varsity sport (204)
Board votes $400 for polo team support (207)
Administrative reforms adopted for athletics (234 ff)
New athletic association constitution approved (238)
Stadium turned over to University (128)

1928

University takes over control of athletic funds (238)
Stadium debt paid off (129)
Dr. Wilce resigns as head football coach (149)
Rockne sought as replacement (149–150)
Golf team first in Big Ten meet (201)
Negotiations authorized for survey of golf sites (217)

1929

Willaman promoted to head football coach, Hauser and Miller added to staff (150)
Wright succeeds St. John as baseball coach (178)
Ohio State first in NCAA track championships (187)
Polo recognized as Varsity sport (207)
H. S. Wood made intramural director (209)
Purchase of site for golf courses approved (217)
Field committee reports ambitious athletic building program (223)
Partial reorganization of Athletic Board effected (240)

1930

Rifle team wins 5th Corps match and Conference title (206)
Board tables request to recognize boxing as Varsity sport (208)
Another new athletic constitution presented (238)

1931

Added football game played with Minnesota for charity (244–245)
Castleman ends active track coaching, succeeded by Snyder (182)
Natatorium dedicated, Mike Peppe begins long career as swim coach (223)
Men's gymnasium built (221)
Revised method of electing team captains adopted (239)
Cleveland delegation seeks post-season charity football game there (244)
Issue of broadcasting athletic events raised (250)
North Central Association takes look at Big Ten affairs (260)

1932

Changes made in football coaching staff, Fesler added (152)
Simpson and Keller on U. S. Olympic track team (185, 186)
Marzolf becomes golf coach (201)
Pistol team in competition (206)
Some sports put into intramural program because of depression (241)

1933

Southwest Stadium tower converted to dormitory uses (129)
Pressure mounts on Willaman to resign (152)
Stahl becomes baseball coach (178)
Basketball team ties Northwestern for title (190)
Olsen takes over golf coaching duties as economy move (201)
Athletic belt tightened because of reduced income (241)

1934

Schmidt replaces Willaman as head football coach (151, 153)
Contracts for purchase of golf course land modified because of depression (219)

1935

Football team ties Minnesota for Big Ten championship (155)
Loses memorable game to Notre Dame (154–155)
Jesse Owens sets three world records, ties fourth in Conference meet at Ann Arbor (184)
Athletic budget reviewed for further economies (241)
Governor charges football players with subsidization and professionalism; accusations refuted (242–243)

1936

Football team loses return game to Notre Dame but beats Michigan for third straight time (156)
Board adopts detailed rules for athletic broadcasting (251–252)
Three-year agreement with Schmidt renewed (156)
Owens stars in Berlin Olympics (186)
Golf course construction made possible through WPA project (219)
Board resumes modest financial support for lesser sports (245)

1937

Ohio State beats Michigan for fourth straight time (156)
Nihousen wins Conference singles tennis crown (203)
Golf course project extended to complete 36 holes, plus clubhouse (220)
New policy adopted for athletic broadcasts (252)

1938

Football team does less well, loses to Michigan (156)
Varsity swimmers win first Conference title (197)
Kepler begins long career as golf coach (201)
Rifle team revived (206)

ATHLETIC ADMINISTRATION 297

1939
Football team wins second Conference title under Schmidt (157)
Mackey new baseball coach (178)
Basketball team again tops Big Ten, loses to Oregon for NCAA title (190)
Special field house committee set up (224)

1940
Football team, in Schmidt's final season, breaks even (157)
Committee named "to consider the general football situation" (157–158)
Gilbert first Ohio State golfer to win Conference individual title (201)
Downes wins NCAA wrestling title (205)
Last of athletic indebtedness to banks paid off (246)

1941
Paul Brown replaces Schmidt as football coach, with six new assistants (158–159)
His first team wins 6, loses one, and ties one—Michigan (159)
President Bevis takes active place on Athletic Board (240)
Smaller Ohio colleges urge consideration of abandoning Ohio State football broadcasts (253)

1942
Conference grants permission to play 10 football games, relaxes other rules (247)
Football team wins Conference title; two games with service teams (159)
Game with Illinois shifted to Cleveland municipal stadium (247)
Track team wins Conference indoor title, followed by outdoor (182)
Various coaches go into active war service (247)
Fencers win NCAA title (206)

1943
Freshmen permitted to play on Varsity because of wartime conditions (160)
Football team wins only 3 of 9 games—one the "overtime" game with Illinois (160)
Game with Purdue played in Cleveland municipal stadium (160)
More members of coaching staffs go into war service (161)
Baseball team wins Conference title, and swimmers Big Ten and NCAA team titles; Ohio State duo takes Big Ten doubles crown (178, 193, 203)

1944
Widdoes becomes acting head football coach with Brown in Navy (160)
Football team unbeaten but Conference denies Rose Bowl permission (161)
Widdoes named coach of year, Horvath wins Heisman Trophy as player of year, team No. 1 in nation (161)
Basketball team again tops Big Ten, and tennis pair wins Conference doubles crown (189, 203)

1945
Brown resigns as football coach, Widdoes named successor (162)
Football team wins 7 of 9 games (162)
Wrigley baseball coach (178)
Swimmers win NCAA crown (196)
Baker and Lorms co-champions Big Ten golf, squad wins team title, also NCAA crown, Baker individual titlist (201, 202)
Ohio State pair again tops in Big Ten tennis (203)
Athletic Board actions made subject to trustee control (248)

1946
Widdoes asks to be relieved as head coach, succeeded by Bixler (162)
Olsen resigns after 24 years as basketball coach, "Tippy" Dye successor (191)
Cage team again wins Conference crown (189)
Swim team tops in Conference and NCAA (196)
Bollas wins NCAA heavyweight wrestling title (205)
Larkins chosen athletic director-designate (249)
Conference enters into first 5-year Rose Bowl pact (261)

1947
Bixler steps down as head coach, Fesler named successor (163)
Football team wins only 2 of 9 games but Board commends Fesler (164)
Taylor retires after 26 years as ticket head; Tony Aquila also retires (250)
Stahl again baseball coach (178, 180)
Swimmers repeat in Conference and NCAA (205)
Manos wins Big Ten gymnastics individual title (204)
Changes made in Athletic Board; Postle succeeds Pollard as Conference representative (240)
St. John steps down as athletic director after 34 years (249)

1948
Football team does better, winning 6 of 9 games (164)
Track team Conference indoor champions (182)
Whitfield sets Olympic record for 800-meter run (186)
Three Ohio State swimmers in Olympics, Peppe U. S. diving coach (199)
Fredericks becomes wrestling coach (205)
Trustees bring athletic appointments and budget under closer control (249)
Board grants help for pistol team but withholds awards (206)
Lacrosse club gets University recognition (207)
Question of telecasts of football games comes to fore (243)

1949
Number of changes made in football coaching staff (164)
Conference football title shared with Michigan (164)
Janowicz wins Heisman Trophy as player of year (170)
Track team ties Wisconsin for indoor title (182)
Swimmers again first in Conference and NCAA (196)
Golf course turned over to University trustees debt free (220)
Stadium gets new press box at cost of more than $200,000 (231)

1950
Ohio State beats California in Rose Bowl, Marching Band gives memorable performance (165)
Administration takes unusual steps to reassure Fesler, he agrees to stay (166)
Football team wins 6 of 9 games (166)
"Snow Bowl" game with Michigan one of all-time football highlights (166–167)
Fesler resigns 14 days later but soon takes Minnesota coaching job (167, 168)
Track team wins Conference indoor crown (182)
Dye resigns as basketball coach, succeeded by Stahl (191)
Conference considers television problem, trustees oppose Conference stand (254)
Cagers again Conference champions, swimmers repeat two main crowns (189, 196)

ATHLETIC ADMINISTRATION 299

1951

Despite pressure for return of Brown, "Woody" Hayes is named football coach (168–169)
Karow takes over as baseball coach, team wins Conference title (178)
Golf team first in Big Ten, Nieporte tops in NCAA (201, 202)
Wrestling team Big Ten champions (205)
Rose Bowl agreement renewed for three years (261)

1952

Whitfield again wins Olympic 800-meter run, Cole also on team (186)
Thirteen Ohio State swimmers in Olympic games (199)
Board approves lacrosse as Varsity sport (207)
Athletic receipts pass $1,000,000 for first time (266)

1953

Soccer revived as Varsity sport, Bennett coach (204)
Third set of plans developed for field house group (227)
Limited number of athletic scholarships provided (262)

1954

Football team wins all 9 games along with Conference title (170)
Cassady wins Heisman Trophy as nation's No. 1 player (170)
Athletic Board formally commends players and staff (171)
Swimmers again win both Conference and NCAA titles (196)
Golf squad tops Big Ten (201)
Construction of Arena begun (228)
Whitfield wins Sullivan Award (185)

1955

Team wins Rose Bowl game from Southern California in mud, controversy over band show (171–172)
Team wins second straight Conference title but cannot go to Rose Bowl (172)
Baseball team tops Conference, makes summer trip to Japan (178, 179)
Swimmers again triumph in Conference and NCAA (196)
Contract let for Field House (229)
Special faculty committee authorized to study campus athletic situation (262)

1956

Football showing off somewhat, team wins 6 and loses 3 (172)
Glenn Davis sets new Olympic mark along with NCAA and AAU records (184–185)
Blue Paper takes minority view on Big Ten subsidy plan (265)
First basketball games played in Arena (265)
Freeman scores 46 points in game against Michigan State (191)
Swimmers repeat Big Ten and NCAA titles—7 compete in Olympics (196, 199)
Harper sets record as NCAA champion in two sports (200)
Jones wins NCAA golf title (202)
Conference puts Ohio State on probation, NCAA follows suit (263, 264)

1957

Football team loses opener then wins 8 straight games and third title under Hayes (173)
Wins top national ranking (174)
St. John Arena and French Field House dedicated (265)
Freeman leads Conference basketball scoring (192)
Conference indoor track meet held in Field House (265)
Grants-in-aid increase athletic financial burden (268)
Fullington Committee reports on athletics (268–270)

1958

Football team makes fourth Rose Bowl appearance, narrowly beats Oregon (173–174)
Taylor made head basketball coach (188)
Harper again double NCAA champion (200)
Ersing succeeds Knuttgen as soccer coach (204)
Indoor intramural track meet revived (210)
Faculty Council reaffirms principle of faculty control of athletics (270)
Athletic Board becomes Athletic Council, Conference representative to be elected instead of appointed (270)
Davis wins Sullivan Award (185)

1959

Athletic Council votes for renewing Rose Bowl pact, but Faculty Council instructs representative to vote against it (261)

INDEX

A

AAU, 195, 196
Adelbert (see Western Reserve)
Alumni Monthly (or *Quarterly*), 23, 24, 37, 65, 68, 71, 91, 93, 100, 106, 109, 118, 119, 120, 132, 140, 144, 155, 171
American Legion, 127, 128
Anderson, Miller, 196, 197, 198, 199
Aquila, Tony, 88, 250
Armory and Gymnasium, 3, 14, 15, 17, 34, 54, 58, 61, 97, 111, 182, 188, 194, 208, 213
Athletic Association, 4, 5, 6, 7, 8, 9, 13, 14, 26, 33, 54, 55, 56, 57, 58, 80, 91, 92,93, 106, 108, 238
Athletic "benefit," 9, 10, 56, 64
Athletic Board, 16, 57, 58–171 *passim*, 188–204 *passim*, 209, 218, 224, 226, 229, 238–41 *passim*, 243, 247, 251, 254, 255, 258, 259, 261, 263, 266, 270, 276, 283, 285
Athletic Council, 261, 270
Athletic House, 110, 131, 258
Athletic scholarships, 262, 266, 268, 271
Atkinson, H. S., 92, 159, 221, 243, 249
Auburn, 138

B

Baird, Dow A., 102, 112
Band, 45, 68, 76
Barricklow, Don, 109, 134
Barrington, Walter D. "Rink," 88, 102
Baseball, 4, 6, 7, 8, 11, 25–29, 55, 67, 72, 90, 101–102, 115, 177, 178–81
Baseball Association, 7, 27
Basketball, 90, 97–101, 115, 177, 188–94, 216, 247, 251, 275
Bellows, George, 101
Bevis, President Howard L., 129, 159, 227, 228, 240, 248, 262, 263
Big Nine, 21, 79, 97, 112, 113, 114, 136, 258
Big Six, 4, 8, 29, 73, 94, 95, 96, 111, 112, 113
Big Ten, 161, 264, 280
Bixler, Paul, 158, 159, 162, 163, 175
Block "O" section, 283
Bomb explosion, 145–46
Boyd, Prof. James E., 24
Boxing, 177, 207–8
Bradford, Prof. J. N., 23, 24, 120
Bricker, John W., 138

Broadcasting (radio), 248 ff.
Brown, Paul, 157, 158–61, 162, 168, 175
Brumley, Dr. O. V., 113, 240
Buchtel College, 18, 27, 43
Buckeye Grove, 287
Butcher, Fred E., 53, 56

C

California, Univ. of., 139, 140, 142, 164, 165, 170, 261
Camp, Walter, 89, 91, 142
Camp Sherman, 117, 118, 138
Canfield, President J. H., 15, 19, 20, 21, 50, 55, 56, 59, 98
Caniff, Milton, 287
Canton, 48, 49, 50
Capital Univ., 6, 26, 27, 126
Captain's Breakfast, 286–87
Carlisle Indians, 83, 84
"Carmen Ohio," 85, 121
Case Institute, 21, 52, 67, 74, 78, 83, 84, 85, 87, 88, 89, 91, 92, 93, 94, 107, 132, 135, 137, 138, 139, 284
Cassady, Howard "Hopalong," 170
Castleman, Frank R., 115, 134, 182
Centre College, 47
Cheerleaders, 81, 111, 137 fn., 282–83
Chicago, Univ. of, 83, 107, 110, 112, 139, 142, 144, 145, 146, 154, 156, 157, 182, 248, 277, 280
Cincinnati, Univ. of, 19, 47, 48, 51, 92, 94, 132, 151
Clark, Lyal, 163, 168
Class Day, 3, 4, 8, 9, 24, 25, 29–35, 94
Clotworthy, Bob, 196, 198, 199
Cockins, Edith D., 116
Cole, George N., 37
Colgate Univ., 89, 144, 154
Coliseum, 213–17, 236, 247
Columbia Univ., 145, 284
Columbus Barracks, 51
Columbus *Dispatch*, 9, 17, 18, 26, 27, 28, 29, 30, 31, 32, 33, 34, 35, 36, 38, 41, 43, 44, 45, 46, 47, 48, 49, 50, 52, 56, 74, 75, 76, 77, 78, 79, 94, 98, 108, 171, 174, 230
Columbus Driving Park, 29, 33, 94
Cooke, Clement C., 96, 97, 185, 186
Corneal, George D., 95
Cornell, Fred A., 85, 282
Cornell Univ., 142, 157

301

Courtney, Harold J. "Hap," 138
Cross Country, 94, 95, 114, 115, 177, 188
Crumit, Frank, 86

D

Davey, Gov. Martin L., 242
Davis, Glenn, 183, 184–5, 186, 187, 188
Davis, Gov. Harry L., 121, 143, 244
Davis, Vernon H., 83, 86
Denison Univ., 3, 17, 18, 19, 27, 41, 43, 45, 83, 84, 85, 88, 99, 132, 138, 139, 144 146
DePauw Univ., 28, 29, 85
Dougherty, William A., 86
Duke Univ., 172, 175, 282
Dye, Dean Clair A., 108
Dye, W. H. H. "Tippy," 189, 191, 193

E

Eckelberry, Prof. George W., 126, 201
Eckstorm, Dr. J. B. C., 74, 75, 76, 77, 79, 81, 89, 275
Edwards, David F., 52
Eggers, Prof. Ernst, 20, 54, 55
Ersing, Walter F., 204
Essman, Walter, 136, 148
Evans, Prof. M. B., 200
Evans, Prof. W. L., 66, 67, 92
Ewing, Harry E. "Mother," 88, 283

F

Faculty, 12, 14, 15, 16, 20, 50, 54, 55, 56, 57, 58, 106, 107, 270
Farber, C. H., 29, 202
Farrar, Sid, 49
Farrell, Stephen J., 90, 94, 95, 96, 97, 111, 112, 135
Fawcett, President Novice G., 261, 265, 267, 269
Fencing, 177, 178, 202, 205–6, 241, 245
Fesler, Wesley E., 147, 152, 158, 163–67, 175, 176, 181, 286
Field Day, 3, 4, 5, 6, 8, 12, 24, 25, 28, 29–35, 36, 41, 59, 94, 105, 273
Field House (see French Field House)
Fisher, Dick, 163, 168, 192
Football, 5, 6, 7, 11, 24, 30, 36–53, 74–93, 111, 131–76, 233, 247
Foulk, Prof. C. W., 40, 41, 42, 43
Franklin Medal, 30, 31, 32, 273
Fredericks, Casey, 205
French, Ed, 19, 32, 50
French Field House, 3, 210, 213, 222, 223–29, 265, 287

French, Prof. Thomas E., 32, 37, 65, 107, 108, 109, 113, 117, 119, 120, 123, 125, 133, 139, 141, 148, 189, 238, 239, 240, 258, 260
Fullington Committee report, 268–70, 288

G

Galbraith, J. H., 107, 108
General Assembly, 14, 45, 125, 237
Godfrey, Ernie, 152, 158, 162, 169
Godman, Mike, 201
Golf, 28, 177, 178, 200–2, 203
Golf course, 217–20, 222, 224, 245, 287
Great Lakes, 159, 160, 161, 248, 282
Griffith, John L., 242, 259, 260
Gymnastics, 9, 177, 178, 202, 203, 204

H

Hale, Perry, 81, 82
Harlan, Bruce, 196, 197, 198, 199, 200
Harley, Charles W. "Chic," 136, 137, 138, 139, 176, 205, 286
Harley Fund, 286
Harper, Don, 196, 197, 199, 200, 204
Hauser, George, 150, 152
Hayes, Wayne W. "Woody," 158, 168, 169–75, 263, 264
Heidelberg College, 74, 85
Heisman Trophy, 161, 170
Hendrix, John W., 203
Herrnstein, Al, 86, 88, 89
Hewlett, Joe, 203
Hickey, Charles A., 49, 50
Hopkins, Prof. James R., 162
Horvath, Les, 161
Hoyer, Ralph W., 86, 92, 240
Howard, Homer C., 33, 44 fn., 46, 48, 107
Hull, James R., 190, 191, 192, 194, 274
Hunt, Prof. Thomas F., 14

I

Illinois, Univ. of, 69, 82, 83, 107, 109, 110, 137, 138, 139, 141, 142, 143, 144, 145, 146, 151, 152, 154, 156, 157, 159, 160, 161, 162, 163, 164, 165, 166, 170, 171, 172, 173, 174, 177, 182, 187, 231, 242, 247
Indiana, Univ. of, 29, 69, 82, 85, 99, 107, 110, 115, 135, 137, 138, 146, 151, 152, 154, 156, 157, 159, 160, 161, 163, 164, 165, 166, 169, 170, 171, 172, 173, 174, 189, 242, 284

INDEX 303

Iowa, Univ. of, 110, 142, 143, 144, 145, 146, 151, 154, 161, 163, 164, 166, 170, 171, 172, 173, 174, 241, 280
Intramural athletics, 108, 208–11

J

Janowicz, Vic, 165, 170
Jones, Howard, 68, 90, 91, 92

K

Karow, Marty, 178, 180
Kauffman, Dean George B., 59
Kays, Prof. D. J., 120, 240
Kennedy, John K., 217, 218, 219
Kentucky, Univ. of, 47, 48, 154
Kenyon College, 3, 8, 10, 17, 18, 19, 27, 42, 43, 44, 45, 47, 49, 51, 74, 75, 77, 79, 83, 85, 87, 89, 94, 98, 101, 207
Kepler, Bob, 201, 202, 224
Kibler, Tom, 100, 101, 102
Konno, Ford, 197, 198, 199, 200
Kraner, H. Wade, 250
Knuttgen, Howard, 204, 207

L

Lacrosse, 207
Lantern, 4, 6, 7, 8, 9, 10, 14, 15, 17, 18, 19, 20, 21, 23, 25, 28, 29, 30, 34, 36, 38, 39, 41, 42, 43, 46, 47, 48, 49, 50, 51, 52, 56, 57, 58, 61, 62, 64, 71, 73, 74, 81, 82, 83, 84, 86, 87, 88, 89, 90, 94, 95, 97, 98, 99, 102, 107, 109, 133, 135, 139, 200, 208, 230
Larkins, Richard C., 8, 152, 167, 168, 169, 216, 220, 226, 227, 228, 229, 230, 231, 249, 254, 255, 256, 261, 262, 263, 267, 268, 282
Laylin, Prof. Clarence D., 107, 108, 109, 146, 240, 241
Lazarus Prize, 31
Lazarus, Simon, 119, 126
Lazenby, Prof. W. R., 7, 9, 11, 13
Legislature (see General Assembly)
Leighton, Prof. J. A., 107, 204
Lilley, A. S., 37, 38
Lilley, M. C., 38, 46
Linhart, Prof. C. P., 15, 54, 58, 62, 82
Lincoln, J. F., 86
Lincoln, Paul, 40, 42
Little, George E., 115, 135, 136
Lloyd, E. G. "Rastus," 75, 76
Lord, Prof. N. W., 7, 54, 81

M

Mackey, Fred C., 159, 178, 180, 268
Makio, 8, 36, 56, 65, 88, 89
Marching Band, 165, 171, 174, 284–86
Marietta College, 74, 76
Martter, Perry, 205
McCarty, W. D., 95
McFarland, Prof. R. W., 26
McPherson, Dean William, 32, 58
Means, Dr. J. W., 87
Miami Univ., 19, 78, 83, 93, 94
Michigan, Univ. of, 27, 28, 52, 66, 67, 68, 69, 71, 72, 77, 78, 79, 82, 83, 85, 87,88, 89, 90, 91, 101, 107, 111, 113, 137, 139, 143, 144, 145, 146, 148, 151, 152, 153, 154, 155, 156, 157, 159, 160, 161, 163, 164, 166, 167, 169, 170, 172, 173, 174, 175, 177, 182, 187, 195, 237, 248, 253, 256, 265, 278, 280, 285
Michigan Pants Club, 153
Michigan State Univ., 92, 133, 169, 170, 175, 195, 280
Military department, 135, 206, 284
Military drill, 13, 15, 93
Military "O" Association, 73
Miller, Don, 150, 152
Mills, Dr. W. C., 62, 70
Minnesota, Univ. of, 83, 99, 110, 141, 142, 152, 155, 156, 161, 162, 163, 164, 166, 245, 285
Missouri, Univ. of, 157, 161, 163, 164, 165
Mooney, B. F., 205, 275
Morrey, Dr. C. B., 8, 39, 40, 41, 43
Morrill, J. L., 119, 126, 190, 240, 252, 275, 285
Morris, Prof. Clyde T., 123, 124, 224, 240
Muskingum College, 77, 83, 87, 146

N

Nakama, Keo, 197
Natatorium, 1, 194, 195, 196, 213, 220, 221–23, 224, 241, 244, 245
Navy (Annapolis), 151, 152, 281
NCAA, 106, 177, 179, 187, 190, 194, 195, 196, 199, 200, 202, 205, 206, 241, 256, 257, 263, 264, 265, 269, 287
Nebraska, Univ. of, 172
Nesbitt, Hugh E., 225, 240
New York Univ., 127, 156, 281, 284
North Dorm, 5, 23, 24, 36, 37, 38
Northwestern Univ., 28, 107, 110, 112, 115, 135, 137, 138, 146, 151, 154, 155, 157,

159, 160, 162, 163, 164, 165, 166, 170, 171, 172, 173, 174, 175, 189, 190, 277, 284
Norton, "Effie," 27 fn.
Norton, Fred, 138
Notre Dame Univ., 149, 154–55, 156, 175, 179, 241, 244, 281

O

Oberlander, A. J., 148
Oberlin College, 18, 21, 50, 51, 52, 67, 76, 78, 87, 89, 93, 94, 96, 97, 100, 107, 111, 132, 135, 137, 139, 141, 143, 182, 204, 207
Ohio Conference, 8, 21, 63, 70, 84, 281
Ohio Field, 3, 23, 60, 65, 66, 67, 69, 70, 85, 90, 91, 93, 96, 106, 114, 117, 118, 135, 136, 139, 178, 275, 288
Ohio Intercollegiate Athletic Assn., 8, 17, 18, 20, 94
Ohio Medical Univ., 51, 52, 74, 76, 77, 78, 81, 87
Ohio Relays, 188
Ohio Stadium, 85, 117–130
Ohio Stadium Committee (see Stadium Committee)
Ohio State Journal, 29, 38, 39
Ohlson, H. C., 194, 205
Ohio Wesleyan Univ., 3, 19, 21, 22, 26, 29, 31, 38, 39–41, 51, 52, 75, 80, 82, 88, 94, 96, 99, 105, 112, 133, 137, 138, 139, 142, 143, 144, 146, 152
Ohio Wesleyan Transcript, 40, 41
Olentangy River, 34, 119, 120, 121, 123, 130, 208
Olsen, H. G. "Oley," 189, 190–1, 193, 201, 275
Olympic Games, 97, 183, 196, 198
Oregon, Univ. of, 173, 174, 190, 287
Otterbein College, 3, 7, 19, 42, 47, 48, 49, 50, 51, 52, 75, 77, 78, 83, 84, 86, 89, 92, 114, 132
Owens, Jesse, 32, 183–4, 186, 187, 188
Oyakawa, Yoshi, 197, 198, 199, 200

P

Paterson, Robert G., 272
Patnik, Al, 197, 200
Pearse, Arthur, 95
Pennsylvania, Univ. of, 152, 170
Penn Relays, 95, 96, 115, 241
Penn State, 132–33, 172, 282

Peppe, Mike, 194, 195, 196, 197, 199, 204, 223, 275
Physical education building, 110
Physical education dept., 106, 143, 168, 249
Pistol shooting, 206, 241, 245
Pittsburgh, Univ. of, 151, 152, 156, 157, 159, 160, 161, 162, 163, 164, 165, 166, 170, 248, 253, 280
Pollard, Prof. James E., 240, 259, 261
Polo, 206–07, 241, 245
Postle, Dean Wendell, 240, 255, 256, 261
Potter, Frank D., 181
Power, Donald C., 249, 254
Press box, 130, 230, 231
Princeton Univ., 25, 38, 52, 146, 147, 175, 281
Purdue Univ., 95, 97, 99, 110, 139, 142, 144, 156, 159, 160, 162, 163, 164, 170, 171, 173, 174, 175, 242, 247

R

Radio broadcasting, 250–57
Raymond, Stockton R., 101
Recreation Park, 41, 43
Richards, John R., 106, 111, 112, 114, 131, 132, 133, 134, 141, 144, 182, 208
Riebel, Dr. F. A., 205, 206
Rifle team, 206, 241, 245
Rightmire, President George W., 33, 60, 64, 68, 70, 71, 72, 82, 83, 91, 92, 95, 105, 106, 107, 108, 109, 110, 112, 113, 217, 235, 236, 237, 238, 240, 243, 251, 260, 272, 278
Rockne, Knute, 149, 150, 243
Rose Bowl agreement, 261
Rose Bowl game, 134, 136, 139–41, 161, 164, 165, 170, 171–2, 173–4, 255, 260, 261, 285, 287
Rothgeb, Carl, 114, 134
Royer, R. M., 108, 238
Ryder, Fred B. "Jack," 44, 46, 48, 74

S

Sargent, George, 201
Schmidt, Francis, 150, 151, 153–58, 175
Schueller, Jr. John B., 14
Scott, President William H., 11, 12, 15
Sigrist, John L., 80, 81
Smith, Howard Dwight, 117, 121, 195, 219, 221, 222, 225
Smith, Bill, 196, 197, 198, 199, 200
Snyder, Larry, 182, 186, 196, 247
"Snow Bowl" game, 166–67

INDEX 305

Soccer, 115, 204
Southern California, Univ. of, 156, 159, 160, 163, 164, 170, 172, 177, 187, 281
Southern Methodist Univ., 166, 170, 174
Stadium (see also Ohio Stadium), 3, 6, 142, 178, 220, 221, 223, 229–32, 238, 245, 275, 287, 288
Stadium Building Committee, 122, 123, 124, 126
Stadium campaign, 118, 119, 120, 275
Stadium Committee, 119, 122, 125, 129
Stadium Fund, 118, 124, 126, 234
Stadium subscribers, 118, 125, 276, 277
Stahl, Floyd, 178, 180, 189, 191, 192
Staley, Leo G., 203, 209
Stanford Univ., 172, 187, 257, 264, 282, 287
Starling Medical College, 47
State fair, 46, 236, 237
State fair grounds, 29, 33, 182, 188, 213, 247
Staten, George, 171, 250
Steeb, Carl E., 82, 107, 119, 120, 126, 129
Steel, Harry, 205
Stinchcomb, Gaylord "Pete," 136, 139, 141, 188
St. John Arena, 3, 188, 213, 221, 223–29, 265, 287
St. John, Lynn W., 37, 87, 105, 106, 111, 114, 115, 120, 127, 129, 130, 133, 142, 146, 148, 149, 152, 157, 158, 160, 163, 178, 180, 193, 208, 224, 225, 226, 228, 233, 235, 239, 243, 246, 248, 249, 259, 260, 272, 281, 282
Strobel, Harry, 164, 169
Strong, Dean Frank R., 168, 240
Subsidy program (see Athletic scholarships)
Sullivan Award, 185
Summer, Samuel N., 119, 120, 121, 126, 220, 240, 241
Sweetland, E. R., 82, 84, 85, 86, 94
Swimming, 177, 194-200, 222, 275
Syracuse Univ., 70, 92

T

Taylor, Fred, 180, 188, 191, 192
Taylor, Henry D. "Hen," 250
Taylor, Jacob B., 227, 228, 268
Taylor, Prof. Joseph R., 68, 100, 101
Television, 250–57, 287
Tennis, 11, 12, 24, 28, 29, 90, 202–3
Tennis association, 27
Texas Christian Univ., 151, 156, 173, 281, 282

Thanksgiving Day game, 10, 43, 44, 45, 47, 49, 51, 53, 64, 75, 77, 79, 83, 85, 87, 133, 142
Thomas, Prof. B. F., 10, 13, 56, 57, 60
Thomas, Oscar L., 250
Thompson, President W. O., 19, 59, 61, 73, 80, 93, 107, 114, 117, 120, 121, 125, 126, 135, 141, 143, 240, 272, 274
Ticket distribution, 120, 265, 267, 275–80
Toledo alumni, 148
Townsend, Col. G. L., 240, 274, 275
Track, 4, 6, 24, 72, 94–97, 111, 115, 177, 178, 181–88
Training table, 75, 84
Trautman, George M., 86, 138, 188, 193, 201, 209, 220, 233
Trustees, board of, 12, 13, 15, 17, 54, 63, 65, 94, 106, 107, 110, 121, 122, 128, 159, 169, 171, 195, 214, 229, 238, 239, 241, 243, 248, 249, 262, 279
Tuttle, Prof. Albert H., 9, 30
Tuttle, Prof. Alonzo, 107, 108, 109, 114
TV broadcasting, 250–57

U

University colors, 24, 25
University Field, 59, 64, 82, 94
University Hall, 4, 23

V

Vanderbilt, 66, 69, 88, 89, 151, 152
Varsity "O," 73, 88, 92, 100, 114, 116, 135, 204, 206, 207, 272–75, 283
Varsity "O" Association, 93, 100, 115, 147
Vaughn, Harry, 91, 92, 93, 109
Victory Bell, 287

W

"Wahoo, wahoo, etc.," 24, 76
Ward, Grant P., 136, 147–48, 209
Washington State, 170, 173
Washington, Univ. of, 174, 282
Weaver, J. Edward, 250, 268
Weigel, Prof. Eugene J., 275, 284
Welch, "Doc," 90, 92
Wells, L. R. 'Prep," 91, 92, 109
Western Conference (see also Big Nine or Big Ten), 4, 8, 62, 63, 69, 70, 71, 72, 86, 92, 99, 105, 106, 107, 109, 112, 113, 114, 131, 136, 162, 179, 246, 251, 254, 256, 257, 258, 259, 260, 261, 264, 265, 266, **288**

Western Reserve Univ., 21, 27, 28, 43, 45, 74, 76, 80, 92, 94, 107, 126, 135, 153, 154
West Virginia Univ., 51, 77, 78
White, Bob, 174, 175
Whitfield, Mal, 183, 185, 186, 196
Widdoes, Carroll C., 158, 159, 160–62, 174, 175
Wikoff, Garnett, 94, 96, 97, 185, 186
Wilce, Dr. John W., 74, 115, 131–50, 169, 175, 176, 200, 209, 286
Willaman, Sam, 148, 150–53, 175, 209
Wilson, K. L. "Tug," 260, 263
Wingert, Dr. H. Shindle, 62, 63, 82, 88, 92, 93, 102, 106
Wirthwein, Herman, 203
Wisconsin, Univ. of, 83, 92, 99, 110, 112, 115, 131, 135, 137, 138, 139, 141, 144, 151, 152, 159, 162, 163, 164, 165, 166, 170, 171, 172, 173, 174, 182, 189, 192, 242, 280
Wittenberg College, 19, 22, 42, 46, 50, 51, 75, 85, 87, 89, 99, 145, 146, 151, 264
Women cheerleaders, 137 fn.
Wood, Harold S., 148, 209
Wooster, College of, 17, 18, 21, 27, 38, 41, 85, 87, 88, 89, 94, 105, 112, 144, 178
WOSU (WEAO), 250, 251, 252, 256, 264
WPA, 218, 219, 220
Wrestling, 115, 177, 202, 203, 204–5
Wright, Wayne, 178, 180
Wrigley, Lowell, 178, 180

Y

Yale University, 90, 93, 177, 178
Yost, Fielding H., 52, 53, 83, 89
Youngstown alumni, 237

www.ingramcontent.com/pod-product-compliance
Lightning Source LLC
Chambersburg PA
CBHW030128240426
43672CB00005B/64